Essential
Islington

PAMELA SHIELDS

Pamela
Jan 05

SUTTON PUBLISHING

First published in the United Kingdom in 2000 by
Sutton Publishing Limited · Phoenix Mill
Thrupp · Stroud · Gloucestershire · GL5 2BU

Reprinted in 2003

British Library Cataloguing in Publication Data
A catalogue record for this book is available from the British Library.

ISBN 0-7509-2573-6

Typeset in 9/11.5 pt Gill Sans.
Typesetting and origination by
Sutton Publishing Limited.
Printed and bound in England by
J.H. Haynes & Co. Ltd, Sparkford.

Introduction

Outside Central London, it's still possible to get a feel of the unique identities of places such as Islington (coyly described in guide books as a 'village' even though it has a population bigger than many towns) which sprang up outside the old City walls.

To the casual visitor, the name Islington may mean little or nothing compared with Westminster, Chelsea, Kensington or other destinations on the tourist trail, but to the Londoner the borough has an equally distinctive personality. This tiny inner borough is never out of the news. At the time of writing, there are two major documentaries on BBC TV about its failing schools and even Radio 4's Food Programme went to Islington Ecological Centre of all places to talk about cooking autumn berries!

Most large cities around the world have a residential haven hidden away somewhere. New York has its Greenwich Village, Paris has its Montmartre and London has Islington. The ancient City is right on its doorstep and the West End, the commercial centre, is within easy reach.

A mere six miles by four, the borough has played an extraordinary part in world events, the scene of many Royal progresses, barbaric executions, religious and political plots against the throne, home of the Knights Hospitallers, free health care and even Punk rock. It has an astonishing history of rebellion against the established order. From Wat Tyler and the Peasants' Revolt, George Fox's Quakerism, John Wesley's Methodism and Tom Paine's *Rights of Man*, Islington can fairly claim its place in history as the cradle of modern Western democracy.

Long-familiar names step out of these pages, from Elizabeth I, Sir Walter Raleigh, Shakespeare, Dr Johnson, Dickens, Benjamin Franklin, Lenin and Alfred Hitchcock, to Dr Crippen, Joe Orton and Johnny Rotten. These and many other world-famous personalities are recalled here to strut their hour upon the stage of London's liveliest borough.

Many landmarks are still here and can be visited, many more have sadly gone, washed away by successive tides of speculative development – but *Essential Islington* is all about change. Today the borough is enjoying a mini-renaissance as an arts, shopping and entertainment centre, where TV personalities, film stars, politicians, City wheeler dealers and media celebrities who could afford to live anywhere are happy to call Islington 'home'. *Essential Islington* is a book for everyone, residents and visitors alike, a 'tour guide' through the ages, to fascinate and inform.

This book is not history proper, it doesn't increase a body of knowledge or say anything new. It's a synthesis of information from books borrowed from Islington libraries or bought, usually second-hand, from bookshops in the borough. A single paragraph can be an amalgam of books, newspapers, tv/radio programmes, CD Roms and the world wide web. Nothing has been omitted simply because it's common knowledge and been said a thousand times already but it's hoped that some anecdotes at least are new.

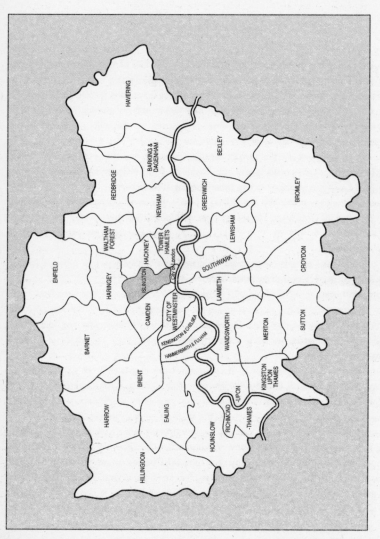

London Borough of Islington

ADAMS, Douglas (1952–)
Writer and broadcaster
1979 In A *Hitch-Hiker's Guide to the Galaxy*, Zaphod Beeblebrox meets Arthur Dent at a party in Islington.
1980 Hotblack Desiato, estate agents in **Upper Street**, achieve a certain kind of fame in *The Restaurant at the End of the Universe* when the creator of Slartibartfast and Yooden Vranx, looking for an equally silly name for his rock star character, sees *Hotblack Desiato* on a 'For Sale' board, although Adams bought in **Duncan Terrace** N1 through a rival agent. Islington provides Mr Adams with the answer to *Life, the Universe and Everything* when he writes this book here: the answer to the '*ultimate question of life*' is 42.
1999 Having also written *So Long and Thanks for All the Fish* (1984) *Dirk Gently, Holistic Detective Agency* (1987) *The Long Dark Tea-Time* (1988) and *Mostly Harmless* (1992), Adams departed for Hollywood to film '*Hitch-Hiker*' for Disney. He remarked that he would have had to move anyway to get a half-decent education for his daughter (for Islington schools see Boyson, Sir Rhodes; Owen, Dame Alice, *et al.*).

AFRICAN NATIONAL CONGRESS (ANC)
1988 African National Congress, **Holloway Road**, campaigns in exile for Nelson Mandela's release. South African military intelligence tried to dig a tunnel under the office to blow it up. Later moved to 28 **Penton Street** N1.

AGRICULTURAL HALLS (The 'Old Aggie')
Upper Street N1
See **Business Design Centre**

ALBION PLACE
off **St John's Lane** EC1
Formerly known as St George's Court or George Court.
1721 Christopher <u>Pinchbeck</u> makes watches, astronomical clocks and musical automata (tunes from operas, bird songs, flutes, minuets, jigs and psalms for churches with no organ). He invented an alloy, 80 per cent copper, 20 per cent zinc, as a cheap substitute for bronze used in jewellery and watch making. Later, by association, the word '*pinchbeck*' is used to describe anything counterfeit, not worth having.
1776 Thomas <u>Bewick</u>, famous for his engravings of British birds, who lent his name to Bewick's swan, arrives from Newcastle to work with old friend Thomas <u>Hodgson</u>

(apprentices together). He looked up another old friend, fellow engraver, Robert Pollard in nearby Baynes Row (now **Exmouth Market**) and the pair attended St Andrew's, Holborn, where the notorious Henry Sacheverell was once incumbent (see **St John's Square**). Apart from Westminster Abbey and John Wesley's sermons, Bewick didn't like London and although much in demand and earning a lot of money, returned home, saying he '*would rather herd sheep in Newcastle for five shillings a week than live in London.*'

1987 Janet Street-Porter, newspaper editor and TV broadcaster, commissions Piers Gough ('*the Vivienne Westwood of architecture*') to build a home on the site of an old warehouse on the corner of Albion Place and **Britton Street**. Designed on a theme of diamonds and triangles, it has a blue glazed Belgian pantile roof, graded colour brickwork resembling rising damp, log-effect lintels and aluminium windows left untreated. An outside staircase leads to Ms Street-Porter's office and a skull and crossbones flag flies from the roof. The most talked about house for years was likened to '*something by Gaudi*' and caused uproar in the press: '*extraordinary … highly eccentric … reflects client's taste for the outrageous … a study in jokes.*'

....

ALI, Tariq
Writer

1968 Ali, LSE student, leads an anti-Vietnam War march to the American Embassy, Grosvenor Square.

1981 Marxist friend of John Lennon, Ali opens The Other Book Shop, 328 **Upper Street** N1, an alternative bookshop for left-wing literary politicos, feminists and anti-racist groups selling as well as books, 'angry' newspapers, T-shirts and badges. He called it The Other Bookshop because T. Miles bookshop, a few doors down at 325, had been there since 1812, run by only its fifth proprietor in 200 years (now in St Paul's Road N1). Ali also edited the Trotskyite magazine *Black Dwarf*. (The original *Black Dwarf*, a radical magazine of the Regency period, was published in **Rosebery Avenue** in premises now occupied by Amnesty International.) Ali has been a *Street Fighting Man* (the lyrics to which he published when the song was banned by the BBC) since he was six years old when he urged his servants in Lahore (where he was born and brought up) to go on strike for higher wages.

2000 Writes *Snogging Ken*, a politically angry satire for the **King's Head Theatre**, about Ken Livingstone's (ultimately successful) London mayoral election.

....

ALMEIDA THEATRE
Almeida Street N1

1832 Islington Literary and Scientific Society (The 'Lit & Sci') meet in the Canonbury Tavern. To finance a permanent base, they offered £10 shares, which included lifelong membership and free admission to lectures. Architects Roumieu and Gough designed an impressive, pseudo-classical building in newly-built Wellington Street (now **Almeida Street**).

The foyer had an imposing staircase of Portland stone with bronze balustrades, the lecture theatre seated 500 and the reading room (forerunner of Finsbury Free Library), with over 5,000 books, was lit by gas lamps of Florentine bronze. The 'Lit and Sci' ran lectures on topics such as magnetism, music and the manners of North American Indians. The curate of St Mary's (across the road) wrote to the newspapers criticising the Society's policy of excluding religion as a suitable topic for discussion.

One of the Society's best attended evenings was a reading of *Uncle Tom's Cabin* (not a dry eye in the house) by Mrs Webb, a black woman from Philadelphia on a lecture tour funded by Harriet Beecher Stowe, the book's author. Inside the packed house on another evening was the famous cartoonist George Cruikshank, who lived near **The Angel**. He had gone to witness the unwrapping of a 2000-year-old Egyptian mummy which the Society bought for £200 from the British consul in Egypt, with a guarantee that the casket had never been opened. When the lecturer, Dr Pettigrew, dramatically raised the lid, it became clear that all the funerary ornaments had been stolen except for a ring bearing the 'evil eye' of Osiris.

1871 The 'Lit & Sci' moves to the Athenaeum, **Camden Road**. The building was sold to the Wellington Music Hall.

1890 The failing music hall is taken over by the Salvation Army to house down-and-outs. There were so many Wellington Streets in London, this one was renamed **Almeida Street** after one of the Iron Duke's famous victories in Portugal.

1952 Beck's Carnival Novelties (of **Camden Passage**, **Cross Street** and **Upper Street**) buy the building as a factory and warehouse.

1971 Malcolm Heaysman, manager of Beck's, Upper Street, unrepentant transvestite, is murdered by his son-in-law Roy Searl in the Welsh farmhouse he bought for his retirement. Beck's building was put on the market, Searl got life.

Harry Secombe puts in a bid to open the Orange Music Centre (musical comedy and light opera). The popular singer and former Goon was turned down when locals objected. Dan Crawford, landlord of the **King's Head** pub (q.v.), also had his plans turned down.

1978 Planning permission to turn the building into a theatre is granted to The Almeida Theatre Company, supported by Greater London Council (GLC), The Arts Council, Greater London Arts (GLA) and Islington Council, to the tune of £150,000. The theatre has since hosted touring companies such as Traverse, Abbey Theatre, Cheek by Jowl, Theatre de Complicité and the young, unknown, Kenneth Branagh's 'Not The RSC', which later became the Renaissance Theatre Company.

1990 Becomes a producing theatre and attracts stars including Glenda Jackson, Claire Bloom, Nicola Paget, Harold Pinter, Diana Rigg, Eleanor Bron, Martin Shaw and designer Jasper Conran.

....

AMERICA

Until 1783, when America became independent, criminals found guilty of serious offences sentenced at Hicks Hall, **St John Street** *or the Middlesex Sessions House,* **Clerkenwell Green** *EC1, had a stark choice: hanging or transportation. Thus, many became Americans.*

1585 Walter Raleigh (or Ralegh) is knighted for colonising Virginia, named after England's 'virgin' queen. After her father, Henry VIII, closed the religious houses that previously fed them, Elizabeth passed the Vagrancy Act to deport '*beggars, incorrigible rogues and vagabonds*' and put the able-bodied to useful labour in the New World.

1644 George Fox (age 20) founder of the Society of Friends (Quakers), moves to Clerkenwell and preaches in the Meeting House, **St John Street** EC1. By 1661 the Society had its own Meeting House, 21 **Roscoe Street** EC1.

1669 Fox marries Margaret Fell (widow of Judge Fell). Together they took the Quaker religion to North America. Fox returned to **Clerkenwell** where he is buried (see Fox, George).

1686 Charles Morton, headmaster of the famous Dissenters' Academy (see Dissent), **Newington Green**, teaches Charles Wesley (John's father), Daniel Defoe and Isaac Watts. He later emigrated to New England, where he supervised the notorious prosecutions for witchcraft in Salem.

But the traffic is not all one-way . . .

1724 Benjamin Franklin arrives in Islington and becomes friends with William Caslon, Clerkenwell printer. Caslon achieved fame after Franklin used his type fount to print the *Declaration of Human Rights* (a bit of Clerkenwell forever in a foreign field – see also Caslon, William).

Franklin, age 18, found himself stranded in Clerkenwell after arriving with (so he thought) letters of credit from the Governor of Pennsylvania to buy type founts. Either the promised letters were never written or were lost or stolen, so not only could Franklin not make his purchase, with no money he couldn't even get home. Taken on by the Samuel Palmer Printing Office, **Bartholomew Close** EC1, Franklin lodged in nearby **Little Britain** EC1. Unlike his colleagues, Franklin was a teetotal workaholic and could not believe how lazy Londoners were:

'7 am and not one shop open although the sun has been up since 4. They moan about the price of candles yet they sleep by sunshine and live by candle-light . . .' He also explained why Islington was so popular: 'London is one great smoky house and every street a chimney, the air full of floating sea coale soot, you never get a sweet breath of what is pure.' After two years, Franklin had saved enough for his passage home.

1757 Franklin returns to London a rich man and renews acquaintance with old friends William Strahan, whose son George is the vicar at St Mary's, **Upper Street** N1 and Edward Cave, editor of *The Gentleman's Magazine* at **St John's Gate** EC1.

1768 Franklin witnesses the Wilkes and Liberty riots (q.v.). Wilkes championed America in its struggle and was known as 'the colonists' best friend' (towns in America are named after him). *Sons of Liberty* in Boston and the House of Assembly in South Carolina sent birthday presents to him in Fleet prison. (See Wilkes, John and other entries.)

1774 Tom Paine, after meeting Franklin, is convinced America must annexe itself from England. With letters of introduction from Franklin, he travelled to America and helped galvanise eleven disparate states into action with his book, *Common Sense* (see Paine, Thomas). Paine took American citizenship and died forgotten.

1820 Washington (*Rip Van Winkle*) Irving rents his hero Oliver Goldsmith's old room in **Canonbury Tower** to write his biography (see Goldsmith, Oliver).

1821 Junius Booth, actor, emigrates to America from Clerkenwell. One son, Edwin, became America's leading Shakespearean tragedian. The other, John Wilkes Booth, assassinated President Lincoln (see Booth, Cherie).

1827 George Peabody, philanthropist from Danvers, Mass., settles in London and finances cheap housing for workers in Islington.

1877 A fragment of the 1620 Plymouth Rock is sent to **Union Chapel** (see Union Chapel).

1883 James Bailey, of Barnum & Bailey fame, brings the World Fair to the Agricultural Halls, otherwise known as the Aggie (see Business Design Centre).

1913 Charlie <u>Chaplin</u> and Stan <u>Laurel</u> appear many times at music halls in Islington (Collins, Holloway Empire, Rosemary Branch and Sadler's Wells) before emigrating to America. (See entries on Chaplin, Collins music hall, Sadler's Wells *et al*.)

1919 American companies Bex Bissell Carpet Sweepers, Singer Sewing Machines, Columbia Gramophone Company (recording studios at 102/108 **Clerkenwell Road**) and Edison Phonograph open branches in Clerkenwell. Edison Bell were at 143 **Rosebery Avenue** and 5 **Chapel Street**. The Paramount Picture Corporation founded Islington Film Studios and started the career of Sir Alfred <u>Hitchcock</u>. 'Hitch' emigrated to America in 1939. (See entries under Islington Film Studios; Hitchcock, Alfred, *et al*.)

1938 C. Howard <u>Crane</u> who built Radio City in New York designs the Gaumont Cinema, **Holloway Road**. (See Cinema)

1945 Jessica <u>Tandy</u>, actress, of **Highbury Crescent** emigrates to America.

1959 Anglo-American societies pay for a statue of Sir Walter <u>Raleigh</u> in Whitehall, unveiled by the American Ambassador. (Plans are afoot to remove it to Raleigh's old home at Sherborne, Dorset: see Raleigh, Sir Walter.)

1969 Dan <u>Crawford</u> from New Jersey buys **The King's Head** pub and converts part of it into a fringe theatre.

....

ANGEL (The) N1

The Angel is the name given to the area that surrounded the old Angel Inn. 'London begins here in earnest' says Noah Claypole in Oliver Twist *(see Dickens, Charles).*

1225 Henry III grants citizens the privilege to hunt once a year within 20 miles of London. They use a disused royal hunting lodge at the top of **St John Street**. It's possible that pilgrims and drovers who arrived after Alders Gate and Cripple Gate closed for the night sheltered in the lodge and this was the beginning of the famous Angel Inn.

The 'angel' on the sign was probably Gabriel with Mary (until <u>Henry VIII</u> banned all pictorial references to the Virgin). There are 'Angel' inns all over England, but The Angel, Islington – close to St Mary's Nunnery, St John's Priory, the priory of St Bartholomew the Great, Bart's Hospital, Bartholomew Fair, Cloth Fair, Smithfield Market and the great City of London – is the most famous.

1548 A lead mill (survives until 1800) is powered by the river Walbrook which starts at the Angel and enters the City via Cripplegate. With water costing a penny a pail, the poor built their shanties and the rich their houses along the riverbank, which became first a lane, then a road. The Wall Brook is now **City Road** (see Rivers).

1638 Angel Inn rebuilt. Its galleried coachyard doubled as a theatre. Its superb location guaranteed financial success until trains replaced stagecoaches.

1665 Bubonic plague, the worst London has known. 593 die in Islington, 14 in one week. A victim was boarded into his house in the city (as was the custom) but broke out. He was turned away at the Angel Inn so staggered down the road to the Pied Bull (Sir Walter Raleigh's old house) where they gave him a room. Next morning, he was found dead.

1666 The Great Fire of London. The merchant class, forced out of London during the Great Fire, not wanting (and in many cases not able) to move back because of the high cost of rebuilding with stone, settled around The Angel so the aristocracy moved out. (See Great Fire of London.)

1747 William <u>Hogarth</u> paints *The Stage Coach at the Angel Inn, Islington.*

1773 Henry <u>Penton</u>, MP for Winchester, Lord of the Admiralty, builds **Penton Ville**, London's first designed suburb. (See entry under Pentonville Road.)

1782 *The Diverting History of John Gilpin; Showing How He Went Further Than He Intended And Came Safe Home Again.* This very funny poem written by William <u>Cowper</u>, a suicidal depressive, is about a 'Train Band' captain who sets off along Goswell Road, The Angel, Lower (then Essex) Road and Balls Pond Road to Edmonton with his wife, to celebrate their wedding anniversary at the Bell. His horse bolts, he loses his wig and ends up at Ware, ten miles further on.

1836 *Police Gazette* reports that 64 omnibuses carrying 4,000 passengers pass The Angel 375 times a day (see <u>Shillibeer</u>, George). Drivers were repeatedly fined for racing each other down City Road. This stopped only when a pedestrian was killed.

Charles <u>Dickens</u> makes frequent mention of the area. Porter and Smithers stay at The Angel Inn and Morfin lives here in *Making A Night of It.* Mrs Lirriper, Joe Willet, Barnaby Rudge, Mr Brownlow, John Browdie, Nicholas Nickleby, Esther Summerson, the Artful Dodger and Oliver Twist all come to The Angel. (See Dickens, Charles.)

1880 The Angel Inn is rebuilt (present building) with an 'angel' frieze (still there) which <u>Pevsner</u> (Sir Nikolaus, 1960s editor of *The Buildings of England*) described as '*jolly commercial vulgarity*'.

1899 The Silver Grille at the Angel Hotel serves 800 lunches a day.

1900 The Angel gets the first electric underground railway when the Northern Line opens. In 1901, City and South London Railway was extended from Moorgate to the Angel.

1905 Smith's erect a clock at the top of **City Road** (still there).

1907 City and South London Railway extended from the Angel to Euston.

1913 Islington's most luxurious cinema, the Angel Picture Theatre, opens. Its 100-foot Italianate campanile, or bell tower, is still one of the borough's best-loved landmarks. The cinema had a copper-domed roof, black and white marble floors, ornate plasterwork ceilings and housed the Angel Orchestra.

1921 The Angel Inn becomes a Lyons Corner House (until 1959). Joe Lyons was the first in Britain to offer fast-food, mass catering with white linen tablecloths and uniformed waitresses called 'nippies' (they 'nipped' around the tables). He offered a high standard of service at reasonable prices but went out of business in the 1970s.

1926 The Angel Picture Theatre becomes the Gaumont.

1934 *Monopoly*™ is invented by Charles Darrow in Atlantic City, New Jersey. Waddingtons of Leeds bought the UK rights, anglicised the board and made The Angel famous. As a slum that is, being one of the cheaper blue squares nobody wants. Today, The Angel is the third most popular area of London in which to live after Chelsea and Hampstead – and the sixth most expensive.

1960 The Angel Inn closes after 300 years.

1972 TV has killed the cinema. The remains of The Angel cinema were hidden behind a hoarding. Only its tower survives (listed Grade 2, see Cinemas).

1973 A pub in **Prebend Street** N1 is named after and opened by Carl <u>Giles</u>, famous cartoonist born at The Angel, who created the truly awful Grandma Buggins for the *Daily Express.* His original drawings line the walls.

1981 Now-derelict Angel Inn is taken over by the Co-op Bank.

1996 4,000 vehicles and 1,500 pedestrians pass The Angel every hour. Pollution damage to the lungs equals 60 cigarettes a day.

1999 *Islington Gazette* suggests: '*an angel for the Angel . . .*' St Martin's School of Art is commissioned to design one.

ANIMAL HOSPITAL
Sonderburg Road N7

1968 Princess Alexandra opens the Sir Harold <u>Harmsworth</u> (Viscount Rothermere) Hospital, built with a gift of £130,000. Sir Harold's (Associated Newspapers) brother is Viscount Northcliffe (Amalgamated Press). Between them they owned *The Evening News*, *The Daily Mail*, *The Daily Mirror*, *The Sunday Pictorial* and *The Sunday Dispatch*. Known locally as The Harmsworth, the hospital became famous in 1994 when it appeared each week in the hugely popular BBC-TV series *Animal Hospital*, presented by Rolf Harris.

ARCHWAY N19

So called after 1812 when the architect John <u>Nash</u> built an arch to span a huge (unplanned) hole in the road.

1370s Dick <u>Whittington</u>, bent on leaving the city, gets as far as Highgate before he 'turns again' (see Whittington, Sir Richard).

1386 The main route north (now the A1) is built through Highgate Village.

1473 William <u>Pole</u> founds a leper colony and spital (hospital) between **Salisbury Road** and **MacDonald Road,** called The Lazar House. People placed food and clothes for the lepers on a stone outside. They call it The Whittington Stone. When leprosy died out, the hospital took in plague victims.

1550 Bart's (St Bartholomew's Hospital) transfers its dying patients to Whittington Hospital. Each took his own mattress, bolster, sheets and bedcover.

1810 Hills are inconvenient for horses and carriages, so a tunnel is planned through **Highgate Hill**. After just 130 feet, the tunnel collapsed and the scheme was abandoned. How could traffic get across the hole? Ask famous architect, John <u>Nash</u> to build a bridge! He designed it in the style of a Roman aqueduct, one big arch supported by three smaller ones. The area became known as Arch Way (**Archway**).

1884 San Francisco comes to Islington when a cable car service opened between **Archway Tavern** and **Highgate Village**. Andrew <u>Hallidie</u>, a Scot, invented the cable tram for the steep hills of San Francisco after many horses suffered broken legs and had to be shot. He got his idea patented by The Cable Tramways Corporation of San Francisco and returned to London. **Highgate Hill** was perfect. The cable car operated for 30 years. Rails, 3½ feet apart, ran as far as **Southwood Road**. The power station and depot were opposite **Waterlow Park** gates.

1892 The cable car closes after an accident.

1900 LCC re-open the cable car. Nash's brick arch was replaced with the present bridge by Sir Alexander <u>Binnie</u>, chief engineer, London County Council (LCC).

1912 Highgate Station opens (re-named Highgate and Archway 1941, re-named Archway, 1947).

1910 The cable car is electrified.

1912 The Electric Palace, a magnificent cinema, is built next door to (the original) Highgate Station.

The huge, scalloped entrance led into a fairytale world resembling an Arabian palace. It was taken over by ABC cinema chain in 1937, closed for the duration of World War II, refurbished in 1958 and demolished to make way for **Archway Tower** (see Cinema).

1914 Mass murderer George '*brides-in-the-bath*' Smith lodges in **Bismarck Road** (see Smith, George).

1945 Rod Stewart, singer, is born at **Archway**. His parents owned a newsagents. He went to school with brothers Ray and Dave Davies of *The Kinks*. He didn't fancy being an accountant like his brother, so left school at 16 and became a gravedigger ... In less than a decade *Every Picture Tells A Story*, *Reason to Believe* and *Gasoline Alley* made him very rich (£150 million) and internationally famous.

1969 Actor and Goon Peter Sellers, crossing Binnie's 'Suicide Bridge' (first suicide occurred just after the bridge was built) with fellow actor Wilfrid Hyde-White, sees a crowd around a would-be jumper and persuades the man down (see Sellers, Peter). In 2000 Mad Pride holds a sunset vigil at Suicide Bridge.

1975 Archway Tower is built, hated even before it is completed.

1996 Glenda Jackson MP opens the first alternative clinic within a NHS hospital (Whittington). Archway Clinic of Herbal Medicine is the only facility of its kind in the UK.

....

ARSENAL FC
Avenell Road N5

The oldest football club in London, Arsenal has won the League Cup eleven times, the FA Cup seven times, the Double (Cup and League) twice (1970–71 and 1997–98). The club was started in 1886 in The Royal Oak pub next door to **Woolwich Arsenal** station by employees of the Royal Arsenal Armaments Factory, hence the team became known as The Gunners.

1893 Arsenal join the Football League.

1913 With a meagre £19 in the bank, the club is looking for a permanent ground. It had to be in a densely populated area within Greater London near good public transport (to attract huge crowds). Harringay and Battersea were considered before the chairman, Henry Norris, spotted the grounds of St John's College of Divinity, **Highbury**. Residents objected to a football club moving in. Negotiations continued for months, the Ecclesiastical Commissioners tried to put the club off by demanding a prohibitive £20,000 for a 21-year lease (the eventual deed of transfer was signed by the Archbishop of Canterbury, no less). Islington Council too vetoed the idea; however, before the Town & Country Planning Act planning permission was not needed so the move went ahead. Being on a hill the pitch had to be raised by 11 feet at one end and lowered by 4 feet at the other. The Club was unable to afford the work, so the builder agreed to be paid from turnstile takings.

When war broke out a year later (1914), the players were called back to work in the munitions factory they had just left.

1925 Herbert Chapman, ex-Huddersfield Town, makes The Arsenal the most famous football club in the world. The first thing he did was to drop 'The' from the name, so that Arsenal was alphabetically the first club in the League (until Aldershot joined). The next was to get London Underground to change the name of **Gillespie Road** station (opened 1906) to Arsenal so fans could find the ground. (Gillespie Road is known to locals for *Henry Stephens & Co., Ink Manufacturers*, here since 1892). The third was to buy the freehold of the ground. The College of Divinity became the club's tenant.

1929 Arsenal win FA Cup for the first time.

1930–31 Win FA Cup again at Wembley. The *Graf Zeppelin* flies over the ground to dip a salute to King George V.

1932–33 Chapman builds the famous West Stand – and, after seven years of lobbying, succeeded in getting Gillespie Road station changed to Arsenal.

1936 FA Cup winners. New manager, George Allison rebuilds the East Stand.

1938 Highbury Film Studios, **Highbury New Park**, release the Boulting Brothers' *Arsenal Stadium Mystery* featuring the 1938 line-up, including captain Eddie Hapgood, manager George Allison and trainer Tom Whittaker. Islington filmgoers cheered every time the curtain went up.

1957 Legends of the England team, Sir Stanley Matthews, Duncan Edwards ('Busby Babe', died in the Manchester United air disaster at Munich) and Billy Wright train at Arsenal for the match against Scotland, the last game Matthews (d. 1999) played for England, winning his 54th cap at the age of 42.

1964 Hornsey Road Baths opened by Billy Wright CBE, 90 times captain of England, Manager Arsenal FC 1962–66. Married to Joy, one of the Beverley Sisters, he was proof that great footballers do not necessarily make good managers.

1970–71 The Double: FA Cup and League Cup. Also top of the 1st Division.

1972 Club awarded Freedom of the Borough.

1988 Corporate entertainment arrives. Eight-seater luxury executive boxes unveiled at the South End with en-suite catering, closed-circuit and satellite TV.

1992 Nick Hornby publishes *Fever Pitch*, a best-selling novel about Arsenal (see Hornby, Nick).

1993 Following the Taylor Report on safety after the Hillsborough stadium disaster, Arsenal introduces all-seater North stand.

1994 All-seater stadium opens. The waiting time for a £500 season ticket was now four years. A museum was also opened in the North stand.

1998 Channel 4 TV debate on whether homes should stand in the way of expanding the stadium.

2000 Talks in progress on closing the historic stadium and building a new one a mile away opposite Holloway Road Tube station.

AUSTRALIA

King George III finally acknowledged in 1790 that he no longer owned America. So now where were we going to send convicts sentenced to transportation from the Sessions House, **Clerkenwell Green**?

1812 Thomas Homer, overseer on the **Regent's Canal** is up for embezzlement before the magistrate at the Sessions House and transported (see Regent's Canal).

1834 Six farm labourers from Tolpuddle in Dorset – trade unionists Thomas Standfield and brother John, George Loveless and brother James, James Hammett and James Brine –

collectively known as The Tolpuddle Martyrs – are sentenced to transportation (see **Tolpuddle Street**, also Wakley, Thomas). 120,000 trade union members led by Robert Owen gathered on **Copenhagen Fields** to demand their release and marched to Whitehall with a petition. Wakley, local MP, finally got them pardoned. George Loveless, the first to return, was given a hero's welcome at the White Conduit House (q.v.), **Pentonville**.

1846 Caroline Chisholm, 'the emigrants' friend', moves to 3 Charlton Crescent N1 (now 32 **Charlton Place**, blue plaque 1983) where she based her Family Colonisation Loan Society. Married to an English army officer posted to New South Wales (where she remains a legend), she set up a chain of women's hostels. Returning to London, she travelled the country tracking down relatives of transported convicts and persuaded the government to give them free passage to Australia. A close friend of Dickens, he said that her children were 'badly behaved'. (Both faces are familiar: Mrs Chisholm ended up on the Australian $5 note, Dickens on our £10.)

1861 Australia refuses to take any more criminals and in 1900 gained its own constitution and Parliament.

1950 Post-war **Charlton Place** is earmarked for demolition but Islington Council didn't get around to it. Today the houses are listed as architecturally important, many valued at over a quarter of a million pounds.

....

BABBAGE, Charles (1791–1871)

Mathematician and father of the computer

Nineteenth-century Islington was represented in Parliament by four members in the constituency of **Finsbury**. One contender was mathematics wizard, Charles Babbage, who ran twice with no luck. When the Reform Bill of 1832 extended a newly enfranchised electorate, he stood as the Candidate for Science. Already a national figure, he received good press coverage when he addressed meetings in Canonbury Tavern and at the Crown on **Clerkenwell Green**. He campaigned for state intervention in education. One of his opponents was Wakley, saviour of the Tolpuddle Martyrs (q.v.) who, like him, lost on that occasion to Sir Robert Grant.

1834 Babbage tries again when Grant is made governor of Bombay but loses to Duncombe (see Duncombe, Thomas). He wrote a comic play about his defeats. Founder of the Astronomical Society, Babbage spent 40 years trying to perfect an automatic calculator he called the Difference Engine, a prototype computer. (Lord Byron's daughter, Ada Lovelace worked as his assistant).

1991 British engineers, following his detailed drawings and specifications, reconstruct the Difference Engine. It worked flawlessly. Babbage's idea was simply 100 years ahead of its time and the technology needed to make it work had not yet been invented.

....

BACON, Sir Francis (1561–1626)

Politician, poet and 'Renaissance Man'

1616 James I's Lord Chancellor, Keeper of The Great Seal of England, moves into **Canonbury Tower** N1 and stays until his death, ten years later. Solicitor and Attorney General, Bacon owned a town house on the Strand and a country mansion at St Albans. An avid gardener, local legend has it he planted the mulberry tree which grows here. (Possible. Hundreds of thousands of mulberry trees were planted by the gentry as a seventeenth-century experiment to encourage the silk worm industry, however they were mostly of the wrong type and Continental – later American silk – was cheaper.)

1618 Having seen off one old friend (<u>Essex</u>), Bacon helps to remove another, Sir Walter <u>Raleigh</u>, on trumped-up charges, successfully arguing for his execution. 'Sly', 'vindictive', 'icy-hearted', 'repellent', 'duplicitous', 'reptilian' are some of the nicer descriptions we have of Bacon. Even his doctor, William <u>Harvey</u> (of 'circulation of the blood' fame, see Harvey, William), said he had 'the eyes of a viper.'

1621 Bacon becomes Viscount St Albans. Three days later, he was charged with corruption. A trained lawyer, he pleaded guilty, was banished from Court, stripped of office and fined £40 thousand, an enormous sum.

1626 Death of Bacon.

According to John <u>Aubrey</u>, the Nigel Dempster of his day, Bacon left Canonbury Tower by coach with his friend Dr Witherborne, the king's GP, to visit the Earl of Arundel in High Gate. It was winter, and they discussed whether meat would preserve as well in snow as it did in salt. In the true spirit of scientific inquiry, they knocked on a cottage door to buy a chicken, and asked the peasant to pluck it. Bacon stuffed the bird with snow but got chilled himself in the process. He took to his bed and died three days later. (Other sources suggest he died of a drug overdose.) Local legend has it that a featherless chicken still haunts **Pond Square**.

1681 John Aubrey again: 'Sir Harbottle Grimston (only The Goons could beat that), Master of the Rolls, on being told there is no room at St Michael's Church for his tomb, removes that of Francis Bacon who had lain there sixty years.'

1886 The Francis Bacon Society moves into Canonbury Tower. In 1769 the theory was first put forward that a mere 'Stratford rustic' could not possibly have written the plays attributed to Shakespeare, and that Bacon was the real author. The Society was formed to examine the evidence.

....

BARNSBURY N1, N7

Local legend has it that in AD 66 not only was there a Roman camp here but <u>Suetonius</u>, the Roman general and historian, lay in wait for <u>Boadicea/Boudicca</u> on her way home to Norfolk after burning down Londinium and that battle (see Battle Bridge) took place between **Sheen Grove** *and* **Boxworth Grove**.

1066 <u>William the Conqueror</u> gives Geoffrey <u>de Mandeville</u> the Lordship of north Islington, owned by the Bishop of London.

1200s Ralph <u>de Berners</u> owns the Lordship.

1430 Margery, daughter of Sir James <u>Berners</u>, gives part of Barnsbury to <u>Charterhouse</u>.

1515 John <u>Bourchier</u>, Lord Berners, is Chancellor of the Exchequer. He went with Henry VIII and Thomas <u>More</u> to the Field of the Cloth of Gold. (Oliver <u>Cromwell</u> married a Bourchier).

1523 Lord Berners translates Froissart's *Chronicles* and makes Sir Walter <u>de Manny</u>, founder of Charterhouse, famous.

1539 Sir Thomas <u>Fowler</u>, Lord of the Manor, Deputy Lieutenant for Middlesex, is a close friend of Henry VIII. His daughter, Margaret Fowler <u>Savile</u>, 19, died in childbirth. There's a brass of her in St Mary's dated 1546. Queen Elizabeth's Lodge in Mansion House Garden (**Cross Street**), built for her by Fowler, was still there in 1655. The manor house survived until 1845. (Sir Thomas was a juror at Raleigh's trial.)

1642 Sir William <u>Halton</u>, wealthy royalist landowner, is married to Ursula, daughter of Sir Thomas <u>Fisher</u>, Lord of the Manor.

1752 Thomas <u>Lord</u> starts the White Conduit Cricket Club in **Barnsbury Road** N1, precursor of the Marylebone Cricket Club (MCC) which plays at the famous Lord's ground in St John's Wood. (See MCC)

1754 Sir William Halton gives the manor of Barnsbury to William <u>Tuffnell</u>, provided he agrees to style himself Joliffe. The Joliffes owned the manor until 1925.

1824 Charles <u>Barry</u> builds Holy Trinity Church, **Cloudesley Square** (see Barry, Sir Charles).

1827 Barnsbury Square is laid out.

1829 Barnsbury, on the social map for the White Conduit House cricket matches and pleasure gardens, gets caught up in the building boom. Its fields were ploughed for clay to make the bricks to build the houses surrounding the kilns. Businessmen needed to live within walking distance of the city, so moved into the newly-built squares (see Traffic Problem, the).

1831 Every Sunday, Michael <u>Faraday</u>, the 'father of electricity', can be seen walking to or from his local Sandemanian Church (q.v.).

1841 Ebenezer <u>Landells</u> launches *Punch* and *Illustrated London News* from **Thornhill Road**.

1842 Pentonville prison opens in **Caledonian** Road (see Pentonville Prison, *et al.*).

1846 Charles **Chubb** of Chubb's Patent Lock and Key fame dies at home – 8 **Barnsbury Park**.

1849 White Conduit House is demolished. Barnsbury is completely built-up and views of the city lost.

1861 Foundation stone of the **Agricultural Halls** laid by Lord Berners.

1918 Sir Gerald <u>Tyrwhitt-Wilson</u> succeeds as 14th Baron Berners. Friend of Fascist leader Sir Oswald Mosley; writes musical scores for **Sadler's Wells Ballet**.

1925 The Lordship of the manor of Barnsbury, but not the title, becomes defunct.

1931 Walter <u>Sickert</u> RA moves to 14 **Barnsbury Park**.

1953 Robert <u>Carrier</u> arrives in London for the Queen's coronation. He moved to Barnsbury Square, opened a restaurant in Camden Passage and started a TV 'personality chef' trend with *Carrier's Kitchen*.

1960s Juggernaut drivers use the squares for overnight parking. Residents proposed a Keep Out scheme which the Council adopted. Streets were humped with 'sleeping policemen' and became virtually inaccessible by car (see Traffic Problem, the).

1968 Anna <u>Scher</u> takes over an empty chapel in **Barnsbury Road**, opens a drama club for underprivileged kids and ends up creating a 'Fame' factory (see Scher, Anna).

1976 Poet Laureate, Sir John <u>Betjeman</u> opens **Battishill Gardens**. The 70-feet long stone frieze came from the 1842 Hall of Commerce, Threadneedle Street, demolished 1922.

1992 The title Baroness Berners is inherited by Pamela Kirkham (b.1929).

1994 Media attention beams on a Mr Tony Blair MP, of **Richmond Crescent**, when John Smith, Leader of the Labour Party, dies unexpectedly at Bart's.

BARRY, Sir Charles (1795–1860)
Architect

1824 Master of the fashionable Gothic style, is commissioned to build four churches in Islington. The first was Holy Trinity, **Cloudesley Square** N1. *The Gentleman's Magazine*, **St John's Gate**, criticised him for the boring view from **Liverpool Road**. Other churches designed by young Barry were St Paul's, Hopping Lane (now **St Paul's Road** N1) closed 1980, St John's, **Pemberton Gardens**, Holloway N19 and St Peter's, **Devonia Road** N1 (closed 1982). Externally, St John's and St Paul's were almost identical.

1836 Barry becomes famous when he is commissioned to design the Palace of Westminster (Houses of Parliament, occupied him until he died in 1860). He preferred to forget his early churches in Islington, so burnt the plans.

1842 The portcullis entrance to **Pentonville Prison** is by Barry.

BARTHOLOMEW FAIR
Smithfield EC1

1133 Fundraising for *Bart's Hospital*, the Prior holds a fair (another life-enhancing custom imported from France) every 24 August on St Bartholomew's Holy Day. Bartholomew Fair (Bartelmy to locals), an international success, survived until the 1850s. Ben Jonson, Thomas Hardy, Charles Lamb, William Wordsworth *et al.* all wrote about it. Dickens immortalised it in *Oliver Twist*. Huge revenues were collected from Cloth Fair, the most commercially important part of the fair held along the churchyard's north wall.

The first bale of cloth from the loom was cut by the Lord Mayor to declare the fair open, a ceremony repeated all over the world every time someone cuts a ribbon to open an event.

The inn sign of the Hand and Shears, **Cloth Fair** EC1, commemorates the cloth-cutting tradition. Upstairs, a 'Pie Powder Court' dispensed summary justice while the fair was on (held at all large fairs until as recently as 1971. The name comes from Londoners' mispronunciation of pieds (feet) and pouldrous (dusty). Members of the Worshipful Companies of Mercers (silk merchants) and Merchant Taylors ensured 'fair' trading; after nine hundred years we still have an office of Fair Trading (OFT).

1614 Ben Jonson's *Bartholomew Fair* gives a wonderful flavour of the time, full of the drunks and 'cut purses' who lived near Ruffians Hall (local name for **Smithfield**). His characters included Little Wit, Well Born, Trash, Punk Alice and Purecraft. 'Puring' (pooper scooping) was still going on in Dickens' day (doggy-do was used to cure leather).

1855 After seven hundred years, the fair is closed.

2000 The Butchers and Drovers Charitable Institution revives the Fair for the same reason it was started, to raise funds for Bart's Hospital. It's opened by TV personality cook, One Fat Lady, Clarissa Dickson Wright.

BART'S (Hospital) EC1

1420 St Bartholomew the Great Priory and Hospital (with, say some sources, 200 beds, others 2000), built in the 1100s, divides into two independent institutions. This proved fortunate when Henry VIII later closed the priory but due to public outcry had to allow the hospital to remain open. As a sop to his ego, his statue was erected over the door, the only surviving outdoor statue of him. Bart's became a teaching hospital and was established as a parish in its own right. Saint Bartholomew the Less was converted from a medieval chapel within the hospital tower and west wall.

1550 Terminally ill patients are sent to Whittington Hospital (see Archway).

1572 Architect, Inigo Jones is baptised in St Bartholomew the Less.

1609 William Harvey is a physician here. He demonstrated how the blood circulates, to the derision of colleagues who said it ebbed and flowed like the tide. Harvey was court physician to both James I and son Charles I (whom he accompanied throughout the Civil War). The Harveian Oration is still given in his honour every year at the Royal College of Physicians.

1760s Little Wolfgang Amadeus Mozart has his tonsils out.

1835 John Leech, local Charterhouse boy, is studying medicine but gives it up to become a cartoonist.

1874 Later-to-be Poet Laureate, Robert Bridges qualifies as a doctor.

1877–79 Dr Bridges is in charge of the casualty department (see Bridges, Robert).

1879 Cricketing legend, Dr W.G. Grace qualifies (and donates his bat).

1880 Bart's offers training for nurses (married women are excluded).

1887 Sherlock Holmes and Dr Watson first meet here in Sir Arthur Conan Doyle's *A Study in Scarlet.* The hospital still gets Holmes fans asking to be shown where they met.

1992 Despite Henry I's promise to '*maintain and defend this place even as my crown ... and let this place be perpetually defended by the protection of kings*', and despite 98.6 per cent of those concerned disagreeing, the Tomlinson Report says Bart's must close: there were 'too many' hospital beds in London. By Christmas there were half a million signatures on the protest petition and thousands joined a torchlight procession.

1995 The Accident and Emergency (A&E) ward closes.

1996 Plans are afoot to turn part of Bart's into a museum. Peg legs, amputation saws, pestles and mortars, Dr Grace's bat and the largest medical archive in the UK lie three vaults below, many of them hidden since 1127.

1997 Mrs Monica Willan, 81, born and brought up in Clerkenwell, plagued with arthritis, lives in sheltered housing on the Peabody estate. She fronted the *Save Bart's* campaign which tackled Health Secretary, Mrs Virginia Bottomley, head-on in court and won. Bart's was reprieved.

1998 Pathologists at Bart's and Edinburgh specialising in breast cancer pioneer diagnostic links over the Internet.

....

BATTERSEA DOGS HOME
Started in Holloway.

1860 Mary Tealby (**Tealby Court**, George's Row, Ring Cross Estate N7) opens the world's first animal refuge, *The Temporary Home for Lost and Starving Dogs*, behind her house at 15 Hollingsworth Mews, Hollingsworth Street, Lower Holloway (now completely disappeared), known as Holloway Dogs Home.

Her neighbours, naturally, were not best pleased when she died in 1865 leaving hundreds of barking dogs. Her work was carried on by a committee, but complaints continued to pour in, so in 1869, over eight hundred dogs were taken away.

1871 Holloway Dogs Home moves to Battersea. One wing was named after Mrs Tealby. She is said to haunt the Home though she died long before it came into existence.

....

BATTLE BRIDGE N1

Which battle? No-one knows. Possibly Celts v. Romans (Boadicea v. Suetonius) or Saxons v. Danes (Edmund v. Cnut). Academics still have no real idea where the battle took place; so, until they do, the Icenean Queen remains an honorary Islingtonian. In 1937, Buckingham Street was re-named **Boadicea Street** *N1.*

61 AD Celtic Queen Boudicca, a 40-year-old widow, after burning down Londinium (lumps of her fire are still being found) commits suicide rather than surrender to the Romans. The battle (see Barnsbury), it's said, took place near the bridge (the only one) which crossed the 'river of wells' (later re-named the Fleet).

A succession of Battle Bridges survived until 1862, when tracks were laid along the river bed for the world's first underground railway. Battle Bridge is now The Scala Cinema and local legend has it that Boudicca is buried underneath (in King's Cross station, platform number varies between 8 and 13, depending on the guide book).

1016 Saxon King Edmund (Ironside) battles with Danish King Canute/Cnut. Edmund won and a well sprang up at his feet, which he dedicated to St Chad (place of pilgrimage for centuries). **St Chad Street** is still in King's Cross WC1.

1660s Charles II builds a summer home at Bagnigge Wells (pronounced Bagnidge, probably the name of the landowner) for Nell Gwynne, his favourite mistress (plaque 61–63 **King's Cross Road**). The Fleet flowed through the gardens.

1756 Battle Bridge village disappears when **Pentonville Road** is built.

1772 Hundreds take the waters at Chad's Well.

1826 Hundreds still queue every morning to take the waters, said to cure rheumatism, gout, liver problems, dropsy and scrofula (a tubercular swelling of the glands).

1830 Battle Bridge loses its ancient name.

By now it was a vast area of rolling hills. Not grassy green ones, but hills, mountains even, of horse and cattle carcasses, cinders, domestic refuse, animal dung, dead babies and human excrement, known quaintly to the Victorians as 'dust heaps'. These were worth up to £40,000 a year to the owners. Local legend has it that the Russians bought both King's Cross and Mount Pleasant rubbish tips as infill to rebuild Moscow after Napoleon. If true, there is another part of a foreign land that is forever Islington. In any case, the tips were cleared because the authorities wanted to build a monument to the reviled George IV – and Battle Bridge became King's Cross.

1997 Speculators and developers move in. Marketing people revert to the old names as **King's Cross** (q.v.) is now synonymous with crime, drugs, prostitutes and pimps. Battle Bridge becomes 'The Gateway to Europe' and is renamed **Ice Wharf**. Flats overlooking the canal fetch half a million pounds.

....

BEARDSLEY, Aubrey (1872–1898)

Oscar Wilde's illustrator

1888 Beardsley, 16, of the weird haircut and beaky nose, leaves Brighton Grammar School and starts his first job in the District Surveyor's office, 5 **Wilmington Square** WC1. Some sources say he rented a studio at No. 20. His boss was Ernie Carritt, his salary £16 a year and he stayed nine months until he found a better paid job with Guardian Fire and Life Assurance.

....

BEDLAM
Lunatic asylum. Founded 1247 in Bishopsgate, burnt down 1666 (Great Fire of London).

1675 The first psychiatric hospital in Europe (possibly the world) is built near present day **Finsbury Circus** EC2. The magnificent, palatial Bethlehem Royal Hospital was designed by Robert Hooke, Surveyor of London and friend of Sir Christopher Wren. Patients stayed 12 months after which they were discharged as cured or incurable. Violence against patients was forbidden. Cold and hot baths, purgatives, blood letting were the order of the day before manacles were resorted to.

1680 Caius Cibber (actor/dramatist son Colley will live in **Colebrooke Row**) sculpts two huge stone statues, *Raving Madness* and *Melancholy Madness* (symptoms of manic depression), from Portland stone for the entrance. His model, a patient, was one of Cromwell's soldiers from his New Model Army. The poet Alexander Pope called them *'great Cibber's brazen brainless brothers.'*

1693 Tourists do The Tower, Westminster Abbey, London Bridge and Bedlam (pay to see the patients), in that order.

1735 Hogarth visits to sketch patients for *The Rake's Progress*; he has them wearing jesters' hats, scribbling on the walls.

1770 Bedlam closes its doors to the paying public when John Howard of the Penal Reform League denounces the practice.

1815 Bedlam is closed. 120 patients were taken in Hackney carriages to the new Bedlam in Lambeth. Among them James Hatfield, who had tried to shoot George III at Drury Lane Theatre, and Margaret Nicholson, who tried to stab him. In 1851, architect Augustus Pugin, whose parents are buried in St Mary's churchyard, was a patient.

1999 Plans are on the drawing board for a museum charting the history of treatment of the mentally distressed. It will have the foundation stone of the original Bedlam and Caius Cibber's sculptures.

....

BENNETT, Arnold (1867–1931)
Novelist

1888 Aged 21, leaves Staffordshire and comes to London as a solicitor's clerk. He lodged at 46 **Alexander Road** N19, off Holloway Road, described in *Hilda Lessways* as: *'... the longest street she had ever seen, ten thousand small new houses all alike and vistas of endless, endless railway arches ... dark torrents of human beings ... covering the platforms with tramping feet'.*

1916 Has a stall in **Caledonian Market** N7 to support War Allies and raises £20,000. Lloyd George offered him a knighthood, which he refused.

1922 Explores Islington by taxi, a strange sight in those days, to research *Riceyman Steps*. Set in 1919, the novel is about a miserly bookseller in **King's Cross Road**. Historic steps leading from the road to **Granville Square** are now protected. Officially **Gwynne**

Place WC1 (after Nell Gwynne who lived there), locals called them Plum Pudding Steps or Riceyman Steps. Many Islington locations are mentioned in the book.

1937 St Philip's, Granville Square (built 1831), featured in *Riceyman Steps*, is demolished.

BETJEMAN, Sir John (1906–1984)
Poet Laureate

Fourth generation of the Islington Betjemans. Loved the Highbury of his parents and grandparents and looked upon it as home: 'It's north of the Thames for me.' His father and father's brother were baptised in St Mary's, **Upper Street***; other family members attended Union Chapel,* **Compton Terrace***. George (great-grandfather) came from Germany and married Eleanor Smith, a London girl.*

1820 George starts a cabinet making business in **Ashby Street** EC1 off Northampton Square. His son and daughter married another brother and sister, children of William <u>Meyrick</u>, a Welshman living in **Northampton Square** (William Meyrick Jnr married Rebecca Betjeman, George Betjeman Jnr married Mary Anne Meyrick).

1860 George Betjeman moves his (manu)factory from Ashby Street to 36 **Pentonville Road** N1. The company made dressing-tables, writing desks and the Betjeman-patented Tantalus, a contraption for locking alcohol away from the servants. The poet wrote: '*The Tantalus with an en-grade lock was invented I believe by my grandfather, who died of the things he was locking up ... e.g. brandy, whisky and gin, which were presumably in those square-cut decanters.*' He remembered exploring upstairs at 'The Works' and discovering: '*a dusty drawing room, completely furnished, where great grandfather had lived above his work before moving up to sylvan Highbury.*'

1870 John (grandfather) marries local girl Hannah Thompson in newly-built St Saviour's, **Aberdeen Park** N5 (parish redundant 1981, merged with Christ Church, Highbury). His cousin, Gilbert <u>Betjeman</u>, Musician to Queen Victoria, lived in nearby **Hillmarton Road** N7.

1873 John and Hannah move to 329 **Holloway Road**. Their son Ernest (poet's father) attended Highbury Park School.

1882 Family moves to 13 **Compton Terrace** N1 and stays until old John Betjeman dies (1897).

1902 Ernest enters the family business. He, like his father, was married in St Saviour's. His bride was Mabel (Bess) Dawson. Both were born and raised in Highbury.

1919 Young John convinces his disappointed father that his will not be the fourth generation to carry on the family business.

1945 The Betjeman factory in Pentonville Road closes.

1948 JB attends St Saviour's where his parents and grandparents were married.

1955 Revives popular interest in Islington duo, George and Weedon Grossmith's *Diary of a Nobody*.

1960 Publishes autobiographical poem, *Summoned by Bells*. St Saviour's Aberdeen Park and other Islington locations become famous.

1962 Leaves home in **Cloth Fair** EC1 dressed in old overcoat with patched elbows, safety pins holding it together, to unveil <u>Cruden</u>'s plaque in **Camden Passage** N1 (q.v.). Cruden's house is now Portofino's Restaurant so the plaque is on the nearest house.

1969 Knighted.

1972 Poet Laureate.

1974 Revisits family haunts in Highbury, Holloway and 'The Works' in Pentonville Road (now Medici Society Greeting Cards). Bits of the old factory (a door, the Counting House and the parlour with its original fireplace) remained.

1976 Sir John opens **Battishill Gardens**, Barnsbury N1.

2000 His poems are among those voted most popular in *Radio Times* poll *The Nation's Favourite Poems of Childhood*.

....

BLAIR, Tony (1953–)
Prime Minister

1986 Labour MP for Nottingham, Sedgefield, moves to **Stavordale Road**, Highbury.

1988 Shadow Cabinet. Portfolio for energy.

1991 Shadow Employment Secretary.

1992 Shadow Home Affairs. Moves from Highbury to 1 **Richmond Terrace**, Barnsbury N1.

1994 May. John Smith, Leader of the Labour Party, unexpectedly dies. Collapsing in the **Barbican**, he was rushed around the corner to **Bart's** but pronounced dead on arrival. Local legend has it that Blair met with Gordon Brown MP, Shadow Chancellor, at the Granita Restaurant, **Upper Street** N1 to, so the story goes, ask him not to challenge for the leadership. The restaurant is circumspect over who eats there but rumour has it that the pair sat at table 12, also frequented by Princess Margaret. Douglas Adams eats here, as do showbiz luminaries Simon Callow, Angus Deayton, Sidney Lumet, Harold Pinter, John Schlesinger, Zoe Wanamaker, *et al*.

1994 July. Gets 57 per cent of 'one member, one vote' to become leader of the Labour Party.

1996 Ditches sacrosanct Clause Four: *'To secure for the producers by hand or by brain the full fruits of their industry upon the basis of common ownership of the means of production'*, sidelining the Unions, who formed the original Labour Party (in **Farringdon Road**), in favour of 'New Labour' and the as-yet undefined Third Way. (See *New Statesman* and other entries.)

1997 Second Islington Labour politician to bring down a Conservative government (Barbara Castle did it in 1963). 1 May, after eighteen years of Tory rule, under Blair Labour won a landslide victory. Of the Islington MPs, Jeremy Corbyn, Islington North ('old' Labour) polled 24,834, Chris Smith (Heritage Secretary), Islington South ('new' Labour) polled 22,079 (Tony Blair clocked up 33,526 in Sedgefield).

Islington's remaining Tories suggested former Social Security minister Peter Lilley, who lives in **Canonbury Road**, should be the new leader of the Conservative Party. William Hague was elected instead. Political pundits mutter about the Islington caucus of Tony's cronies (Chris Smith MP, Jack Straw MP, Margaret Hodge MP, Stephen Twigg MP), all one-time Islington councillors and close neighbours singled out for PM attention.

1999 In the House of Commons, Hague dubs Blair *'The Angel of Islington.'*

2000 Property prices make front page of national newspapers. Flats in the old Thames Water building, **New River Head**, cost £400,000 each. The former Blair home has a Council Tax assessment of £1,756 per annum (10 Downing Street is only £590).

....

BLISHEN, Edward
Writer

1960s Blishen, a teacher at Archway Secondary Modern School, is determined to force some culture down the throats of his tough, street-wise pupils. He was often seen on Islington streets, leading his flock. His wonderfully ghastly experiences inspired *Roaring Boys*, a shattering description of schools in slum areas. It propelled him into the limelight as an authority on education.

Blishen registered as a 'conchy' (conscientious objector) during World War II, was sent to work as an agricultural labourer and wrote about it in *A Cackhanded War* (1972). Later books included: *Sorry Dad* (1978) (his father disapproved of writers), and *Shaky Relations* (1981). The latter won him the J.R. Ackerley Award for autobiography. A Fellow of the Royal Society for Literature and presenter of BBC Radio 4's *A Good Read*, Blishen died in 1997, age 76.

....

BOOTH, Cherie QC (1953–)

QC, married to Tony Blair, Prime Minister (q.v.)

1986 The Blairs buy 10 **Stavordale Road**, Highbury N5 from Peter Stothard, editor of *The Times*. Their three children attended nearby Joan of Arc Catholic School. Had Cherie Booth returned to her roots? (See below.)

1992 Moves to 1 **Richmond Crescent**, Barnsbury N1.

1997 Moves to 10 Downing Street, Whitehall, Westminster.

THE BOOTH FAMILY SAGA

Father, actor Anthony Booth (Alf Garnett's 'Goldilocks' in BBC TV's Till Death Us Do Part*) believes his family is connected to* **John Wilkes Booth***, who assassinated President Lincoln. He may in fact be descended from two old Clerkenwell gin distilling families, the Booths and the Wilkes. Booth (probably) bought out Wilkes, the families (probably) intermarried and joined the more famous Wilkes name (see* Wilkes*, John) with the Booth family name.*

1550 Hermitage Fields at The Angel is bought by Thomas Wilkes, a local brewer.

1567 Alice Wilkes (15), daughter of Thomas, has a go at milking a cow. As she stood up, the legend goes, an arrow landed in her hat. Grateful for her life, she vowed that if ever she became rich (richer?) she would build a school for the poor in Islington (see Owen, Dame Alice). She did.

1582 Middlesex Sessions Roll lists Robert Wilkes, 'beare brewer', of Islington.

1596 Middlesex Sessions Roll lists Christopher Wilkes, 'vintner' (wine merchant), of Islington.

1688 Booth's Gin opens in **Cowcross Street**.

1727 St James Court, **St John Square**, Clerkenwell. John Wilkes, famous radical politician, is born.

1821 Junius Booth, actor, emigrates to America.

1825 Over from America, he appears at Sadler's Wells.

1832 Edwin, son of Junius Booth, is born. He became America's leading Shakespearean tragic actor.

1837 Henry Wilkes Booth, 20, dies at home, 8 **Albemarle Street**, Clerkenwell EC1 and was buried in St John's churchyard.

1839 Junius Booth has a third son he christens John Wilkes.

1865 Ford's Theatre, Washington: John Wilkes Booth, disaffected confederate, shoots dead President Lincoln on opening night.

Booth broke a leg escaping from the theatre. The unsuspecting Dr Mudd was imprisoned for treating him (giving rise to the expression 'your name is Mudd around here'). The career of brother Edwin, America's most illustrious actor of his era, received a boost from the publicity. A portrait of him by John Singer Sargent hangs in The Players Club, Gramercy Park, New York. John Wilkes Booth refused to surrender and was shot in a barn in Virginia.

2000 A lock of John Wilkes Booth's hair is auctioned and fetches £40,000. A piece of the towel used to stem Lincoln's wounds went for £10,000, the sheet which covered his body for £20,000.

BOYCOTT, Rosie (1952–)
Editor

1972 Launches feminist magazine, *Spare Rib*, from 27 **Clerkenwell Close** EC1, Britain's first magazine to give a voice to the Women's Movement. The cover models were ordinary women without make-up. Topics such as battered women's refuges, an abortion referral unit in Liverpool and NHS vasectomies are covered. Erica (*Fear of Flying*) Jong visited. Writers include famous names such as John Berger, Margaret Drabble, Eva Figes, Edna O'Brien and Fay Weldon. Subjects included equal pay, abortion law, women and the law, sexual equality and sexual harassment in the work place. When *Spare Rib* became a women's collective, Boycott lost interest and left (see also Feminism).

2000 Ms Boycott is Editor, the *Daily Express*.

BOYSON, Dr Rhodes (Sir) (1925–)
MP and pedagogue

1960s The Wilson government (Education Secretary Shirley Williams) has abolished grammar schools. Labour-run Inner London Education Authority (ILEA) closes high-achieving **Dame Owen School** and **St Aloysius College** (Peter Sellers's old school) in Islington.

1966 Fully paid-up member of the Labour Party, ex-grammar school boy and strict disciplinarian, new Head, Dr Boyson's brief is to combine Highbury Grammar School (academic subjects, every pupil passed the 11+), Barnsbury Secondary Modern School (non-academic subjects, no pupil passed the 11+) and Laycock Street School (no subjects, 'problem boys' expelled, trouble with the law, etc.,) into one 'comprehensive' school, Highbury Grove, where 1,350 pupils are all to be given the same education.

(1966) Michael Duane, head of the failing Risinghill (**Hermes Hill, John Street**) Comprehensive School, in the news for banning corporal punishment, is sacked. In *Risinghill: Death of a Comprehensive School*, Leila Berg wrote: '. . . out of one of the dirtiest, ugliest, most despised parts of London, where two prisons bar the streets like warning fingers, a co-educational comprehensive school shot into the newspaper headlines . . .' The Press was also camped outside the Head's door at the failing William Tyndale School; while, when Pink Floyd needed children to sing 'We don't need no education' (*The Wall*), where did they go, but to the failing Islington Green School?

1971 On entrance to Highbury Grove many eleven-year-olds had a reading level of eight. The school, with its impressive academic results, was besieged by parents who wanted their children to go there. A furious ILEA ordered them to enrol at their nearest school in their own area, so parents moved to be nearer Highbury Grove. In Boyson's catchment area, property prices rose rapidly.

1972 White Lion Free School opens, run by pupils who did as they pleased, including not attending lessons. Pupils could choose what, if, and when they learned.

1974 Boyson accuses the *'loony left'* of *'trying to inculcate a socialist revolution via the classroom'*, giving *carte blanche* for slack teaching and expecting pupils to learn to read *'by discovery.'* He resigned from Highbury Grove after eight years and became dyed-in-the-wool Thatcherite Conservative MP for Brent North.

1983 Minister for Social Security.

1990s Islington schools have one of the worst reputations in the UK.

1999 Damning Ofsted report (GCSE results 'lowest in London'). Islington Labourites, including the Blairs, were already sending their children to schools outside the borough.

2000 Henry Jones, acting head teacher at Highbury Grove, has his ear slashed by youths outside the school. Education is handed over to private management, Cambridge Education Associates winning the seven-year contract.

BRIDEWELL
Prison, Clerkenwell, see **Sans Walk** EC1

BRIDGES, Robert (1844–1930)
Poet Laureate

1874 Qualifies as a doctor at **Bart's**.

1876 Eton-educated Bridges reports for duty at the Great Northern Central Hospital, **Caledonian Road** N1 (now swimming baths).

1877–79 In charge of Bart's casualty department.

1879 Great Northern Hospital with Dr Bridges moves to **Holloway Road**.

1882 Suffers ill-health so leaves medicine to devote his life to poetry. He published the unknown Gerard Manley Hopkins, was made poet laureate in 1913 and founded *The Society For Pure English*.

BRITAINS
Islington: Home of the Toy Soldier

1845 William Britain Snr (1828–1906) is a Toy Maker of 28 **Lambert Street**, Hornsey Rise N19, a large, detached house. Son and grandson followed in his footsteps.

1860 William Jnr born.

1893 William revolutionises his father's toy business when he invents hollow casting in lead. He bought next door, demolished both houses and built a factory where 300 employees moulded, cast and painted toy soldiers. Britain sold sets of Life Guards with fixed arms on a heavy oval base, five in a box, for one shilling, followed by Imperial Yeomanry, Royal Horse Artillery and Boer War cavalry and infantry.

1903 Dennis Britain born.

1910 Sets of Infantry commemorate the coronation of George V (very rare, one sold for £8,000 in 1988). St John Ambulance range introduced. Now 500 employees.

1931 After the horrors of World War I, soldiers are non-PC, so Britains introduce farms, zoos and circuses. A second factory was built in Walthamstow.

1933 When William Jnr dies, Dennis Britain takes over.

1939 Moustaches disappear from toy soldiers. They're never seen again (was this because Hitler had one?). The peaked cap was replaced by a steel helmet. Because production lasted only two years (stopped 1941 because of the war) helmeted soldiers are now extremely rare and worth a small fortune.

1955 The invention of plastic spells the end of hollow casting. Britains buy Herald Toys and introduce 'Swoppits', plastic figures with interchangeable parts (forerunners of today's *Star Wars* figures).

1966 Plastic replaces lead soldiers. The new *Deetail* range has heavy metal bases to overcome the problem of plastic soldiers toppling over.

1968 After 123 years, the factory in Hornsey closes.

1982 Collectors pay £15,000 for boxes of foot guards, £20,000 for Royal Artillery (steel helmets) and £50,000 for Royal Horse Artillery.

1994 Britains' archives sold at Christie's for £120,000.

1996 Dennis, third generation, dies. Britains name bought out by Ertle.

....

BRITTEN, Sir Benjamin (1913–1976)
Composer

Britten, the most English of Englishmen, conscientious objector and musical genius, was once considered the enfant terrible of British music.

1966 Britten and lifelong companion, singer Peter <u>Pears</u>, move to **99 Offord Road** N1 and stay four years. They worked, on and off, at Sadler's Wells from the time Lilian Baylis took over in 1931 (see Sadlers Wells), and helped her found English National Opera. In 1939 when theatres were closed for the duration of the war, Sadler's Wells Ballet and Opera were forced to go on tour. Britten and Pears, both pacifists, went to America where they stayed with 'Britain knockers', poet W.H. Auden and his friend, playwright Christopher Isherwood, both of whom had American citizenship. Taking a risk on being imprisoned as *'conchy homosexuals'*, the couple returned and enrolled for National Service. They were exempted from combat to give morale-boosting concerts.

1970 Britten (working on *Death in Venice*) and Pears move from Offord Road to **8 Halliford Street**.

1985 Halliford Street gets a blue plaque, unveiled by Sir Peter Pears.

....

BUNHILL FIELDS EC1
Nonconformist cemetery

1549 Wagon loads of corpses are moved from St Paul's Cathedral charnel house to land it owns near the Honourable Artillery Company training ground. Dubbed Bone Hill by the locals, Bunhill it still is.

1657 London is running out of burial grounds, so the City allows Nonconformists and Dissenters (from the Church of England), forbidden to be buried in consecrated ground, to be buried here (railings partition off holy ground). John <u>Lilburne</u>, Leveller brother of Robert (one of the regicides), was buried here, as were two centuries of Nonconformists.

1688 Not all Nonconformists are Dissenters, Wesley was a Nonconformist, not a Dissenter (but all Dissenters are Nonconformists). Blake was a Swedenborgian (see Swedenborg, Immanuel); John (*Pilgrim's Progress*) <u>Bunyan</u>, a Puritan, is buried here. Once imprisoned for twelve years for Nonconforming, at 59 he rode forty miles to Islington from Bedford on an errand of mercy in pouring rain. He became ill while preaching and within days was dead from pneumonia.

1692 Lt General Charles Fleetwood, husband of Bridget Cromwell, daughter of the Protector, is buried.

1731 Daniel (*Robinson Crusoe*) Defoe is buried.

1742 Susannah Wesley, mother of Charles and John (and seventeen other children) buried.

1831 William (*Jerusalem*) Blake (who, many years later, will have a bust in Westminster Abbey and a plaque in St Paul's) and his wife Catherine are buried here.

1748 Isaac Watts, '*father of the English hymn*', buried here.

1797 John Wilkes is buried here.

1854 Last burial. It's estimated that 120,000 people were buried here.

1869 Gates and railings are put up recording the history of the burial ground. A manufacturer's error says that 'Samuel', not Susanna, Wesley is buried here.

1879 139 years after his death, Daniel Defoe still has no monument so young readers of *Christian World* launch a fund to build one.

1996 English Heritage lists Bunhill Fields on its *Buildings At Risk Register* for the third year running, criticising the City of London which owns them but does nothing much to maintain them.

....

BUSINESS DESIGN CENTRE Upper Street N1

Started life as The Agricultural Halls (the 'old Aggie')

1798 Smithfield market traders launch The Smithfield Cattle Club for livestock shows.

1861 Frederick Peck designs a 130-foot roof span (bigger than Alexandra or Crystal palaces). Part of Hedge Row was demolished to make way for the **Upper Street** entrance to the five-acre site. The original, in **Liverpool Road**, had twin towers that are still there. Hedge Row, here since the 1600s, was a row of shops next to the Three Wheatsheaves. Behind was a cattle lair used to fatten animals before they were taken down **St John Street** to **Smithfield Market**.

1862 UK venue for trade fairs (bakery, drapery, brewing, shoes, leather, cycles, furniture etc.), horse shows and circuses. The cattle show took a back seat when entertainment became the predominant activity. Smaller halls, such as The Blue Hall, were added.

1877 Cycling and walking races are held.

1880 The Grand Military Tournament becomes The Royal Tournament after being attended by royalty. It was held here annually until 1906, when it transferred to Earl's Court.

1883 The World Fair is put on by the American James *Barnum* Bailey. He advertised *Zulu War Dances, Mexican Knife and Indian Tomahawk Throwing* and a model of Canterbury Cathedral made from 300,000 sea shells.

1891 Charles Cruft, local dog cake salesman, launches Cruft's Dog Show (see Cruft, Charles).

1894 Charles Blondin (70), who crossed Niagara Falls on a tightrope, repeats the stunt here.

1895 The Aggie, patronised by royalty, becomes The Royal Agricultural Hall.

1898 The Motor Show arrives.

1900 3 August, Britain's first proper film show is part of the Mohawk Minstrel Show. On the bill were *Count Zeppelin's Warship*, *A Visit to the Spiritualist* and *Rush Hour at The Angel*.

1906 The Motor Show transfers to Earl's Court. MPs had passed the Channel Tunnel Bill and a scale model was put on show here. The War Office, convinced it was not in Britain's best defence interests, had the Bill scrapped.

1936 Crufts has 9,000 entries.

1939 WWII. Crufts transfers to Earls Court

1940 Mount Pleasant, GPO parcel sorting office, is bombed so moves here.

1976 Sorting Office moves out. The old Aggie was derelict. Trees were growing inside. Islington Council toyed with the idea of turning it into a *Dickens' London* theme park. Sam Morris, Chairman, City Industrial Ltd, a shopfitting company in the borough since 1954, put in a bid to bring back exhibitions to the large hall and use the small ones as showcases for interior designers.

1986 Britain's first cinema, St Mary's Hall, although officially listed, is demolished when Morris opens The Business Design Centre. Everything architects and designers could need was under one roof. Many companies who rented space needed a London base for corporate hospitality/PR/product launches. Over 300,000 visitors a year means that it is seldom out of the news.

1997 HM Inspector of Anatomy saw a newspaper photograph of a silver-coated plaster cast of a head and torso on sale. The sculptor nephew of the Duke of Norfolk was prosecuted for stealing body parts from The Royal College of Surgeons and spent six weeks in Brixton prison.

1999 BAFTA (British 'Oscars') Awards Ceremony. 1,900 guests include Gwyneth Paltrow, Michael Caine, Cate Blanchett, Tim Roth, Martin Clunes, Richard E Grant, Andie McDowell and Pierce Brosnan. A frail, white-haired Elizabeth Taylor was helped on stage to receive a BAFTA Fellowship Award. Sons of Sam (Morris) bought out rival exhibition centres Earls Court and Olympia, for £183 million.

CAMDEN PASSAGE N1

Often used for filming (Hitchcock and Polanski have filmed here, as has Claire Bloom in local author Nina Bawden's Family Money), Camden Passage is a bustling shopping centre for antiques.

Islington: Home of Concordance to the Bible

1737 Alexander Cruden publishes 225,000 references in his life's work, *Complete Concordance of the Holy Scriptures of the Old and New Testaments*. Born in Aberdeen, Cruden moved to London after completing his MA. Sacked as tutor to the Earl of Derby's children because of his bad French, he opened a bookshop beneath The Royal Exchange and was appointed Bookseller to the Queen. When Queen Anne died, people lost interest. The public embarrassment at the Concordance being a financial flop sent him mad but he lived to see it reprinted three times.

After John Wilkes published *Liberty*, the slogan 'Wilkes and Liberty' was daubed all over London, so Cruden carried a sponge with him to scrub it from walls. This earned him the nickname *Cruden the Esponger*.

1770 Cruden dies at home.

1776 A row of sixteen houses is built, called Camden Passage after Earl Camden, who owned the land.

1807 The Camden Head pub is built.

1820 The Gun is renamed Duke of Sussex (they were at it even then, changing historical pub names).

1896 Frederick Beck opens a toy shop at 28 (still there). Local legend has it that Kate Carney, when appearing at Collins' music hall across the road, bought young Charlie Chaplin a rocking horse here.

1925 The Passage is a slum. Gaslit streets around the power station (now Mall Antiques), built to run the trams, were filled with drunks, buskers, Punch and Judy, escapologists, 'guess your weight', violinists and organ grinders. Shops sold day-old chicks (piled high in windows heated with light bulbs) umbrellas, hats, sweets, fish and chips, fresh fish – a bookie (betting is illegal) was there too, posing as a printer.

1959 John Payton, 'Passage' music shop keeper, gives the Passage a new lease of life. Shops were still boarded up with corrugated iron from the war, the area used as a dumping ground for old mattresses, tyres and other unmentionables. Fellow traders were a newsagent, printer, cobbler, upholsterer and undertaker. Others sold sewing machines, hardware, dartboards, bikes, toys, records, secondhand clothes, wallpaper and prams.

Payton, who ran a music shop at 112 where he was born and brought up, discovered that the Council planned to demolish the Passage and build yet more flats. (His 'mole' at the Town Hall was one of his customers, young Paul Jones, who went on to become lead singer with Manfred Mann. Payton formed the Camden Passage Traders Association and arranged an outdoor art exhibition which was opened by local celeb, actor/producer Michael Medwin, and a local trader's glamorous wife, 'Bond Girl' Sheree Winton (suicide 1976, mother of TV presenter Dale).

Islington was dubbed the new Chelsea and the celebs who lived there (Sir Basil Spence, Dame Flora Robson of 19 **Alwyne Villas** and Beatrice Lehmann of 23, Arnold Wesker and Cyril Cusack) were dubbed *The Islington Set*. (The Cusacks lived in **Vincent Terrace**.)

1961 Camden Passage, well and truly on the London map, holds another art exhibition opened by Stanley Baxter, attended by other locals – Professor Jacob Bronowski, Peter Dimmock and wife Polly Elwes.

1962 Celebrity chef, Robert Carrier gives slummy Islington a new trendy image. Taken aback by the low standard of English catering he opened a restaurant. John Betjeman unveiled a plaque commemorating Cruden (q.v.) (his house is now Portofino's so the plaque is on the nearest house, see Betjeman, John). An art exhibition was attended by locals Derek de Marney (actor) and Angus McBean (theatre photographer). The Passage got its first antique dealer and began to go up-market (antique mania spilled out into **Upper Street** and **Essex Road**).

1970 Alexander Walker, *Evening Standard* film critic, dines with Romaine (*Screen on the Green*) Hart and Sir Laurence Olivier at Carrier's. Walker was moderator between Olivier and the Screen on the Green audience at a showing of his film, Chekhov's *The Three Sisters*.

2000 Dealers and international collectors make up the greatest concentration of antiques in Europe, with 350 specialist dealers in 200 yards (seven arcades). This causes confusion for many tourists who think they are in Camden Market ...

CND

Islington: home of the Campaign for Nuclear Disarmament

1908 Fenner (later Lord) <u>Brockway</u> (founder of CND) – conscientious objector, Labour candidate for Finsbury Council – moves into Claremont Square Mission then to 60 **Myddelton Square** EC1, where the Independent Labour Party (ILP) was based and half a dozen or so socialists lived communally.

1945 Secretary, ILP.

1954 CND founded (based in **Holloway Road**) to campaign for Britain's abandonment of nuclear weapons. CND spread world-wide. Thousands carried its famous logo on marches. Brockway, Monsignor Bruce <u>Kent</u> (priest at St John's, **Duncan Terrace**) and Bertrand <u>Russell</u> led 9,000 on the first Easter march from the Atomic Weapons Research Establishment, Aldermaston, Berkshire to Trafalgar Square. All ages, classes, religions, ordinary people across the board marched with their children wrapped in plastic macs in driving rain. When in 1983 7,000 linked arms around the nuclear weapons centre, a cynical Michael Heseltine (Defence Secretary) dismissed them as 'naive'.

1963 International Nuclear Test Ban Treaty. CND stopped its protest marches.

1964 Brockway created Labour Party's first peer.

1975 Unveils blue plaque on his old home in **Myddelton Square**.

1984 Opens the Philip Noel-Baker Peace Garden, **Elthorne Park**, Hornsey Rise N19 in memory of the Nobel Prize Winner's work for world peace. The Islington Peace Sculpture in the park was unveiled by Bruce Kent. A statue of Lord Brockway, 96, was unveiled in **Red Lion Square** by Labour Leader Michael Foot in Lord Brockway's presence.

2000 CND Holloway Road now has more members than in the days when its protesters filled Hyde Park.

CANONBURY

William the Conqueror gave the Geoffrey de Mandeville land in 1066, previously owned by the Bishop of London.

1253 <u>de Berners</u> family gives **St Bartholomew the Great** a huge piece of Barnsbury which becomes known as the Canon's Borough (Canonbury). A sizeable chunk of real estate not to be sneezed at (then or now), Canonbury comprised **Canonbury Lane/ Park/Place**, **Compton Street**, **St Mary's Grove**, the **Alwyne Villas** area, bounded by **Upper Street**, Lower Road (**Essex Road**) and Hopping Lane (**St Paul's Road**).

Some sources say Hopping Lane was so narrow, people had to hop out of the way when riders passed (they still do when an articulated truck thunders by); others that it cut through hop fields. When Sir Charles <u>Barry</u> built St Paul's Church on the corner with Essex Road, the name changed to St Paul's Road.

CANONBURY PLACE N1

1776 Marquess of <u>Northampton</u> leases this land to John <u>Dawes</u>, stockbroker and property developer, who built a row of houses (date on one of the downpipes). He demolished a Tudor wall and one wing of Prior <u>Bolton</u>'s Elizabethan mansion. The surviving wing (Canonbury Academy) is how it used to look.

1780 Canonbury House is built on the corner (not to be confused with Canonbury Tower [q.v.]).

1838 No. 6 is a girls' school.

1854 Nos 1 and 2 are named Gothic Villas.

1855 The school reverts to a private house (Northampton House).

1878 No. 6 is a school again, Highbury and Islington High School For Girls. Nos 18, 19 and 20 are known as Gothic House.

1888 Ronald <u>Carton</u>, first compiler of the *Times* crossword, lives at No. 5. Revd William Hagger <u>Barlow</u>, Vicar of St Mary's, moved into Canonbury House while his architect cousin, William Henry <u>Barlow</u>, who designed St Pancras Station, was building him a new vicarage.

1891 Weedon <u>Grossmith</u> moves into No. 5, known as The Old House (now No. 2) where he lives ten years. Some sources say he shared with bohemian brother George.

Punch serialised *The Diary of a Nobody*. Written by George, illustrated by Weedon, it chronicles the daily life of Charles Pooter, a humble clerk with social pretensions, who lives in Holloway. Sons of a law reporter, both Grossmiths had interesting careers. George was a law reporter for the *Times* before joining Gilbert and Sullivan's Savoy Opera. For twelve years he toured the UK and America, creating many of the leading roles. Weedon went to the Slade School of Art but followed his brother on stage specialising in small downtrodden men who stand on their dignity, men exactly like Mr Pooter.

1911 The Girls High School at No. 6 closes.

1930 No. 6 taken over for HQ North London District Nursing Association.

1956 Professor Basil <u>Spence</u>, architect, moves in at No. 1, the year the foundation stone of his new Coventry Cathedral is laid. He won an open competition to rebuild the bombed out cathedral. Knighted 1960, his practice was around the corner at Northampton Lodge, **Canonbury Square**.

1965 The Nursing Association moves out of No. 6. The Medical Missionary Society moved in and re-christened it Harcourt House.

1980 Raymond <u>Mortimer</u> at No. 2 (Grossmiths' old house) (84), writer, art critic, book reviewer for *Vogue, New Statesman, Sunday Times*, dies.

1993 Canonbury Academy Conference Centre hosts a seminar on terrorism. Roads were sealed off and police marksmen were on the roofs. Residents ordered to move their cars were not impressed to be told that Stella <u>Rimington</u>, the first woman Head of MI5, attending the seminar, lived in Canonbury.

CANONBURY SQUARE N1

1807 Henry <u>Leroux</u>, architect, flushed with the success of his Union Chapel (q.v.), **Compton Terrace**, leases land from the Marquess of Northampton. He designed Canonbury Square and built his first Gentleman's Villa, Northampton Lodge (39, once the practice of Sir Basil <u>Spence</u>, now the Estorick Gallery of Italian Art). He probably lived here while building the square.

1812 A road is needed to divert traffic from the City to Archway. This came as bad news to Mr Leroux, who hadn't known about it when he signed the lease. The new **North Road** (to join Holloway Road) cut straight through his beautiful square (modern visitors assume wrongly it was built after the square was completed), rendering it unattractive to wealthy buyers. Leroux was bankrupted.

1823 Nos 1–12 built.

1830 Nos 25–28 built.

1840 The houses become 'bedsit land', inhabited by clerks, teachers, printers and dressmakers. Many of those who could, moved to the suburbs, now accessible by the new railways.

1844 Actor manager Sam Phelps moves into No. 8. He was to revive Sadler's Wells (q.v.), and Shakespeare.

1864 George Daniel at No. 18, friend of Charles Lamb (*Recollections of Charles Lamb*) satirist, journalist, poet, playwright, book collector, dies during an epileptic fit. When his house was opened for a 10-day sale, his four original Shakespeare Folios were sold for £15,865.

1918 Arthur Popham, Keeper of Prints and Drawings at The British Museum, moves into No. 4.

1920 The Marquess sells off much of his Canonbury estate.

1928 Novelist, satirist, self-professed snob, Evelyn Waugh moves in to No. 17 with new wife, The Hon. Evelyn Gardner. Sadly, the marriage doesn't last (see Waugh, Evelyn).

1943 WWII. Mr Stokes of 343 **Essex Road** gives Islington Council an Italian statue for the gardens (stolen in the 1990s).

1944 George Orwell, wife Eileen and Richard, their adopted baby, move in at No. 27.

1955 Canonbury Square is a war-damaged slum.

While many tenants couldn't wait to be re-housed, speculators were building pastiche replacement houses on the bomb sites. When estate agents brought buyers to view the new houses, many fell in love with the derelict older properties and bought those instead, to 'do up' with 50 per cent improvement grants offered by the Council. So it was that, once the 'smokeless zone' (resulting from the 1956 Clean Air Act) was introduced by Stanley Cohen, Councillor for Farringdon Without (**Stanley Cohen House** EC1), the mania to own these tiny houses was born and the love affair with the borough began.

1955 Vanessa Bell, RA (Virginia Woolf's sister) and theatre designer Duncan Grant, leading lights of the Bloomsbury Group, are living in No. 26. The couple knew Picasso and Matisse and helped Roger Fry organise the first exhibition of French Impressionist paintings in London. One Sunday, a scene painter at the Tower Theatre around the corner was explaining the technicalities to the old chap who had wandered in to watch, and invited him to have a go. When told this was Duncan Grant, the man was unimpressed. He'd never heard of him.

1963 Local legend has it that when Sylvia Plath left Ted Hughes she rented rooms here with her children before moving to Camden, where she committed suicide. Local legend also has it that Christine Keeler was living here at the time of the Profumo affair.

2000 Considered by many to be *'the most perfect square in London'* (inasmuch as it remains closest to the original).

CANONBURY TAVERN Canonbury Place N1

1735 Either built or re-built?

1785 Tea Gardens and Bowling Green open.

1803 *The Times: 'On Thursday last, the Gentlemen of the late Corps of Loyal Islington Volunteers dined together at Canonbury Tavern for the purpose of presenting a magnificent Silver Cup of the value of 250 guineas to Alexander Aubert Esq, their late Commandant, in testimony of their esteem and affection.'*

1805 The new owner opens tea gardens attended by four hundred at a time. He built new kitchens, a bakery, cow sheds, piggeries, coach houses and stables. Attractions included bowling, shooting, fishing, quoits and cricket.

1832 The Islington Literary and Scientific Society ('Lit & Sci') hold their meetings here (see Almeida Theatre). Charles Babbage addressed crowds in his election campaign for state intervention in education.

1846 Rebuilt (present pub).

1899–1902 After the South African (Boer) War, the pub is used as a hospital for war veterans. A young nurse died here in unknown circumstances and was said to haunt the pub, usually on a Sunday. Looking pale and ill (as ghosts do) she sat in the bar wearing her regulation uniform (long grey dress) or clumped up and down the stairs.

CANONBURY TOWER Canonbury Place N1

Twenty-four ley lines (lines of geomagnetic energy often related to the alignment of religious sites) are said to run through the pre-Roman foundations.

1509 William Bolton (architect who built Henry VII Chapel, Westminster Abbey, one of the most beautiful buildings of the late Middle Ages), also Prior of St Bartholomew's (**Prior Bolton Street** N1), rebuilds the country seat. As towers were all the rage, it got one. It's still here, as is his 'rebus' (pictorial pun on a name), a bolt (arrow) through a tun (barrel), on the octagonal summerhouses, which survive (**7 Alwyne Road** and **4 Alwyne Villas**) with original Tudor diaper brickwork.

1532 Bolton dies, blissfully unaware that soon Canonbury Tower (and his beloved Priory) will be appropriated by Henry VIII.

1533 Thomas Cromwell moves in.

1536 Cromwell is promoted to Lord Privy Seal, given Canonbury Tower, the remains of Highbury Castle and its 300 wooded acres.

1541 After he arranges Henry's disastrous marriage to Anne of Cleves, Cromwell loses Canonbury Tower, Highbury Castle and his head. His property reverted to the crown.

1547 John Dudley (father of the more famous Robert) KG, Duke of Northumberland swaps the Tower with Edward VI for Teignmouth Priory. He may have wanted it as a temporary home for his son and daughter-in-law, the unfortunate Lady Jane Grey, named by Edward as his successor.

1557 Following Northumberland's execution for treason, Canonbury Tower is again Crown Property. Mary Tudor swapped it for Lord Wentworth's (privy councillor) Cheney Gate Manor, Westminster.

1570 Wentworth sells it to Sir John Spencer, who features throughout Elizabeth I's reign.

1572 Arthur Atye, PPS to Robert Dudley, rents Canonbury Tower.

1598 Lord Compton of Bruce Castle (see William the Conqueror) has gone through his inheritance. He arrived to borrow £28,000 from Sir John Spencer to pay his debts and fell in love with Eliza, Spencer's beloved only child. Dad was not best pleased. Neither was he impressed, because was he not himself one of Queen Elizabeth's favourites? Compton may have been a Lord, but he was broke.

1599 Compton pulls strings to get Spencer put in prison while he elopes with Eliza, heiress to £800,000, which includes Canonbury Tower and Crosby Hall.

Compton sent a baker and his basket to the Tower and Eliza was lowered out of the window on to a cart (the Compton family has a painting commemorating the event). They married in London, she was 21, he 37. Their first child, Spencer, was born at Compton Wynyates (the present Marquess of Northampton is also called Spencer, not to be confused with Earl Spencer of Northampton). Elizabeth I agreed to be Spencer's sponsor (not then called godparents). Aware of the rift between father and daughter, she tricked Sir John into being co-sponsor. When he discovered the child was his grandson, he was overjoyed.

Baroness (Countess in some books) Compton's second child, a daughter, was born at Canonbury Tower and baptised in St Mary's. William died of pneumonia in his 50s after swimming in the Thames, son Spencer died in his 30s fighting for Charles I against Cromwell. Fate decreed Eliza would return to Canonbury Tower an impoverished grandmother.

1601 Spencer redecorates Canonbury Tower. Some of his chimneypieces, ceilings and panelling are still there (one of the original chimneypieces is in the Big Hall, Castle Ashby).

1610 Sir John dies. Lord Compton (via Eliza) inherited his vast fortune and became temporarily unhinged. All his life he had been in debt and he could not immediately adjust to his new found wealth.

1616 Sir Francis Bacon moves in.

1626 After Bacon's death, Sir Thomas Coventry arrives. He was Lord Keeper of the Great Seal, Solicitor-General, Recorder of London, Attorney General, MP for Droitwich.

1635 James Stanley, KB, MP, Lord Strange, earl of Derby moves in. A Royalist, he was executed by Cromwell and dubbed The Martyr Earl.

1643 Lord (Spencer) Compton (42) Earl of Northampton, Royalist, dies at Hopton Heath. Cromwell deprived his son of Compton Wynyates and Castle Ashby, so the family returned to Canonbury Tower, the old family home. The third earl was the last to live here.

1653 A son is born to Sir William but dies age 5.

1654 Sir William forms *The Sealed Knot*, a secret society to organise royalist resistance. The family sells Crosby Hall and takes out a mortgage of £1,751 on Canonbury Tower.

1719 The grand days of Canonbury Tower are long gone. It was now a rooming house in multiple occupancy.

1728 Mr Ephraim Chambers, England's first important encyclopaedist, publishes his two-volume *Cyclopedia: Universal Dictionary of Arts and Sciences* (translated into French, it was influential in France too).

1761 John Newbery, publisher, moves in with Oliver Goldsmith.

1769 H.S. Woodfall, who invented the characters *Darby and Joan* (brother of William, founder of Hansard) moves from Colebrooke Row into Canonbury Tower. Here he edited *The Public Advertiser* and published *Letters of Junius*.

Unsolved mystery, who was Junius? 'Junius', like John Wilkes, was opposed to the monarchy and wanted to reform both Houses (Lords and Commons). Woodfall never revealed his identity but admitted only to being the 'go-between' between Junius, the eponymous writer, and Wilkes. 'Junius' kept up his attacks on <u>George III</u> for three years until Woodfall was prosecuted for seditious libel. Many people said Junius was Wilkes.

1770 Marquess of <u>Northampton</u> leases Canonbury Tower to John <u>Dawes</u>. The megolomaniacal, speculative builder demolished the south range of the Tudor quadrangle to build **Canonbury Place**.

1817 (circa) Robert <u>Seymour</u>, who will one day be Dickens' illustrator, has rooms here.

1820 Washington (*Rip Van Winkle*) <u>Irving</u>, a lawyer, arrives from America and rents <u>Goldsmith</u>'s old room to write his hero's biography. He soon got fed up with the caretaker bringing visitors to look at 'Goldsmith's Room': *'peeping through the keyhole . . . on returning home one day, I found a coarse tradesman . . . gazing over my manuscripts.'*

1872 Used as a school.

1920 Now a lodging house.

1952 **Tower Theatre** (Tavistock Repertory Company) is granted a fifty-year lease. Gracie <u>Fields</u>, Edith Evans, Compton McKenzie, Thornton Wilder sent donations. (Ex-luminaries include Jessica <u>Tandy</u>, Richard Baker, Ronald Eyre, Michael Gambon, Bob Hoskins, Ken <u>Loach</u>, Alfred Molina, Roger Lloyd Pack and his daughter Emily Lloyd).

1953 First Tower Theatre production. In the audience was the Marquess of Northampton.

Professor Jacob (*The Descent of Man*) <u>Bronowski</u> wrote a play which was performed at the Tower. In the audience with him were fellow intellectuals and writers, J.B. Priestley and Kingsley Martin, editor of *The New Statesman (q.v.)*. The Royal Academy of Dramatic Art (RADA) lent Tom Courtney and Sian Phillips to the Company.

1958 The Tower comes into Harold <u>Pinter</u>'s life at a turning point in his career. *The Birthday Party*, premiered at the Lyric, was savaged by West End critics and slammed by theatregoers so was withdrawn after three performances. The more adventurous Islington audiences loved it. Pinter wrote to The Tower: *'May I say that the Tavistock production of The Birthday Party was the best there has been and I am sure the best there will be of that play. It meant a great deal to me.'*

1968 Barbara (now Baroness) <u>Castle</u> MP (see Castle, Barbara), who lives around the corner (**John Spencer Square**), takes her mum to see Aristophanes' *Lysistrata*.

1976 Sir Bernard <u>Miles</u>' *Lock Up Your Daughters* is a great success. Also living around the corner (**Alwyne Villas**), he was in the first night audience.

2003 The lease on the theatre expires.

....

CASLON, William (1692–1766)

Type-founder

In the eighteenth and nineteenth centuries, Islington, particularly Clerkenwell, was the centre of the London printing industry.

1716 Moves from Worcestershire to **Clerkenwell** and opens type foundry.

1720 The King's Printers (George II) use Caslon's new, distinctive Arabic, Roman and Hebrew fonts. In fact, until 1780 almost every work printed in England used Caslon type.

1725 Moves to 5 **Helmet Row** EC1.

1727 Moves to 39 **Ironmonger Row** EC1.

1738 Moves to 22 **Chiswell Street** EC1.

1766 Dies world famous thanks to friend Benjamin Franklin's American *Declaration of Independence*, which was printed using his fonts. He was buried in St Luke's, **Old Street**. His descendants continued the foundry for 150 years (plaque says closed 1909). Building bombed in WWII.

....

CASTLE, Barbara, Baroness (1911–) MP.

Mrs Barbara 'I was reared in irreverence' Castle, crusading Labour MP for Blackburn, and husband, Alderman Ted Castle (of Conservative Hornsey), sang The Red Flag *on the steps of Hornsey Town Hall after every Council meeting.*

1957 Moves to John Spencer Square, **St Paul's Road** N1.

1963 Brings down the Tory government.

Castle was furious with PM Harold Macmillan for dismissing rumours that Jack Profumo, his Minister of War, was having an affair with Christine Keeler (who was sleeping with a high-ranking Russian naval attache at the same time). Not because of the sex, which she said could apply to any half of any Cabinet in any government, but because the Conservatives were getting away with something Labour would never be allowed to. She invited Labour grandees Harold Wilson, Richard Crossman and George Wigg (Chairman of the Betting Levy Board) to dinner and told them she intended to raise the matter in the House. They agreed to back her. Her question: *'Is it true that the Minister of War is involved?'* brought Profumo to the dispatch box to lie that there had been *'no impropriety whatsoever'* in his relationship with Keeler, which Macmillan accepted. Six months later, following the trial and suicide of Keeler's pimp, society osteopath Stephen Ward, Profumo finally admitted he had lied, and resigned. Lampooned in *Private Eye*, Macmillan went soon after and the ineffectual Sir Alec Douglas Home took over.

1964 Harold Wilson is PM and Barbara Castle in the Cabinet as Minister for Overseas Development. Wilson asked her to switch to Transport because, desperate for an effective transport policy, he needed: *'a tiger in his tank'* (advert for Esso petrol). She replied that she couldn't drive, which didn't stop her bringing in seat belts and the breathalyser . . . Road deaths fell by 23 per cent.

1968 The country is plagued by a series of strikes. Barbara settled down in **John Spencer Square** to write her anti-Union power White Paper *In Place of Strife*, pausing only to take her mum to a performance of *Lysistrata* (an early feminist tract, in which women strike against men) at the Canonbury Tower Theatre.

1970 Just before the Labour government is ousted, Castle brings in the Equal Pay Act.

1975 Campaigns in the referendum against joining the EEC. Needing a political adviser on the NHS, husband Ted, now Alderman for Islington Council, recommended former student activist Jack Straw, vice-Chair of Islington Council Housing Committee (1971–78), now Home Secretary in the Blair government. His father was a conscientious objector, his mother an Islington councillor.

1976 Ted Castle dies. Mrs Castle resigns from government, Jack Straw is elected as MP for Blackburn. When asked why he was chosen, Barbara Castle said *'for his guile and low cunning'*.

1990 Life peerage for Baroness Castle. Described as *'the best Labour Prime Minister Britain never had'* she is still campaigning on a range of issues, including reinstating the link between pensions and earnings.

CAVE, Edward (1691–1754)

Magazine editor

Son of a poor cobbler, who 'discovered' Dr Johnson.

1725 Following an apprenticeship with a printer, Cave lives in Norwich working for the Post Office while submitting country news to London papers. When he moved to London, he submitted city news to country papers. Working non-stop, he saved every spare penny to launch his own publication.

Islington: Home of the First Magazine

1731 Cave launches *The Gentleman's Magazine* at **St John's Gate**. It was to remain popular for 200 years. For the first few years he wrote most of it himself as *Sylvanus Urban*. His was the first quality monthly to be published in England and he was the first person in publishing to use the term *'magazine'*.

1737 Described as fat, slow and stingy, Cave paid hard-up writers to contribute for a pittance. One of them was Dr Samuel <u>Johnson</u>, lexicographer, satirist and friend of Boswell.

1738 Denounced in Parliament for publishing George II's answer to an address before it had even been reported from the chair (Parliamentary proceedings could not be reported before <u>Wilkes</u>).

1754 Aged 63, Cave dies at The Gate and was buried in St James' Church, **Clerkenwell**.

CAVELL, Edith (1865–1915)

World War I heroine

Edith Cavell Close, Hornsey Rise Gardens N19.

1862 Frederick <u>Cavell</u> (ordained as a priest in 1852) is curate to Revd John Lees, first Vicar of St Mark's, **Tollington Park** – consecrated 1854. He married Louisa Warming, daughter of his housekeeper, before becoming Vicar of Swardeston, near Norwich.

1867 Florence Nightingale appoints Mabel Torrance first matron of Whittington Hospital, together with twelve 'Nightingale Nurses'.

1901 Nurse Edith Cavell, Night Superintendent at the Whittington, will be dubbed the *Angel of Mons*. She spent her off-duty hours relaxing with other nurses in Waterlow Park and once walked thirty miles to Rickmansworth.

Edith started her nurse's training later than most. She was now thirty-five and anxious for promotion. In 1903 she became Assistant Matron at the Shoreditch Infirmary, Hoxton (later St Leonard's) *'. . . glad to have obtained some day work after my three years on night duty . . . the salary is better . . .'* In 1907, she was invited to Brussels as Matron to open Belgium's first training school for nurses. By 1914 she was working in the Red Cross Hospital, an underground haven for Allied soldiers. A year later, age 50, she was captured and shot by the Germans for helping two hundred French, Belgian and British soldiers escape to Holland. She wrote home: *'Patriotism is not enough, I must have no hatred or bitterness towards anyone'.* There was a national outcry. Her statue is outside the National Portrait Gallery, London.

CHAPEL MARKET N1

Originally Chapel Street led to St James, Pentonville (built 1787) and to St Silas, Penton Street (built 1865).

1790 Beginning of the end for Chapel Street, a middle class residential area. Dr Grosvenor at No. 19 complained to the Vestry that a butcher had set up a stall outside his house.

1796 Essayist, Charles <u>Lamb</u> lives in Chapel Street for four years.

1859 Adverse health report: inhabitants get their water from a well where costers throw unsold fish, meat, fruit and veg.

1873 Declared official street market (one day, the father of Samantha Fox, archetypal *Sun* 'Page Three' girl, will have a stall, and Ralph <u>Fiennes</u> and wife Alex Kingston, actors, will live here).

1882 John Sainsbury opens a shop here.

1936 Because of the market which has been here since 1868 it finally gets a name change to Chapel Market.

1996 The market is an unlikely place of pilgrimage for seekers of enlightenment. Fergie's (Duchess of York) mystic medium, <u>Madame Vasso</u>, has published a book. People who had never heard of Chapel Market, where she had a stall, beat a path to her curtain; alas, she and her purple pyramid had relocated to the front room of her council flat in **Southgate Road**.

CHAPLIN, Sir Charles (Charlie) (1889–1977)

Actor, composer and film producer

1891 Charles Chaplin Snr is appearing at Sadler's Wells. Charles Jnr was two years old. The family lodged around the corner in **Arlington Way** EC1.

1906 Chaplin and fellow comedian Stan <u>Laurel</u> were appearing in Casey's Court Circus at The Holloway Empire, **Holloway Road**.

1913 Joins brother Sydney on stage at Collins Music Hall with Fred Karno's Mumming Birds, one of his last appearances in England. Films being the future, after Chaplin and Stan Laurel were asked to tour America they didn't come back.

1988 Houses are demolished in Arlington Way to build the Lilian Baylis Theatre. One was where Chaplin lodged. Another is where Mr Barnett <u>Deitch</u> lived 28 years making ballet shoes for, among others, Pavlova. As he worked, he could hear children playing in the street while their parents rehearsed. He remembered Chaplin as a little boy dropping in for tea.

1992 Richard Attenborough films *Chaplin* in **Cheney Street**, King's Cross.

1993 Annie Chaplin (33) follows father and grandfather treading the boards of Sadler's Wells (q.v.).

CHARTERHOUSE
Charterhouse Square EC1

Medieval plague pit, Carthusian monastery, Tudor palace, hotbed of Catholic intrigue, famous public school (home of English football) and a home for elderly gentlemen, Charterhouse has been a cosmopolitan centre of activity for over 900 years. It's open to the public during the summer.

1326 Walter de Mauny (anglicised to Manny), relative and young page to the even younger (13) Princess Philippa of Hainault in Belgium, accompanies her to London. Two years later she married Prince Edward, also 15 (crowned King Edward III, 1330). This was the Edward who founded the Order of Knights of the Garter (KG), still awarded. Sir Walter was among the first, possibly the first, to be admitted.

1348 The Black Death decimates London. The graveyards were full so bodies were scooped up and thrown into rivers. De Manny, sixteenth richest man in England (£4 billion) came to the rescue of the city he loved, buying 13 acres from **Bart's** using three as a plague pit.

Because the dead couldn't get to heaven until masses were said to release their souls from purgatory, de Manny built a temporary chapel before founding a monastery modelled on that of Saint Bruno, founder of the Carthusian Order. In 1084 Bruno moved to a 'chartreuse' (isolated country house) in Grenoble with six monks (it became famous for sweet Green Chartreuse liqueur. Chartreuse, pronounced 'chartr'ouse' by locals, has nothing to do with charters). De Manny commissioned Henry Yvele, the king's Master Mason, foremost architect in England, founder of the English Perpendicular style, to build it.

1371 Sir William Walworth (slayer of Wat Tyler, leader of the Peasant's Revolt, see Tyler, Wat) lays the first stone of the first cell.

The life of a Carthusian, on the face of it, looks good. For six days a week he wasn't expected to do anything but pray, Sundays were for socialising. Far from the popular image, the monks' 'cells' were actually two-storey cottages with four rooms (wood panelled for warmth) each with its own herb/physic garden. The wall abutting the cloister had a service hatch. A servant (lay brother/monk responsible for the running of the monastery) delivered meals from the cloister and closed the door. The monk opened a door his side and took his 'vittles' – a sort of medieval 'meals-on-sandals'. The garden wall had a service hatch too, so that the night soil collector could collect the monk's excreta. When a novice was given his white habit he was told it was also his shroud. When he died he had no coffin and no memorial. He was laid face down in the earth in an unmarked grave (today a nameless wooden cross is alllowed to mark his grave).

1372 Sir Walter dies and is buried before the high altar in Charterhouse chapel. His funeral was attended by Edward III and Queen Philippa. He made front page news again nearly six hundred years later, when WWII bombs blasted open his resting place.

1430 Margery Bernersbury gives a part of Barnsbury to Charterhouse. The Prior of St John's granted a licence to the Prior to pipe water from a well there (corner of **Barnsbury Road/Maygood Street**) to the twenty-five cells (lettered A–Y). A map of the plumbing system is still in Charterhouse.

1436 Charterhouse, started 1348, is completed.

1534 Bishop of London asks Prior Houghton to sign the Act of Succession (so that Elizabeth, Anne Boleyn's daughter, a Protestant, not Mary, Catherine's daughter, a Catholic, will succeed).

John Houghton, Essex gentry, studied law at Christ's College Cambridge, became a Carthusian in 1515 and was appointed Prior in 1531. He refused, because to sign was to agree that Henry's marriage to Catherine was not valid. He was taken to the Tower, where fellow Carthusians persuaded him that a marriage, even a royal one, was not a good enough reason to martyr himself, so he signed and was released. Nine months later, the Act of Supremacy was passed in which Henry named himself Supreme Head of the Church in England. This, Houghton definitely could not sign.

1535 Charterhouse is the centre of world attention. Houghton, with Prior Lawrence of Beauvale and Prior Webster of Axeholme, who were visiting Charterhouse (how unlucky can you get?), were charged with treason (*desiring to deprive the king of his title as Supreme Head of the Church*) by Thomas Cromwell and thrown in the Tower. Europe now saw something undreamed of. The three tortured Carthusian priors in their white habits were tied, upside down, to hurdles and pulled from the Tower through the streets to Tyburn. There, they were hanged and – still conscious – drawn (disembowelled) and cut into four pieces (quartered) while Henry watched. Prior Houghton's arm was nailed to Charterhouse gate. When it fell off, the arm and the surplice he was wearing were given a Carthusian burial (see Torture).

The monks still would not bow to Henry, so eighteen were '*boyled in oyle*' at **Smithfield**. In Bruges, Martin Chauncey, friend of the martyred Prior, eye witness who survived the purge, published *A History of Some of the Martyrs of Our Age*.

1550 Charterhouse used as a store for Henry's equipment for Smithfield jousts.

1970 The Pope makes Houghton a saint, one of 40 martyrs of England and Wales.

2000 Two hundred men apply every year to be English Carthusians.

TUDOR PALACE (the only one left in London).

Charterhouse is where Lord North *(***Lord North Street***) prepared* Elizabeth I *for her coronation, and where the Duke of Norfolk prepared* James I, *her successor, for his.*

1547 Sir Edward North, Chancellor of the Exchequer, who has already bought St Mary's Nunnery, buys Charterhouse.

1553 Treason is afoot. John Dudley, Duke of Northumberland (father of Robert, Elizabeth I's future paramour) has married son Guildford to Lady Jane Grey, named by Edward VI as his successor. He was determined to get Jane on the throne and use Charterhouse as a temporary palace (he stored furniture for it at **St John's Gate**). If Edward had lived longer, Jane and Guildford would have moved into Charterhouse. Sadly, Edward died and elder sister, Mary Tudor, succeeded to the throne.

1553 'Bloody Mary' invites the Carthusians back. Unable to face the memories, they opted for Sheen instead. North breathed a sigh of relief. He had secretly sold Charterhouse to Dudley, although no money had exchanged hands. Nor would it. Dudley's cover was blown and he died on Tower Hill. Even though North signed the paper agreeing Mary must be deposed, she promoted him to Lord North, Peer of the Realm.

Fellow plotter Sir William (Baron) Parr, who lived in **Charterhouse Square**, an avid supporter of 'Queen Jane', sentenced to death, was also not only pardoned but created Marquess of Northampton.

1558 Catholic Mary dies, Protestant Elizabeth is Queen. Carthusians again leave England. Whitehall is not ready to receive her and Mary is still lying in state in St James' Palace, so North invites Elizabeth I to Charterhouse to prepare for her coronation. Elizabeth stays five days.

1561 Second visit. 10–13 July, another Royal Progress. Her host is again Lord North, though this is costing him financially.

1565 The Queen has left North financially ruined. He sold Charterhouse to Thomas Howard, Duke of Norfolk, who re-named it Howard House.

1567 Howard brings his third Duchess, Elizabeth, daughter of Sir Francis Leyburne, to Charterhouse where they have their portrait painted together. Not a case of third time lucky, this poor woman fared no better than her predecessors. She died in September the same year.

1568 Treason is afoot. Again. It was suggested it would be good for England if Howard married Mary Stuart, Queen of Scots, put her on England's throne and became king of Scotland and England. Catholics were all for the idea. His sister, in charge of Queen Mary, imprisoned at Carlisle Castle, acted as go-between. When she heard the gossip, Elizabeth I made her third visit to Charterhouse, as guest of her *'dear coz'*.

1569 Elizabeth, staying at Hampton Court, is convinced that Howard is serious in his ambition to marry her arch enemy so sends to Charterhouse for him. She seized him by the elbow, gave him a meaningful pinch and warned him to 'take heed on what pillow' he laid his head. He protested, calling Mary Stuart an adulteress and murderess but never his intended wife. Before leaving, he signed an undertaking that he would have nothing to do with Mary, then returned to Charterhouse to arrange her rescue ... A royal pursuivant was again sent to Charterhouse to take Howard to Elizabeth but, pleading illness, instead of reporting to court, Norfolk left for Suffolk ... Elizabeth again summoned him to court, this time at Windsor. Howard was arrested and put in the Tower.

1570 From the Tower, Howard, Duke of Norfolk, continues his plot. In August there was an outbreak of plague in Tower Hamlets, so Elizabeth, bizarrely, allowed him to return home to Charterhouse under surveillance. He built an arcade leading to his tennis courts and bowling alley. Was he improving his mansion, hoping the Queen of Scotland would move in?

THE RIDOLFI PLOT

Ridolfi is posing as a Florentine merchant banker settled in London. He is supported by Philip II of Spain, who wants rid of Protestant Elizabeth in favour of Catholic Mary, now imprisoned at Chatsworth. Ridolfi is in fact a Senator of Florence. He is also a spy, undercover agent to both Pope Pius V and Philip II (Mary Tudor's ex-husband, unsuccessful suitor of Elizabeth and godfather to Norfolk's son). The plan is to send troops from Holland; Howard is to raise a further 40,000 here. Ridolfi asks the Duke to sign an agreement but he refuses, so Ridolfi forges his signature.

After discussing the plot with Norfolk at Charterhouse, Ridolfi, seen to the Gate by Barker, Norfolk's secretary (main witness at Norfolk's subsequent trial) was so excited, he foolishly blurted out the details of their conversation. The Duke was no better as he had hidden an incriminating letter under the mat in his study (some sources say under the roof tiles). The French were also plotting for Mary against Elizabeth. The French Ambassador, who lived in **Charterhouse Square**, received a huge sum of money from her supporters in France and sent it via his servant to Norfolk, who wrote Mary a letter and enclosed it with the money. The messenger read the letter and told William Cecil, the Queen's right hand man and spymaster, of the plot to kill her. Norfolk was arrested at Charterhouse and taken to the Tower. Once more Europe's attention was focused on Charterhouse. During the trial, the extent to which Charterhouse had been used in the plot was detailed. Mary's ambassador, the Bishop of Ross, confessed to many secret visits always made by appointment, always met by the great gate and escorted into the palace. He admitted to bringing messages and tokens from Mary (rings set with diamonds, Mary's famous embroidered cushions and handkerchiefs, a pair of writing tables and a gold tablet with Mary's portrait on it.

1572 January: The trial in Westminster Hall of the Premier Peer in England is ushered in with the pomp, ceremony and splendour fitted to his high station. His appointed counsel, Chief Justice Sir James Dyer, Speaker of the House of Commons, his neighbour in Charterhouse Square, proclaimed that in law, a peer accused of treason could be heard only by his peers. Although Cecil had enough evidence to convict Norfolk ten times over, the trial lasted all day; and, as evening approached, the Lords gave their verdict. The Queen reluctantly agreed to Norfolk's execution, arranging for 11 February, but then cancelled the order. It took months for her advisers to get her to give the go-ahead. Norfolk was beheaded in June. His old tutor, John Foxe, of *Book of Martyrs* fame, who lived in nearby Grub Street, was with him. Thomas Howard, Duke of Norfolk, lies buried in St Peter's Chapel in the Tower where cousins Anne Boleyn and Katharine Howard lie alongside John Dudley.

1573 Charterhouse reverts to the Crown and is leased to the Portuguese Ambassador. He celebrated the Catholic Mass, which was permitted. However it was not permitted for the Queen's subjects to join him (to worship as a Catholic was illegal until the Catholic Emancipation Act, 1829). One evening when he knew Mass was being celebrated, the Recorder of London accompanied by two Sheriffs appeared at the Porter's Lodge. The Portuguese porter slammed the Recorder's foot in the Great Gate, but he managed to barge into the room where Mass was being said and ordered all Englishmen to leave.

1589 Philip Howard, 38, (Norfolk's first son, godson of Philip II of Spain) has a Catholic Mass said for the Spanish Armada and successful invasion of England. Found guilty of treason, he was executed and buried in the Tower.

1593 George de Clifford (family line started with the wonderfully-named Walter FitzPonce, a Norman baron), Earl of Cumberland, naval commander, rents Charterhouse (Crown property) and stays two years with his wife and children. One was his heir, three-year-old Anne, who had to fight Sir Joseph Williamson, Secretary of State to Charles II (ruined by Titus Oates' Popish Plot, q.v.) to claim her inheritance: '*I have been bullied by a usurper, I have been neglected by a Court, but I will not be dictated to by a subject*'.

Elizabeth I, very fond of Cumberland, gave him a glove set with diamonds, which he put in his cap and wore till he died. He commanded one of her ships, the *Elizabeth Bonaventura*, in the battle against the Armada. Knowing Sir Francis Drake as well as he does, it's tempting to imagine Drake visiting him at Charterhouse. The Queen lent Cumberland her ship *Golden Lion* for one of his ten pirate raids on Spain, all of which were unfortunate. On the *Victory* to the Spanish main, he captured the treasure galleon of the West Indian fleet worth £100,000. The ship sank with all its treasure on board (probably still there).

1594 The Earl of Cumberland on yet another of his abortive trips brings three Spanish grandees back to Charterhouse as prisoners in honourable captivity while he waits for their ransom to be paid. He had a long wait. The noblemen were with him for a whole year.

1601 Elizabeth leases Charterhouse to Thomas Howard, whose father and half brother were executed for treason. This is the son of Norfolk's second marriage to Margaret Audley, daughter of Lord Chancellor Audley (North and South Audley Street W1). In the Armada, he commanded the *Golden Lion* with a crew of 250, was knighted for gallantry aboard the Ark Royal and made Admiral of the Fleet.

1603 The first place Elizabeth visited on becoming Queen is one of the last she visits before ending her long reign of 45 years. 17 January, age 70, she paid her fourth visit to Charterhouse to dine with *'my good Thomas'*. The Queen gave him Charterhouse and made him Lord Howard of Walden. Two months later, she was dead.

ARRIVAL OF KING JAMES

*In Charterhouse now sits the son of Elizabeth's sworn enemy, Mary Queen of Scots. James I (sixth in Scotland) Stuart, King of Britain (England and Scotland). This great grandchild of Henry VII rests at The Kings Head, **Upper Street**, on the last leg of his long journey from Scotland to Charterhouse to prepare for his coronation.*

At Woods Close (later **Northampton Street**) James, like his predecessor, left the King's Highway and took to the fields. She had been avoiding the winter mud, he was avoiding the summer dust. At Charterhouse he was met ceremoniously by seventy City Fathers dressed in velvet and gold. *'He was most royal received by the Lord Thomas, where was such abundance of provisions and all manner of things that greater could not be both of rare wild fowls and many rare and extraordinary banquets to the great liking of His Majesty and contentment of the whole train. He lay there four nights (7–11 May). He made divers knights whose names are there.'*

In the Great Chamber, one of the finest Elizabethan rooms in existence, then and now, where Liz danced in her young days, 133 hangers-on received a knighthood from the new King.

PUBLIC SCHOOL

The richest commoner in England (£5 billion), Thomas Sutton married Elizabeth Dudley, a rich widow. (Was she the Elizabeth Dudley who very nearly lived in Charterhouse when her husband, the traitor John Dudley, owned it for a few weeks? Or was that Elizabeth Dudley executed with her husband? Coincidentally, there once was a Sutton de Dudley). Sutton started working life (as did de Manny, who founded Charterhouse) as a mercenary, a 'free-lance' (soldier), but grew rich by shipping coal to London from Berwick-on-Tweed.

1580 Thomas Sutton (**Sutton Place**), old Etonian, ex-Lincoln's Inn, moves to London.

1611 Thomas Howard wants money for Audley End (his grandfather was Chancellor Audley), his country seat in Essex, so sells Charterhouse to Sutton, who has become a moneylender and is getting even richer (Ben Jonson's play *Volpone*, about a rich miser without children, is said to be a savage portrayal of him). But he can't have been that mean, as he converted Charterhouse into an almshouse for 80 male pensioners (today the number hovers around 35) and a school for 40 boys age 10 to 17.

Scholars or Gown Boys are sons of gentlemen of good breeding but little money, who might one day be influential, inherit money, titles or land. The boys are poor but their families are well connected. Prospective pensioners, brothers, have to produce a certificate of good behaviour and soundness of religion. Priority is given to retired servants of the court. The first brothers are ex-Armada, old men of lost fortunes, with good references. Preference is given to: 'decrepit old Captaynes, either at Sea or Land, Souldiers maymed or ympotent, decayed Marchaunts, men fallen into decaye through shipwrecke, Casualtie or Fyer or such evill Accident, those that have been captive under the Turks, etc.'

Sutton piped-in water from his well north of Charterhouse (**Penton Street**), covered the conduit and faced it with white stone, known thereafter as The White Conduit (q.v., later re-named The Penny Farthing pub). He died, age 79 (like de Manny before him) soon after completing the conversion of Charterhouse. The only known portrait of him is by Rubens. Among the first school governors was Solicitor General, Sir Francis Bacon (q.v.).

1613 A belfry is built. The curfew bell is rung at eight o'clock every evening in winter, nine o'clock in summer. The number of strokes equals the number of brothers in residence.

1615 The first pupil is admitted, son of a barber surgeon from nearby **Bart's**.

1651 Oliver Cromwell is a Governor.

1654 The water supply is low so the school is connected to the New River.

1682 Joseph Addison meets Richard Steele, fellow pupil, and they become lifelong friends, always referred to as Addison & Steele (never the other way round). Addison wrote for Steele's *Tatler* and they founded *The Spectator* magazine together. Addison was a poet, playwright, MP, Under-Secretary of State, married the countess of Warwick and retired on a fat state pension of £1,500 p.a. He helped launch the *Guardian* newspaper, edited by Steele, was a friend of William Blake and is buried in Henry VII chapel, Westminster Abbey. Steele, who outlived his friend by ten years, also became an MP.

1714 The Duke of Buckingham nominates John Wesley (10) for a scholarship.

Wesley was to spend fifty-six of his eighty years in the borough. One of fifty schoolboys, he stayed at Charterhouse until 1720 when he went up to Oxford. His parents had 19 children (he was the 15th). Three were boys, only ten survived childhood. He founded the largest Protestant denomination in the world, 14 million Methodists celebrate his birthday, and countless hospitals, schools, colleges, churches and missions are named after him. At Charterhouse, Wesley slept two to a bed, rose at 5 a.m. and breakfasted on beer and cheese.

1730 Opposing teams (Gown Boys v. Scholars) lay down a code of practice for 'cloister' football played in the 10 feet wide, barrel-vaulted arcade. The door at each end was 'goal'.

1737 Johann Christoph Pepusch (calls himself John) is appointed resident organist.

Pepusch, conductor of the Brandenburg orchestra, came to London with his friend, George Frederick Handel. In 1728, he wrote the music for *The Beggars Opera* (pop songs such as *Over the Hills and Far Away*) and, along with John Gay (lyricist) and John Rich (producer), was embroiled in the public outcry. They were accused of causing juvenile delinquency, violent crime, theft, riots and general immorality. It was said that highway robbery increased after the opera, with copycat holdups. Its impact was comparable with Kubrick's *Clockwork Orange* or Kerouac's *On the Road*.

The hero, Captain Macheath, a romanticised highwayman, is based on real-life local hero Jack Sheppard (see Sheppard, Jack). The opera (inspiration for *The Threepenny Opera*) is anti-establishment. It parodies serious opera and glorifies low-life. Instead of traditional heroes and heroines, it's about the thieves, prostitutes and gangsters of nearby 'Hockley-in-the-Hole'. Hogarth engraved scenes from it.

Old boy Wesley often comes back to visit Charterhouse and becomes friends with Pepusch.

1818 Thomas Milner-Gibson, whose family owns parts of Islington, is one of 238 pupils. He was at prep school with Disraeli.

1820 William Makepeace Thackeray is enrolled. He said he hadn't been there five minutes before a senior boy shouted *'Here! New boy! Come and frig me!'* Homosexual rape was not the only trauma. All portraits of Thackeray show his broken nose, which he got fighting fellow pupil Venables when he boarded at 7 **Charterhouse Square**.

The area is teeming with undesirables. Parents object to their sons being mugged by the lower orders, so to protect them from being stoned and spat at, a tunnel is built from the school to the board houses in Charterhouse Square (pupils ate off a board).

1822 Thackeray moves into **Berry Street**, Clerkenwell and stays two years, then another two years at 10 Wilderness Row (**Clerkenwell Road**). Despite fighting and rape, he looked upon Charterhouse with affection and wrote *The Newcomes* based on his experiences there (Charterhouse is 'Slaughterhouse').

1824 Edward Blore (commissioned to complete Buckingham Palace after John Nash was sacked for not keeping within budget) redesigns parts of Charterhouse.

1825 480 pupils.

1827 John Leech is enrolled. A contemporary of Cruikshank, he trained as a doctor at **Bart's** but preferred cartooning so worked for *Punch* specialising in political satire (*Punch* bought three thousand of his drawings). He also illustrated Dickens' *A Christmas Carol*. He attended Old Boy re-unions with Thackeray.

1835 The area is so rough the number of pupils is down to 99.

1838 William Horsley, school chapel organist, composes *There is a Green Hill Far Away*.

1856 Islington: Home of Football

Charterhouse v Westminster. Soccer hooligans are born. Flowering of Football Association (FA), using unwritten rules of charging and offside. Goal is the only member of the eleven to whom a post is assigned, the other ten simply try to get control of the ball and keep it (forward, wing, centre back introduced later). Handling the ball is allowed, otherwise the game is much as it is now.

1863 Duke of Wellington is a Governor. The old Etonian duke said Charterhouse was a far better school. 12 December, Thackeray, author of the hugely successful *Vanity Fair*, attended his last Founders Day dinner with John Leech. Twelve days later, he was buried at Kensal Green.

1867 Robert Baden-Powell is enrolled. An inspirational leader, he held Mafeking in South Africa for seven months against Boer insurgents in 1900 (he had to eat his own horse) and founded the international Boy Scouts, Sea Scouts and Wolf Cub movements.

1872 Clerkenwell is now a slum so after 250 years at Charterhouse the school moves to Godalming, Surrey where it remains today. The old school was rebuilt as Merchant Taylor's School and some of the land reverted to Bart's.

1906 Developers try to get their hands on Charterhouse but fail.

1931 Merchant bankers, Baring Brothers are freeholders and trustees.

1935 Merchant Taylor's School moves to Middlesex.

1941 WWII, parts of Charterhouse are gutted by an incendiary (oil filled) bomb.

1947 Restoration of war damage. Consultants from the London Museum worked under Lord Mottistone. So much was revealed of the original monastery, the calamity was now seen as a blessing. The Victorian stucco had fallen off revealing the original Tudor brickwork. Cell B, built 1371, was discovered – as was founder de Manny's grave. A blocked-up squint window was found in the old monastic treasury through which the monk on duty in charge of the valuables could follow Mass. It was known that de Manny was buried before the high altar but no one knew where. By following the line of sight from the squint in the Treasury to where the altar once was, de Manny was found. Professor Jones, Royal College of Surgeons examined the 600-year-old remains and pronounced they were of '*a man over 60, from Belgium*'.

1990 Museum of London finds five more cells and the great cloister.

2000 Residents of Charterhouse are male, Church of England, over 65, ex-Army/Navy officers, clergymen, doctors, lawyers, artists, etc. Means-tested assets must not exceed £23,000 and annual income must be below £9,000. Each has a comfortable bedsit and takes meals in the Great Hall.

CHARTERHOUSE SQUARE EC1

1529 John Neville, Lord Latimer, buys No. 10 '*because it stands in good air out of the press of the City*'. He brings Catherine Parr, his third wife, here (he is her second husband). Her brother, Sir William Parr also lives here (he stole parts of Charterhouse to build his house).

1543 Henry VIII has set his sights on Catherine Parr (33) wealthy widow (of both Sir Edward Burroughs and Lord Latimer) who has set *her* sights on Sir Thomas Seymour, who visits her here. Seymour (the king's brother-in-law, his sister Jane married Henry) has set *his* sights on young Princess Elizabeth. Catherine leaves Charterhouse Square not to marry Seymour, the love of her life, but to be Henry's sixth and last wife. She does, however, marry Seymour when Henry dies.

1598 Stowe's *Survey of London* writes about a stone cross dated 1349, commemorating 50,000 dead of plague (the actual figure was nearer 60,000 some books say 100,000); but in 1349 the population of London was only 45,000.

Islington: Home of Opera (in England, 1656) (see D'Avenant).

Islington: Home of Artificial Stone

1760 Mrs Eleanor Coade lives in Charterhouse Square. She opened Coade Artificial Stone Manufactory on the south bank of the Thames to produce artificial stone on a mass scale. Gifted artist, chemist and businesswoman, she invented the most weatherproof, durable, artificial stone ever made. When the factory closed (1840) the secret of its manufacture was lost until modern chemical laboratories cracked Coade's code, so to speak. The factory was demolished 1948 to build Festival Hall. In 1996 on the BBC *Antiques Road Show*, a Coade stone plinth minus its statue was valued at £4,000.

1805 John Cunningham Saunders, distressed by the blinding conjunctivitis suffered by thousands of troops returning from the Napoleonic wars, founds The London Dispensary for Curing Diseases of the Eye, the first eye hospital. In 1820 it was rebuilt in **Eldon Street** and renamed London Ophthalmic Infirmary. In 1899 it moved to **City Road** in the old moor fields, and became **Moorfields Eye Hospital**. Today it's still a world leader. Surgeons perform five thousand cataract operations a year.

1841 Charles <u>Dickens</u> has a fistula removed at The Infirmary for the Relief of the Poor Afflicted with Fistula and Other Diseases of the Rectum, at No. 38. As Dickens was not poor, presumably he was charged.

1935 Florin Court is built, a modern, stylish block of flats on land owned by Charterhouse. It has a cantilevered steel canopy and the curving walls and windows typical of '30s architecture. The design showed off new materials such as aluminium, reinforced glass and concrete. Residents of the 126 bedsits were wealthy businessmen who needed a *pied a terre* close to the City. The block had roof terraces, squash courts, restaurant, cocktail bar, residents' club and underground garage. Jacuzzis and a swimming pool were added later. The name 'Florin' is a mystery but it's better known to TV viewers as 'Whitehaven Mansions', art deco home of Agatha Christie's Hercule <u>Poirot</u>, played by David Suchet.

1999 A hostel for **Bart's** medical staff is converted into a 76-bedroom hotel.

CHISWELL STREET EC1

'Chysel' *(Saxon for stony/gravelly)* or 'Ceosol' *Well (old English for flint/pebble).*

1738 William <u>Caslon</u>, founder of funky fonts fame, moves in.

1739 George <u>Dance the Elder</u> designs Mansion House.

1741 George <u>Dance the Younger</u> born here. Moved out 1775 when he married.

1750 Samuel <u>Whitbread</u> closes his tiny brewery in **Whitecross Street** and erects a huge one here in its place. James <u>Watt</u> built the steam engine needed in the brewing process and Scots engineer (builder of Waterloo, London and Southwark Bridges) John <u>Rennie</u> installed it.

1768 Dance the Elder dies.

1770 George Dance the Younger re-builds Newgate Prison.

1775 James <u>Lackington</u> borrows £25 from John Wesley's Mission and opens a bookshop at No. 46.

1796 Whitbread dies owning fourteen pubs, his brewery exporting to Ireland, South Africa, Hong Kong, Australia, New Zealand and America.

1956 Val Guest films *The Weapon* on a bomb site near the brewery.

1958 Whitbread exports to sixty countries.

1976 Whitbread ceases brewing on the site.

1999 Whitbread is the UK's leading food/drinks empire and owns *Brewer's Fayre, Wayside Inns, Hanrahans, Café Rouge, TGI Friday, Pizza Hut, Marriott, Country Club, Travel Inn, IPA, Flowers, Boddington, Murphy's, Heineken, Stella Artois* and *David Lloyd Gyms.* It also sponsors the Whitbread Book Prize.

CINEMAS (see also entries under **Archway**, **Essex Road**, **Holloway Road**, **Seven Sisters Road**, etc.)

Islington: Home of Britain's First Cinema – which, although protected, listed and recognised as historically important, astonishingly was demolished in 1986.

Islington is film mad and in its heyday had 40 cinemas, converted from shops and church halls. Going down the 'flea pit' or 'bug hole' as they're affectionately called was a social occasion where friends met and romance blossomed. Fans went every time the programme changed (two or three times a week). Strict fire regulations, two wars and the advent of television mean that today there are just two: the Odeon, **Holloway Road** *and the Screen on the Green.*

1900 3 August. Britain's first proper film show is part of the Mohawk Minstrel Show in the 'Aggie' (q.v.). Films shown were *Count Zeppelin's Warship, A Visit to the Spiritualist* and *Rush Hour at the Angel.* To meet the huge demand for the 'flicks', empty chapels, church halls, meeting rooms and shops were taken over, given pretentious names and punters fell over themselves to pay a penny to the gaffer/owner (penny gaffs). Plate glass windows were boarded over and a sheet hung on the wall. Projectors broke down, music was played on out-of-tune joannas (pianners) and patrons sat on wooden benches. At best, the pictures flickered (hence, flicks); at worst, the unstable nitrate film caught fire. When the London County Council was formed (1910) cinemas had to comply with fire safety regulations to get a licence. Many closed (down from forty to twenty-nine).

An empty shop at 325 **Caledonian Road** became The Variety Picture Palace. Refused an LCC licence, it was closed during WWI. At the derelict church on **River Street**, Rivers Electric Theatre, cinemagoing was a communal experience. Although pitch black inside, there were no attendants. People's enjoyment was interrupted by cries of *'Where's a seat?'* with angry patrons screaming directions. *'Shut that door'* was a familiar cry when people stumbled to the loo because light filled the auditorium, whiting-out the film. The projection was so appalling, patrons yelled *'Higher! Lower!'.* . . It too closed during the first war.

The Lower Stanley Assembly Hall, **Junction Road**, became the Electric Theatre but it was always known as the Stanley. Very popular, it opened in the afternoon and closed at 11 p.m. Performances were continuous so there were no queues to get in, no waiting for the film to begin and no intervals. Patrons were shown to their seats by an usher with a torch. It too closed during the war and never re-opened.

The old chapel at 16 Church Street, (**Gaskin Street**) became The Picture Palace, where the first film shown was untitled. The first patron to guess the title won an umbrella. Local residents complained of the non-stop piano playing.

1911 A row of houses in **Hornsey Road** is converted into Hornsey Palace and survives until the outbreak of WWII. No. 335 was the foyer, No. 345 the exit, the auditorium at the rear connected them. The houses between were unaffected. The cinema had green leather seats and thick carpets. It underwent a name change to The Star – but, Palace or Star, it was always called the 'flea pit'.

1912 The Victoria, 272 **New North Road**. The piano player teased the audience by playing sad pieces during funny bits and vice versa. His reward was to be pelted with orange peel and nutshells. Winners picked out at random by spotlight were given prizes of smoked kippers. The Vic survived two wars but couldn't compete with TV. It closed in 1957.

153 **Hungerford Road** was The Empire Picture Theatre, 138 **Copenhagen Street** the Copenhagen and the purpose-built Scala opened at 15 The Parade, **Stroud Green Road**. Soon closed for the duration, after the war it was called The New Scala but closed in 1924.

1913 Before the war the borough has twenty-seven cinemas, after, it has seventeen.

1923 The Holloway Empire Theatre is converted into a cinema designed for the talkies, which won't arrive in Britain for another ten years.

1924 The Flying Scotsman opens a cinema on its **King's Cross** to Leeds run. The converted railway carriage had forty-four comfortable seats and the films were of excellent technical quality.

1928 The old 1859 Vestry Hall, on the corner of **Florence Street** and **Upper Street**, is converted into The Lido. It had an orchestra and ran grand piano playing competitions judged by the audience.

1930 Northern Polytechnic, **Holloway Road** is showing a film of the South African War (Boer War). The Revd Donald Soper's holy picture shows at the Central Methodist Hall, **Drayton Park**, drew huge crowds. Vast super cinemas were opened by celebrities with massed bands, all over the borough. They had huge auditoriums, impressive entrance halls, comfortable lounges, tea rooms, telephone booths, cloakrooms and armies of uniformed attendants. Queues were so long, buskers entertained them (piano-accordionists, spoon players, one-man bands and sand dancers). Designed to awe and impart a sense of occasion, they offered undreamed-of luxury.

1932 The Grand Theatre Islington High Street is now called The Empire.

1935 The Flying Scotsman cinema amazes patrons with the new talkies, including the Jubilee celebrations, Pathe news and sport.

1936 The Lido, corner **Florence Street/Upper Street**, now an Odeon, is mobbed when film star Anna Neagle and film producer husband Herbert Wilcox visit.

1937 Hornsey Palace closes. Gracie Fields opened The Mayfair, 474 **Caledonian Road**. Although opposite the tube, it had two car parks. Our Gracie thrilled the audience with *Sally* (written in Islington, see Sally Place) *Sing as We Go*, *Little Old Lady* and *Walter, Walter, Lead Me to the Altar*. Larger cinemas had commissionaires and attendants in uniforms made by the Uniform Clothing & Equipment Company, **Clerkenwell Green**, who promised to transform an *'insignificant working individual into an imposing and awe-inspiring personage.'* Opulent cinemas contrasted starkly with huge tracts of Islington which were designated official slums. After WWII, chains took over the running of many cinemas. The Empire, **Islington High Street** and The Mayfair, renamed the Essoldo, **Caledonian Road**, were now ABCs.

1938 The Holloway Empire is demolished. A 3,000-seater, the last Gaumont built was opened in Holloway Road. The design was by American C. Howard Crane, who built Radio City in New York. Walnut was used throughout, with columns, mirrors, chandeliers, balustrades and a café terrace overlooks the shops. It had an Italian renaissance-style auditorium painted gold and blue, Corinthian columns, domes, panels of crimson, gold and blue, ivory dados in gold and crimson, pink plush upholstered seats. Uniformed staff wore blue with silver trim. Below the cinema was a waiting area for two thousand patrons so that they didn't have to queue in the cold and wet.

1953 TV arrives. The coronation of Elizabeth II sent everyone out to buy a set on Hire Purchase. The hordes strolling the streets shopping until late at night dwindled as people stayed mesmerised by their firesides and cinemas closed one after another.

1955 Highgate Odeon, **Junction Road**, is the last cinema to be built in Islington. A grand affair, it had cream terracotta outside, inside were red plush seats and carpets, blue and cream pay boxes and confectionery kiosks, mahogany-panelled staircase, Vistavision™, Cinemascope™ and other wide screen formats.

1961 The Odeon/Lido in **Florence Street** was demolished (now a petrol station). The old Philharmonic (opened 1860, aka The Grand, The Empire) now an ABC, **Islington High Street** was demolished (Royal Bank of Scotland) (The Museum of London has its facade of classic columns and caryatids).

1965 The Mayfair, **Caledonian Road**, is now a Bingo hall.

1973 The Odeon, **Junction Road**, less than twenty years old, is demolished.

....

CITY UNIVERSITY
Northampton Square/St John Street EC1

1802 Northampton Square is laid out.

1819 James Hook RA, renowned for his English coastlines (*The Samphire Gatherer* is in the Tate) praised by John Ruskin, is born at No. 27.

1843 George Baxter of Baxter Prints fame at No. 11 invents high-definition oil colour printing which makes coloured prints commonly available – and now, quite collectable.

1880 The British Horological Institute (science of clock/watch making) founded 1853 in St John Square moves to No. 35 Northampton Square. The correct time was relayed here via Greenwich Observatory.

1891 Following The Great Exhibition there is a national obsession with technology. Many Technical Education institutions were opened. Northampton Institute was built on land given by Lord Northampton. City churches now had few parishioners so the City Parochial Fund was generous. Livery Companies were also very generous. Large, commercially-led businesses in the City needed an educated workforce so also contributed. The government made up the shortfall. Designed by E.W. Mountford, architect of the Central Courts of Criminal Justice (called Old Bailey after the street) and Mountford House in nearby **Britton Street**. Late-Victorian architecture was eclectic, including baroque, rococo, Queen Anne and French Renaissance features, the building was also a salute to William Morris' Arts and Crafts movement (faithful to local materials, i.e. extensive use of brick with bands of Portland stone). However, the Institute was better known for its world-leading innovations.

1896 The old manor house is demolished and the land given by Lord Northampton to build a technical institution.

1901 A turret clock is added as a tribute to the watchmakers who worked in these streets. Nicknamed 'Little Ben' it was by Dent's, the same people who made 'Big Ben'.

Islington: Home of the Sandwich Course

1904 Northampton Institute introduces the 'sandwich course' so students can gain practical experience between two six-month academic courses. The term made it into *Encyclopaedia Britannica*.

1907 Revolutionary new courses are offered in submarine cable work and radio-telegraphy, aero-engineering and cinematography. Acknowledged world leader in ophthalmology. (Moorfields Eye Hospital, see Charterhouse Square, was just down the road).

1910 The Principal, recognising the popularity of cinema, was the first to offer a course for the training and certification of projectionists. Local boy-made-good, Robert Paul (father of British cinema, born nearby, see Paul, Robert) designed the first fireproof projection box.

1919 Majority of students are war veterans.

1946 Graduate and post-graduate arts courses are now offered as well as technical subjects.

1947 National College of Horology opens.

1950 New courses include making contact lenses.

1955 Re-named Northampton Polytechnic. In 1945, Thomas Wilson, President of IBM, predicted there would only ever be a need for five computers in the world. Northampton Poly, already using ultrasonic cameras, installed the world's eighth and offered courses in computer programming. The machine weighed-in at around one ton, was 16 feet long, used 4 kW/hr electricity and took up a whole room.

1957 Re-named Northampton College of Advanced Technology.

1963 Introduces faculties in Management, Social Sciences and Humanities.

1966 Re-named City University. Architects desecrated the elegant 1802 Northampton Square to build an extension. Despite local opposition, the north side and two adjoining streets were bulldozed. In their stead was built a concrete monstrosity. One of the houses demolished was where George Baxter lived. Islington Coat of Arms includes a book of 'learning' to represent City University.

1996 Joe Loss (bandleader) memorabilia is presented to the new music department, opened by singer Frankie Vaughan.

....

CLERKENWELL EC1

1066 <u>William the Conqueror</u> gives land to Baron Jordan de Briset (**Briset Street**).

1100 First mention of the clerk's well. The de Brisets gave land for a Benedictine nunnery, *Ecclesia Sanctae Mariae de Fonte Clericorum* (the church of Saint Mary by the Clerk's Well). It can still be seen at 14 **Farringdon Road**, just half a mile from St Paul's. To reach it took no time walking along the banks of the Fleet, so it was frequented by parish clerks who escaped the noxious City with a stroll along the river to their favourite watering hole. The well became known as the **Clerken** (Anglo-Saxon plural for clerk) **Well**, as did the village which sprang up around it.

One of the chief duties of The Worshipful Company of Parish Clerks was to stage plays to teach stories from the Scriptures. When the churches, then the churchyards, became too small for the hordes who attended, open air venues had to be found. The Clerk's Well was perfect. The Fleet Valley with its steep banks provided a superb natural amphitheatre.

1174 Monk, William <u>FitzStephen</u>, writes about the well.

1536 Until the nobles move in, Clerkenwell is very quiet. <u>Henry VIII</u> had closed Charterhouse, the knights, monks and brothers were gone, as was everyone who worked for the priory and the nunnery.

1553 Queen <u>Mary Tudor</u> brings back the Knights of St John.

1558 Elizabeth I disbands the Order again. Instead of the Knights in and out of The Gate, it was actors trooping along to see the Master of the Revels (see Theatre).

1562 418 Clerkenwell residents, 112 of whom live in **Turn Mill Street**, are assessed for the Poor Rate.

1598 Stowe's *Survey of London* refers to: '*Clarke's Well, a curbed-about square with hard stone.*'

1660 The Great Plague, followed shortly by The Great Fire, sends city folk fleeing here. Many never went back.

1661 418 houses.

1675 The game of bowls is all the rage. Four public greens were laid out.

1685 The French hate their Protestants as much as the English hate their Catholics ... After the Edict of Nantes, half a million Huguenots (French Protestants) deprived of civil rights, fled France. Refugee craftsmen, especially watchmakers from northern France, settled in Clerkenwell. The City banned them from the Guilds (closed shop unions) but they were free to practise outside the city walls.

1668 Shrove Tuesday, apprentices burn down the brothels and are gaoled in Clerkenwell Bridewell. Their friends tried to burn the prison down to get them out.

1711 1,146 houses are here.

1720 Earl of <u>Northampton</u> gives the well to the parish. The Vestry leased it to John <u>Crosse</u>, brewer, on condition locals had access. He turned the well into a fountain.

1727 John <u>Wilkes</u> is born in St John's Square.

1783 Robert <u>Hindmarsh</u>, Clerkenwell printer, founds The Swedenborg New Jerusalem Church.

1798 Clerkenwell teems with engravers, publishers, printers and, because of the abundance of water, distillers and brewers. Being near Hatton Garden it was important for watchmakers and jewellers, and a world centre for scientific instrument makers.

The wealthy kept thousands of precision metalworkers busy with their demand for barometers and clocks. The Clerkenwell Watchface was highly fashionable, other countries sent their clocks and watch casings to have them put on. The government imposed a heavy tax on gold and silver, so much of the trade on which Clerkenwell residents depended for their livelihoods moved to Switzerland, throwing thousands on to poor relief. Undeterred, the government then levied a further massive import duty on watch and clock casings. The watchmaking industry halved, seven thousand out of the 21,000 population were unemployed.

In the first eleven weeks of its opening, a soup kitchen in Coppice Row fed 3,000 families.

1801 Population now 23,396. The well was brought up to pavement level and a pump installed to make drawing water easier.

1826 Because of local industry and housing development, the water table is falling. A windlass (winch to lower and raise a bucket) was installed.

1832 The well is wedged between two shops, one selling pottery, the other caged birds. The water table continued to fall.

1836 Dickens' *Oliver Twist* puts Clerkenwell and its infamous 'rookeries' – overcrowded slum dwellings – on the international map.

1851 Clockmakers exhibit ornate timepieces at The Great Exhibition.

1856 The Vestry closes the well. It was built over and forgotten.

1861 Population of 65,681 includes 1,877 clock and watchmakers, 725 goldsmiths, 720 printers, 578 shoe makers, 1,477 milliners, 314 bookbinders, 164 engravers and 97 musical instrument makers.

1900s Local factories are connected with food processing, radio battery assembly, furniture making, chemicals, printing and toy making. Household names included Scholl, Freeman, Hardy & Willis and Lilley and Skinner (shoe firms), Bovril, Robert Dyas ironmongers, Ingersoll watches, Bravington's rings, toys and Tom Smith's Christmas Crackers.

1901 Because of slum clearance, Islington is now three times more densely populated (335,238) than Finsbury (101,463).

1924 The well is re-discovered in the cellar of *The New Statesman* offices. Until it was found, a plaque hung on the wall of nearby St James Church, **Clerkenwell Close**. The magazine helped fund the excavation and granted Islington Council a lease on the well. The *Church Times* wrote: '*These downtown neighbourhoods conceal more buried history than Tutenkhamun's tomb.*'

1965 London Local Government Act merges Clerkenwell with Islington.

1985 *The New Statesman* helps fund the Clerken Well Museum.

1990s Scholl's Paramount Building, **St John Street** is sold for loft-style living, with flats priced at £1m each. The same happened to the 1897 Bovril factory in **Old Street**. Marketing gurus began to call Clerkenwell, **Cityside**.

....

CLERKENWELL CLOSE EC1

1541 Sir Thomas Chaloner, diplomat, royal envoy to Spain, Scotland, France and the Netherlands, Clerk to the Privy Council, given land here for services to the Crown, builds a mansion. He was also given Guisborough Priory, Yorkshire – which would help cost a future king his head.

1558 Elizabeth I asks Sir Thomas as her representative in the Netherlands to bring her back some 'good horses'.

1599 Sir Thomas Chaloner the Younger, son of the diplomat, is a naturalist. He discovered valuable alum on the family land in Yorkshire (alum was used for, among other things, hardening tallow candles).

1642 Oliver Cromwell, MP for Cambridge, whenever he is in London on parliamentary business, stays in the splendid home of fellow republicans, brothers Thomas and James Chaloner (third and fourth sons of the naturalist).

James was MP for Aldborough, Yorkshire and Governor, Isle of Man, Thomas MP for Richmond, Yorkshire. Thomas's alum mines brought in (according to John Aubrey's *Brief Lives*) £2,000 p.a. When Charles I confiscated the mines and called them The Royal Mines, lust for revenge turned Thomas into a regicide. One of Charles' judges, after the Civil War he signed the King's death warrant.

1653 Cromwell dismisses Thomas from Parliament, calling him an incompetent drunkard, but returns the mines to him.

1660 According to the *Dictionary of National Biography*, on the restoration of the monarchy, James Chaloner committed suicide in Peel Castle, Isle of Man. His brother, Thomas escaped to Holland where he died a year later (1661). According to Aubrey's *Brief Lives*, however, it was Thomas who committed suicide and James who died in Holland.

1662 William Cavendish, Duke of Newcastle, seventh richest man in England (£6 billion) demolishes the north and west range of old St Mary's, along with the nuns dining hall, to build a mansion. He remained here for the rest of his life. A fervent Royalist, he spent £1m in service to the monarchy but, treated badly at the Restoration, left the court – although Charles II visited him here. He was Ben Jonson's patron, as was his Duchess, nicknamed Mad Madge. After her death she lay in state at Newcastle House before being buried in Westminster Abbey.

1672 Dr <u>Garencieres</u>, physician to the French ambassador, translates and publishes *Nostradamus*, the most famous prophet in Western history.

1676 The old duke dies. His son Henry Cavendish was Master of the Robes and Lord of the Bed Chamber.

1780 When James <u>Carr</u> rebuilds St James Church, he demolishes the Duke of Newcastle's mansion and builds a row of houses.

1972 Rosie <u>Boycott</u> founds *Spare Rib* (q.v.), Britain's first feminist newspaper, at No. 27.

1984 *Dance With a Stranger* is filmed in **The Close** with Miranda Richardson as Ruth <u>Ellis</u> (last woman hanged in Britain, for murder, see **Holloway**) and Rupert Everett as her lover. Georgie Ellis, who was three when her mother died, had her photograph taken with an uncomfortable-looking Richardson.

....

CLERKENWELL FIRE STATION
Rosebery Avenue EC1

Site of the mansion of Sir John <u>Oldcastle</u>, Lord <u>Cobham</u>, confidant and drinking partner of the young prince Harry of Monmouth (Henry V).

Cobham was Public Enemy Number One in Rome – which is hardly surprising as he repeatedly and publicly denounced the Pope as the Antichrist. He was leader of the Lollards, who paved the way for Protestantism. (*Lollaert* is a derisory Dutch term for '*mumbler*'.) Oldcastle's Rebellion denounced transubstantiation (wine into blood, bread into flesh), war and capital punishment. He was sent to the Tower following a conviction for heresy and immediately dropped by the young king.

1414 When Sir John, adored local hero, escapes from the Tower, friends in Clerkenwell shield him from the authorities. But he was recaptured.

1417 '*Good Lord Cobham*' is hanged in chains and burnt alive on Christmas Day. In 1563 he appeared in John <u>Foxe</u>'s *Book of Martyrs* (see Grub Street). In 1597, <u>Shakespeare</u> read about him and his friendship with Prince Hal (Henry V) in Holinshed's *Chronicles* and put him in *Henry IV* as the prince's riotous and dissolute drinking partner. The play was premiered in Shoreditch, Oldcastle's haunt of 150 years earlier. Shakespeare had Sir John rollicking in the taverns and brothels in **Turnmill Street**, but as soon as he appeared on stage there was uproar. Locals objected to their hero being used as a figure of fun and complained to the censor, none other than Lord Cobham, through his mother a direct descendant of Sir John. He ordered the character to be removed. Shakespeare went back to Holinshed and substituted Sir John Fastolfe (in later versions Falstaff), another historical character (a coward in Henry V's wars on France) as the prince's companion instead.

1716 Volunteer fire fighters are introduced.

1728 Cobham's Head opens on the site of Cobham's old mansion and advertises *fishing for carp and tench*.

1860 Cobham's Head collapses, its foundations undermined by the bursting of New River water main when tunnelling was carried out to build the world's first underground railway in time for the second Great Exhibition of 1862.

1872 The Metropolitan Fire Brigade replaces volunteer fire fighters and builds a fire station, said to be the oldest (purpose built) in London.

1910 The fire station is rebuilt. Engines are still horse drawn.

CLERKENWELL GREEN EC1
Home of Political and Religious Dissent

1174 With St John's Priory on one side and St Mary's Nunnery on the other, by the time William FitzStephen wrote about it, not much remained green.

1381 Wat Tyler sets up camp here (see Tyler, Wat).

1641 The Crown opens, a popular meeting place for printers and watchmakers.

1649 Izaac Walton, biographer of John Donne, moves in. He is 56.

1650 Izaac's wife has a son who survives only four months. The following year the couple had another baby who also died young. Both are buried in St James'.

1653 Walton publishes *The Compleat Angler*, a philosophical treatise on fishing, which was re-printed five times in his lifetime. There are *Compleat Angler* pubs in Buckinghamshire and Derbyshire and *Izaac Walton* pubs in Enfield, Staffordshire, Derbyshire and Hampshire – but none in Clerkenwell.

1670 Nicholas Culpeper gathers herbs from Little Saffron Hill (re-named Herbal Hill 1937) for his *Medicament for the Poor*. Sawbridge Booksellers, Clerkenwell Green published it.

1738 Thriving dairy farms need milkmaids so local farmers recruited them from Wales and a large Welsh community sprang up. Education was a priority of the Welsh so they converted No. 37, an old dairy (cows seldom saw the light of day) into The Welsh Charity School. A figure of a charity boy was in the oriel window niche.

1772 The Welsh School admits girls as well as boys so moves to **Grays Inn Road** to bigger premises. The school was converted into workshops for cabinet makers and upholsterers and by 1782 had become a pub, The Northumberland Arms.

1779 Serious crimes were tried in Hicks Hall (q.v.), **St John Street**, but it had become too small. An open competition was held for the design of a new Sessions House and plans submitted to Thomas Rogers, architect and county surveyor. He rejected them all and drew up his own, published in the trade magazine *The Builder*. John Carter, a rejected competitor who wrote for the magazine, claimed to recognise his own plans. Some sources say the new court was finally designed by Roland Gilbert.

1787 A woman in the pillory outside the Sessions House is pelted to death.

1794 Trial of members of the London Corresponding Society (q.v.). Found not guilty!

1806 Bells are rung and cannons fired as the foundation stone of The Sessions House (now Grade I listed) is laid by the Duke of Northumberland. He marched at the head of a procession followed by the Lord Lieutenant of Middlesex and county magistrates. Stonemasons, bricklayers and carpenters each carried the implements of their craft.

The building had offices, accommodation for visiting judges and dungeons as well as courtrooms (present incumbents, the Freemasons, say it also has ghosts). The fireplace and Jacobean overmantel were brought from the old Hicks Hall, as were the fetters worn by Jack Sheppard. The plaster frieze outside is by Joseph Nollekens RA, eccentric miser, the most fashionable sculptor of his day. It shows the Arms of the County of Middlesex and Roman heralds carrying bundles of rods with projecting axe blades (emblem of authority).

The Sessions House was called New Hicks Hall, and all British mileage was measured from here, until Charing Cross took the honour. The back door opened straight on to the river Fleet, by which transported convicts were taken on boats to join the hulks (rotting prison ships, derelict since the Napoleonic Wars) on the Thames. Those to be hanged at Newgate were given a drink at the St John of Jerusalem on the way. (The hangman was said to have gone back and forth from Newgate via a tunnel under Clerkenwell Green.)

1826 William Cobbett, of the famous *Rural Rides*, thunders against the Corn Laws. If anybody wanted to rouse public feeling for a cause they came here. The Green became the centre for everything repugnant to the establishment: radicalism, republicanism, revolution and atheism.

1830 Samuel Bros Uniform Clothing Company and Livery Tailors opens to sell army surplus clothing. The company was commissioned to make Doggetts Coats, Tower Warders 'undress' (summer uniforms), uniforms for Trooping the Colour, footguards, mounted musicians, trews for Scots and Irish pipers, bandmasters' frock coats, Royal Horse Artillery and the Royal Yacht. All were bespoke 'Sealed Patterns'.

1831 The People's Charter with a million signatures is drawn up by the National Union of Working Classes. Three members were tried at the Sessions House for inciting a riot and acquitted.

1832 The Reform Act increases the electorate by half (from 5 per cent of the population to 7½ per cent) and introduces proportional representation of a sort. New parliamentary constituencies were created but the vote was still for property owners only (10,300 electors out of pop. 224,839). There are two MPs for Finsbury (includes Islington, Stoke Newington, Bloomsbury and Holborn).

1836 *Oliver Twist: 'Mrs Mann, I'm a going to London . . . to depose to the matter before the quarter sessions at Clerkinwell.'*

1837 More Chartist riots.

1839 Seven thousand attend another Chartist Rally.

1840 Riots over religion, politics and that perennial problem, starvation.

These were the hungry '40s, when Corn Laws kept the price of bread, a basic necessity, artificially high. The law, which prohibited the import of wheat cheaper than home grown, had just had its third reading. Loaves of bread carried on hearses draped in black and purple were paraded around the Green in mock funerals. 20,000 assembled outside Parliament but were dispersed by the military so instead attacked the houses of Corn Law supporters. One was Fred Robinson, whose effigy was hanged from a tree in Islington.

1842 Henry 'Orator' Hunt rages against the Corn Laws. Another Chartist Rally. Three million signatures demanding votes for all were presented to the House of Commons. Sir Robert Peel (Prime Minister 1834–5 and 1841–6, eventually repealed the Corn Laws) banned the Green as a meeting place..

1848 Seditious leaflets abound. Freedom of the Press (won by local hero, John Wilkes) allowed them to be published but not sold, so straws were sold and the pamphlets given away free. Peel (founder of the modern police force) sent in 5,000 police and a squadron of Horse Guards to break up yet another political meeting. Clerkenwell Green resident: *'We had the police every night . . . We had the horse troops one night . . .'* Policeman: *'The police were always coming into conflict with the mob . . . There was plenty of space on* *the Green for fighting and many houses in which the Chartists could hide and throw things at us ...'*

1851 The Crown is re-built with a music hall on the first floor. A big attraction was a clock from Rye House (where nearly 200 years earlier there had been a plot to assassinate Charles II and his brother, the Duke of York).

1861 The red brick of the Sessions House is covered with stucco and an extension added.

1862 Meetings of Karl Marx's International Working Men's Association are held in The House on Clerkenwell Green (q.v.). It may be that Marx himself attended (he is buried at Highgate cemetery). England (which nurtured his genius for thirty years) unlike Russia, China, Korea, Vietnam, Hungary, Cuba and Czechoslovakia, remained (generally) immune to his seductive prose. In despair he wrote that, in England: *'the new society is stifled even in the womb.'*

1865 London Trades Unions and the Manhood Suffrage and Voter by Ballot Association reform into The National Reform League.

1867 Four thousand gather to protest at the impending execution of three Fenians in Manchester (see entry under IRA).

1870 Tiny Eleanor Marx, daughter of Karl, campaigning for votes for women with Emily Pankhurst, is greeted by thousands so goes into the Crown for a beer crate to stand on.

1871 Five hundred rally to support the Paris Commune's appropriation of Crown property for the nation, separation of Church from State, free education and abolition of the death penalty. Red flags and red caps of liberty were everywhere and the band played *La Marseillaise*.

1872 Landlords lose their licence if they let rooms for republican meetings so The London Patriotic Society, launched to campaign for the nationalisation of land, called itself The Robin Hood Discussion Society.

The Society supported trades unions, was committed to radical reform and, unusually, admitted women. In response to a petition drawn up by rival pubs, the police suspended the licence of the pub where they met, so they advertised in The National Reformer £1 shares to raise money for a permanent meeting place. John Stuart Mill (born in **Pentonville**) and Pasmore Edwards bought them and the society took over No. 37.

The secret ballot for elections is introduced. Ten thousand turned out (to watch – not, of course, to vote) in the Finsbury election.

1887 13 November, 'Bloody Sunday'.

Police Commissioner Warner banned a march planned for Trafalgar Day to protest against government policy in Ireland. George Bernard Shaw, William Morris, Eleanor Marx and Annie Besant demanded the right to demonstrate. They led the Clerkenwell contingent, singing La Marseillaise, to join the march to Trafalgar Square. 15,000 constables cordoned it off, 3,000 more guarded Nelson's column, a hundred mounted cavalry had rifles with fixed bayonets and mounted police were issued extra-long batons. 2,500 Reserves surrounded Charing Cross and a hundred more were at Hyde Park. The Grenadier and Lifeguards were on standby. Two hundred rioters ended up in hospital and several were killed.

1890 The World's First May Day March starts from the Green with members of 28 local radical associations demanding an eight-hour working day. Speakers Corner moved from Clerkenwell Green to Hyde Park.

1893 Twentieth Century Press, the first legal Communist press, opens in No. 37 to print *Justice*, the mouthpiece for the Social Democratic Federation (SDF). William Morris sold his library to fund the venture, guaranteeing the first year's rent, and designed the membership card inscribed *'Educate, Agitate, Organise'*. He also made them a banner (still there), a present from Hammersmith socialists, and lectured here many times. Harry Quelch, editor, was leader; so the first statements of Marxist theory available in English came from The House on the Green.

Islington: Home of the Russian Revolution

1902 Vladimir Ulyanov Ilich Lenin arrives to plan the Russian revolution, the most ambitious social experiment ever seen (see Lenin, V.I.)

1920 Tom Quelch, son of Harry *Justice* Quelch, is in Moscow as a delegate of the British Socialist Party at the second Communist International. He visited his father's old friend Lenin at the Kremlin. The Soviet Leader greeted him with: *'So, how is everybody at Clerkenwell Green?'*

1921 The Sessions House transfers to Newington Butts, Southwark. Avery Scales took on the lease for its head office. The company had been founded in 1817 by James Watt, and was taken over in 1895 by William Avery.

1922 The last issue of *Justice* rolls off the presses on Clerkenwell Green (it staggered on for three more years in Southwark). A waste paper merchant took over the building.

1933 Marx Memorial Library and Worker's School is set up at 37 Clerkenwell Green to commemorate Marx after the Nazi Party in Germany burnt his books on the 50th anniversary of his death. The Workers School held evening classes and ran summer schools.

1935 Jack Hastings, earl of Huntingdon, pupil of Diego Rivera, paints a fresco dedicated to the overthrow of capitalism on the wall in The Marx Memorial Library. Someone put a bookcase in front of it and it was 'lost' for 50 years.

1963 Tunnels are discovered in the basement of the Marx Memorial Library (are they from the medieval St Mary's Nunnery? Do they lead from St James' Church to the Sessions House? Are they Fleet arches or perhaps Lenin's hideout?).

1978 Avery Scales experiences a hostile takeover by GEC and moves out. Freemasons moved in.

1991 TV documentary *Marx On The Wall* is about the re-discovered fresco painted by Jack Hastings.

....

CLOUDESLEY SQUARE N1

1517 Richard Cloudesley, local landowner, leaves his 'stoney fields' to the parish of St Mary in return for a thousand masses to be said three times a day to save his soul. This created a fund which, by 1999, was worth £17 million and yielded £500,000 annually for charity.

1826 Square laid out around Charles Barry's Holy Trinity Church, an imitation of King's College, Cambridge. Cloudesley is commemorated in the east window. Farmer Rhodes, one of the two largest landowners in the borough, great-grandfather of explorer-colonist Cecil, moves in.

COLD BATH SQUARE EC1

1697 Walter Baynes, lawyer, of Middle Temple, finds one of Clerkenwell's old wells. He built Cold Bath Spa (see Spas and Pleasure Gardens) and three-gabled Cold Bath House. From then on this part of Islington was known as **Cold Bath Fields**. The Spa opened from 5 a.m. to 1 p.m. every day and Baynes advertised it as being in: *'Sir John Oldcastle's field (the oldest pub in London) and able to cure ... convulsions, creeping fevers, dropsy, disorders of the spleen, deafness, dizziness, distemper, drowsiness, heaviness of head, jaundice, lethargy, rickets, redness of the face, rupture, rheumatics, sore eyes, stiffness of limbs, shortness of breath, weakness of joints.'*

1737 Resident Eustace Budgell, barrister of Inner Temple, cousin of Joseph Addison, commits suicide. He lost his fortune in the South Sea Bubble of 1720 and thereafter earned a crust writing for Addison's *Spectator* (36 pieces published, signed 'X'). When Addison died, his only source of revenue dried up. Accused of fraud in connection with a Will, he hired a boatman to row him across the Thames and half-way over, jumped in.

1794 Huge 'Cold Bath Prison' is built and the square slides downmarket.

1816 Mrs Jane Lewson, known locally as Lady Lewson, dies, aged 116. The *Observer* published a piece on her. Born in 1700, she lived here 90 years as a rich recluse with one servant. She allowed few visitors, and never ventured beyond her garden, allowed her windows to be cleaned or bought new clothes. She wore the flounced and padded gowns made for her when George I was on the throne. The unslept-in beds were made up regularly. Some sources say she was the inspiration for Dickens' Miss Havisham.

1847 Cold Bath Spa is closed.

1889 The square disappears to make way for **Rosebery Avenue**, and is remembered only by a street name.

....

COLEBROOKE ROW N1

1728 Starts with four houses (present Nos 56–59).

1733 Colley Cibber, actor/dramatist to Sadler's Wells, poet laureate to George II, son of famous sculptor Caius Cibber (who carved the huge figures outside Bedlam) moves into No. 56. Known for comic portrayals, he wrote thirty plays. His son Theophilus, also an actor, married Susanna Arne, sister of the composer of *Rule Britannia*. Handel (q.v.) composed pieces for her and gave her singing lessons. Cibber lived here with Charlotte, his youngest daughter, also an actress.

1740 Charlotte is appearing at Sadler's Wells. She became a grocer, quack doctor, puppeteer in Brewer Street (**Paget Street**), published a successful autobiography, opened a pub in Islington, went bankrupt and died a pauper. She was found dead in a hovel near **New River Head** with her pet cat, dog, magpie and monkey.

1744 Two more houses built (Nos 54 and 55).

1760 Colebrooke Cottage (a detached house) is built. Its most famous resident was to be the essayist Charles Lamb and his sister Mary (see Lamb, Charles).

1767 Six new houses built (Nos 60–65).

1769 H.S. Woodfall, creator of *Darby and Joan*, brother of William Woodfall (founder of the Hansard reports of Parliamentary proceedings) moves from Colebrooke Row to Canonbury Tower.

1808 Benjamin <u>Disraeli</u>, future Prime Minister, attends Dame Roper's Academy (see Disraeli, Benjamin).

1937 Fred <u>Murphy</u>, 57, a resident, working for Harding's Furnishers, 22 **Islington Green**, telephones Head Office to say he has found the body of a woman in the cellar. The police identified the corpse as Rosina Field, a prostitute who plied her trade from 13 **Duncan Terrace**. Police records showed that Murphy had previously been accused of the murder of another prostitute but was let off through insufficient evidence. This time, he was hanged.

1955 Cyril <u>Ray</u>, broadcaster, comic punster, is living in No. 57.

1963 Angus <u>McBean</u>, society photographer, moves to No. 58. He was asked to do the cover for a Beatles album – at the same time, Joe <u>Orton</u>, living around the corner (in **Noel Road**) was commissioned to write a screenplay for the Beatles' film *A Hard Day's Night*. Neither did.

....

COLLINS MUSIC HALL
Islington Green N1

1790 Publican of The Lansdowne Tavern, **Old Paradise Row**, opens a 'singing room' (music hall in embryo).

1861 Sam Collins <u>Vagg</u> converts the singing room into the 600-seat Collins. Ex-chimney sweep, born and bred in London, Vagg pretended to be Irish and specialised in songs such as *No Irish Need Apply*, about the ban on Irish labour at The Great Exhibition. He died three years later, age 39, and was buried at Kensal Green. His famous Irish hat and shillelagh are carved on his headstone. Islington, acknowledged centre for London music hall, was dubbed The Golden Mile.

1870 Collins gets its very own Oliver Reed ... Flamboyant George Leybourne, Britain's first superstar, lived at nearby 136 **Englefield Road** (blue plaque, 1970). The tall, handsome mechanic from the Midlands arrived in London with the manuscript for *Champagne Charlie*. Portrayed as the elegant, charming Lord Dundreary, he wore a monocle, Piccadilly Weepers (side whiskers), shiny top hat and an overcoat with huge fur collar. He surrounded himself with beautiful women in his carriage-and-four (rivals poked fun at him by riding in a cart pulled by donkeys).

'*That Daring Young Man on the Flying Trapeze*', inspired by the French acrobat Leotard, and '*Champagne Charlie*' were smash hits. Royalties exceeded £120 a week. Johann <u>Strauss</u>, on his only visit to London, recorded them in *Songs from Covent Garden*. Champagne Charlie came on stage dressed in immaculate evening dress and, pretending to be tipsy, sang about what it was like to be a man about town. The problem is, he wasn't acting ... Leybourne drank his way to a short but happy life. As bar profits rose sharply after his famous drinking song, pubs gave him free champagne. This, in addition to the generous supply from Moet and Chandon. By the end of each act he was almost comatose. Britain's first pop singer died, age 42, of a surfeit of champagne.

In 1944, the film *Champagne Charlie* was made as a tribute starring Tommy Trinder and Stanley Holloway. A few of the many others who trod Collins' boards were Marie Lloyd, George Robey, the Tommy's Cooper, Trinder and Handley (Cooper had his first paid gig here). Collins was Handley's favourite gig, he appeared here in *Disorderly Room* and *ITMA*. Stanley Holloway, Dan Leno, Tessie O'Shea, Vesta Tilley, Harry Lauder, Norman Wisdom and Benny Hill also appeared.

1896 Britain's first public film show. Also on the bill were George Robey and Dan Leno.

1897 Re-built and electricity installed. Inside a glass case was a photograph of Belle Elmore (Mrs Crippen) wearing a brooch destined to become famous as evidence in Islington's most celebrated whodunnit.

1912 Charlie <u>Chaplin</u> on the bill.

1913 Chaplin joins brother Sydney with Fred Karno's Mumming Birds.

1915 Gracie <u>Fields</u> on the bill.

1957 *Davy* starring Harry <u>Secombe</u> is filmed here. But time was being called for Collins. Seats were filled only by *tableaux vivants* (policed by the Lord Chamberlain, girls must not move on stage). Music Hall was on its last legs, defeated by TV and stricter safety regulations.

1958 When John <u>Osborne</u>'s *Look Back in Anger* is put on at The Royal Court, Laurence <u>Olivier</u> is so impressed he asks to have a part in his next play, so Osborne writes *The Entertainer* for him. He chose Islington's shabby, dying Collins theatre and its has-been entertainers as the symbol for the demise of England: '*The Collins ... was about to be swept away. Bulldozers and iron balls were poised. I was especially keen that we* (he, Vivien Leigh [2nd Mrs Olivier] and Sir Laurence) *should go a few times to Collins, where I had witnessed some of the very worst acts imaginable.*'

For the 'angry' young playwright, the dying music hall was an allegory for an England facing cultural redundancy. *The Entertainer* is about a mediocre, small-time music hall comedian, Archie Rice (modelled on Max Miller, The Cheeky Chappie with his loud stage costume and blue jokes) who perseveres with his corny patter to an audience only there for the strip tease. By the time the film came out, Vivien Leigh was Olivier's ex-wife – he married Joan Plowright, his co-star on the film.

1958 Collins closes. A fire guts it soon after their visit.

1962 Collins' memorabilia auctioned by Tommy <u>Trinder</u>, who made his first stage appearance here in 1910. When he left school he became a butcher's boy at Hart's, **Smithfield**, where he was remembered as forever wisecracking.

1993 Waterstone's Books take over the site.

1997 £13m Lottery bid to build a modern theatre joined to Waterstones by a café bar is turned down.

2000 Plans are afoot to re-erect the 600-seat oak mock-up of The Rose Theatre built for the film *Shakespeare in Love*. Dame Judi Dench, who played Elizabeth I, sent eight removal vans to save the set and donated it to Islington.

....

COMPTON, Lord
Ashby Grove/Street, Compton Avenue/Passage/Place/Road/Square/Street/ Terrace, Northampton Park/Place/Road/Row/Square/Street/Terrace and Alwyne (family name) Cottages/Lane/Place/Road/Square/Villas)

Islington's landed gentry goes back to Saxon times, but the history of the area is inextricably bound to the Compton family, earls of Northampton. Their descendants still visit Canonbury Tower, which the Comptons inherited through a marriage to Eliza <u>Spencer</u> during the reign of Elizabeth I (see Canonbury Tower).

1075 Earl of Northampton owns land here, marries Judith, niece of William the

Conqueror. **Yardley Street** (he lived at Yardley Hastings and Yardley Chase, Northampton) is named after him.

1205 Philip de Cumton builds Compton Wynyates, Tysoe, Warwickshire, one of the most beautiful country estates in England.

1490 William Compton is born and in 1501, age 11, was appointed page to the two-year-old Prince Henry (King Henry VIII)

1512 William Compton buys Castle Ashby from the earl of Kent. He was now Henry's Groom to the Royal Bedchamber. Knighted, he had the exceptional privilege of adding the Royal Lion to his coat of arms. Henry gave him Bruce Castle, which the Comptons were to own until his great-grandson sold it in 1630.

When Henry is hunting in the Islington area, which is very often, he: *'reserved for himself all the games of hare, partridge, phesaunt and heron from his palace at Westminster to Hornsey and Highgate including Islington'* and stayed frequently with Compton.

1516 The King goes to *'maister Compton's house beside Tottenham'* to welcome his sister Margaret (married James IV of Scotland) to London.

1528 William dies. His only son is dead so no adult Comptons inherit.

1562 Henry Compton has a son, William.

1572 Henry is made a peer.

1574 Henry, Lord Compton, re-builds Castle Ashby, Northamptonshire.

1589 William (21) succeeds to father Henry's estates.

1593 Secretary of State, Sir Julius Caesar (truly) writes to Baron Compton begging use of Bruce Castle: *'during this time of sickness in London'* (plague).

1596 Sir William is Master of the Leash, keeper of the Royal Greyhounds.

1598 John Norden, traveller, writes: *'At this place* (Tottenham) *Lord Compton hath a proper ancient house.'* William went to Canonbury Tower to borrow money from Sir John Spencer, and promptly fell in love with Eliza, his only child. (Full story: see Canonbury Tower). They eloped and the Queen tricked Spencer into recognising the marriage.

1610 Sir John Spencer dies. William, via Eliza, inherited his vast fortune and temporarily went mad.

1612 James I stays at Castle Ashby.

1613 William, Privy Councillor, is made an Earl. As Lord Lieutenant of Wales he lived in Ludlow Castle, Shropshire.

1616 James I stays at Castle Ashby again. Sir Spencer Compton, 15, close friend of Charles, Prince of Wales, was made knight of the Bath.

1617 The Earl is treated by Dr Hall of Hall's Croft, Stratford, for *'toothache, hot urine and stinking stools'*.

John Hall was Shakespeare's son-in-law, having married daughter Susanna (24) in 1607. Born in Bedfordshire, Hall may have trained at Cambridge with William Harvey of Bart's. He treats Lord and Lady Compton, their son Spencer and Spencer's pregnant wife. He says in his notes that the Countess: *'very fair and beautiful lying with her baby daughter in her arms, has charm'*.

1618 William is made Lord Compton, Bruce Castle is renamed Lordship House.

1621 Sir Spencer is MP for Ludlow.

1622 Lady Eliza, 44, falls at home in Ludlow Castle. Dr Hall rides forty miles to treat her.

Clearly smitten, he noted that she was *'pious, beautiful and chaste'*. He also tended to Spencer's wife, who has given birth to James, their first son, named after the king.

1623 Spencer has a second son, Charles, named after James' son.

1625 Spencer has a third son, William.

1626 Spencer is made Master of the Robes.

1629 Old William invested as KG. Spencer has a fourth son, Spencer.

1630 Spencer has fifth son, Francis. His father, William, dined at White Hall Palace then died after bathing in the Thames. Spencer succeeded to the Northampton title. (Ludlow Castle was taken over by the Earl of Bridgewater, new Lord Lieutenant of Wales. <u>Milton</u> (q.v.) wrote a masque celebrating his appointment). Not wanting Lordship House/Bruce Castle, Spencer sold it.

1632 Spencer has a sixth son, Henry (Bishop of London who crowned William and Mary).

1642 William, 17, third son of Spencer, fights for Charles I at Banbury and is knighted.

1643 Spencer, 42, dies for childhood friend Charles I in the battle of Hopton Heath. James, 21, succeeded as third earl but <u>Cromwell</u> seized Compton Wynyates and Castle Ashby. The family returned to Canonbury Tower (where Spencer grew up). With them was his brother Henry.

1653 James, 31, is forced to take out a mortgage of £1751 on Canonbury Tower. His brother William formed The Sealed Knot, a secret society dedicated to organising Royalist resistance, and had a son (the second Compton baby born here).

1658 Sir William's son, 5, dies.

1660 Monarchy restored, the Compton lands are returned. Sir William was appointed Master of Ordinance and left Canonbury Tower, the last Compton to live here.

1664 James has a son, George.

1673 James has a second son, Spencer (Earl Wilmington, Prime Minister).

1675 Henry Compton, last son of Sir Spencer is appointed Bishop of London.

1681 James (third earl) dies. George (fourth earl) leased Northampton House in the manor of Clerkenwell (**St John Street**).

1688 Bishop Compton and six laymen secretly invite <u>William of Orange</u> to land an army in England so that James' daughter Mary can succeed to the throne.

Bishop Compton was one of The Immortal Seven, architects of The Glorious Revolution to depose <u>James II</u>. James, a Catholic, issued a Declaration of Indulgence urging religious toleration but was petitioned to withdraw it. Only one ecclesiast, Bishop Compton, signed. James put the petitioners on trial but they were acquitted and he was forced to leave England, opening the field to the Dutch Prince William of Orange.

1689 The Archbishop of Canterbury refuses to crown William and Mary (in case James II comes back) so Bishop Compton does the honours.

1695 William III is staying at Castle Ashby.

1727 Prince George is in Richmond when Sir Robert <u>Walpole</u> arrives to tell him his father George I has died and he is now king. George loathed Walpole and told him to report instead to Sir Spencer Compton. Speaker of the House, his closest friend, the only Englishman the German king could tolerate. His Vice Chamberlain wrote: '. . . (King George) *hated the English, looked upon them all as king killers and Republicans . . . forced to* *distribute his favours here very differently from the manner in which he bestowed them at Hanover. There he rewarded people for doing their duty ... here, he said, he was obliged to ... buy them not to cut his throat.'*

Sir Spencer is unable to form a cabinet, forcing George to appoint Walpole, who stays in power fifteen years.

1730 Sir Spencer is created Lord Wilmington (**Wilmington Square**).

1740 George makes Lord Wilmington Head of the Treasury when Walpole resigns as Prime Minister.

1755 The Earl's sister, Lady Catherine Compton, marries John <u>Perceval</u>, Earl of Egmont. Her second son, Spencer <u>Perceval</u>, was assassinated at the House of Commons in 1812, the only British Prime Minister to end this way.

1891 6th Marquess gives Clerkenwell manor house to the Vestry as a home for Northampton Institute of Technology (see City University).

1946 Spencer Compton born.

1954 Northampton estates in Islington are sold except for Canonbury Tower.

1973 Spencer has a son, Daniel (Earl Compton).

1978 Spencer succeeds as 7th Marquess.

1990s Tudor wing of Canonbury Tower is converted into Canonbury Academy.

....

CRIPPEN, Hawley Harvey, Dr (1862–1910)
<u>Wife killer</u>
Islington has been home to some of Britain's most notorious murderers ...
1905 A couple from New York move to 39 **Hilldrop Crescent** N7 and never leave Islington again. Mrs Crippen remained in Islington cemetery. Her husband was hanged for her murder and buried at Pentonville Prison (q.v.). It was called '*The Murder of the Century*' (but the century was only ten years old ...).

No. 39 was one of sixty-two imposing, semi-detached houses with large gardens. Many parts of Islington were slum areas but Hilldrop Crescent was not one. (Robert <u>Seeley</u>, biographer of John <u>Wesley</u> once lived at No. 59 and one day Sir Eugene <u>Goossens</u>, world famous conductor, would live here). Dr Hawley Harvey <u>Crippen</u> was a partner in Yale Tooth Specialists, Albion House, 61 New Oxford Street and his wife was the unsuccessful but flirtatious actress, Belle Elmore ...

1906 When Crippen finds Belle in bed with their lodger, he, humiliated and henpecked, dreams of a new life with Ethel Neve, his adored secretary. He bought 313 **Hornsey Road** for her, and they started an affair. She had a miscarriage and begged him to move in with her.

1910 19 January, Crippen collected hydrobromide of hyocine (henbane/deadly nightshade) from Burroughs Chemists near his consulting rooms. Nothing unusual in that, he was well known at the shop, a regular who had bought many poisons over many years. As was the law, he signed the Poisons Register. Crippen was one of the few people familiar with this poison having seen it administered to the violently insane when he worked at **Bedlam** (q.v.). 31 January, Mrs Crippen invited friends to dinner, the last time anyone saw her alive. It was 1.30 a.m. before they bade each other goodnight. Mrs Crippen would have a very bad night indeed, being dismembered and filleted by her husband.

Next day, Ethel was overjoyed to find a message from her beloved on her typewriter saying that Belle had 'returned to America', and spent the night with him for the first time at Hilldrop Crescent. Harvey sent a letter to The Music Hall Lady Artistes Guild Committee on behalf of Belle (Honorary Treasurer), saying she had had to visit a sick relative in California so was resigning her position, and apologised for the short notice. Crippen pawned Belle's jewellery except for her favourite brooch, a distinctive diamond rising sun. Ethel moved in with Crippen. Ecstatically happy (often seen arm in arm shopping in Holloway Road), they went by boat to Dieppe for a holiday, and Crippen threw Belle's head overboard. On return he told everyone she had been taken ill in California with pleuro-pneumonia, and days later announced that Belle had died, would be cremated and her ashes sent back to England. He published Belle's obituary in ERA, trade theatrical weekly newspaper (editor, Richard Baines lived at 73 **Calabria Road**, Highbury).

31 March, Belle's friend reported her disappearance to Chief Detective Inspector (Blue Serge) Dew of Scotland Yard (he always wore a blue serge suit). In 1887, Dew had been spectacularly unsuccessful in solving the Jack the Ripper mystery. She told him that Belle had no relations in California, only New York. Also she was a Catholic and Catholicism banned cremation. Dew needed more evidence. 28 June, Belle's friends in New York hadn't heard from her in five months so came to London to look for her. They went to Scotland Yard and saw DCI Dew. 8 July, Dew and his Sergeant called at 39 Hilldrop Crescent. Crippen was at work but they noticed that Ethel was wearing the same brooch as Belle in her promotional photographs. Dew visited Crippen in New Oxford Street and interviewed him between dental appointments. He and two policemen returned to Hilldrop Crescent where, after searching the house, Dew advised him to get in touch with Belle. In front of the Inspector, Crippen drafted an ad for the American papers and signed his statement. After they left, he shaved off his moustache, abandoned his spectacles and disguised Ethel as a young man (you do wonder what he said to her). They took the night boat from Harwich to the Hook of Holland. 11 July, Dew visited Hilldrop Crescent again. No-one was in, so he went to Crippen's consulting rooms to be told he hadn't been at work for two days.

Dew returned to Hilldrop Crescent and ordered a search of the three-storey, nine-room house but found nothing. They dug up the garden of roses in full bloom. The search lasted two days until only the cellar was left. After digging six inches a foul stench filled the tiny room. Bits of Mrs Crippen were rotting under the brick floor. Oddly, for a doctor, Crippen had mistakenly used lime, a preservative, instead of quicklime. Belle's head was missing (in the English Channel), as were her internal organs, genitalia and bones. Her body was hard to identify, however, a metal haircurler was found with a tuft of hair, dark at the roots, blonde at the ends (she bleached her hair) and on her abdomen, a scar (she had had her ovaries removed). Hydrobromide of hyocine was found in the remains. The label Jones Bros (Holloway) Ltd on the gent's pyjama top in which bits of flesh were wrapped was from a department store in **Holloway Road** (there until 1990).

15 July, Crippen read in a newspaper that Belle's remains had been found and a warrant issued for his arrest. 20 July, booked passage on the SS Montrose bound for Quebec. He

now had a beard. Ethel was still dressed as a young man but her body language, shape, voice, etc., gave her away. 22 July, The Captain recognised the pair and sent a radio message to shore using the ship's new Marconi wireless. 23 July, Dew left Liverpool on a White Star liner. 25 July, the progress of the murder was being reported daily in the newspapers thanks to the new transatlantic wireless. Bookmakers were taking bets on which ship would reach Quebec first. 27 July, Dew's ship overtook SS Montrose. 31 July, Crippen and Ethel were arrested. 28 August, the couple arrived at Liverpool. 29 August, Bow Street Magistrates Court. 26 September, the Coroners Court verdict which led Crippen to the gallows was signed by all 17 jurors: 'On view of human remains to wit: the heart, the lungs, the stomach, the kidneys, the liver, the spleen, the pancreas, portions of the intestines, portion of the windpipe and gullet and other parts of a body which were found buried underneath the floor of a cellar at No. 39 Hilldrop Crescent, Islington.' 18 Oct, four thousand people applied for seven hundred tickets for the trial.

The Old Bailey then saw the first appearance in court of the young, gifted Bernard Spilsbury dubbed the 'detective pathologist'. 23 October, the jury took just twenty seven minutes to find Crippen guilty. He was taken to Pentonville to await the results of his appeal, turned down by Home Secretary Winston Churchill. 27 October, Ethel, remanded in Holloway (q.v.), was tried for being an accessory but acquitted. 23 November, Crippen was executed at Pentonville and buried with Ethel's photograph. She was granted probate (including the house in Hornsey), changed her name to Harvey and headed for Toronto.

Some sources say Ethel stayed in Canada until 1967, married a book-keeper and raised two children, never revealing her identity to her family. Others that she returned to London after WWI under the name of Nelson, married Stan Smith, a bookkeeper, and had two children. Stan died in 1943 never knowing her story. No. 39 became a Black Museum filled with Crippenalia, personal effects and mementoes left in the house vacated in a hurry. Vilified by locals, the owner converted it into a boarding house for music hall performers.

1940 WWII. No. 39 is bombed.

1954 Ethel (or her brother) tells her story to novelist Ursula Bloom, who writes The Girl Who Loved Crippen, one of 37 books on the affair (Ernest Chandler wrote We The Accused).

1954 Margaret Bondfield House is built on the site. As a shop assistant in Somerset, Bondfield started the National Union of Shop Assistants, co-founded the National Federation of Women Workers, was appointed first woman Chair of the TUC, became an MP and Minister for Labour, the first woman to hold a Cabinet position.

1967 Ethel dies in Dulwich (some say Croydon), age 84.

1999 The Coroners Court verdict which led Crippen to the gallows is auctioned at Christie's with a reserve price of £1,500.

....

CROMWELL Oliver (1599–1658)

MP for Cambridge. Lord Protector. Regicide

Until 1642, when he takes a house in Holborn, whenever in London on parliamentary business, Cromwell stays with James and Thomas Chaloner in Clerkenwell Close EC1.

According to William Heath <u>Robinson</u>'s biography, he also owned a house with a huge studded front door opposite **Waterlow Park** next door to his general, Ireton. He defended the city with battery and breastwork from royalists at **St John Street**, **Seward Street** and **Goswell Road** (see HAC).

1643 Lord <u>Compton</u> dies in battle at Hopton Heath. Cromwell deprived his heir of Compton Wynyates and Castle Ashby but left the Compton family in possession of Canonbury Tower (q.v.).

1649 Charles I is charged with treason against his people and executed. Cromwell declared himself Protector.

1650 Governor of Charterhouse. *'We the said committee do likewise think that the Arms of the late king* (he was wrong, not those of Charles I but of James I) *standing above the gates be forthwith pulled down and defaced and that the arms of the Commonwealth be put up ...'*

1651 James <u>Stanley</u>, KB, MP, Lord Strange, Earl of Derby (who once lived in Canonbury) is executed by Cromwell and dubbed The Martyr Earl.

1653 Cromwell dismisses Thomas <u>Chaloner</u>, fellow regicide, erstwhile landlord and friend, from Parliament, calling him an incompetent drunkard. Appoints the Honourable Artillery Company official escort of the Lord Mayor (as it still is). Mr Vowel, a local teacher (truly) and monarchist who plotted to kill Cromwell, was hanged at Charing Cross, where he was arrested.

1654 William Compton living in Canonbury Tower forms The Sealed Knot, a secret society to organise Royalist resistance.

1657 John <u>Lilburne</u>, Leveller brother of Robert, one of the regicides, is buried in **Bunhill** cemetery.

1658 Cromwell dies.

1660 Restoration of the monarchy, followed by the trial of 29 Regicides at Hicks Hall (q.v.) **St John Street**. Colonel <u>Okey</u> of Cromwell's New Model Army, drayman in an Islington brewery, one of Charles I's judges had escaped to Holland, but was brought back and hanged.

1661 Perpoole Lane (**Baldwin Street**) Clerkenwell. Sir Arthur Hesilrige (or <u>Haselrig</u>) MP, hero of Cromwell's wars, had, naturally, many enemies among the nobility. On his way home to **Holloway Village** from the House of Commons, he was attacked by the earl of Stamford and died later the same year in the Tower.

1692 Lt Gen. Charles <u>Fleetwood</u>, husband of Bridget <u>Cromwell</u>, daughter of the Protector is buried in Nonconformist Bunhill Fields, as were many other Cromwells: Major Henry (53) son of Oliver second son of the Protector, d. 1711, with his widow and sons William, Thomas and Henry. Eleanor, d. 1727 (aged 2 months). Mary, 41, spinster, d. 1731. Hannah, 79, d. 1732. Mrs Mary, 62, d. 1752 and Mrs Letitia, 56, d. 1789. in 1869, Henry Cromwell's body was discovered with his son Richard, 7 feet beneath the surface.

CRUFT, Charles (1852–1938)

Lived at 325 **Holloway Road** and worked for *Spratt's Dog Cakes*.

1891 Islington: Home of Crufts

Charles Cruft dog food salesman puts on a dog show at The Aggie. Queen Victoria exhibits four dogs. Within a short time, Crufts is annual and international, the largest celebration of dogs in the world.

1913 Moves to 12 **Highbury Grove** N5 (demolished to build Highbury Grove School, plaque on the block of flats opposite).

1936 The Jubilee Show attracts 9,000 entries.

1938 Cruft dies. His Show is taken over by The Kennel Club.

1939 The Aggie is closed because of the war. Crufts transferred to Earls Court.

2000 NEC Birmingham. 20,000 dogs, 110,000 visitors, 350 trade stands. It's a huge commercial business – yet the Supreme Champion wins a mere £100.

....

CRUIKSHANK, George (1792–1878)

Cartoonist/Illustrator

Apart from the occasional foray treading the boards in Charles <u>Dickens'</u> amateur productions, Cruikshank spent every day of his life in north London. He lived in Islington from the age of 26 to 58.

1818 Mother moves to **Claremont Square** EC1 with George, daughter Eliza (who died young) and son Isaac.

1820 Power and influence already considerable. Print shops displayed his cartoons, the only places where the masses could see their own dim views of the monarchy and the Government reflected. One of the world's greatest and most gifted illustrators, known by every publisher in Britain, on James <u>Gillray</u>'s old work-table he illustrated (among others) Dickens, Smollett, Fielding, Defoe, Sterne and Ainsworth. George, like his father a heavy drinker, was often away from home for days, weeks, months or even at one time, a year.

1822 Goes to Sadler's Wells where he draws a cartoon of the famous yearly race (six Shetland ponies raced on a platform around the pit). He had dinner at his favourite local, the Sir Hugh Myddelton (re-named Shakespeare's Head) where he met cronies from The Crib Club (Joe <u>Grimaldi</u> (q.v.), president).

1824 Moves to Myddelton Terrace, where he stays 25 years (blue plaque). The family occupied numbers 22 and 23 (now re-numbered and re-named as 69 and 71 **Amwell Street**).

1825 Meets cronies at Walter Raleigh's old house, The Pied Bull, **Upper Street**, '... *for the purpose of looking at this house previous to it being pulled down* ... *George Cruikshank, David Sage, whose father David Sage the elder is about to pull down the house* ... *William Hone* ... *(drank) toasts* ... *to the Country of Sir Walter and ourselves, 'Old England' – we came here for the high veneration we feel for the memory and character of Sir Walter and that we might have the gratification of saying hereafter that we had smoked a pipe in the same room that the man who first introduced tobacco smoked in himself* ...'

1827 Age 35, marries Mary Ann Walker when she reaches her majority (21).

Cruikshank completed a piece of work every three days throughout his long life. He breakfasted at 8 a.m., smoked a pipe and started at 9 a.m. working, except for a snack at mid-day, without break until 3 p.m. Then had a substantial meal with a jug of porter and a pipe but was back at his desk by 6 p.m. Worked through until 9 p.m. (unless he was entertaining or Grimaldi was appearing at Sadler's Wells).

1828 <u>Randell and Evans</u> build massive kilns in **York Way**, where they thrive for fifty years. Cruikshank was dismayed at these kilns churning out thousands upon thousands of bricks to build more houses just like his and criticised the very development he was enjoying. He painted the scathing *London Going out of Town: The March of Bricks and Mortar* deploring the loss of countryside. Fields were leased to speculators and 'merrie Islington' inexorably disappeared. Spa, Moor, Finsbury, Pipe, Cold Bath and Canonbury Fields were buried under rows of streets until only the names remained.

1832 Produces a book of drawings *'Sundays in London'* and illustrates Charles <u>Lamb</u>'s *Satan in Search of a Wife*. Lamb had moved to Edmonton where he was very unhappy (see Lamb, Charles). Did the homesick Lamb come back to Islington to talk to Cruikshank about it?

1833 George and Mary move next door to 23 (71 **Amwell Street**). Perhaps the hated brickworks could not be seen from this house. Launched *The Comic Almanac*, which George produced for 19 years. 20,000 readers bought the first issue.

1836 Illustrates <u>Dickens</u>' *Sketches by Boz*.

Dickens based Fat Boy in *Pickwick Papers* on Joe Sleap, Cruikshank's apprentice. Addicted to opium, he passed his days in a dream and died, aged 15.

When first approached to illustrate Dickens, Cruikshank refused. He was twenty years older than Dickens, a successful and established caricaturist, son of an equally famous caricaturist and himself famous before the writer was born. He had been caricaturing Londoners all his life, the greatest pictorial satirist since Hogarth. Dickens delayed publication of *Oliver Twist* because he wasn't happy with Cruikshank's engravings. A scandal erupted over their collaboration. Cruikshank claimed (as Robert <u>Seymour</u> had claimed before him) that Dickens stole his ideas, and that *Oliver Twist* was his story. He said he had been planning to publish his own book about London life – including the story of a young thief. This made Cruikshank unpopular, as Dickens was adored.

1840 Founder member of the Philanthropist's Club, launched in The Skinners Arms, Coburg Street (renamed **Goode Street**), which campaigned for the nationalisation of all land.

1849 Mary, 33, dies of TB. Feeling guilty about the dance he had led her, George (57) signed the pledge (not to drink).

1850 Remarries. After a 22-year childless marriage in Islington, Cruikshank moved to Camden where he had a 27-year childless marriage to Eliza Widdison. Age 66, he took a mistress around the corner at 31 **Augustus Street**. Posing as George Archibald he fathered ten children by Adelaide Archibald. The first, George Robert, was 23 by the time the youngest was conceived (George was by then 82). It's thought his wife turned a blind eye to his parallel life.

1854 Alcoholism is a big problem in London. Cruikshank chaired a Total Abstainers meeting at Sadler's Wells (forerunner of the AA).

1878 Dies (of bronchitis).

D

DANCE, George, the Elder (1700–1768)
City Architect, Surveyor to the City of London, lived in **Chiswell Street** *EC1 for most of his life.*
1722 James, his first son is born. He became a successful actor using the stage name of Love. Among his contemporaries were Mrs Jordan, John Kemble and Mrs Siddons. Charles <u>Lamb</u> saw him play Sir Toby Belch in *Twelfth Night* at Drury Lane.

1739 Designs Mansion House, official residence of the Lord Mayor (plans are in Soane Museum).

1741 Second son is born. George Dance the Younger (1741–1825).

1768 Dance the Elder dies and is buried in St Luke's, **Old Street**. George the Younger succeeded him as City Architect and City Surveyor to the City of London. Rioters threw stones at Mansion House because it was not lit to celebrate John <u>Wilkes</u>' election as MP. They broke the windows and chandeliers.

1770 Re-builds Newgate Prison.

1775 Age 34, George is commissioned to build **Finsbury Square** and, some sources say, his friend John <u>Wesley</u>'s Methodist Chapel in **City Road**. He moved from Chiswell Street. In 1780 the Gordon Rioters (q.v.) burned down his Newgate prison and again stoned his father's Mansion House. He rebuilt the prison and repaired the damage to Mansion House. His son Charles Dance follows his uncle James and becomes an actor.

....

D'AVENANT, Sir William (1606–1688). (Davenant Road N19) Like Daniel Foe, Avenant invented the 'De'. He insisted he was Shakespeare's illegitimate son.

Islington: Home of Opera (in England)

1638 Poet laureate.

1643 Knighted by Charles I.

1656 London sees its first opera when Sir William, poet, playwright and actor moves into Rutland House, Charterhouse Square and stages *The Siege of Rhodes*. Permission is granted by Cromwell which is surprising because not so long ago (1652) he put him in prison for active service in support of Charles I and his son Charles II.

1660 When Charles II grants him a theatre patent (monopoly) he builds a new theatre in Dorset Gardens (Duke's Theatre) but dies before it's finished. His wife took over the project.

1663 Waxes lyrical at the sight of Moor Fields drying grounds, where laundresses stretched their washing over tenter hooks (not that he could smell fresh laundry, his nose fell off through syphilis and he wore a false one).

....

DEFOE, Daniel (1661–1731)

Writer

Creator of Robinson Crusoe. Born plain 'Foe', he added the 'De' in 1703, when he was 42.

1675 Age 14, attends Charles <u>Morton</u>'s famous Dissenters Academy on **Newington Green** N1 with Samuel <u>Wesley</u>, father of the more famous John. The Academy was similar to a university (youths were accepted after grammar school). Here he got a good education and was fluent in Latin, Spanish, Italian, Greek and French. Foe was born into a Dissenting family (Presbyterian), some say his father was a butcher, others a tallow chandler, perhaps he was both.

1686 Marries Mary <u>Tuffley</u>, daughter of a wealthy Dissenting merchant who gives her a large dowry (£4,000). They were happily married for fifty years and had eight children, six of whom survived into adulthood. The first, Daniel, was christened in St James', **Clerkenwell** so they must have lived in the parish. Defoe is described as: *'middle sized ...*

spare ... brown complexion ... dark brown hair ... but wears a wig ... hooked nose, sharp chin, grey eyes and a large mole near his mouth.'

1719 Age 60, gives the world Man Friday's enduring footprint in England's first novel, *The Life and Strange and Surprising Adventures of Robinson Crusoe of York, Mariner.* Defoe, a driven writer, probably wrote it in his splendid house in Stoke Newington (blue plaque, 95 **Stoke Newington Church Street** N16, put up 1932). Present-day **Defoe Road** cut through his back garden. He lived here 20 years, enjoying the 12-room house and 4 acres.

1725 Defoe, to escape his creditors, is writing in a Clerkenwell lodging house in **Rope Maker Alley**, Moorfields, using the pseudonym Andrew Morton.

1731 Defoe, hiding from creditors, dies of a stroke in his rented room despite having a fine house in Stoke Newington. He was buried at Bunhill Fields (q.v.) but had to wait 139 years for a memorial. In 1879, 1,700 young Sunday School readers of *Christian World* launched a fund and raised the money to erect a stone.

....

DICKENS, Charles (1812–1870)
Writer

1837 Dickens, 25, is house hunting in Islington. His literary circle included Carlyle, Harrison Ainsworth and the Leigh Hunts so he needed to be somewhere that reflected the status of an up-and-coming writer. With the whole of London at his feet he chose **Pentonville**, a fashionable area he knew well through his illustrators, Robert Seymour who lived in **Liverpool Road** and George Cruikshank (see above). Also, Dickens first researched the area while writing *Sketches by Boz*, looking for somewhere for Nicodemus Dumps to live in *The Bloomsbury Christenings*.

Just as once the world knew Islington because of Smithfield Market and Bartholomew Fair, now it will know it through Dickens. His undying fascination with the borough was reflected in his books. Islington recognised its debt to him, there was once talk of opening a permanent 'Dickens Experience' in the old Aggie, **Upper Street**. In *Sketches by Boz*, The White Conduit House features in '*First of May*' and The Angel Inn in '*Making a Night of It*'. Balls Pond Road is where the Butlers live in '*Sentiment*', City Road is in '*Miss Evans and The Eagle*', and Coldbath Fields Prison is in '*Prisoner's Van*'. In Pickwick, Mr P. lodges with Mrs Bardell in **Goswell Road**, Jack Hopkins is a medical student with Slasher the surgeon at **Bart's**, while **Whitecross Street** debtors' prison is a constant threat.

Taken aback by the inflated prices (then as now), Dickens walks down the road to cheaper **Bloomsbury**. '*I strolled about Pentonville thinking the air did my head good and looked at one or two houses in the new streets. They are extremely dear, the cheapest being £55 a year with taxes.*' He took a lease on 48 **Doughty Street**, a private road with uniformed porters (blue plaque, 1903). Out of all his London homes this is the only one to survive. He was amused by the house agent showing him around, mistakenly calling him 'Mr Pickwick'. On 1 April, his first wedding anniversary, Dickens '*enjoys the pleasant occupation of moving*' to Doughty Street with his wife Catherine, baby son Charles, brother Fred and Mary Hogarth (17), Catherine's sister. His sister Fanny (who lived in Islington) was to be a frequent visitor. He began writing *Oliver Twist*, the story of a slum boy living in **Saffron Hill**, a five-minute walk away (there was no **Rosebery Avenue** then).

Until **Clerkenwell** was cleared to build the world's first underground railway (1863) it was a no-go area, where even clergy giving last rites had to be police escorted. One of the most squalid areas in London, with a high murder rate, it was called Jack Ketch Warren (name of the hangman) because so many ended up on the gallows. The book was inspired by the recently refined Poor Law, but bits were based on Dickens' own impoverished childhood. He was to return to the theme of underprivileged, abandoned children (Pip, Little Nell, David Copperfield, Nicholas Nickleby, Florence Dombey, Amy Dorrit) and the threat of debtors' prison all his life. The name Oliver was that of a local bus conductor. Mr Laing, the magistrate at Hatton Garden, became Mr Fang and Ikey Solomons, a Clerkenwell 'fence' who drinks in The Three Cripples on Saffron Hill, became the thiefmaster, Fagin.

The novel made Dickens' name and that of Clerkenwell internationally famous. The book opened people's eyes to a side of London they hadn't known existed. Dickens wrote *Oliver* for many reasons, the need for an income being just one. Because of his own appalling childhood he felt passionately about injustice. London, nicknamed The Great Oven or The Big Wen, stank. It was the first thing visitors commented on. In Clerkenwell, the stench was worst. The Fleet was an open sewer, the same water supplied street standpipes for drinking and washing. Sanitation and hygiene were unheard of. Floor boards were taken up and the cavity used as privies, excrement was piled in cellars and yards. Abandoned children were cold, starving or dying. The average age of mortality was 22, half the funerals were for children under ten. Corpses were eaten by rats. Cholera, dysentry, smallpox and typhoid were common. Burial grounds were overflowing, with bodies piled on top of one another. Dickens was simply recording what he saw.

Clerkenwell's 'fences' (people who handle stolen property) lived on the corner of Field Lane and Saffron Hill. Here, where pickpockets and prostitutes plied their trade, police rarely ventured. When they did, it was in daylight and in pairs. Attics of dilapidated buildings accommodated up to four families. In lodging houses, thirty men, women and children crowded into one fetid room to shelter for the night. Oliver was used as a vehicle to vent his anger against these conditions and set him up as the social conscience of his day, doing for nineteenth century England what Dostoevsky was to do for Russia.

But the culture was rich and the language colourful. Picking pockets especially for expensive silk handkerchiefs (wipes) which end up in *dolly shops*, was *tail buzzing*. Inventing begging stories was being *on the blob*, prostitutes were *Judy's tails*, stealing from street stalls was *sneaking*, look outs were *crows*, child cat burglars *snakesmen*. When the poet Longfellow asked Dickens to take him to Clerkenwell to see the rookeries, Dickens called it *'the attraction of repulsion'*. After Oliver, he began research for *Barnaby Rudge*, a story about the Gordon Riots partly set in Clerkenwell.

1884 Canon Benham, a Dickens fan who lives in Finsbury, explores the locations in his books. The Artful Dodger takes Oliver via the back door to Fagin's Den in **Saffron Hill** (thought to be Field Lane Ragged School, one of Dickens's favourite charities). Bill Sikes plods up **Highgate Hill**, Noah Claypole and Charlotte trudge under **Archway Bridge** and when they get to **The Angel**, Noah says: *'London begins here in earnest'*. Rich Mr Brownlow's *'neat house in a quiet shady street near Pentonville'*, Fagin's Den in Field Lane, Saffron Hill and the Sessions House, **Clerkenwell Green** are embedded in our consciousness. Mr Brownlow has his pockets picked by the Artful Dodger and Charley Bates outside a bookshop on Clerkenwell Green.

1838 Edits *Life of Grimaldi*. Despite the fact he considered it 'twaddle' it sold 1,700 copies the first week. Second child, daughter Kate, was born.

1839 Finsbury Savings Bank opens in **Sekforde Street**. Dickens became a customer. Third child was born. No. 48 was too small for his growing family and servants so he moved to 1 Devonshire Terrace W1, but for the rest of his life continued to tramp the streets of Islington.

1841 *Barnaby Rudge*. Joe Willet stays at The Angel Inn, Gabriel Varden lives at his locksmith shop, The Golden Key, in **Clerkenwell**. Prisoners are released from The New Prison by Gordon Rioters, and in **Smithfield**, Barnaby helps his father get rid of his fetters after his release from Newgate Prison. In *The Old Curiosity Shop*, Old Maunders keeps eight dwarfs and eight giants in a cottage in **Spa Fields**.

1843 *Martin Chuzzlewit*. 3 **Terretts Court** (Place) off Upper Street is thought to be where he puts Tom and Ruth Pinch in lodgings. *'A singular little old-fashioned house up a blind street which had two small bedrooms and a triangular parlour. No doll's house ever yielded greater delight to its young mistress.'*

1848 Dickens' sister, Fanny Burnett, dies at home 4 Sutherland Villas (71 **Hanley Road**). *Dombey and Son*. Betsey Prig is a nurse at **Bart's**, Morfin lives at The Angel Inn and the Perches live in **Balls Pond Road**. *The Haunted Man*, **Jerusalem Passage**, is Tetterby's house and shop.

1850 *David Copperfield*, Betsey Trotwood's husband is born and buried in **Hornsey**. **City Road** is where Mr Micawber lives and Uriah Heep lodges near **New River Head**.

1853 *Bleak House*. Esther Summerson and Inspector Bucket take a coach from The Angel. Phil Squod, the tinker, works in **Saffron Hill**, the Smallweed family live near **Mount Pleasant**, Mrs Guppy lives in 302 **Old Street** and at 87 **Penton Rise** lives Mr Guppy.

1857 Dickens, a middle-aged, much-married man, falls in love with Ellen Ternan, a young woman living off **Balls Pond Road**. (Full story, see Ternan, Ellen.)

Little Dorritt. Cavalletto is a patient at Bart's, **Bleeding Heart Yard** is where the Plornishes live near the Doyce & Clenman Factory and *'the private residence of Mr Pancks'* is in **Pentonville**.

1859 *Tale of Two Cities*, Jarvis Lorry lives in **Clerkenwell**.

1865 *Our Mutual Friend*, The Wilfers live near the dust heaps in **Holloway**, *'a tract of suburban Sahara.'*

1871 *Christmas Stories*, Mrs Lirriper has her first lodgings at **The Angel** and the narrator of '*Holly Tree*' stays at The Peacock Inn.

1924 Walter Dexter, editor of *The Dickensian*, who lives at 84 **Highbury New Park**, successfully campaigns to buy 48 **Doughty Street** for Dickens House Museum.

....

DISRAELI, Benjamin (1804–1881)

Prime Minister, novelist

*Date unknown, Isaac d'Israeli moves from behind Canonbury Tower to Trinity Row (9 **Upper Street**, now 215) where he lives for a year. It may be that Benjamin was born in Islington, Disraeli was very secretive about his early years. The family moved to 6 King's Road, Bedford Row, now 22 **Theobald's Road** where one of his biographers says Benjamin was born (Disraeli himself said he was born at the Adelphi). Certainly the first steps on his educational path were taken here.*

1808 Benjamin is enrolled at Dame Roper's Academy, **Colebrooke Row** N1 which he said was a 'very high-class establishment'.

1811 Age 7, leaves for prep school in Blackheath. Thomas Milner-Gibson, whose family owned parts of Islington, was there at the same time. He too would become an MP.

1852 Chancellor of the Exchequer.

1868 Prime Minister (and 1874–80). Much slum clearance undertaken during his time in office.

1876 Created Earl of Beaconsfield.

DISSIDENCE

When John Bird launched The Big Issue *(to give street dwellers a leg up on the social ladder) in* **Clerkenwell** *(now in* **Pentonville**) *in 1991, he had 'no idea' of the borough's radical past. Islington in fact has an astonishing history as a focus, both of religious dissent and social change, perhaps owing to the concentration of the printing trade encouraging the growth of pamphleteers and magazine editors, and its low-rent housing attracting young artists, refugees and radical thinkers.*

CHRONOLOGY OF DISSENT

1530 Outraged locals prevent Henry VIII from closing **Bart's**. **1605** Thomas Sleep helps Guy Fawkes. **1649** James and Thomas Chaloner help Cromwell execute Charles I. **1667** Charles Morton founds Dissenters Academy. **1738** John Wesley shocks people by telling them all souls are equal. **1745** Wm Hogarth first artist in England to expose condition of the poor. **1762** John Wilkes helps bring about a free press. **1792** Mary Wollstonecraft writes the first feminist manifesto, *Rights of Women*. Tom Paine writes *Rights of Man*. Thomas Hardy founds The London Corresponding Society to champion the cause of workers. **1837** Tom Wakley gets the Tolpuddle Martyrs reprieved. **1840** Cruikshank, founder member of The Philanthropist's Club campaigns for the nationalisation of all land. **1842** Thomas Duncombe presents the Chartist petition, gets rid of prison hulks and fights to keep open spaces. **1846** Caroline Chisholm helps families join transported relatives in Australia. **1862 The House on Clerkenwell Green** is Marx's International Working Men's Association. Wm Morris lectures here. **1865** Torrens Act improves living conditions and Torrens' London School Board Act introduces free education. **1872** The London Patriotic Society campaigns for nationalisation of land. **1875** John Groom, first voice of the disabled. **1890** World's first May Day March starts from Clerkenwell Green. **1893** Twentieth Century Press, first Communist press. **1902** V.I. Lenin plots Russian Revolution. **1921** Dr Marie Stopes pioneers birth control. **1936** Campaign for Abortion Law Reform opens in Islington High Street **1954** CND founded by Fenner Brockway **1958** John Betjeman, founder member of The Victorian Society, champions Euston Station and saves St Pancras. **1959** John Payton saves **Camden Passage** from Islington Council. **1961** Amnesty International established in **Rosebery Avenue**. **1965** Barbara Castle produces *In Place of Strife*. **1972** Rosie Boycott launches *Spare Rib*. *Index on Censorship* launched in **Highbury Place**. **1986** London Greenpeace 'McLibel' Campaign. **1986** Esther Rantzen's *Childline* in **Theberton Street** takes 1.2 million calls for help a year. **1988** African National Congress, **Holloway Road**, campaigns for Nelson Mandela's release. *Charter 88* set up to secure a Charter for human rights, a written constitution, constitutional change, accountable government, proportional representation, reform of the judiciary and House of Lords, and Scottish and Welsh devolved parliaments (last three achieved 1999). **1990s** Troops Out campaign for an Irish Republic at 27 **Horsell Road** N5. **1991** International PEN moves to **Goswell Road** (see entry under Goswell Road). *Conscience* at 601 **Holloway Road** N19 campaigns for a law to divert the 10 per cent of taxes which goes to the arms industry.

1995 *The Book*, a directory of UK Campaign Groups, is published. Islington is home to Activ88, Advisory Service for Squatters, ARROW (Active Resistance to Roots Of War, started by Gulf War resisters in 1990) Campaign Against the Arms Trade, Dream Creation, The Green Party, Reclaim The Streets, Squall (exposes hidden agendas) Squash (Squatters Action for Secure Homes). It could have listed many more. *The Book* could also have included Amnesty International (Nobel Peace Prize 1976), *The Big Issue* (campaigns on behalf of the homeless), British Union for Abolition of Vivisection, Earth First, Friends of the Earth, Green Party, Greenpeace, The People's Press, Troops Out (of Ireland) or WEN (Women's Environmental Network).

1996 Outraged locals campaign to prevent Virginia Bottomley MP from closing **Bart's** (see Bart's).

1999 Tony Blair PM abandons Clause Four, launches Scottish and Welsh devolution, the Good Friday Peace Agreement, proposes an elected Mayor for London, modernises House of Lords and introduces Minimum Wage.

2000 Labour Day, one thousand Reclaim The Streets anti-capitalist activists based in Finsbury Park march on Parliament Square.

DROVERS

We don't know when drovers first walked with their beasts (swam if they lived on Skye, much of the famous Roast Beef of Olde England came from Scotland) the length and breadth of Britain to **Smithfield** Meat Market (q.v.), the oldest in the world, but it was long before 1066. Drovers were about as popular as today's juggernauts but far more important to the growth of Islington as they came through on their way to Smithfield. Before a drove, they wrapped stiff brown paper made waterproof by soap around their socks, and dry soaped the inside of their hard wooden clogs. 'Fast food' on the road was a handful of oats washed down with spring water and a ram's horn of whisky to help start them on frosty mornings and to warm them before settling down at night among the herd, which they dared not leave. Until the 1600s they were on the lookout for wolves and, until 1782 when an Islington man, Abraham Newland, invented the banknote, wary of footpads and highwaymen.

10th century onwards Inns spring up all over Islington (23 on **Islington Road/St John Street** alone) to cater for drovers. Many put on entertainment. Bets were taken on bare-knuckle boxing matches between local farmers and drovers. Islington was teeming with vintners, victuallers, brewers, farmers, saddlers, horse collar makers, coopers, wheelwrights, blacksmiths, cobblers, weavers, bakers, glaziers, carpenters and tailors. The city's back garden, playground and hospital provided hay for horses and a constant supply of fresh dairy products: butter, milk and cream.

A thousand cattle a drove was normal, so the noise (let alone the mounds of dung) was deafening, with drovers shouting, dogs barking and the huge beasts themselves making their dissatisfaction very vocal. Farmers started fencing in their fields, which prevented drovers 'accidentally' ending up at Islington with more beasts than they started out with. Drovers were the postmen and news reporters of their day. Walking at two miles an hour they had plenty of time to catch up with gossip along the way.

Near London, cattle drovers were joined by sheep drovers from Lincolnshire, Suffolk and Norfolk. Pigs, notoriously stubborn, refused to be driven so had to be raised near Smithfield. To preserve their feet on the long march, geese and turkeys had them dipped in warm tar, then coated with sawdust and crushed cockleshells, before being wrapped in canvas 'shoes'. Passing carts gave them a ride if they had room. Turkey drovers had to be wary as dusk fell, because the birds tried to roost in the trees overnight and hours of precious light were wasted next day getting them down. Although unwelcome and unpopular intruders into Islington's rural peace, drovers were respected for their honesty. In addition to looking after their masters' cattle they were the Securicor of their day, in trust to local traders to deliver large sums of money and act as guides escorting travellers and pilgrims. The job was stressful, so how they cheered when they got to High Gate and finally looked down on the tallest spire in Europe (450 feet until it was destroyed by lightning in 1561) of St Paul's Cathedral and the great City of London spread out beneath them. After three tortuous weeks on the road it was downhill all the way; and when they climbed once more up High Gate hill to return home, at least they were cattle-free. Those who did well at market could pay for a lift home.

Where the Hollow Way meets (present-day) **Hornsey Road** they let out another cheer if the rotting corpse of a highwayman hung from the gibbet. The corpses were baked and covered in tar so that they lasted for months, years even, until a replacement comes along. Here, drovers tied a personal possession to the collar of a dog and sent it on ahead to their favourite Islington inn to make sure of a bed for the night. Drinking establishments had to be licensed according to a strict code: an ale house could sell only ale (beer), a tavern had to serve food, an inn must offer accommodation. When they arrived they could relax because in Islington a 'closed shop' was practised, concerning the procedure for the sale of cattle. Salesmen drovers licensed by the City put the emaciated beasts out to their final pasture to be fattened up for sale. Yet a third drover contingent led the animals down Islington Road to **Smithfield Bar** (barrier). On the last leg these official drovers, suitably bribed by pickpockets, sometimes stampeded the cattle to cause chaos amomng the crowds of marketgoers (hence the saying, 'a bull in a china shop'). After the sale a fourth set of drovers, paid by butchers, took the cattle on to the slaughterhouses along the banks of the Fleet.

1689 Michael Warton, farmer and MP for Beverley, Yorkshire, records the accounts for sending his cattle to Smithfield. His cattle left home on Monday 11 February (droving was not allowed on Sundays) and he paid drover, John Shearwood, £7 17s 11d to drive seventeen oxen to Smithfield. They arrived in Biggleswade, Hertfordshire on 21 February and Islington on 23 February. At Islington he paid £1 for twelve trusses of hay to feed the animals.

1860 It's not only people who can travel by rail. So could cattle, which meant Islington soon saw the last of the drovers. A familiar sight for over eight hundred years, the

Drover's Hall Day Centre near the old **Caledonian Market** is today Islington's only memory of the cattle men who brought prosperity to the area.

....

DU MAURIER, George (1834–1896)

Artist and novelist, father of Gerald and grandfather of Daphne

1851 Age 17, arrives in Islington from Paris. His father Louis had a brother, Robert, living locally and Louis (who fancied himself as a scientist) insisted that George should study chemistry at University College. All George wanted to do, despite the fact that he was blind in one eye, was paint. When George's grandmother (ex-mistress of the Duke of York) died, his mother Ellen inherited the annuity wrung out of the royal family. Husband Louis used it to set up a laboratory in Paris, where George was expected to work. It was a spectacular failure.

1852 George's family (and their five cats) come to Islington to be near him. They rented 44 **Wharton Street**, Pentonville N1 and stayed five years. George graduated in chemistry but after his father's death returned to Paris to study art. One of his fellow students was a mesmerist (hypnotist) who inspired du Maurier's novel *Trilby*.

Du Maurier gave Britain the eternal dilemma of *The Curate's Egg* in one of his *Punch* cartoons. His son, Gerald (*Bulldog Drummond*), was a chain smoker who had the du Maurier cigarette named after him, although he never smoked them because they were cork tipped. Daphne gave the world *Frenchman's Creek*, *My Cousin Rachel*, *The Birds* and *Don't Look Now* ...

....

DUNCAN TERRACE N1

1843 After three hundred years it's now legal to be a practising Catholic (1829 Catholic Emancipation Act). St John the Evangelist was built for Irish Catholic immigrants who settled here after building the **Regent's Canal**. The Catholic architect was Joseph Scoles. Pugin (who had strong family connections with Islington) scathingly called it: '*the most original combination of modern deformity ever*' and Pevsner, editor of *The Buildings of England*, condemned it as '*bleak, barn like ...*'

1954 Monsignor Bruce Kent, incumbent priest, led nine thousand in a peaceful protest from the Atomics Weapons Research Establishment, Aldermaston to Trafalgar Square (see CND). He resigned when he thought his political activities might embarrass the church.

1970 Beatle, Ringo Starr and Apple Records with 100 members of London Sinfonietta record John Tavener's *The Whale*.

1999 Having helped to ban (almost) nuclear weapons, Mr Bruce Kent of Finsbury Park, President of CND, campaigns to abolish war. He tried to set up a World Wide Criminal Court and get legislation passed to ban the sale of arms from Britain.

....

DUNCOMBE, Thomas (1796–1861)

Radical MP

(Duncombe Road N19)

1834 Immensely popular ('Honest Tom' or 'Finsbury Tom'), ex-Coldstream Guard, rich aristocratic dandy, Harrow public school, is voted in at every election from now until he dies.

1842 Presents the Chartist petition and campaigns to get rid of the 'hulks' (rotting ex-

Napoleonic War prison ships moored on the Thames. In the 1990s Michael Howard, Home Secretary, suggested bringing them back).

1844 Outraged to learn that the government is keeping anti-Monarchist <u>Mazzini</u> under surveillance in **Little Italy**, opening his mail and informing his enemies of their contents, Duncombe makes an official complaint in the House. The subsequent enquiry exonerated the government.

1851 *Friends of Italy* Council Member. Campaigned to keep Finsbury Park an open space.

1878 Duncombe Road Board School opens.

1885 Duncombe Road Chapel built.

1901 Duncombe Road Hall built.

1951 Duncombe Road School becomes Archway Secondary Modern (see entry under Archway).

1965 The 1877 Board School in **Cottenham Road** moves to **Sussex Way** and is re-named Duncombe Primary School.

E

ELIZABETH I
Queen of England
Local legend has it that Henry VIII secretly courted Anne Boleyn at St John's Priory. If true, could it be that Elizabeth I was conceived in **Clerkenwell***?*

1558 Wednesday 23 November, Elizabeth (25) leaves Hatfield House, Hertfordshire with a retinue of a thousand courtiers and rides south to London for her official reception at **Charterhouse**.

At High Gate, the bishops kissed her hand. As the retinue passed through low-lying lands between Islington and Charterhouse, the mist was rising. The Queen's Highway was so muddy, the company abandoned it and took to the fields, arriving at the back of Charterhouse instead of using the road to the entrance. That evening, greetings in the shape of a jewelled ring arrived from Philip II of Spain. Next day, Elizabeth held her first reception. The Tapestry Room (temporarily the Throne Room) was thronged with titled subjects paying homage to 'the splendid Tudor girl'. Among them was a lady-in-waiting bearing rings taken from Mary Tudor's corpse.

Elizabeth stayed five days. Excited crowds outside grew bigger each day. 29 November, she set out for her coronation at Westminster Abbey. A splendid company met in the entrance court behind the Gate. When the Queen took her place, the procession moved forward among the crowds outside, proceeding through the newly gravelled, banner-bedecked streets to the Tower for the traditional prayer vigil undertaken by all new monarchs (especially if they witnessed the demise of six queens and two kings). The whole of London arrived to cheer their new, young and (even better) Protestant Queen on her way. Her procession from Charterhouse is well documented:

'. . . the Queen removed to the Tower from the Lord North's plasse which was the Charter

Howsse. The stretes ... was newe gravelled ... and afor rod gentyllmen and knyghtes and lordes and after cam all the trumpets blohyng and cam all the haroldes in aray: and my lord of Pembroke bare the Quen's sword: Then cam her Grace on horsebake in purple welvett with a skarpe abowt her neke after rod Robart Dudley her master of her horse: and so the gard with halberds. There was shyche shutying of Gunes as never was hard afor.' (Henry Machyn's diary, published by the Camden Society.)

Master of the Horse, <u>Dudley</u>'s was no lowly position, he was third chief officer in the royal household and rode next to the monarch on all State occasions. Sir Walter <u>Mildmay</u> (probably owned land in Islington), Chancellor of the Exchequer and Revenue Commissioner, issued the new coinage and the Queen asked Sir Thomas <u>Chaloner</u>, her Representative in the Netherlands, to send her some good horses.

1559 Disbands the Order of St John. Visiting friends in Islington, she was surrounded by *'seventy four begging rogues'* so, furious, rode home again. They were rounded up and imprisoned.

1561 10–13 July, another Royal Progress to Charterhouse. Her host again being Lord <u>North</u>, this one was more lavish than three years before: *'... over the feldes to the Charter Howse my lord North's plase ... and the feldes of pepull gret number as ever was sene and ther tared till Monday.'* During her stay she rode: *'... from the Charterhouse by Clarkynwell over the feldes unto the Sayvoy unto master secretore Dysselle to soper ... after gret chere tyll mydnight . .. she ryd to bed at the Charterhouse.'* Once again, on the fourth day the streets were newly gravelled and sanded. The procession formed in the courtyard for a royal progress via **Smithfield** to the City was even more splendid than the last time she left Charterhouse: *'... all thes plases where hangyd with cloth or arres and carpetes and with sylke ... Cloth of Gold and Cloth of Sylver and velvett of all colours and taffatas ...'*

Later the same month the Queen left St James' Palace to visit Enfield but refused to use the roads and went across Islington Fields instead. Whenever the Queen rode over Moor/Finsbury/ Islington fields, ditches had to be filled in, the ground levelled and hedges removed. **St John's Road** (changes name to 'Street' inside City, there are no 'roads' in the City of London) was so bad the Queen refused to use it when she visited Islington, which she did on many occasions to see Robert <u>Dudley</u> and his stepson the earl of <u>Essex</u> in Lower Road (**Essex Road**), Sir John <u>Spencer</u> of **Canonbury Tower**, Sir Thomas <u>Fowler</u> at Mansion House (**Cross Street**), Sir Walter <u>Mildmay</u> of **Newington Green** and Sir Walter <u>Raleigh</u> of **Upper Street**.

Fowler (land bordered Canonbury Tower) was Lord of the Manor of Barnsbury and Deputy Lieutenant for Middlesex. Sir Thomas was to be one of the jurors at Raleigh's trial. Elizabeth's Lodge was still standing in Mansion House Garden in 1655 (some sources say as late as 1861), the house itself survived until 1845.

1564 Visits **Highbury** Fields to inspect one of the sources of London's water.

1568 Hears of the Ridolfi Plot (see entry under **Charterhouse**). Makes her third visit to **Charterhouse** to embarrass Thomas Howard.

1572 Cousin Howard, Duke of Norfolk (of Charterhouse) beheaded for treason.

1579 Appoints Edmund Tilney/<u>Tylney</u> Censor and Master of the Revels and gives him **St John's Gate**.

1580 Gives Robert Dudley Shipcote House in **Essex Road**.

1581 Walter Raleigh of **Upper Street** arrives at Court.

1603 The first place Elizabeth visited as Queen is also the last. 17 January, age 70, she paid her fourth visit to Charterhouse to dine with *'my good Thomas'* Howard. She died a few months later.

ENO

Islington: Home of English National Opera

England enjoyed its first opera in the 1600s when William D'Avenant staged The Siege of Rhodes in **Charterhouse Square***. (See D'Avenant.)*

1931 Sadler's Wells Opera is founded.

1945 Sadler's Wells Opera, exclusively English language, re-opens after the war with Benjamin Britten's *Peter Grimes* (see also Britten, Benjamin).

1968 Moves to London Coliseum.

1974 Becomes English National Opera.

ESSEX ROAD N1

Originally Lower Road, geographically lower than **Upper Street** *(Islington is on a hill), property owners got it renamed* **Essex Road***. 'Road' comes from Anglo-Saxon 'ride' (horse-riders), a traffic diversion.*

1580 Although Elizabeth I doesn't forgive Robert Dudley, Earl of Leicester, for his betrayal (he got married) and won't let him return to court, she wants to see him when the whim takes her and, presumably, not wanting to trek to Kenilworth, gives him Shipcote House, King John's Place (later Ward's Place) between Green Man Lane and Paradise Place (**Peabody Square** is now on the site). The huge mansion with magnificent stained glass windows was built by Sir Thomas Lovell, Speaker of the House of Commons, Chancellor of the Exchequer to her grandfather, Henry VII and father, Henry VIII, and rebuilt by her favourite *'coz'* Henry Carey, Lord Hunsdon. Dudley was delighted. He told the Queen that Islington was *'one of the most ancient and best towns in England, next to London'* and praised *'its cheeses and salt butter, custard curds and wheys tarts and other pastry cook delicacies'.*

Robert Laneham, actor friend of Dudley (MC at the lavish festivities put on by Leicester at Kenilworth for Elizabeth) agreed: *'The worshipful village of Islington in Middlesex is well known . . .'* After Dudley's death, Shipcote was among other things, a smallpox hospital, soap factory and poor house, but by 1800 there was no trace of it.

1774 The Thatched House, 119 Essex Road, is kept by the proud father of Dr William Hawes who resuscitated half-drowned people from the Thames (whether they wanted it or not) and founded The Royal Humane Society.

1807 Thomas Hood, poet, moves to No. 50.

1836 A new cattle market opens to replace Smithfield but is a financial flop so closes.

1900 Islington folk spend two or three evenings a week at the cinema (see Cinemas). No. 58, an empty fruit and veg. shop, became The Picture Hall and the old post office at No. 46, the Coronet.

1921 Veterans still unemployed three years after the war ended occupy Essex Road Library for a six week protest.

1930 The Egyptian-style Carlton cinema is opened by royalty, Mayor of Islington, British Legion, Grenadier Guards and Scots Guards. Marble and mirrors everywhere, amber lights, colonnades, a ceiling dome of buff, amber and silver, the gold drapes had green and scarlet pelmets and the telephone booths were gold. Large tea rooms and an elegant lounge were provided. The opening film starred Harold Lloyd in his first talkie.

1931 The Coronet is part of the Blue Hall cinema chain. Closed during WWII (now William Bedford antiques).

1962 Joe Orton and lover, Kenneth Halliwell, found guilty of stealing and defacing library books from South and Central Libraries. The soon-to-become *enfant terrible* of British theatre launched his career as a playwright from gaol (see Orton, Joe).

1999 Well-loved local landmark, Alfredo's Café, closes. The fight scene in *The Who* rock opera *Quadrophenia* was filmed here in 1978.

....

EXMOUTH MARKET EC1

1685 A recently re-discovered spring results in the building of The Fountain Inn.

1754 The Fountain Inn closes.

1765 Walter Baynes, lawyer of Middle Temple, who owns Cold Bath Spa, builds Baynes Row.

1770 Thomas Rosoman leases land from the Marquess of Northampton and sub-lets Ducking Pond House to a Mr Craven, who demolished it to build a huge pantheon (Church of The Holy Redeemer is on the site). The People's Pantheon, a pleasure dome for the masses, was 'a humble imitation' of the one in Oxford Road (Street) patronised by the nobility. Apprentices, tailors, hairdressers, dressmakers, milliners and servants frequented this large, beehive-shaped building. Advert in *The Theatrical Magazine*: 'Pantheon – The **NOB**ility's Oxford Road, the **MOB**ility's Spaw Fields.' (Spaw was a deliberate mispronunciation of Spa, made popular by Dr Johnson (q.v.) with his strong Staffordshire accent.)

1776 The Pantheon is so notorious it's closed by the authorities. The owner went bankrupt and rented the building as a showroom for carriages.

1779 Owner of the Pantheon sells it to Selina, Countess of Huntingdon to use as a Nonconformist place of worship. She renamed it Spa Fields Chapel and moved in next door where she stayed for the rest of her life. Wesley was a good friend of hers, as was Dr Johnson. She began a long struggle with Reverend Sellon, Vicar of St James, Clerkenwell who objected to her and her chapel. He also objected to her paying her chaplains, not charging pew rents and undercutting his price for burials (the Pantheon Gardens are now Spa Fields Chapel cemetery). Revd Sellon wanted the chapel closed so urged the Church of England to bring an action against her in the Ecclesiastical Courts, which (not surprisingly) they won. Selina launched the Lady Huntingdon Connection (to Methodism), left the C. of E. and declared her chapel outside church jurisdiction. Her organist, William Shrubsole, wrote *All Hail the Power of Jesus' Name*.

1782 Robert <u>Pollard</u> (see Pollard, family), artist, moves to No. 15. Pupil of Richard Wilson RA, painter of landscapes and seascapes in oils, he turned to more profitable print making.

1790 Lady Huntingdon (84) dies at home next door to her beloved Spa Fields Chapel. She asked to be buried in the white silk gown she wore when she opened it.

1792 James, seventh child of Robert Pollard is born here.

1810 After twenty-eight years, Robert moves to 11 **Holloway Place**, Holloway Road to set up a print business with son James.

1822 Joey <u>Grimaldi</u>, quintessential clown and actor-manager of Sadler's Wells, moves into No. 4 (he stayed seven years). Richard <u>Earlom</u>, successful engraver, dies here, age 80.

1829 Baynes Row is renamed **Exmouth Street** after Edward <u>Pellew</u>, Admiral Lord Exmouth MP, was given the freedom of the city for naval deeds.

1834 John <u>Caley</u> dies here. He was the Keeper of Records, Westminster Abbey Treasury, sacked for dishonesty.

1845 Spa Fields Chapel cemetery, intended to hold 1,361 bodies, is full up within its first year. Fifteen hundred more were buried the next. Within 50 years, 80,000 had been accommodated. Gravediggers were continually exhuming, cremating or dismembering corpses, burning coffins and piling corpses on top of one another to make room. Locals were scandalised when these activities were discovered and the cemetery was closed (now a public garden).

1847 Archibald <u>Leighton</u> at No. 55, inventor of bookbinding cloth, dies.

1854 Harriet Beecher <u>Stowe</u>, author of *Uncle Tom's Cabin* (English edition illustrated by George <u>Cruikshank</u>) on a world tour campaigning to abolish slavery, lectures at Spa Fields Chapel.

1863 Exmouth Street is in danger of collapsing after tunnelling was started for the world's first underground railway.

1886 Spa Fields Chapel is demolished. The Marquess of Northampton gave the land instead to build the Anglo/Catholic Church of the Holy Redeemer, the only church in London built in the Italian basilica style. Architect John <u>Sedding</u> had been longing to have a go at Italian Renaissance and Henry <u>Wilson</u> (who took over when he died) wanted to get away from 'cheap Gothic.' Gladstone laid the foundation stone. The font came from St Giles Cripplegate. The organ, from the Chapel Royal, Windsor, was previously owned by Prince Albert, a keen organist. The campanile still dominates the street.

1894 Officially designated a street market.

1939 Re-named **Exmouth Market**.

1950s Local legend has it that Glenda <u>Jackson</u> (film star turned MP) worked in Boots the Chemist (now a betting shop).

FAMILY TREES (Public Records)

Islington is <u>the</u> place to come if you are hoping to trace your ancestors.

1911 The Society of Genealogists was founded in **Charterhouse Street** EC1. It holds records going back to the 1500s but researchers are advised to trace family trees elsewhere until they get down to parish registers.

1965 The ancient Saxon county of Middlesex and the county of London established in 1900 are combined, together with their record archives, under the Greater London Council (GLC).

1982 Prime Minister Margaret Thatcher abolishes the GLC. The Greater London Records Office and History Library (London Metropolitan Archives include Middlesex, Essex, Herts, Kent and Surrey) transferred to **Northampton Road** EC1. Every census from 1801 is here, plus 10,000 volumes, 6,000 bundles of official records, half a million photographs, 5,000 maps and 40,000 prints.

1998 Documents specific to family history (birth/marriage/death certificates from 1796) from the Public Record Office at Kew, Somerset House, St Catherine's House and Chancery Lane transferred to The Family Records Centre, **Myddelton Street** EC1. American and Australian visitors who think their ancestors may have been transported from London or Middlesex will also find The Clerkenwell House of Detention useful, it has (some) records of prisoners incarcerated there.

FARADAY, Michael (1791–1867)

Scientist

Faraday Close N7

1806 Leaves school and gets a job as an errand boy.

1831 Invents the electric generator. Every Sunday the 'father of electricity' could be seen walking to or from the Sandemanian Church, (q.v.) 7 **Barnsbury Grove** (corner of **Bridge Street**). He was an Elder of the church and gave sermons until just before he died. He often smiled to see passers-by run round the block to get a second look at him. Former lab assistant, Faraday became science adviser to the Government of the day, but refused all honours. He could equally well be known as the 'father' of cryogenics, experimenting with low-temperature physics (he got down to minus-110 degrees C.)

1867 Dies at the 'grace and favour' home in Hampton Court given him by Queen Victoria and is buried at Highgate Cemetery. As was the Sandemanian custom there was no service, no prayers and no hymns.

1886 Faraday's chapel closes when a new Sandemanian Meeting House is built in **Furlong Road** (co-incidentally a Joseph Sandeman lived at No. 9). It thrived until 1945 (now Leeson Hall, Conservative Party HQ).

1906 Plaque to Faraday unveiled on the site of the old chapel in Barnsbury.

1959 Chapel moves to **Highbury Crescent** (now closed).

1976 Faraday's ivy-covered grave is rediscovered by the 'Friends of Highgate Cemetery'.

FARRINGDON ROAD EC1

Old course of the river Fleet (this was the Fleet valley, see Fleet, river; also Rivers).

1080s William the Conqueror builds Fleet prison (east side of **Farringdon Road**) for those committed by the Star Chamber. It survived in one form or another for 766 years.

1100s The Clerk's Well (Nos 14–16) on the river bank is just half a mile from St Paul's.

1642 Fleet Prison is a debtors' prison but on the outbreak of the Civil War was used for political offenders.

1686 The Butcher's Arms opens in **Pear Tree Court** (the court is mentioned in Dickens' *Oliver Twist*).

1727 Known as Hockley-in-the-Hole. When it rained, the Fleet overflowed and low-lying land was flooded. The huge Clerkenwell Workhouse was built (The *Guardian/Observer* offices now cover the site). Before old age pensions, the workhouse was a resented but accepted fate for many old people.

1731 Part of the Fleet is filled in and arched over, linking Holborn Bridge to Fleet Bridge to make Fleet Market.

1750 Advert for pre-TV entertainment in Hockley-in-the-Hole: *'Mad bull to be dressed in fireworks and turned loose. Dog to be dressed in fireworks and turned loose with the mad bull. Bear to be turned loose with a cat tied to its tail.'*

1774 Town End Lane, known as Rag Lane, is renamed Ray Street.

1811 The Coach and Horses in Ray Street replaces the tea gardens used for bear baiting and cock fighting. During demolition, a leather bag was found with the name R. Turpin.

1836 Dickens' *Oliver Twist*: '. . . *by the side of the workhouse across the classic ground which once bore the name of Hockley in the Hole thence into Little Saffron Hill and so into Saffron Hill the Great.'*

1840 Built by William the Conqueror, burnt down by Wat Tyler, where Sir Walter Raleigh was imprisoned, home for a year to John Wilkes, burnt down again by the Gordon Rioters (q.v.), where Dickens' Mr Pickwick languished for breach of promise, Fleet Prison is demolished. The Congregational Memorial Hall was built on the site.

1855 More of the Fleet is filled in. Ray Street, Cod Piece/Coppice Row and Oldham Street, slums in Hockley-in-the-Hole, are razed to make way for Victoria Street, re-named Farringdon Road.

1865 Dr Thomas Wakley, MP for Finsbury, castigates Clerkenwell Workhouse in the *Lancet* as the worst in London (see Wakley, Thomas).

1882 Peabody Buildings are built in **Pear Tree Court**.

1883 Clerkenwell Workhouse is demolished.

1884 Frank Swinnerton is born at No. 150. Office boy for publishers J.M. Dent and Chatto & Windus, friend of Arnold Bennett, he wrote 55 books including a biography of Bennett.

1913 *The New Statesman*, a weekly political journal, is launched at 14–16 Farringdon Lane as the mouthpiece for The Fabian Society.

1930 The People's Press funded by the British Communist Party publishes *The Daily Worker* from No. 75 (became *The Morning Star*). So popular, it put out four editions every night (after the collapse of Communism in the 1990s it's now lucky to sell 6,000 copies a week). It was here too that *Tit Bits* and *Marxism Today* became uneasy bedfellows. Arnold Bennett contributed to *Tit Bits*, as did Joseph Conrad. The popular weekly magazine founded 1881 by George Newnes had cartoons, comic strips, crosswords, jokes, puzzles, serials, short stories, snippets of news and sports coverage.

1936 Russia, Germany and France help General Franco invade Spain. Hundreds of Islingtonians joined The International Brigade and walked over the Pyrenees to fight against fascism in the Spanish Civil War. *The Daily Worker* gave them full public support.

1976 Corporation Buildings, on the site of the old Workhouse, is demolished. The *Guardian/Observer* newspaper offices are now here.

1984 The Butcher's Arms, **Pear Tree Court**, is re-named *Betsey Trotwood* (great-aunt of David Copperfield) to commemorate Dickens. Until recently when a pub in Essex Road was re-named The Artful Dodger, the 'Betsey' was the only visible memory of Dickens ever having walked these streets. This is where the 'Cogers', the oldest debating society in England, meet. It was formed in 1755 by politicians and law students who wanted to improve their public speaking.

1996 Chris Smith MP, Islington South and Minister for Culture, campaigns to get Farringdon Station name changed to Clerkenwell. London Underground argued successfully (for the time being at least) that Farringdon should keep its historic identity as the terminus of the world's first underground railway.

....

FAWKES, Guy (1570–1606)
Terrorist

1600s The web of streets and alleys between **Cowcross Street** and **St John Street** Clerkenwell is where many recusant Catholics live and plot against James I.

1605 England's first terrorist visits Thomas Sleep, printer of seditious leaflets, in St Peter's Lane (off St John Street). 4 November, arrested while laying gunpowder in the cellars of the Houses of Parliament. He never stood a chance, the king's spies were everywhere. 7 November, Calendar of State Papers: *'From Salisbury House to Mr Percival. Informs him of divers houses of recusants in St John St amongst them Mr Thomas Sleep. Guy Johnson (alias Fawkes) is often at Sleep's house'*. Fawkes was tortured and executed, as was, presumably, Sleep.

....

FEMINISM

Mary Wollstonecraft (q.v.) lived in Islington from the 1780s and opened two schools here. Mother of Mary 'Frankenstein' Shelley, she wrote the first modern feminist manifesto, *Vindication of the Rights of Women*. Another resident, Wallace Cheeseman, 27 **Florence Street**, founded the Fawcett Society, for advancing the cause of women. Marie Stopes opened the first birth control clinic here, which gave rise to the Legalise Abortion campaign, in **Islington High Street**. Around the corner The Marx Memorial Library has the history of the suffragettes – so Ms Rosie Boycott, editor of *Spare Rib*, had feminism at her fingertips when she launched her new magazine here in 1978.

1975 Sex Discrimination and Equal Pay Acts passed.

1978 Women picket *Islington Gazette* offices to protest over the use of scantily clad pin-ups. Sisterwrite (first feminist bookshop in the UK) opens in **Upper Street**.

The five-woman co-operative, the first to sell radical feminist literature, was run by women for women about women. It specialised in children's books which used non-sexist language, caustic posters and radical magazines. The Womens Press with its flat-iron logo, a new feminist publishing company, opened in **Clerkenwell** (still there) and Boycott helped launch Virago Publishing. '*This Advertisement Exploits Women*' stickers started appearing on London Underground drawing attention to the strange convention of using nude women to advertise anything from cars to carpets and to male dominated (sexist) language.

....

FINSBURY

1231 Known as *Fens Burh* or *Vinisbur*.

1315 Now spelt *Finesbiri*, possibly after the de Fiennes family. They certainly gave land between **The Angel** and **Smithfield** to the City for the enjoyment of its citizens. *Ride a Cock Horse*, the famous nursery rhyme may have been inspired by Lady Celia Fiennes, who in 1697 rode around Britain ('*. . . to see a fine* (Fiennes?) *lady upon a white horse*').

1582 A two-day festival of archery is held on Finsbury Fields with 3,000 competitors, each with a longbow and four arrows. Winners rode home accompanied by 200 torch bearers.

1784 St Luke's Lunatic Asylum, **Old Street** is built (later Bank of England Mint). Mrs Turner, the artist's mother, was a patient.

1800 Five times as many (55,515) live in Finsbury as in Islington (10,212).

1824 The Eagle Tavern takes over the ancient Shepherd and Shepherdess Ale House, **City Road**: '*Up and down the City Road, in and out of The Eagle, That's the way the money goes, pop goes the weasel.*' '*Pop*' is slang for pawn, '*weasel*' is tailor's slang for a flat-iron. The Eagle features in Dickens' *Sketches by Boz*. Local girl, Britain's first female pop star Marie Lloyd appeared here, age 14.

1883 Finsbury Technical College, **Leonard Street** opens, the first in London.

1885 From now until 1918, Finsbury returns three members to Parliament. The 62 MPs in total included Richard Chamberlain (Joseph's brother) and one was an Indian (see below). 18 were knights or Baronets and 4 became Peers. There were 4 army officers, 12 lawyers, 5 civil servants, 7 local government officers, 7 merchant bankers, 3 'something big in the city' and 3 in education. 3 were women and 6 were 'working class' (3 trades unionists). One unsuccessful contender was the inventor of the computer, Charles Babbage (see Babbage, Charles).

1889 Electricians hold their first meeting at St Paul's Head pub and start The Electrical Trades Union. It established its HQ at Club Union Buildings, **Clerkenwell Road**.

1890 Lord Mayor of London opens Britain's first free library in **Skinner Street**.

1892 Finsbury Central election. Finsbury votes in Prof. Dadabhar Naoroji, Lib. – first non-white MP in the House of Commons. Naoroji was nicknamed 'Narrow Majority'. A professor of Mathematics, he arrived from India in 1855 determined to become an MP and fight British Rule. Naoroji was a mentor to Mahatma Ghandi, whom he met at the Indian National Congress. He returned home in 1906 and died eleven years later. His achievement was barely recognised for 100 years.

1894 At Finsbury Free Library, for the first time ever the public is allowed to browse around the bookshelves at leisure.

1895 Finsbury Town Hall is opened by Lord Rosebery.

1899 The parishes of St James and St John, St Luke, St Sepulchre and Charterhouse are combined as Metropolitan Borough of Finsbury. Its Coat of Arms had the cross of the Knights of St John, running water (wells in the area) four red circles and crescents (arms of Thomas Sutton (q.v.), founder of Charterhouse School) an embattlement (City Wall and towers) and gates (Aldersgate, Cripplegate and Moor Gate – once opened on to the moors).

1901 Population 101,463. Because of slum clearance in Clerkenwell, Islington was now three times bigger than Finsbury (335,238).

1918 Finsbury's three MPs now down to one.

1931 Population down to 69,888.

1934 The council progressively replaces gas street lamps with electric.

1938 Berthold Lubetkin designs the first purpose-built health centre in Britain (see Lubetkin, Berthold).

1951 Further slum clearance. By now, the electorate was down to 35,370.

1965 The borough of Finsbury covering St Luke's, St James, Bunhill, Pentonville and Clerkenwell is absorbed into Islington when the London Local Government Act merged it with the more densely populated borough of Islington. The parliamentary constituency became Islington South.

1967 Islington Council, astonishingly, demolishes the world famous (Lenin used it) Finsbury Free Library and puts up a bland replacement.

1993 Professor Naoroji MP officially commemorated by a plaque on Finsbury Town Hall, unveiled by Diane Abbott MP, Chris Smith MP and former Liberal leader, Sir David Steele. When Insurance Street was renamed **Naoroji Street**, Ghandi's grandson was at the ceremony.

....

FINSBURY SQUARE EC1

1777 The precursor of Harley Street and first public place lit by gas is designed by City Surveyor, George Dance the Younger.

1778 James Lackington, who borrowed £25 from John Wesley to open his first bookshop in **Chiswell Street**, moves into prestigious premises (140 feet frontage) originally intended for William Caslon Type Foundry. It was so huge that as a publicity stunt he hired the York Mail, a coach and six, to drive through the shop. Over 50,000 books were on display. He called it The Temple of the Muses.

1795 Mary Wollstonecraft, early feminist and unmarried mother, moves in.

1804 Dr George Birkbeck of College fame moves in and stays until he dies 40 years later.

1856 Dr David Livingstone, after 17 years in Africa, is being looked after by friends in No. 15. He is recuperating after a lion savaged his arm (**Bart's** still has the cast of the damaged humerus).

1871 Anton Bruckner begins his Second Symphony at No. 39.

1925 Foreseeing the problems the car will bring to residential areas, the Automobile Association suggests the square be dug up for an underground car park but nothing is done. Finsbury Council picked up the idea in the 1930s, but the Second World War stopped all unnecessary building so the plan was aborted.

1961 A company called Les Garages builds London's first underground car park, one and a half acres with 350 parking bays, beneath the square.

....

FITZSTEPHEN, William (d. 1190)

Chronicler monk, biographer of Thomas à Becket

When Becket, the second richest man in England (£19 billion) was murdered in Canterbury Cathedral, FitzStephen, his private secretary, was with him.

1174 *Vita Sancti Thomas* is as much an account of twelfth century London as it is of Becket, giving us the first written records of **Smithfield, St John Street** and **Turn Mill Street**.

FitzStephen wrote about Smithfield Market, the buying and selling of cattle and wives, pursuits such as football on **Clerkenwell Green**, jousting tournaments, javelin throwing, wrestling, hawking, hunting and archery. He described the Wall Brook in the moor fields which overflowed in winter and froze, providing a superb ice rink for apprentices. They tied animal bones from knackers' yards to their feet and used them as skates. He also tells us about the 'moor fields' races, shot putting, battles on horse and foot, games when a shield was fastened to a pole midstream and youngsters hurled lances at it from boats swept along in strong currents. Huge crowds gathered to cheer when they missed and foolhardy lads fell into the swiftly flowing river. He also wrote about the Clerken Well on the banks of the Fleet, where the water was '*sweet, wholesome and clear*'.

FLEET (river, see also Farringdon Road and Rivers)
*For years an important tributary of the Thames, the Fleet had two sources, one at the Vale of Health, Hampstead Ponds, the other at Kenwood. They met at **Camden Town**, where the Fleet went on to **King's Cross**, **Farringdon Road** and **Holborn Viaduct** to join the Thames at Blackfriars. It once formed a natural defence of the west wall of Roman London and at its widest was 650 feet, navigable until it met another of London's lost rivers, the Old Bourne (Holborn).*

704 Celtic *Yseldon* is now Saxon *Isendone* (*isen* is saxon for iron) and the '*river of wells*' is now the *Fleet* (fast flowing).

1080s William the Conqueror builds a prison on the river.

1100 First mention of the 'clerk's well' on the river bank (See: **Clerkenwell**).

1170s Hospitallers build a wharf.

1254 Black Friars downstream complain that double strength incense burners can't disguise the stench.

1300 Totally unnavigable, it's cleaned out.

1417 Used for tanning, wool making and brewing. Butchers outside Fleet prison wash animal entrails in the river at ebb tide (the river here, for obvious reasons, is known as 'The Red Fleet'). Locals (and prisoners) become ill from the stench. The practice is stopped.

1579 Tylney, Master of the Revels and first Censor, is lodged at **St John's Gate**. Theatre props, scenery, etc. were brought here via the river. Actors were obliged to rehearse in front of him before being granted a licence to perform.

1598 Stowe's *Survey of London* lists six bridges over the Fleet. One was Cow Bridge (**Cow Cross Street**), another was **Chick Lane**.

1605 Cleared out again.

1652 Lavatories are now used by the rich. Effluent was flushed straight into the Fleet, already impassable because of the many '*encroachments thereon made by the throwing of offal and other garbage by butchers … and by reason of the many houses of office standing over upon it.*'

1720 Baker's Row, **Great Warner** and **Little Warner Streets** are laid out in the Fleet Valley (today they are 20 feet below **Rosebery Avenue**).

1731 Part of the river is filled in and arched over linking Holborn Bridge to Fleet Bridge to make Fleet Market. The street created was **Farringdon Street**.

1766 Now an open sewer. The authorities enlarged Fleet Market and built a road from Fleet Bridge to the Thames. Parts of the river disappeared from view and from memory.

1782 The back door to the Sessions House on Clerkenwell Green leads straight on to the river for prisoners sentenced to transportation.

1860 Sand and gravel are removed along the banks to lay tracks for The Metropolitan Subterranean Railway.

1862 Forced underground, the river bursts. Flood water, 10 feet deep, stretched back to King's Cross.

1872 The Fleet is now a sewer in a drain (it still flows underneath the Fleet Valley and exits at Blackfriars).

1889 Rosebery Avenue bridges the old Fleet valley.

1996 A group of new Clerkenwell residents fantasise over pasta *al fresco* on the banks of the old river ... Friends of the Fleet, wearing *Free the Fleet* T-Shirts, campaigned to expose a stretch of the ancient waterway.

....

FRY, Roger (1866–1934)
Artist and writer

1919 Roger and sister Margery (known as Sara) set up house in **7 Dalmeny Avenue** and stay until 1926. His book *Vision and Design* is published while here (1920).

Born in Archway into a Quaker family, the Frys knew the area well. Sara spent her life campaigning for prison reform and the abolition of hanging. She was educational adviser to Holloway Prison, Secretary to the Howard League for Penal Reform, following in the footsteps of namesake Elizabeth Fry who campaigned to get matrons appointed in the women's sections of Cold Bath House of Correction and Clerkenwell House of Detention. Roger, leader of the Bloomsbury Group, was a gifted artist, critic, writer and lecturer, champion of modern art and ex-Director of the Museum of Modern Art, New York. He invented the term Post-Impressionism, championed Cézanne, Van Gogh and Picasso at a time when Alma Tadema was still painting themes from ancient Greece and Rome. He also founded the Omega Workshops.

Fry's painting of his garden in Dalmeny Avenue is in Islington Library.

....

GAINSBOROUGH FILMS
Poole Street N1 (See also Islington Studios)

Michael Balcon's Gainsborough Films' logo was a beautiful woman in a huge plumed picture hat nodding a smiling welcome to the audience. She was as familiar as MGM's roaring lion, Rank's he-man with the gong and RKO's crowing cockerel. Many of his films are now classics.

1924 Balcon (26) started as a filmmaker directing adverts. His first forays into film were stabs at a drama, *The Passionate Adventure*, directed by Alfred Hitchcock (q.v.), a crime thriller and a romance. This give him the confidence to put in a bid for Islington Studios, which were up for sale. Paramount Pictures were asking £100,000 but Balcon offered

£14,000 and was astonished when it was accepted. Paramount had no option, the studios were running at a loss. As he didn't have £14,000 either, he was allowed to buy the studios by instalments. A joyous Balcon launched *Gainsborough Pictures* and adopted Thomas Gainsborough's famous painting of actress Sarah Siddons as his logo. Paramount Pictures returned to Hollywood, fame and fortune.

Balcon installed glass walls (to use natural light), darkrooms, printing labs, props, scenery shops and dressing rooms. It was the biggest, most technically advanced film studio in Britain. Under him, the talents that emerged in all fields of the film business – actors, producers, writers, musicians, cameramen, photographers and directors such as Carol (*Third Man*) Reed and Hitchcock – were truly amazing. Hitch's first murder thriller, *The Lodger* – based on Jack the Ripper, and starring (bizarrely) light opera star and impresario Ivor (*The Dancing Years*) Novello, was a Gainsborough Picture. Hitch said his time here was the happiest of his career (see Hitchcock, Alfred). Not only was Balcon the only producer who gave him freedom to do as he wished, everyone knew everyone else because staff get-togethers were regularly organised. Stars associated with Gainsborough (Stewart Granger, Margaret Lockwood, James Mason, Michael Rennie, Jean Simmons, Michael Wilding, *et al.*) are still household names eighty years later.

1936 Having made Gainsborough Films and Islington Studios famous, Balcon leaves and does the same for Ealing Studios.

1938 Gainsborough Films is bought by Gaumont British (GB/Gainsborough) who owned eight of Islington's 18 cinemas. *Fanny By Gaslight*, a Victorian romantic melodrama, is still shown today. Parts were filmed on the **Regent's Canal** outside the studio door.

Gainsborough now specialised in romantic dramas set in a uniquely English past, the eighteenth century novel on film. These were for home consumption, about love, lust and betrayal in the Regency era. *The Man in Grey* was phenomenally successful and three of Britain's biggest box office draws, Margaret Lockwood, Stewart Granger and James Mason, mesmerised wartime audiences in *The Wicked Lady*.

1945 Sydney <u>Box</u>, Gaumont British Executive Producer, tries out a new scriptwriter. Welsh poet Dylan <u>Thomas</u> worked on *Me And My Bike*, *The Beach of Falesa* and *Rebecca's Daughters*, none of which survives.

1947 Gaumont British bought by J. Arthur Rank.

1949 After 170 films, Islington Studios closes. Annual British box office sales had slumped to only £1.4 billion (still ten times more than in 2000!).

....

GELDOF, Sir Bob. (1954–)

Musician

1975 Starts *Boomtown Rats* '... *to get rich, to get famous and to get laid.*'

1977 Joins mates in a squat in **Tufnell Park Road** N7, reeking of dogs, rotting carpets, leaking gas and marijuana. He amused himself by setting up elaborate traps and caught twenty-six mice in one night. One of the gang saw God in a vision while on an LSD trip and joined a monastery, thereby escaping a drugs bust. Up before Clerkenwell Court was Geldof, star in embryo, who would go on to be showered with honorary degrees and music industry awards.

1984 *Do They Know it's Christmas?* for *Band Aid* sells 7 million copies. The following year

Geldof staged the astonishing *Live Aid* concert, which raised £50 million for Ethiopian famine victims and earned the Irish citizen an honorary British knighthood (1986).

GISSING, George (1857–1903)

Novelist and socialist

Gissing Walk N1

1878 Age 21, returns from America. Moved to 5 Hanover Street (now 60 **Noel Road** N1) to write the first of his fourteen novels, *Workers In The Dawn* (pub.1880) describing the degradation caused by poverty. A decade later, he published *The Nether World* (1889) and *New Grub Street* (1891), also set in Clerkenwell. Close friend of H.G. Wells.

GOLDSMITH, Oliver (1728–1774)

Playwright

1757 A penniless Irishman, he leaves the University of Leiden (John <u>Wilkes</u>' *alma mater*) and, apparently, travels straight to Islington where, apart from teaching in Mrs Milner's Seminary, **Cross Street**, he eked out a living writing for *The Monthly Review* and *Critical Review*. When he died, Goldsmith was worse than penniless, he was £2,000 in debt. He styled himself Dr Goldsmith although no evidence for a medical degree has ever been found.

Goldsmith was flamboyant, a dandy with a penchant for purple silk underwear and a scarlet cloak which he wore to Highbury Barn and The White Conduit House.

1761 John <u>Newbery</u>, publisher, moves into **Canonbury Tower** and publishes Goldsmith's successful *Goody Two Shoes* (said to be the first children's book) and 119 letters in his *Public Ledger*, written by Goldsmith, signed *Citizen of the World*. He spotted the commercial viability of nursery rhymes so folllowed up with *Mother Goose Book of Nursery Rhymes*. For two years Newbery paid £1 a week rent to Mrs Fleming, the landlady, for the feckless Goldsmith's Elizabethan oak-panelled room on the first floor (now two rooms). In return, Newbery got him to do hack work.

1762 Produces work of distinction in poetry, essay, novel and drama and begins to be known. He wrote *The Vicar of Wakefield*, for which his other great friend and supporter, Dr <u>Johnson</u>, found a publisher and saved him from being gaoled for debt. Johnson founded *The Literary Club* with his beloved 'Nolly' or 'Goldy', who, he said, was an '*eccentric vagabond.*' They sometimes met at The Old Red Lion at The Angel. Goldsmith worked with Dr Johnson on *The Gentleman's Magazine*, **St John's Gate** as a book reviewer.

1763 26 June, Boswell's *London Journal*: '*I then walked out to Islington and went to Canonbury House, a curious old monastic building now let out in Lodgings where Dr Goldsmith stays. I drank tea with him and found him very chatty ... (Goldsmith) ... is an ugly little man with a face like a pock-marked monkey, a fumbling and ineffective talker because of his transparent eagerness to shine ... absurd, warm-hearted and loveable.*' Goldsmith leaves Canonbury to be near Dr Johnson at the Temple.

GORDON RIOTS, The

1778 Lord George <u>Gordon</u> (1751–1793), MP (at 23), President of the Protestant Association, is furious when Parliament passes the Catholic Relief Bill (up to now Catholics are forbidden to own property and therefore precluded from voting or running for parliament).

1780 Gordon leads his 'no Popery' followers into the House of Commons with a petition to get the Bill repealed. The petition was rejected and Gordon charged with treason. Rioters burned down Catholic chapels of foreign ambassadors, shops, businesses and houses owned by Catholics and non-C. of E. places of worship.

The Lord Mayor refused to call out the troops, so William Hyde JP, of 27 (61) **Cross Street**, ordered out the militia. Bad move. With 10,000 troops on the streets, Protestant rioters stormed his house and made a bonfire of his possessions in the street. The mob then marched to burn down Clerkenwell Bridewell and release the prisoners. On the way they passed Grimaldi's house near Sadler's Wells and ordered him to put up a notice, *No Catholics Here*. Instead he wrote *No Religion At All in This House*. When they got to the prison, the Governor offered a deal. He would free the prisoners if they didn't damage his prison. They agreed.

The Nonconformist Selina, Countess of Huntingdon (q.v.) was held in high esteem, so the mob left her Spa Fields Chapel alone. Wilkes, who had previously led the largest riots London had ever seen, now turned gamekeeper. He braved snipers' bullets and took personal charge of the defence of the besieged Bank of England, shooting down some of the rioters and throwing others into the river. The Pikemen of the Artillery Company, City Road (see Honorary Artillery Company) were called out as rioters tried to burn it down. Wilkes then issued a warrant for the apprehension of 'all idle and disorderly persons' in his ward of Farringdon Without. This, sneered his one time supporters, was a very *general* warrant indeed (Wilkes had fought for years, and had even gone to prison, in order to ban general warrants. See Wilkes, John).

....

GOSWELL ROAD EC1
The well was probably once called God's Well.

1640s To defend the City against royalists, Oliver Cromwell fortifies the road with battery (three sections, each with two guns and four ammunition wagons with a major as battery commander, a captain and three subalterns) and breastwork (mound of earth and trenches).

1748 Gordon's Gin opens at 132 (on land once owned by St John's Priory) to rival Booth's Gin, **Cowcross Street**. As both are still with us today, they clearly survived the competition.

1785 Charles Green, balloonist, is born here.

1821 Green invents the guide rope and makes the first ascent with carburetted hydrogen (coal gas). He filled his balloon from Piccadilly gas main and flew from Green Park to Barnet.

1836 Green flies from Vauxhall to Weilburg, Nassau. He made five hundred ascents but in 1870, relaxing at home in Ariel Villa, 51 **Tufnell Park Road**, died of a heart attack. In Dickens' *Pickwick Papers*, Mr Pickwick is lodging here with Mrs Bardell.

1847 Thomas Hancock invents vulcanised rubber and founds the India Rubber Company.

1934 Finsbury Council compares the cost of lighting Goswell Street between gas and electricity. Electricity was cheaper, so the council progressively replaced the old gas lamps and followed this up in all its major thoroughfares.

1940 WWII, 15 October, a bomb hits gas and water mains under an air raid shelter. 200 locals were never found (See WWII).

1991 International PEN moves in.

Originally Playwrights, Editors, Novelists, now also scriptwriters, translators, historians, *et al.* A non-political, worldwide association of writers. The Prison Committee holds a Day of Imprisoned Writers, 15 November every year. Fourteen thousand members in ninety-four countries speak up for freedom of expression for those in prison or experiencing harassment. They oppose political censorship in times of peace and encourage criticism of governments. Members have included George Bernard Shaw, Joseph Conrad, Paul Valery and Thomas Mann. Past Presidents have been John Galsworthy, H.G. Wells and E.M Forster. Present Vice Presidents include Nadine Gordimer, Arthur Miller and Mario Vargas Llosa.

1998 The road is dug up thirty times because of new technology (BT, London Electricity, Thames Water, British Gas, Cable TV and Frontier Cable TV).

1999 The 200 residents who perished in WWII are, finally, to get a memorial.

GRANVILLE SQUARE EC1

Named after Granville Sharpe, an anti-slavery campaigner and relative of the landowner.

1831 St Philip's Church is built at the top of Granville Steps (next to the present London Ryan Hotel). Of its one thousand seats, 728 were to rent. 272 were free but under windows or in uncomfortable positions with no view of the altar.

1859 St Philip's is the first C. of E. church to abolish pew rents. How to pay the vicar? Send the plate round for a collection! (Possibly the first church collection in England?)

1860 Granville Square in undermined when excavations are dug for the new underground railway in time for the second Great Exhibition of 1862.

1922 Arnold Bennett writes *Riceyman Steps*. The historic steps which lead from King's Cross Road to Granville Square are now protected.

1937 Although featured in Bennett's *Riceyman Steps* (q.v.), this doesn't save the church from being demolished.

GREENAWAY, Kate (1846–1901)

Artist

Lived 32 of her 55 years in Islington. The first 'child centred' illustrator, she revolutionised illustration for children's books and (like Laura Ashley) started a craze in Europe for 'The English Style'.

1851 Kate (5) moves to **Upper Street**, opposite **Islington Green** N1. Her mother opened a shop to sell children's clothes. Her father was a draughtsman for *Punch* and *Illustrated London News*, which she pored over, frightened by Cruikshank's *The Burning of Edward Underhill* in Harrison Ainsworth's *The Tower of London*. Another early memory was seeing Sam Phelps (see Sadlers Wells, Theatre, *et al.*) as *Henry IV, Richard III* and *Henry V* at Sadler's Wells. The family stayed here until a bigger shop became vacant further down Upper Street opposite St Mary's.

The two wings (present-day No. 147) of what was once an Elizabethan country house had been converted into shops. Kate and her family lived in the flat above for twenty happy years until, rich and famous, she bought a house in **Holloway**. Kate, one of four (three girls and a boy) had an idyllic childhood, allowed to play between **Barnsbury Street** and Wellington (now **Almeida**) Street.

1857 Age 11, attends art classes in William Street, Claremont Square. Talented, she was transferred to Miss Springett's Art School, **Canonbury House**.

1873 At 27, publishes *Little Folks*. This enabled her to buy 11 **Pemberton Gardens**, Holloway N19 where she lived with her parents for a further 12 years.

1876 Kate, who seems never to have experienced romance, and Walter Crane publish *Quiver of Love*, a series of Valentine cards.

1877 Publishes *Under The Window*, portraying a world of flowery meadows light years away from congested Islington.

1880 Illustrates Ann and Jane Taylor's *Original Poems For Infant Minds*.

1884 Commissions Norman Shaw, England's most famous architect to design a house in Frognal, Hampstead where she illustrates Robert Browning's *Pied Piper of Hamelin*. A friend and neighbour was George du Maurier who also lived in Islington for many years. Their conversations were not about art but about gardening.

1901 Dies (55). Cremated at Worthing. A memorial was built at Highgate Cemetery but, untended, became overgrown and forgotten. Kate is still commemorated by *The Greenaway Medal* awarded annually for the best British children's artist.

1997 BBC TV *Antiques Road Show*, a tiny Greenaway water-colour is valued at £10,000.

....

GRIMALDI, Joe (1779–1837)
Islington: Home of the Clown

The modern clown, anyway. The one who crops up as light relief in Shakespeare disappeared along with his plays during the Commonwealth under the humourless Cromwell.

1778 Giuseppe Grimaldi, dentist to Queen Charlotte, arrives from Big Italy to settle in **Little Italy** (q.v.), an area bounded by **Farringdon Road**, **Mount Pleasant** and **Clerkenwell Road**, still the focus for Britain's Italian community.

1782 The stage-struck dentist is appointed fencing, dancing and ballet master at Sadler's Wells. Age 65, he had an illegitimate son also called Joseph. Little Joe, aged two, made his first appearance at the 'Wells' where he trod the boards for 50 years. He lived all his life in Islington, was a great local character, actor manager of the 'Wells', where he topped the bill for many years.

1800 Joe introduces slapstick comedy as *Guzzle the Drinking Clown* wearing a Harlequin costume and red half moons on his white painted face. For many years after this all clowns in England were called Joey.

1822 Moves to 8 Baynes Row (**Exmouth Market**).

1827 Crippled, Grimaldi (48), is carried on stage in a chair at the 'Wells' to bid his fans 'adieu'.

1829 Moves to 23 **Garnault Place**.

1837 The much-loved clown dies. Dickens, who often saw him perform, edited his memoirs. Clerkenwell man through and through, the most famous clown in Britain was buried at St James', **Pentonville Road**.

1985 St James', built 1778, is demolished though the facade is kept. Its cemetery was renamed **Grimaldi Park**. Each year, *The International Circus Clowns Association* lays a wreath on Grimaldi's grave. A local pub was renamed The Harlequin in his memory.

....

GROOM, John (1845–1919)
Social worker
Islington: Home of Care in the Community

Young crippled watercress sellers, ragged and dirty, forage for food. Many others are blind or dwarfs, paralysed or limbless. They pick through the flowers and watercress discarded by Farringdon Market stallholders and trudge to Covent Garden to re-sell the best bits.

Encountering such misery every day a local silver engraver, John Groom, 21, pioneered special housing, industrial training, residential care and holidays for the disabled. Born in **Finsbury** he lived most of his life here. Slogan: '*disabled people are people first.*'

1866 Near **Farringdon**, Groom provides food every day at noon for the flower girls. London was Europe's wealthiest capital but these girls had no food, fire or furniture in their slum dwellings. There was no drainage or clean water but plenty of disease, crime, drunkenness and prostitution. Before long he had a soup kitchen, clothing club, evening school and *The Watercress and Flower Girls Mission* to get them off the streets and into domestic service where at least they would have a home.

1875 Buys 8 **Sekforde Street** (some sources say he was born here) and takes out leases on the properties nearby to house homeless girls.

1893 Sir Hugh Myddelton Model School for two thousand pupils is opened by the Prince of Wales. Thanks to Groom, it provided special education for deaf, dumb and blind children.

1894 Groom moves from Forester's Hall, **Clerkenwell Road** to nearby Woodbridge Street Chapel. Girls were housed and fed and work at an occupation they found fulfilling, creative and rewarding. This was his first Industrial Training School. Using their specialist knowledge, they made delicate artificial flowers fashioned from silk and wire which fashionable women wore as corsages.

1908 Takes over a factory on the corner of **Sekforde Street** and **St James' Walk**. 300 disabled girls worked here and lived in the surrounding streets.

1912 The Flower Girls Mission produces 13 million roses for the first Alexandra Rose Day, which raised £18,000 for hospitals.

1932 The Watercress and Flower Girls Mission is now called John Groom's Crippleage. His Sekforde Street factory was too small so he moved it to Edgware where it still is. His old factory became a tobacco warehouse. In 1950 it was the London base for Mono Pumps and in 1980 it was taken over by another charity, *Help The Aged*.

....

GRUB STREET (Re-named **Milton Street**)

(*Grube, a drain*). *Writers in Grub Street, Moor Fields were (and still are) called 'hacks' after 'hacquenee', French for the dray horse hired to pull a carriage. Like hacquenee ('hackney') horses, writing 'hacks' are for hire. Grub Street becomes a generic term for any haunt of* 'poor writers of weak will and mistaken ambition' *hired by anyone who buys words. (In his Dictionary, Johnson self-mockingly defines a lexicographer as* 'a harmless drudge, an underpaid hack'.)

1560 John Foxe, former tutor to Thomas Howard, takes lodgings in Grub St.

1563 Publishes *The Book of Martyrs' Acts and Monuments of Protestant Heroes*, denouncing Thomas More. Reprinted four times in his lifetime.

1655 For Islingtonians used to theatres, brothels, bear baiting, gambling dens and other entertainments, life was no fun under Cromwell. Dancing around the maypole, adultery and celebrating Christmas were forbidden. There were no writers, musicians, painters or concerts – hence *The Farting Club* determined to have fun. It met every week '*to pyson the neighbourhood with noisome crepitations*'.

1735 *Grub Street Journal*, satirical weekly (sort of early *Private Eye*) is launched to make fun of *The Gentleman's Magazine*.

1982 Parts demolished to make way for the **Barbican** development.

H

HAC (Honourable Artillery Company)
City Road EC1

Official escort of the Lord Mayor since 1653. The monarch is still escorted into the City when necessary by the HAC.

1274 Welsh Barons come to London to pay homage to Edward II.

Needing trained archers for defence of the realm, the king established a Territorial Army (TA) out of these loyal volunteers, the world's finest bowmen. The 'English' Longbow was actually Welsh. They invented both the bow and the accompanying two-fingered insult (so powerful it took two fingers instead of one to draw, hence when the French captured English bowmen, they cut off the index and middle fingers of their right hands.)

1537 <u>Henry VIII</u> grants Letters Patent to the Guild of St George and Science of Artillery, known as the Artillery Company (AC).

1543 Henry re-organises the Guild of St George.

He passed a law that every father must give his son a bow and two arrows on his seventh birthday and all men under 40 (clergy excepted) must practise at the butts every day instead of playing football. Butts were stone or wooden targets of differing heights. There were 164 in Moor Fields. Provided an archer shouted 'Fast!' before taking aim he could not be prosecuted for causing any death from a stray arrow.

1588 10,000 members of the AC or Trained Bands fight against the Spanish Armada.

1641 The Artillery Company settles in what will one day be **City Road**.

1685 The word Honourable is used for the first time in front of Artillery Company.

1735 Armoury House re-built.

1751 <u>Frederick, Prince of Wales</u>, heir to the throne, plays cricket here for The London Club. He was struck on the head with a ball, which led to his untimely death. His son became <u>George III</u>.

1771 HAC takes over firing of Royal Gun Salute at The Tower of London.

1780 HAC defend the Bank of England as Gordon Rioters try to burn it down (see Gordon Riots).

1781 The Finsbury Archers, formed 1681, are disbanded. Archery obsessives found The Toxophilite Society, later The Royal Toxophilite Society, patron George IV.

1784 Britain's first hot air balloon takes off from Armoury House.

1786 HAC form guard of honour for King of Denmark, since when the regiment has taken part in the guard of honour for all Royalty, Heads of State and members of the British Royal Family visiting the City.

1815 Battle of Waterloo. The <u>Duke of Wellington</u> includes the HAC in his *'infamous army'* speech, saying it was made up from *'the scum of the earth. I don't know about the enemy but by God, they frighten me.'*

1828 Armoury House re-built.

1857 Joseph <u>Jennings</u>, architect, designs the New Artillery Ground Militia Barracks (Finsbury Barracks) in castellated style with battlements and turrets.

1860 The Artillery Company is officially declared Honourable by Queen Victoria.

1902 One hundred and ten Islingtonians, many from HAC, die in the South African (Boer) War.

1914 HAC, oldest regiment in the British Army, senior unit of the Territorial Army (TA) fight in WWI (as it did in WWII).

1999 Oldest surviving regiment in the world. One of the few bodies allowed to march through the City with drums beating, colours flying and bayonets fixed. (The Regiment is not allowed to be armed inside borough boundaries, so fixes bayonets outside).

....

HALLEY, Edmond (1656–1742)

Astronomer Royal (1721)

Islington: Home of Gravity and Halley's Comet

1665 The Great Plague rages. Edmond <u>Halley Snr</u> buys a house in Islington (location not known), a fashionable rural suburb of the city, and moves here with his family to escape.

1682 Edmond Halley Jnr marries Mary Tooke, a barrister's daughter. His father gives them an allowance of £60 p.a. (worth maybe £25,000 today) and the house in Islington. Halley built an observatory with a 24-inch telescope and used the 5½ foot sextant he had taken with him to St Helena to collate all the observations made of all twenty-four comets so far known. He was the first to realise that a comet seen in 1456, 1531, 1607 and now over Islington in 1682, was the same one taking seventy-five years to orbit the sun and ergo, predicted its return in 1759. Sixteen years after his death, he was proved right.

1683 Writes *Philosophical Transactions*.

1684 Plucks Isaac Newton from self-imposed obscurity.

Halley's observation that there are inequalities in the motion of Jupiter and Saturn led to Newton's law of gravity; while his observation of a transit of Mercury, proving that comets move in elliptic orbits around the sun, inspired Newton's *Principia Mathematica*. Halley introduced the world to trade winds, climbed Snowdon to test a barometer and correctly predicted a total eclipse of the sun (Tuesday 6 March 1715). Edmond Halley Snr died in suspicious circumstances (probably suicide) and his body was washed up in the Thames at Rochester. It looks as if his stepmother claimed everything, because the couple moved out of the house in Islington and Halley, for the first time in his life, was forced to take paid work (appointed Clerk to the Royal Society).

2000 His two hundred observations made in Islington are in the archives at Royal Greenwich Observatory.

....

HALTON ROAD N1

1642 Frans Hals' *The Laughing Cavalier* (Wallace Collection, London), one of the world's most famous paintings, is, some sources say, of rich Islington landowner, the royalist, Sir William <u>Halton</u>, Lord of the Manor of Barnsbury. He married Ursula Fisher, daughter of Sir Thomas <u>Fisher</u>, Lord of the Manor. Halton also had a full-length portrait painted by Van Dyck, He died 1662,.

1726 Descendant, Sir Thomas Halton dies at Newington Green.

HARVEY, Len

World-famous boxer, fought successfully at several weights.

1923 Age 16, leaves idyllic Cornwall for grimy Islington.

1929 British Middleweight champion.

1933 Light-heavy and Heavyweight champion.

1936 Three British and Empire titles, Heavyweight, Light-heavy and Middleweight

1939 Wins World Heavyweight title from Jock McAvoy.

1942 After 418 contests, Harvey, 35, is knocked out for the first time in his career. Losing his Light-heavyweight title to Freddie Mills, he retired from boxing and joined the Army as a PT instructor.

1946 Takes over Star & Garter pub, **Upper Street** (here since 1831 when a licence was granted to convert a private house, 43 Hedge Row, now No. 45, into a pub).

1973 Retires from the Star & Garter

1976 Dies at home in **Penn Road**, age 69. The Star and Garter changed its name (after 142 years) to The Champion in his honour.

1983 Star and Garter, a.k.a. The Champion, is re-named The Passage, then The Steam Passage. Britain's greatest fighter since Randolph Turpin was forgotten.

....

HICKS HALL

Magistrates Court

*Once known all over Britain because journey miles from London, inscribed on every milestone, were measured from here. A derelict WC in **St John Street** EC1 now stands on the historic site.*

1560s Magistrates have been meeting ever since Edward III first appointed them in 1361.

Sir Baptist <u>Hicks</u>, rich silk mercer, MP, JP for Middlesex (London was part of Middlesex until 1900) presided over the Middlesex Quarter Sessions in the upstairs room of The Castle Inn, St John Street. Crime (as defined in the sixteenth century) was rife. Non-attendance at church, punishable by imprisonment, was typical of the cases which came before Sir Baptist.

1588 William Goughe, Islington innkeeper, indicted for overcharging on wine.

1590 Edward Reeve of St John Street indicted for following the occupation of tallow chandler without serving an apprenticeship.

1591 George Dancaster indicted for: '... *living as a vagabond being over age 18, healthy and sturdy in body able to work ... nor exercising any lawful trade, craft or mystery by which he could live and being unable to give any explanation of how he lived.'* This was his second conviction as a vagabond. First offence, punished with a whipping and branded on the ear, second, sentenced to be hanged unless someone 'credible' offered him work.

1610 Sir Baptist is fed up with holding court in a common pub. He told James I that, if given the land, he would build a court house at his own expense. He could afford it, he was the sixth richest man in England (£7 billion).

1613 First Quarter Session at new Hicks Hall. Fourteen knights/squires were appointed Magistrates, Justices of the Peace (JPs). They could determine sentences for any offence against the King's Peace. They also looked after administration of the county, repair of bridges, upkeep of highways, punished vagabonds, licensed innkeepers and maintained the established religion. One of the first up before the bench was charged with abuse of

James I's majesty: *'Recognizance for the appearance of John Leveridge of Clerkenwell to justifie an information that he hath given against Philip Conistoune for speaking diverse threating and darying words against the kinge.'*

Corpses of executed criminals with no relatives were given to trainee surgeons at **Bart's** to be publicly dissected.

1614 Cases heard include those charged with *'refusing to watche, tippling without licence, not cominge to churche for the space of three months, Richard Smith for dividing his house, Thomas Kitchen for assault'.*

1660 The trial of *'29 Regicides, murderers of his most sacred majesty Charles 1. This day the bloody murderers of the late king are removed to the common prison of the county to be tried at the Sessions House, St John Street.'* Colonel <u>Okey</u> of Cromwell's New Model Army, drayman in an Islington brewery, one of Charles I's judges, who escaped to Holland following Cromwell's death, was brought back and hanged.

1685 James, Duke of York, sues Titus <u>Oates</u> for libel.

THE BRAN TUB PLOT

Oates, employed to spy on the Jesuits, had concocted a story about a Popish Plot (called The Bran Tub Plot, presumably because of his name) to 'murder' Charles II. As a result, many (probably innocent) Catholics were executed. The Grand Jury found Oates guilty of perjury and of thirty-five *'judicial murders'*. Hanging Judge Jefferies (who had colluded with Oates in his original story) sentenced him to be pilloried five times and whipped from Aldgate to Newgate before being imprisoned for life. King <u>William</u> and Queen <u>Mary</u> believed arch-liar Oates, ignored the findings of the Grand Jury and ordered him to be released on a pension of £300 p.a., on which he lived to a bad old age.

1780 The crime rate is rising due to rapidly increasing population and new penal laws introduced to deal with it. 220 offences earned the death penalty. Hicks Hall was too small so, after 167 years, a new Sessions House was built on **Clerkenwell Green**. There was talk about putting up a stone column with lamps at the top to act as a milarium, inscribed *'Here Stood Hicks Hall, pulled down 1782. Miles from London were measured from here.'* Nothing came of it.

....

HIGHBURY

Originally High Borough

1066 <u>William the Conqueror</u> gives the Lordship of the Manor to someone called either Ranulf or Dereman (sources differ). The land was bounded by **Crouch Hill**, **Stroud Green**, **Balls Pond Road**, **Newington Green** and **Essex Road**.

1271 Lady Alicia de <u>Barowe</u> (whose antecedents, along with those of de <u>Berners</u>, made up most of the twenty-seven local landowners in the Domesday Book) gives the Lordship to the Knights Hospitallers (see St John's Priory).

1371 Robert <u>Hales</u>, Prior of St John's, First Baron, Lord High Treasurer of England, builds a magnificent moated castle (inspiration for London Underground logo for Highbury & Islington Station).

Hated by the oppressed peasantry, Hales was the third most powerful man in England after the king and Archbishop of Canterbury. Born 1320 in Cheshire, he became a novice knight at St John's, age 16. Sir Robert, *'organiser of fleets and naval expeditions, constructed afresh the manor house of Highbury and made it as elegant as the alternative paradise as good as the garden of Eden.'* The palace *'of considerable beauty'*, built of stone, a rare commodity, was filled with priceless loot from Hales' sack of Alexandria (1365), tapestries purloined from the east, sculptures from Greece and furniture from France. The blatant show of wealth and privilege was to locals what Versailles would be to the *'sans culottes'* in revolutionary France.

1381 Poll Tax Riots. Robert Hales, hated tax gatherer, is dubbed Hob the Robber. While Wat Tyler was burning down St John's Priory Church, Jack Straw burned down Highbury Castle, Hales's country home. It was never rebuilt. The blaze was so intense it was seen by rebels miles away in Hertfordshire on their way to join the riots. The ruins were known for 600 years as *Jack Straw's Castle* (commemorated in the pub on Hampstead Heath).

1483 Locals build a conduit over a spring in Highbury Fields which feeds **St Giles Cripplegate**.

1536 Thomas Cromwell is given the Lordship as reward for seeing through the Act of Supremacy.

1541 Cromwell arranges Henry VIII's marriage to the displeasing Anne of Cleves. As punishment, he lost Highbury along with his head. His goods reverted to the crown.

1564 An annual custom of the Mayor and City officials is to inspect the sources of London's water supply so Elizabeth I visits Highbury Fields. She combined business with pleasure, hare hunting in the morning, fox hunting in the afternoon.

1641 James I grants Highbury to his son Henry, Prince of Wales.

Following his early death (Henry was 16) his brother Charles I sold it to Sir Allen Apsley, Royalist leader, who sold it on to Thomas Austen, who cleared Highbury Woods. This was the last Islington saw of the great Forest of Middlesex. No more oaks or beeches, pigs had to forage for 'pannage' (acorns and horse chestnuts) elsewhere.

1770 Austen sells Highbury to Sir George Colebrooke who sells it on to John Dawes, Islington's first property developer.

1781 Col. Alexander Aubert FRS, astronomer and wealthy stockbroker, retires to Highbury House with its 74-acre park (part became Arsenal Stadium), shrubberies, gravel walks, fishponds and kitchen gardens. (**Aubert Court/Park/Road**)

An English eccentric of French origin, Aubert built a three-storey observatory from where he could view shipping on the Thames as far away as Gravesend, Kent. When in town, the king visited Aubert and his observatory whenever there was anything worth seeing. William Pitt also came here.

1787 A print in Islington library shows haymaking in full swing. London's healthiest village was nicknamed London's Lung. Because it was a rich farming area which supplied milk, cheese, butter, etc. to the city, it was also known as London's Dairy.

1791 Dr William Saunders, physician to the Prince Regent, builds Highbury Hill House.

1792 Aubert, appalled by the growing Republican movement (thousands supported the London Corresponding Society at Copenhagen Fields, hoping for a revolution) forms two private regiments, infantry and cavalry. They drilled in his back garden in dry weather, in the livery stables at Tyndale Place, **Upper Street** when wet. The regiments, dressed in blue and gold uniforms, lasted until 1801.

Islington: Home of the Electric Telegraph (forerunner of the Fax Machine)

1796 Francis <u>Ronalds</u>, 8, moves to 1 **Highbury Terrace** with his family (**Ronalds Road** N5). He pioneered the electric telegraph and was knighted. The prototype was tested over a wire between his house and a nearby cottage.

1803 *The Times: 'On Thursday last the Gentlemen of the late Corps of Loyal Islington Volunteers dined together at Canonbury Tavern for the purpose of presenting a magnificent Silver Cup of the value of 250 guineas to Alexander Aubert Esq., their late Commandant in testimony of their esteem and affection.'*

1852 Leigh Road is the filled-in moat of Highbury Castle. No. 29 is Belfiore Lodge, later the home of Leslie <u>Henson</u>, actor, who made films at Islington Studios (q.v.). *'Our grandest house was Belfiore Lodge. It had a tower with a flagstaff, stables and a really lovely garden.'*

1885 Islington Vestry buys the 25 remaining acres of Highbury Fields (of the original 300) and opens them to the public. They were meant to rival Hyde Park but greed prevailed and Islington ended up with a few pathetic acres.

1905 Australian sculptor, Sir Bertram <u>McKennal</u>, designs the bronze figure of *Glory* on the War Memorial in Highbury Fields, to commemorate local men killed in the South African (Boer) War. Of the men who died, 110 were from Islington, many from HAC **City Road**. Driver Glasock, a Holloway man, was one of four VCs awarded.

1986 Loyal Islington Volunteers' Cup, made in 1802, auctioned in Glasgow, bought by an American collector for £33,000 is saved for the borough by local journalist, John *(Save The Cup)* <u>Oakes</u>. Cup now in V&A Silver Gallery.

....

HIGHBURY CORNER N1

The Cock pub has been on this site since medieval times. When people couldn't read, inn signs were adverts. This one advertised cock fights.

1772 The Cock is a familiar carriage stage post (passengers pay for each 'stage' of their journey). It's still a bus 'fare stage' today.

1800 Pasture land is owned by Farmer Laycock who keeps cattle sheds (**Laycock Street**) where drovers can fatten emaciated beasts cheaper than at **The Angel**.

1830 Horse-bus route, No. 43 established (disgruntled passengers quip that, 170 years later, they're still waiting for it).

John and Elizabeth <u>Wilson</u> were granted a licence to run omnibuses from Holloway Road, Highbury Barn and Archway Tavern into the City. They used the former Laycocks Dairies cattle sheds at the rear of 5 Sebbons Buildings (built 1806, now 235 **Upper Street**) as their depot. When tollgates were abolished, work became easier for their 39 drivers. Wilson's was London's largest horse-drawn omnibus company with a fleet of 48 buses, 500 horses and 180 employees. On Sundays, church services were held for employees at the depot. (Omnibus, see also Shillibeer, George).

1872 Modest Highbury Station (built 1849) is re-built, a grand affair with fancy gables, chimneys and finials. The complex, which incorporated the Cock Tavern, resembled St Pancras Station.

1904 Keir <u>Hardie</u>, MP for Merthyr Tydfil, founder and first Chairman of the Independent Labour Party (HQ **Drayton Park**), and Ramsay MacDonald, later elected the first

Labour Prime Minister, address a mass meeting of the unemployed at Highbury Corner.

1908 Another huge meeting of the unemployed at **Highbury Corner** is broken up by police.

1914 Tidmarsh Window Blinds, founded in Islington 1827, moves to Laycock Street. Although the company supplied all the royal palaces for 172 years, it was not awarded the Royal Warrant until 1993. All the front windows of Buckingham Palace have Tidmarsh blinds.

1928 Revd Donald *(Soap Box)* Soper is a hugely popular Highbury Corner speaker. Famous for his black cassock, socialism, pacifism and teetotalism, throughout his long life he was a friend to the down-and-out. (See Soper, Donald)

1944 WWII. A flying bomb, one of the last German V2 rockets to be launched, wipes out magnificent Highbury Station.

The crater was the beginning of today's roundabout, for years one of the worst traffic bottlenecks in London (see Traffic). The Highbury Corner end of **Compton Terrace** was so badly damaged it had to be demolished. Islington was bombarded with V1s and V2s (see World War Two). The V1 *(Vergeltungswaffe* means revenge) was the doodlebug or buzz bomb, a small, jet-propelled, pilotless aircraft which was simply allowed to crash when its fuel ran out. The V2 was targeted, the first long-range ballistic missile. 47 feet long, it hit its target at a speed of 3,000 mph. One of the 517 which landed on London fell on Highbury Corner, killing 24 people and seriously injuring another 155.

1953 A new Highbury Station is built.

1967 When the Victoria Line opens, the station is renamed Highbury & Islington.

1986 George Orwell's old drinking haunt, The Hen and Chickens opens a theatre upstairs. Its sixty Edwardian seats started life in Drury Lane Theatre.

1996 Mike Newell directs *Four Weddings and a Funeral,* shot on location at **Highbury Corner, Highbury Place, St James' Clerkenwell** and **St Bartholomew The Great**. Stars Charlotte Coleman and Hugh Grant in wedding gear flag down a black cab to take them to St Bartholomew's for one of the eponymous weddings. Screen on the Green patrons clapped at the shots. Grant's first appearance on stage in London was at Dan Crawford's **King's Head Theatre** (q.v.). Coleman, daughter of the actress Ann Beach, lives in the borough.

....

HIGHBURY CRESCENT N5

1907 Jessica Tandy, actress, born at 21 **York House**. She sat for Walter Sickert when she appeared in *Hamlet* with Sir John Gielgud. Emigrated to America 1945. Married Hume Cronyn, who was in Hitchcock's *Shadow of a Doubt*. Played the mother in Hitchcock's *The Birds* (after a Daphne du Maurier story), took the starring role in *Driving Miss Daisy* when she was nearly 90 (Bette Davies wanted it) and won an Oscar.

1936 Sydney Weekes, designer of London Underground posters and HMV record sleeves, is at 7 York House, the same time as Ms Tandy.

1959 Faraday's old Sandemanian Chapel closes in Barnsbury and re-opens here at No. 3 (now closed).

HIGHBURY GROVE N5

1799 Disaffected Anglicans, spiritually unfulfilled by St Mary's worship (calling themselves Unionists), take over Highbury Chapel (built 1793) but move out when Union Chapel (q.v.) is built in **Compton Terrace**.

1806 The disused chapel is converted into two houses. (No. 18 is now a local authority residential home. When No. 16 was demolished, the party wall was covered with a landmark mural, *Wild Islington*.)

1847 When Christ Church is built, the public footpath across **Highbury Fields** is known as Church Path.

1852 Spencers & Sons convert a garage at No. 56 into a hot air balloon factory which, it's said, was visited by the balloon crazy Graf von Zeppelin.

1893 Warwick Deeping, novelist, lives at No. 37. His *Sorrell and Son* castigated the English class system. *Paradise Place* was about Islington.

Islington: Home of Television (Radar, etc.)

1902 The world's first cathode ray tube is made by Cossor's Radio Company (now UNL).

1913 Charles Cruft moves to No. 12, where he lives 25 years (see Cruft, Charles). His wife remained here another eleven years after his death. Because their house was knocked down to build Highbury Grove School, his plaque was put on the block of flats opposite.

1918 Cossor's Radio Co. moves to Aberdeen Works, behind 16–18. Researchers collaborated with Aldo Marconi (28), inventor of radio. He proved that ships needed radios when the *Titanic* sank (1911). Although we remember how many died, through his invention over 700 lives were saved and England gave the Italian a knighthood. Dr Crippen was arrested via Marconi wireless (see Crippen, Hawley).

1962 The first X-ray tubes and radar receivers are made by Cossor's.

HIGHBURY NEW PARK N5

Twenty stone axes dating from 20,000 BC have been found in this area.

1872 Confirmed atheist Edward Aveling, 21, marries Isabel Frank at **Union Chapel**. The couple lived with her mother at No. 178. The marriage didn't last although they never divorced. Ten years later he was living with Eleanor Marx, daughter of Karl.

1882 The Athenaeum, 96 is built for concerts, debates and lectures.

1918 Athenauem converted into Highbury Film Studios.

1936 The Grand National Film Company takes over the studios and sub-lets them to independent film companies such as Tudor Films, owned by the Marquess of Ely. *Sam Small Leaves Town* starring Stanley Holloway, *I Killed The Count* with Ben Lyon and *Law and Disorder* starring Alastair Sim all came from here. Film producers made 'quota quickies' to comply with the law (because of the predominance of American films, the government forced cinemas to show a quota of British films).

1938 *The Arsenal Stadium Mystery* directed by The Boulting Brothers featuring the current team is released. Islington filmgoers cheered when the curtain went up (see Arsenal).

1940 WWII. A resident phones Scotland Yard in a panic to report that German paratroopers and uniformed Nazis have captured the studios. They turned out to be extras for *Pastor Hall*, a Boulting Brothers film starring Marius Goring based on the life of Martin Niemoller who survived eight years in a concentration camp.

1947 Rank takes over the studios to make B-movies, develop special effects, train technicians and establish The Rank Charm School.

Groups of 30 promising young actors were groomed for stardom on six-month courses. The school taught them elocution, deportment and fencing. Joan Collins, Christopher Lee, Diana Dors, Dirk Bogarde and Kay Kendall were all Rank Starlets between 1947 and 1952. Rank paid promising young actors a princely £20 a week. Michael Caine, 17, was kicked out when he was caught smoking in the loo. Rank released *To the Public Danger* starring Dermot Walsh, Susan Shaw and Patricia Hayes, and *Penny and the Pownall Case* starring Christopher Lee and Diana Dors. Studios were rented to television companies.

1950 High Definition Films take over the studios. Islington filmgoers recognised parts of the borough when the curtain rose on the Boulting Brothers' *Seven Days to Noon*.

1953 ATV take over the studios for popular shows *Sunday Night Theatre, Emergency Ward 10, Take Your Pick* and *Double Your Money*.

1963 Studios are demolished for council flats.

....

HIGHBURY PARK N5

1860 Edward <u>Teschemacher</u> (changed his name to Lockton during WWI), leading songwriter of the day, moves to No. 1 (then Aubert Park) and stays seventeen years. He wrote 2,000 songs. Sales ran into millions, including the sentimental smash hits *Because* (*God made you mine I'll cherish thee*) recorded by Caruso, and *Until (you speak to me with accents sweet)* recorded by John McCormack.

....

HIGHBURY PLACE N5

1483 Locals enclose a spring (in front of what will be No. 14). Pipes, some of fired clay, others of lead, carried water via this conduit to **St Giles Cripplegate** in the City. The spring was in use until 1811.

1564 <u>Elizabeth I</u> is in Highbury with the Mayor of London inspecting the city's water supply.

1770 The old conduit is used to fill individually owned reservoirs behind Highbury Place, a Georgian Terrace built without an architect. The shells were copied from *The Pattern Book for Country Houses* and buyers chose their own interiors.

1790 John <u>Wesley</u>'s friend John Horton in No. 25 is the last person he visits. He dined with him 22 February. Next day, Wesley aged 88 preached at Leatherhead, Surrey but, taken ill, returned home and died 2 March.

Islington: Home of the Banknote

1806 Abraham <u>Newland</u>, Chief Cashier at the Bank of England, buys No. 38.

The long war with France forced England to conserve gold reserves so he asked the Privy Council for permission to replace gold with paper as barter. Bank notes, each equivalent to its stated worth in gold, bore his face and signature so were dubbed 'Newlands'. As each one was numbered and easily traced and as forging banknotes carried the death penalty, Newland earned the gratitude of the drovers (q.v., see Drovers), no longer robbed by highwaymen. Newland retired after sixty years' service and died at home the same year, 1807.

1819 Thomas <u>Wilson</u>, rich son of a rich businessman who made a fortune selling hair ribbons, lives at No. 12 (his barrister son lived at No. 35). Wilson Snr built, entirely at his own expense, Claremont Chapel **Pentonville Road** (now Crafts Council Gallery).

1826 John <u>Nichols</u> of No. 14, editor of *The Gentleman's Magazine* since 1792, drops dead on the stairs on his way up to bed. Nichols was educated in Islington as was his son John (Bowyer) Nichols and grandson John (Gough) Nichols, who both succeeded him as editor of the magazine.

1845 The <u>Chamberlain</u> family including Joseph (9) move into No. 25 where Wesley was once a frequent visitor. They were here for twenty years. Joseph attended prep school at 36 Canonbury Square.

1854 Joseph <u>Chamberlain</u>, 18, leaves his beloved Highbury to work for his cousin at Nettlefolds Engineering, Birmingham, determined to make his fortune and devote the rest of his life to his hobby, politics. It took him 22 years. He called his home *Highbury* (now the name of the whole district). His brother Richard was MP for Finsbury. His sons, half-brothers Austen and Neville, followed in his footsteps and did even better. Austen was leader of the Conservative Party, Chancellor of the Exchequer, knighted and awarded the Nobel Peace Prize. Neville became Conservative Prime Minister *('The Appeaser of Munich')*.

1858 The old water conduit can still just about be seen.

1927 Walter <u>Sickert</u> opens an art school at No. 1.

1986 The most expensive house in Islington, No. 38 is where Abraham <u>Newland</u> died two hundred years earlier. It sold for £450,000.

....

HILLS

Extend from Smithfield to Hampstead (as any cyclist will confirm). Some in Islington were given names such as **Back**, **Eyre Street**, **Herbal**, **Hermes**, **Highbury**, **High Gate**, **Pentonville**, **Rising**, **Saffron** and **Vine**.

....

HITCHCOCK, Sir Alfred (1899–1980)

Film Director

Made films here for 20 years after First World War (1919) until the outbreak of the Second (1939). Fate and his passion for films led him to Islington Film Studios (q.v.), and The Master often reminisced about his happy years spent there learning his craft.

'Hitch' was enrolled at St Ignatius College, **Stamford Hill** the same year that Dr <u>Crippen</u> of Holloway was hanged. He read every gory detail in the *News of the World*, as he did with Islington's, George 'brides in the bath' <u>Smith</u>. He hated his name, so re-invented himself simply as Hitch.

1919 Age 20, Hitch is living with his widowed mother in Leytonstone, working for Henley Telegraph and Cable Company. Film mad, he bought all the trade papers and in *Bioscope* spotted an ad by Paramount Pictures based at Islington Studios for a sub-titler (silent films). The company was planning *The Sorrows of Satan* so he read the novel, made up story cards and put a portfolio together. By the time of his interview the film had been abandoned in favour of *The Great Day* and *The Call of Youth*. Overnight he made new drawings and next day took them to the studios. He was to spend 20 creatively fulfilling years there.

Hitch arrived a lonely young man yearning for recognition and left, the most famous film director in Britain, with a loving wife and daughter, a country house and a flat in town. Paramount made eleven films here, none survive. Shot with hand cranked cameras, they were filmed outside (lack of light inside) until the talkies arrived. They were then filmed at night (less traffic noise), in soundproof studios. Hitch did the title cards for every film for the next two years. Desperate for fame and fortune, he was the first to arrive each day and the last to leave, determined to experience every aspect of film making.

1921 Working with Scottish director Donald Crisp on five films. None survives.

1922 Working on four crime thrillers, none survives. His colleagues were Mordaunt Hall who became film critic for *The New York Times* and Tom Geraghty who went on to write films for Douglas Fairbanks Snr.

For all their advanced technical equipment, Paramount's films flopped so, to raise money, the company started renting studio space to independent film makers.

1923 Writing scripts, designing sets and costumes, production manager and assistant director to Graham Cutts on *Woman to Woman* (Seymour Hicks: *Always Tell Your Wife*): *'Halfway through . . . the Director was taken ill. A fat youth who was in charge of the property room . . . volunteered to help me. It seemed a forlorn hope but . . . we carried on as co-directors. His name was Alfred Hitchcock'.*

1924 Paramount Pictures returns to America (in 1953 Hitch was to work for them again in Hollywood). His career for the next 12 years was interwoven with that of Michael <u>Balcon</u> and Gainsborough Films. Their first picture together was *The Passionate Adventure*, co-produced by Myron Selznick (in 1939 Hitch was taken on by David O. *'Gone With the Wind'* Selznick, Myron's brother). Hitch was mentor to his assistant director, Roy <u>Ward</u> <u>Baker</u> who worked on 38 films at Islington. He went on to be a successful director, lauded for his 1957 *A Night to Remember* and 1967 *Quatermass and the Pit*. Together, he and Hitch enjoyed six uninterrupted years of constant work.

1925 Hitch's *The Rat*, written by and starring Ivor Novello, is released.

An outstanding success, two more *Rats* were in the pipeline (*Triumph of The Rat* and *Return of The Rat*). Balcon sent Hitch and tiny, red-haired film editor Alma Reville to Germany to film *The Pleasure Garden*. She was a brilliant film editor and screenwriter with whom he had worked for three years since she joined the studio. Hitch had now directed three films so, with a secure future ahead, popped the question: *'It was unthinkable for a British male to admit that a woman has a more important job than his and I waited until I had the higher position – assistant director'* he wrote. Hitch, 25, fat and lonely, now had Alma (first and only friend) as soulmate. The marriage was based on professional symbiosis, lifelong devotion, mutual admiration and competitiveness and it survived.

1927 Two Hitch films, *Downhill* and *Easy Virtue*. Gainsborough released Hitch's first murder thriller *The Lodger*, based on Jack The Ripper. Despite distributors keeping it on the shelf for two months because they didn't like it, this impressive example of what was to become his trademark horror genre opened to huge critical acclaim. *Biocope* said it was *'possibly the finest British production ever made.'* This was the first true Hitchcock film, full of his familiar, dramatic visual touches. He said: *'It was the first time I exercised my style . . . you might almost say it was my first picture.'* Locals were taken on as extras in the final scene, which showed Novello pursued by a lynch mob. Hitch at 28 was the highest-paid film director in Britain.

1927 Headhunted by British International Pictures (BIP) while still contractually committed to Gainsborough, as was Alma.

1934 Signs a five-picture contract with Balcon.

1936 Balcon leaves Islington for Ealing.

1938 Gainsborough catch the mood of impending war in *The Lady Vanishes*, one of Islington Studios' all-time greats and Hitch's 97-minute passport to Hollywood. His most famous English film confirmed his reputation. Hitch said he would film it in a month (it took 5 weeks). His wife Alma and daughter Pat, 10, were on the set with him. Although the dumpy, middle-aged lady in tweeds (Dame May Whitty) disappeared from the train in a realistic-looking Europe, the film was actually shot in **Poole Street**.

1939 Gaumont British buy Gainsborough Films. Balcon had left Islington, war was in the air and parents were advised to evacuate their children. Invited to Hollywood by David Selznick, Hitch accepted. He wasn't to know it but his happiest days as a film maker were over. Now, the big studios would control his artistic output. In old age he returned in memory often to his beloved Islington, but he never came back.

HOGARTH, William (1697–1764)

'Father of English Art'

Britain's most famous satirical artist was born in **Bartholomew Close** *and christened in St Bartholomew's the Great (the font is still there). Artists were painting scenes from classical mythology of no relevance to ordinary Londoners. Hogarth was the first to depict low-life, holding a mirror up to the society of his day. A Governor at* **Bart's,** *his murals of The Good Samaritan and The Pool of Bethesda can still be seen on the staircase. His 'Evening' shows Sir Hugh Myddelton and Sir Walter Raleigh 'drinking' tobacco at the Myddelton Head (adjacent to Sadler's Wells).*

1703 William's father, a classics master, opens a coffee shop in **St John's Gate**. The menus were in Latin. The venture was not a success, he went bankrupt and was imprisoned for five years. Mrs Hogarth was reduced to peddling Gripe Ointment and other patent medicines on the streets. William never forgave him.

1713 William is indentured for seven years to a silver plate engraver.

Islington: Home of Copyright

1735 Fed up with being pirated by copyists Hogarth gets the Engraving Copyright Act, dubbed The Hogarth Act, passed. He visited Bedlam (q.v.) in Moor Fields to sketch the patients and showed them in The Rake's Progress wearing jester's hats.

1737 John Gay's The Beggar's Opera glorifies thieves, prostitutes and gangsters of nearby Hockley-in-the-Hole, depicting the depraved side of life. Hogarth loved it and engraved scenes from it.

1740 Publishes *Gin Lane*. Four Acts of Parliament had failed to close unlicensed gin palaces. There were 7,000 gin shops in London. Cheap corn adulterated with turpentine equalled cheap gin and people unconscious in the gutters were a common sight. The public outcry which ensued carried through The Gin Act of 1751. Embarrassed by *Gin Lane*, parliament increased the tax on gin.

1747 Paints *The Stage Coach at the Angel Inn*

1762 Carving out his place in High Society, Hogarth falls out with his friend, the radical John Wilkes, who accuses him of selling out on his art of '*gibbeting in colour*'.

1764 Dies at 67. It's said that twenty-five years later, when his vault in Chiswick was opened to receive his wife, his remains were missing.

....

HOLLOWAY PRISON

Built in 1852, grand 'Holloway Castle' with its towers and turrets (J.B. Bunning, City Architect, copied Warwick Castle) dominated the skyline for 100 years. City Prison, built on a cemetery owned by the city, was called just 'Holloway' by locals.

1895 Oscar Wilde inside for two months awaiting trial. No stranger to Islington, in 1883 he appeared, aptly, in *New Babylon* at The Philharmonic, **Islington High Street**. Visited by Bosie (Lord Alfred Douglas) every day, they were allowed fifteen minutes but the din was so bad and Oscar so deaf, Bosie had to shout to make himself heard. It must have been a shock to Wilde to see that prison uniform really did have the broad arrows beloved of music hall comics. He was so huge, his had to be especially made for him, so at least it was new and it fitted.

1903 Now women-only: prostitutes, drunks, failed suicides and those found guilty of abortion. 3 February, the brothers Billington hanged 'baby farmers' Amelia Sachs of East Finchley and Annie Walters of Islington.

BABY FARMING

What to do with thousands of unwanted babies, pre-Abortion Act? That was the question (not to find the men responsible!) facing Mrs Sachs, who ran a home for single mothers and charged them £30 to get their babies adopted by '*wealthy parents who will leave the children their fortunes*'. When the babies were born, Mrs Sachs telegrammed Mrs Walters of 11 **Danbury Street**, who took them home and drowned them in a copper bath (said to be still hanging in the back yard as late as 1989). One day she asked a fellow lodger to buy carbolic acid and chlorodyne, strange things to have on anyone's shopping list, especially if your landlord is one Police Constable Seal. He put a tail on her who stopped her and asked to see inside her bag. Inside was the corpse of a two-day-old baby boy. The women were found guilty of the joint murders of an unknown number of children. The case brought about the 1908 Children's Act, in which '*notice must be given to the Local Authority by any person undertaking for financial reward the nursing and maintenance of any infant under the age of seven and to inform the authorities of any change of address*'. Paid Infant Protection Visitors were appointed.

1906 Sylvia Pankhurst and other suffragettes brought in a Black Maria with drunks and prostitutes are imprisoned for two months with no privileges. They wore prison clothes and found black beetles in their food.

1912 Catherine Griffiths, a nurse from Finsbury, is imprisoned for trying to break into the House of Commons to put nails on PM Lloyd George's seat '*to make him sit up and take notice of women.*'

1913 Hunger strikes begin. Suffragette martyrs were force-fed by a rubber tube pushed up the nostril or down the throat. Later, women were no longer allowed to die, at least not on government property. Hunger strikers at the point of death were let out on 'temporary release'. The government was determined they would not be martyrs for the cause.

1928 All women over 21 are given the vote. The Women's Movement disappeared until the 1960s (see Feminism).

1939 WWII. Lady Diana Mosley (held her wedding reception at Goebbels's house in Germany) is detained under Defence Regulation 18B. Her friend Lord Berners sent in food parcels. The prison received a hit from one of her hero's bombs while she was here.

1943 Husband, fascist leader Sir Oswald Mosley in Brixton prison is given permission to join his wife at Holloway. They had their own kitchen, bathroom and garden and their children spent the occasional night. At the end of the year they were released although Churchill thought they'd be safer in prison because, given a chance, the mob would lynch them.

1944 Helen Duncan, a medium, accurately predicts the sinking of two British warships. Considered a threat to national security, she was convicted of being a witch and gaoled, the last to be tried under the Witchcraft Act of 1735.

1954 13 December, Mrs Christofi is hanged by Albert Pierrepoint for the murder of her daughter-in-law. No-one took much notice, Mrs Christofi was foreign, middle-aged and unattractive.

LAST WOMAN HANGED IN ENGLAND

A year later it's a different story. Hundreds gathered, watched by mounted police. Albert Pierrepoint was to hang Ruth Ellis, 28, for killing lover David Blakely, 25. Ellis' solicitor was Victor (later Lord) Mishcon (famous forty years on for handling the divorce of Diana, Princess of Wales). The condemned cell was 15 x 14 feet, the bed had a pink and brown cover, there were three chairs and a table and a wardrobe on castors, which hid the door leading to the execution chamber (trapdoor just 15 feet from the bed). Albert Pierrepoint (£15 per execution) practised the drop with sandbags the same weight as the condemned. The traditional last wish of the fifteenth and last woman to be hanged in Britain was to have carnations put on her lover's grave. Seven months later, Pierrepoint, subjected to public vilification, resigned as Public Hangman. Ruth Ellis was buried within the prison grounds; in 1971 she was re-buried in Amersham. (In 2000, Home Secretary Jack Straw was wavering over the question of a pardon.)

1960s Moors murderess Myra Hindley is held here, as was Christine Keeler (perjury, a sop to public opinion). Hindley's social worker (a nun) tried to help her escape.

1965 Abolition of the death penalty on a five-year trial. It was never brought back. The execution chamber was dismantled.

1968 The prison is re-built. It now bears no resemblance to Warwick Castle.

1984 *Dance With a Stranger*, a film about Ruth Ellis, is filmed in **Clerkenwell Close**.

1996 Rosemary West is held, awaiting trial.

....

HOLLOWAY ROAD N7, N19

*There are 'hollow ways' all over England which often led to a market but none as famous as this one, leading to the most ancient of markets, **Smithfield**, the largest in Europe. Once a steep hill, Saxons called it Hohl Weg (hole way) because the cattle wore it away (see Drovers).*

1284 A hermit on High Gate fills the potholes with gravel and charges drovers to pass. The place he took the gravel from in time formed another hole, which became a pond in rainy seasons (**Pond Square**).

1364 Edward III orders tolls to be collected to gravel the road.

1695 Ralph Thoresby, antiquary, topographer, museum curator, close friend of Bishop Burnet, reports on the *'terrible state of the holey way and the danger of riding along it with its deep ruts full of water'*.

1717 Turnpike collects tolls to mend the road.

1737 Dick Turpin, famous highwayman, holds up coaches in Hornsey Lane, a favourite place for footpads (Cruikshank, Islington resident, illustrated Harrison Ainsworth's *Rookwood*. One drawing was *Dick Turpin Leaps Hornsey Toll Gate*). Another infamous highwayman who worked the same area was Claude Duval (**Duval's Lane**), arrested in **Hornsey Road**. Gay's *The Beggars Opera*, first shown that year, glorified highwayman Jack Sheppard, famed for his four amazing escapes from Newgate (see Sheppard, Jack).

1787 Among the *Cries of Old London* is: *'Holloway cheesecake, makes yer teeth ache.'*

1790 People living along the road sell goods from their front rooms, giving rise to Marshal Ney's, *'A nation of small shopkeepers'*. It was the beginning of the end of *The Cries of Old London*.

1806 Edward Lear, poet and illustrator, is born in **Bowman's Place** (see Lear, Edward).

1810 Robert and James Pollard, famous print makers, move to Holloway (see Pollard).

1815 Highbury Brewery opens at No. 54, where a well yields a thousand gallons of water every hour.

1818 After more than 1,000 years Islington has a second Church of England. St Mary Magdalene, a Chapel of Ease, takes the overspill of St Mary's.

1830 In *Our Mutual Friend*, Dickens has the Wilfers living here.

1860 Mary Tealby opens the world's first animal refuge (See Battersea Dogs' Home).

1865 James Collinson (once engaged to Christina Rossetti) co-founder of the pre-Raphaelites with Holman Hunt and Dante Gabriel Rossetti (fellow students at The Royal Academy) moves to 15 St John's Park (now **St John's Grove**).

1873 The Betjemans move to 329 (see Betjeman, John)

1879 The Great Northern Hospital relocates here from Caledonian Road.

1887 The water table is dropping. At Highbury Brewery the well is bored a further 50 feet.

1888 Newly built Great Northern Central Hospital is opened by its president, the Prince of Wales (Edward VII). Philanthropist Angela Burdett-Coutts (founder of the NSPCC) funded the out-patients Department.

1891 Charles Cruft, at 325, shows dogs at the Aggie (see Cruft, Charles).

1900s The Parkhurst Theatre at 401 is converted into a cinema. It had yellow, green and brown decor with green velvet pile carpets, tessellated floor, marble dados and yellow and gold embossed wallpaper. Lit by gas, it had eight fire exits.

1903 Frank Matcham's magnificent Marlborough Theatre (397) opposite the **Nags Head** pub opens with The Carl Rosa Opera Company.

1910 At The Electric Pavilion (643) audiences are given souvenir badges to wear as walking adverts.

1911 The hospital opens an X-Ray Department.

1912 The Holloway Grand Picture House (194) is truly grand. It had castellated towers, a stained glass dome over the entrance hall and lights operated by dimmer switches. Steam-heated in winter, it had a sliding roof for the summer. Electricity came from nearby **Eden Grove** sub-station. Patrons were no longer irritated by whirring projectors, they were behind thick plate glass. Highbury Imperial Picture Theatre (2, near **Highbury Corner**) was another purpose-built cinema. It had a white marble entrance (see Cinemas.)

1914–18 WWI. The Great Northern Hospital has more casualties than it has room for so takes over North Library around the corner in **Manor Gardens**. The People's Picture Palace closed. Highbury Brewery closed (a public house, The Brewery Tap opened on the site. Licensing hours were introduced during the war to encourage diligence among armaments workers).

1919 Marlborough Theatre (No. 397) re-opens as a cinema. It had apple green carpets, tea lounge with cane chairs, palm trees and a 'ladies boudoir'.

1921 Marie Stopes Clinic (see Stopes, Marie) opens at 61 **Marlborough Road**. The Great Northern Hospital was given a Royal Charter. It was now called The Royal Northern.

1923 A war memorial was put up in the doorway of the Royal Northern.

1926 Parkhurst Theatre (401 Holloway Road) closes (now Holloway Arcade).

1935 Holloway Grand (194) is renamed The Regent.

1937 The ABC (643) closes.

1938 The Holloway Empire is demolished. A 3,000-seater, the last Gaumont built was opened (417) by Jessie Matthews and Will Hay. The opening was broadcast live on BBC radio and featured in *The Radio Times*.

1939 WWII. The Savoy (338) is the only new cinema to open during the war.

1954 CND movement starts. (See Campaign for Nuclear Disarmament)

1957 The Gaumont, bombed during the war, re-opens.

1958 Sex Pistol, John Lydon is born in **Benwell Street** off Holloway Road (see Sex Pistols).

1959 Highbury Picture Theatre (2) closes (now Majestic Wine Warehouse).

1960 Joe Meek who wrote the hit tune *Telstar*, moves into No. 304.

1970 Cat Stevens, bearded song-writing pop star, of **Digswell Street** off Holloway Road, records *Matthew and Son*, *My Lady D'Arbanville* and *Moon Shadow*.

1973 The Gaumont is now an Odeon.

1976 Yusuf Islam, the artist formerly known as Cat Stevens, uses his royalties to establish an Islamic school.

1982 Michael Fagan of Holloway (address unknown), painter and decorator, single parent of six, hops over the wall of Buckingham Palace and disturbs the Queen's beauty sleep. He commented that the palace was shabby and could do with a facelift.

1983 Coronet cinema is now a snooker hall.

1987 People's Picture Palace is now the National Youth Theatre of Great Britain. 3,000 young people audition every year for a hundred places. Founded by Michael Croft in 1956, alumni include Kate Adie, Timothy Dalton, Alex Kingston, Daniel Day Lewis, Ian McShane, Helen Mirren, Lisa Tarbuck, *et al.*

1993 First red route in London. No stopping from **Archway** to **The Angel** (see Traffic).

1994 Royal Northern Hospital demolished to build houses. Locals fight successfully to have the war memorial incorporated into the new development.

1997 Death (in Paris) of Diana, Princess of Wales. David <u>Hillman</u>, campaigns officer for the UK Working Group on Landmines (HQ Holloway Road, see Landmines) said she *'put landmines in everybody's living room.'*

HOOD, Thomas (1799–1845)
Poet

1807 Family moves from Poultry to 50 Lower Street (**Essex Road**). His father was a bookseller. The house must have been grand because he couldn't understand why Colebrooke Cottage appealed to Charles <u>Lamb</u>. *'A cottage of ungentility for it had neither double coach house nor wings. Like its tenant it stood alone.'*

1811 Father dies.

1813 Leaves school and works as a clerk, after two years he suffered a breakdown.

1819 Mother dies leaving him responsible for his 4 sisters.

1821 Sub-editor, *London Magazine*. Meets <u>Lamb</u>, Hazlitt, Clare, de Quincey *et al.* He dedicated poems and books to Lamb.

1825 Marries Jane Reynolds at St Mary's Upper Street. They visited the Lambs three evenings a week and enjoyed many parties there. Hood liked recounting a favourite tale of getting drunk with <u>Lamb</u> and Theodore <u>Hook</u> in the Old Queen's Head (their local), and Lamb challenging fat Hook to race him round the garden of Colebrooke Cottage.

1826 Proprietor of the *Athenaeum* magazine.

1827 Their baby son dies. The couple move to **Upper Street**.

1829 Starts *The Comic Annual*.

1832 Leaves Upper Street.

1839 Starts *Hood's Own*.

1841 Editor *New Monthly Magazine*.

1845 Dying, Hood is visited by Dickens. He was buried at **Kensal Green** in a grave of rose granite with a plinth topped by a bronze bust and scenes from *Song of the Shirt*, considered his most important poem. Within a short time everything was stolen, sold for souvenirs.

2000 *Radio Times* poll of 25,000 readers to find the nation's favourite childhood poem. *I Remember, I Remember (the house where I was born)* is Number One. The problem is that no-one knows precisely where Hood was born.

HOPE AND ANCHOR
Upper Street N1
Seminal rock music venue

1973 Many bands make their debut and go on to become world famous (ageing fans from all over Europe still make the pilgrimage here), even though the room was so small that queues stretched two miles around the block. New Musical Express reviewers called it *'the cramped cloister of an Upper Street basement.'*

1976 The Stranglers, The Jam, Tom Robinson Band.

1977 Generation X, The Vibrators, Wayne County and The Electric Chairs, X Ray Specs, Police, Squeeze, Elvis Costello and The Attractions.

1977 Stiff Records Xmas Party. WEA Records released a live double album featuring the groups whom the Hope and Anchor made famous.

1978 Police, Adam and the Ants, The Skids, Joy Division (first London gig).

1979 The Damned, The Specials, Madness, Dexy's Midnight Runners, Cockney Rejects.

FIRST LONDON APPEARANCE OF THE WORLD'S TOP BAND

December, *U2*, first London gig. *Rolling Stone* named *U2* as the leading band of the '80s. After *The Joshua Tree*, *U2* appeared on the cover of *Time*. In 1997 a concert in Phoenix Park had to be cancelled because it was too expensive (£12m) but in 1979 at the Hope & Anchor, only nine people turned up …

1997 The pub gets its music licence back and paints guitars on the windows.

....

HORNBY, Nick (1962–)

Writer

Nick *'I have measured out my life in Arsenal fixtures'* Hornby lives in **Highbury** and puts Islington in his books (it won't be long before fans set up a Hornby Trail).

1992 He puts Arsenal FC in *Fever Pitch*, which (up to 1995) sold 30,000 in hardback and 190,000 in paperback and was a successful film starring Colin Firth. Arsenal FC made him a millionaire. A second-hand record shop in **Holloway Road** features in *High Fidelity* (1995) and *About a Boy* (1999) is, well, about a boy at Highbury Grove School.

2000 *High Fidelity* and *About a Boy* are made into films. *High Fidelity* is set, where else, in America.

....

IRA

1858 Irish Republican Brotherhood in Dublin and The Fenian Brotherhood in New York are launched to overthrow English rule in Ireland, which wasn't to be accomplished until 2000. Finn was a Celtic leader whose followers called themselves *Fiannans* or *Fenians*, 'warriors'. Re-named the Irish Republican Army (IRA) after the Easter Uprising of 1916.

1867 Clerkenwell, traditionally republican, ironically gets the first Fenian bomb.

17 November, **Clerkenwell Green**, four thousand gathered to protest at the proposed execution of three Fenians in Manchester. 20 November, Richard <u>Burke</u> and Joseph <u>Casey</u> were arrested, charged with treason and remanded to Clerkenwell House of Detention. Burke wrote to his sister via his solicitor. In invisible ink on the reverse of the letter was his escape plan. 21 November, Clerkenwell Green, 25,000 gathered to petition Queen Victoria for clemency for the Manchester Fenians. 23 November, Fenians were hanged in Strangeways prison. 12 December, Fenians tried to spring Burke and Casey. They threw a ball over the wall of Clerkenwell House of Detention to warn them to fall out of the exercise line, but then failed to ignite a barrel of gunpowder. The authorities were alerted and the pair removed to another part of the prison. 13 December, three men and a woman trundled a 30-gallon cask containing 548 lb of gunpowder under a blanket down Corporation Lane. They asked a little girl playing in the street to bring them a match. Beneath the prison wall was the gas main. The blast demolished **Corporation Lane. Bowling Green Lane, Coburg Street, Plumber Place, Rosoman Street, St James**

Buildings, **Seckforde Street**, **Shorts Building** and **Woodbridge Street** all suffered damage. Forty of the 120 injured (including prisoners) suffered terrible disabilities and fifteen, including the little girl who gave the match, died. Patrolling police arrested the three men running away from the scene. A plaque on the wall inside commemorates the tragedy, another inside St James' Church **Clerkenwell** was unveiled by Disraeli (q.v.).

1868 26 May, the new 'tube' at Farringdon disgorges two thousand sightseers who have taken the day off to see Mick <u>Barrett</u> (all Irishmen are called 'Mick' after this), Fenian ringleader, who masterminded the Clerkenwell bomb, hanged above the main gate of Newgate prison. He had been found guilty at the Old Bailey of the murder of Sarah Hodgkinson, the little girl who gave the terrorists the match and was blown up. Barrett was the last man in England to be hanged in public.

1888 Twenty years later Gladstone, convinced that Ireland must have Home Rule, is still campaigning. It will be another forty years and a civil war before the Irish Republic is created and more than 100 before The Good Friday Agreement brings a modicum of peace and order.

....

IRVINE, Lucy

Writer and castaway

1980 Irvine, 24, an Inland Revenue clerk living in Islington, is attracted by an advertisement in the Travellers section of *Time Out* for a 'wife' to live on a desert island. The advertiser, Gerald Kingsland, 50, a modern-day Robinson Crusoe, had lived on many desert islands. He received fifty-two replies and interviewed twenty. Four made the short list. He met each three more times before deciding on Lucy. They married 3 April and left for Tuin Island, Brisbane, Australia. The experiment was a disaster and they split up. From one small ad came two best-sellers and the film *Castaway*.

....

ISLINGTON

Islington, or Yseldon in Welsh, was a clearing in The Great Forest of Middlesex. In 1900 it became part of the County of London but definitive boundaries were not drawn until 1967. Sparsely populated until the 1860s (in 1821 people were still stumbling over cows in the dark), it lies in the Thames basin where sand, gravel and limestone provided a superb filter system for crystal clear springs. Water settled between the grains, and (before tarmacadam) wherever it met soggy London clay, it burst through to form a spring. There were at least eighteen wells here and in the main, the water was sweet tasting though a few were bitter with a high iron content. Islington's name, like that of the poet Keats, is 'writ in water ...'

20,000 BC We know people lived here because their axes have been found.

450 BC Celts wander over from mainland Europe. As this place was called Yseldon, Welsh for *the place of wells*, one tribe probably settled here.

AD 61 The Romans build a fort here and do battle with Boudicca (see Barnsbury)

449 AD Saxons call this place *Isen Done. Isen* means 'iron' so presumably referred to those wells with high iron content. Anglo-Saxon *'burh'* became *'bury'* or borough, a fortified settlement armed against invasion. Burhs were self-governing with the right to issue by-laws, grant liberties and privileges by legal charter and be represented in Parliament. It may be that Alfred the Great conferred burh status on Islington.

Some wells are given names. *Bagnigge Wells* (where Nell Gwynne had a country home) was probably named after the owner. *St Chad's Well, Clerken Well* (Anglo-Saxon plural for clerk) *Goswell* (God's Well/Good Well) *Chis Well* ('chysel', stony or gravelly place or old English 'ceosol', flint or pebble), *Loder's Well* in Smithfield, *Sadler's Wells* (holy wells one owned by St John's Priory), *Fagge's Well* is below **Cowcross Street**, *Rede, Tod* and *Rad* wells are yet to be re-discovered – although in 1997 a well was found in a **St John Street** basement. Uniquely for drought-plagued Britain, Islington has an excess of ground water. When it rains, deep tube stations are sometimes closed.

628 AD St Mary's Church, **Upper Street** first built around now.

1017 St Chad's Well (**King's Cross**) has been a place of pilgrimage for centuries. **Chad Street** is still on the same spot, as is, presumably, the well.

1066 <u>William the Conqueror</u> takes all land outside the City. Until 1066, the 'City' was London and London was the City. Then they separated into the old City and the newly created City of West Minster (William was crowned in the abbey), home of the Court.

1349 As the City expands so does Islington.

1562 Ralph <u>Agas</u>, surveyor, draws the first known map of London. The bird's eye view shows sheets drying on tenter hooks in Finsbury Fields (still there 100 years later; see Davenant), windmills and archers practising at the butts and Islington *'on the waye to St Alban'*, with *Schmyt Fielde* (**Smithfield**), *St Bartholomew, White Cross Street, Red Cross Street, Goldinge Lane, Olde Street, Chis Well Street, Charterhouse* and *Canonbury Tower*.

1596 The City takes over **Smithfield Market** and tries to change its name to Newgate Street Market. It, clearly, never caught on.

1600 Bad plague year. 322 burials in Islington (average is 47).

1664 Population is 22,342. Only 2,000 lived in Islington, the rest were in **Clerkenwell**. Roads were so bad, toll gates/turnpikes were built and the money collected used to mend them.

1733 Heyday of **Islington Spas**.

1739 Anglican churchwardens ban John <u>Wesley</u> from preaching at **St Mary's** (see Wesley, John and St Mary's).

1772 The Lighting Act is passed, to the relief of residents who suffered robberies, assaults and murders in the dark. The Marquess of <u>Northampton</u> hands **Islington Green** to the borough. A Watch House, cage and stocks are built.

1784 Thomas <u>Lord</u> starts the White Conduit Cricket Club, WCCC (precursor of MCC) in **Barnsbury** (see Lord, Thomas).

1790 Tom <u>Paine</u> writes *Rights of Man: Part One* at The Angel.

1800 A map shows Penton Ville, London's first planned suburb, built 1780.

1801 Five times as many (55,515) live in Finsbury (includes 23,396 in Clerkenwell) as in Islington (10,212).

1821 Islington is still rural. The manager of the 'Wells', Charles <u>Dibdin</u>, going home in the dark with his wife, tripped over a cow lying in the road.

1832 Cholera is rife. The City acquired ten acres in Holloway for a burial ground. There was a serious outbreak at Coldbath Prison owing to defective sewers.

1841 Islington is known as the 'walking suburb'. Albion Road, Albion Grove and Ripplevale Grove had a city commuter in almost every house. The census showed whole streets of clerks (Dickens wrote about them in *Sketches by Boz*) whose secure employment in the City meant they could afford to live further out and walk to work.

1846 The railway from the Midlands to the docks cuts through Islington. Railways meant the demise of the drovers, then stage coaches and finally, inns.

1850 Public Carriage Office, regulating London's cabs, opens in **Penton Street** (still there).

1851 Islington is now as big as most towns and bigger than many.

1855 Metropolitan Cattle Market, **Caledonian Road** (The Cally) opened by Prince Albert.

No longer would Islington see 50,000 cattle and 500,000 sheep wander through Upper Street. The new market was five times the size of Smithfield. Four hotels, one on each corner, were opened for drovers, The Lamb, The Lion, The White Horse and The Black Bull. Until the railways, 70,000 cattle a week were driven here but they soon started coming by rail and it was not long before Islington waved goodbye to its last drover.

1856 More swathes are cut through the borough's most densely populated areas when the North London Railway demolishes 900 working class homes. If houses lay in the path of the railroad, tenants were evicted; no compensation, no alternative homes offered.

1862 Garrotters and footpads make many places in Islington no-go areas.

1865 Toll Gates, never popular, are abolished.

1871 Population reaches 200,000.

1872 The 'Cally' is known for tinkers and peddlers as much as cattle. They spread their wares on the stones in the huge open-air market. A visitor remarked that: *'Stall holders are dyed in the wool Londoners with cynical expressions of Hogarthian ugliness.'* He described *'acres of tat'* (e.g., second-hand pink stays) *'nothing even a kleptomaniac would want to steal ... £100 would clear the market'*.

1882 Sainsbury's open in Chapel Market (still there). Home deliveries were made.

1886 Population 350,000.

From dawn to dusk streets echoed with raucous cries advertising just about everything for sale. Before breakfast you could find a sweep and a dustman, buy firewood, coal, milk and newspapers. Later, watercress, rabbit and bloater (fish) sellers called. Before nightfall they were joined by muffin, winkle, oyster, shrimp, hot pie, baked potato and lavender sellers.

1891 First Crufts Dog Show at the Aggie (see Cruft, Charles).

1900 Street pumps give way to standpipes, water is turned on for a few hours each day.

Islingtonians now had to travel quite some way to see countryside. **Upper Street** was grand, especially opposite Union Chapel where Rackstraw's Drapery Stores had awnings and a row of elegant street lights.

1901 Population peaks at 436,701. Clerkenwell 'rookeries' had been cleared and the poor forced further north so Islington was now more densely populated than Finsbury. Many parts of Islington were still slums however and alcoholism was a serious social problem. Henry Ansell, leader of the Islington branch of The Band of Hope Temperance League, set up his HQ in Temperance Hall, Church Passage (**Dagmar Passage**, now Little Angel Puppet Theatre). Islington had by now lost the carriage trade which patronised the newly-developed West End.

1910 Dr Crippen, murderer, makes Islington infamous.

1911 Fred Seddon, murderer, does likewise.

1914 As does George (*brides-in-the-bath*) Smith.

1931 English National Opera and The Royal Ballet founded at Sadler's Wells by Lilian Baylis and Ninette de Valois make Islington famous again. Poverty was so bad, some parents were unable to feed their children. The Council opened 'orphanages' (many children had parents whom they sometimes visited). Tracts of Islington were designated official slums by the Medical Officer of Health (e.g. **Bastwick Street** had 45 houses, each home to four families).

1936 For the first time since the 1400s, Islingtonians have clean drinking water. The Public Health Act imposed a duty on local authorities to provide free water to every household.

1937 Population is 295,400.

1946 The concept of a Green Belt around London is approved and eight new satellite towns commissioned. When motorways were built many Islingtonians moved to them.

1950 Rationing on petrol is lifted to promote car ownership and to encourage Londoners to move to the New Towns.

Islington Council started replacing its gaslit public street lamps (lit manually every evening by a lamp lighter on a bicycle and extinguished the following morning) with electric, though gas lamps remained in parts of the borough until the 1960s (Finsbury Council had introduced electric street lighting way back in 1934). Much of bombed-out Islington was a slum and property was cheap. People who thought they would never own their own homes can now afford to buy.

1952 Thousands die of air pollution (smoke + fog = smog) in one of the world's worst (now almost forgotten) environmental disasters.

The weather was freezing, people lit coal fires in every room, the coal smoke mixed with traffic fumes trapped in a freak inversion layer that persisted for days. A cloud of dense, smelly, acrid, yellow smog crept into every crevice. There was no wind and London was choked by sulphuric acid. By three o'clock visibility was nil. The 'Wells' was putting on *La Traviata* but theatregoers couldn't see the stage. The top of Hampstead Heath could just be seen poking above the smog. At Smithfield, stockmen fitted animals with hessian masks but cattle still dropped dead with heart failure. Over two thousand people were killed in London, mostly the old, the very young and those already suffering from 'flu.

1954 CND is founded by Fenner Brockway, one-time **Myddelton Square** resident.

1956 Smokeless zones are created by the Clean Air Act.

1957 Conservatives bring in the Rent Act to make life easier for landlords. This meant that owners like the notorious Peter Rachman could charge what they liked and their properties, tenanted or not, could be sold as prices rose on the open market. Obstinate tenants who had previously enjoyed controlled rents were forced to leave ('winkled out'). Properties were bought by young couples, not tenanted by several families, so the population of bedsit Islington fell drastically. The rent on Barbara Castle's Highgate flat rocketed, so she moved to John Spencer Square, **St Paul's Road** (see Castle, Barbara).

1959 Playwright Joe Orton moves to **Noel Road** (see Orton, Joe). John Payton started his crusade to transform **Camden Passage** from a slum to the fashionable place it is today (see Camden Passage).

1962 Robert Carrier opens a restaurant in **Camden Passage** (see Camden Passage).

1965 Ken Loach's *Cathy Come Home* is filmed in **Popham Street**. It sparked a national debate on the housing crisis and put *Shelter* (charity for the homeless) in the media spotlight. Shortly after filming, slum dwellings in the street were demolished.

1966 Average price for a house is £8,000.

1967 Islington boundaries are re-drawn. Letters Patent granted Islington a new Coat of Arms. Wavy blue lines symbolise water, arrows archery, yellow crescent on red background part of Arms of Thomas Sutton, founder of **Charterhouse School**, yellow rings of Dick Whittington Coat of Arms, Maltese Cross (Knights of St John), book of learning for **City University**.

1969 Dan Crawford opens **The King's Head** theatre (q.v.).

1973 Bryan Johnson of Dagmar Terrace, author of *Albert Angelo, Trawl, The Unfortunates, House Mother Normal* and *Christy Mairy's Own Double Entry*, slits his wrists.

1981 Population is 160,890.

1988 Water is privatised. Again. The Thames Water Company was formed and located its HQ in **Rosebery Avenue**. The Red Flag was flown from the Town Hall and the borough nicknamed The People's Republic of Islington. Author Salman Rushdie was forced to flee Islington and go into hiding under sentence of death for blaspheming Islam in *The Satanic Verses* (fatwa issued by Ayatollah Khomeini, lifted in 1998). Tiny, one-bedroom flats are sold for £80,000.

1990 Islington is once more becoming an international tourist attraction. *Travel & Leisure* magazine (New York): '*This London neighbourhood is exciting, inventive, gritty and alive . . . steeped in tradition . . . as modern as tomorrow . . . it's not pretty but it's fun and feisty and decidedly bohemian.*'

1991 Population is 164,686 of whom 133,601 (68 per cent) are white (112,648 indigenous, 15,066 Irish), 8,320 Black Caribbean, 6,069 Greek Cypriot, 6,009 Black African, 3,440 Asian other, 2,935 Black other, 2,695 Bangladeshi, 2,324 Asian, 2,424 Indian, 2,141 Chinese and 615 Pakistani.

LONDON GETS ITS FIRST RED ROUTE

From Archway to the Angel, there was no stopping the traffic. One of the first casualties was Sisterwrite, the UK's first feminist bookshop. It had just about been holding on with the Council's hike in business rates and a deepening recession. The Red Route was the final nail in its coffin. Union Railways and Railtrack released plans of their overground route for non-stop, high-speed trains from the Channel Tunnel to St Pancras, blighting 1,500 homes with no right to compensation. Despite the majority not owning a car, being on the main route north they are subjected to the fumes. As well as nose-to-tail convoys of lorries, 280,000 cars a day pass through the borough. A pall of smog causes asthma and hay fever. At night, freight trains carry dangerous nuclear waste through the borough. Numerous protest movements started up. A Dr Klein, of **Wallace Road**, *spent five minutes designing an alternative route for the Channel Tunnel line and submitted it for consideration.*

1994 Articles appear daily in the nationals about 'trendy Islington'. Martin Jacques, editor *Marxism Today*, originator of *Demos* think tank, may wear Armani but the borough shared the honours with Lewisham for the highest murder rate in London (one a month). 25 per cent were unemployed, 60 per cent subsidised or no-rent, less than half owned a car.

1996 Despite Dr Klein's five-minute plan costing Union Railways £10m more, the company is forced to accept it. Chris <u>Smith</u>, MP Islington South, whose home was also affected, got the trains put in a tunnel and was voted Green MP of the Year.

1999 Population is 180,000. Most densely populated borough in London. Newspaper headlines: *'Rising ground water levels . . . 35 metres since 1970 . . . underground springs in Finsbury could solve London's water crisis.'* Islington Council (see below) was lampooned in the *Evening Standard* for sending staff on water conservation courses. A house which cost £6,000 in 1966, £15,000 in 1970, was now £500,000. 1960s office blocks were being stripped back to their steel frame underwear, transformed into luxury flats with uniformed porters, underground parking, CCTV, gymnasium, high-tech offices and views of the City. £550,000 each, they were sold before completion. An Islington bedsit took 25 minutes to sell for £65,000.

2000 Although one of the smallest of London boroughs, a mere 6 x 4 miles, Islington has: 11 theatres, (Almeida, Courtyard, Hen and Chickens, King's Head, Little Angel, Old Red Lion, Pleasance, Rosemary Branch, Sadler's Wells, Tower and Unicorn), 6 museums (Arsenal FC, Clerk's Well, Islington, London Canal, St John, Wesley), 20 art/craft galleries, 8 comedy clubs, 15 nightclubs, 40 exhibition venues and 5 annual festivals (International in June, Clerkenwell, Fleadh and Italian in July, London Canal Museum in August and Regent's Canals in September), 21 stations (Kings Cross, third busiest in London, shuffles 38 million passengers a day) and 5 street markets.

2020 (Forecast by Ian Crawley, Islington Council Town Planner.) Predicted population 210,000. Young people with high salaries living in Islington lofts communicate with each other via internet, join car clubs (hiring when they need one). The hated Archway Tower has gone and the glass roof bombed in WWII is back on St Pancras.

ISLINGTON COUNCIL

On any day in its working life, a staggering third of the Council's staff of nine thousand is absent. 8,623 working days lost every year. Staff take every day of their allotted sick leave in addition to seven weeks paid holiday (industry gets two). Social Services is condemned for sex abuse on a massive scale in its children's homes and half its over–11's, because of low standards of education, are taught outside the borough. When *A Capital Divided* is published by The <u>Peabody</u> Trust mapping poverty in Islington, newspaper pundits challenge PM Tony <u>Blair</u> about the Labour-run Council. This is the tenth poorest borough in England with more unemployment, more single mothers and a high mortality rate. Only Hackney has a higher Council tax. The Council may be strapped for cash but it is not bankrupt. It owns properties worth over £1,346m and eight leisure centres worth £26m. (See Postscript)

ISLINGTON FILM STUDIOS
Poole Street N1

The film careers of many of Britain's best known names in cinema history started here. They include: Yvonne Arnaud, Hermione Baddeley, Robert Beatty, Honor Blackman, Dirk

Bogarde, Derek Bond, Phyllis Calvert, George Cole, Cicely Courtneidge, Anne Crawford, Diana Dors, David Farrar, Stewart Granger, Greta Gynt, Robertson Hare, Gordon Harker, Kathleen Harrison, Seymour Hicks, Sonia Holm, Jack Hulbert, Glynis Johns, Mervyn Johns, Malcolm Keen, Evelyn Laye, Margaret Lockwood, Herbert Lom, John McCallum, Victor McLagen, Frederic March, James Mason. Jessie Mathews, John Mills, Robert Newton, Ivor Novello, Bill Owen, Cecil Parker, Eric Portman, Dennis Price, Michael Redgrave, Michael Rennie, George Robey, Flora Robson, Patricia Roc, Guy Rolfe, David Tomlinson, Jack Warner, Naunton Wayne, Googie Withers, Dame May Whitty, Michael Wilding, Mai Zetterling ...

1919 Americans, Adolph Zukor and Jesse Lasky of Famous Players Lasky who own Paramount Pictures, trawl London for a suitable base. Said Lasky: *'We picked a location for The Islington Studios where heavy fog would collect even when the rest of London was in bright sunshine ... the artistic soft focus photography admired by critics ... was simply fog ...'* (90 days are fogbound every winter). Paramount bought the disused electricity power station owned by the Metropolitan Railway on the banks of the Regent's Canal and converted it into the biggest, most technically advanced film studio in Britain. American production standards were introduced into the primitive British film scene.

Borough boundaries are often arbitrary. Today, **Poole Street** is just outside the borough. In 1919, it was probably inside. Until they started selling autographs of the famous stars who arrived in chauffeur driven Rolls-Royces and, in garish make-up and costume ate and drank in the local pubs, kids were mortified to lose their free heated swimming pool (the power station poured hot water into the canal). Their parents, on the other hand, were delighted. There was plenty of work for carpenters, plasterers and labourers (someone had to create desert islands and royal palaces) secretaries, machinists and telephonists. There were film sets on three floors, offices, workshops, sunken tanks for nautical effects, lifts and a restaurant for the studio workforce

1924 Michael <u>Balcon</u> buys the studios for Gainsborough Pictures (see Gainsborough Films, Hitchcock, Alfred and other entries).

1936 Balcon leaves. Gainsborough bought by Gaumont British.

1939 WWII. The Board of Trade moves in. It needed plasterers, carpenters and set designers to build dummy aircraft and tanks which were positioned all over the UK to fool the Luftwaffe. Those most gifted in special effects were recruited into the Special Operations Executive (SOE) for guerrilla warfare (imitation logs contained radio equipment, tyre-bursting bombs inside papier mâché camel droppings were scattered over the desert ...) Despite a ban, films kept pouring out right through the war, a one-studio miracle which kept up the spirits of war-weary Brits.

1946 Sydney <u>Box</u>, Gaumont British Executive Producer, arrives to say the studios are to close. The studios were taken over first by a distillery, then by a carpet factory.

1990s Films are still being made in Islington on the streets, if not in studios, e.g.: *Queen of Hearts, A Fish Called Wanda, Dance With a Stranger, Prick Up Your Ears, Minder, Distant Voices, Still Lives, The Hit, The Fear, High Hopes, Richard III, Anxiety.*

2000 *Diamonds* will be filmed in the old studios. Brad Pitt is to play a boxer in sequel to *Lock, Stock and Two Smoking Barrels*. Ralph Fiennes is here playing *Coriolanus* and *Richard III* for the Almeida Theatre.

J

JERUSALEM PASSAGE

Named after the St John of Jerusalem, an inn in the passage.

1678 Islington: Home of the Music Society

Thomas <u>Britton</u> (1654–1714), a coal merchant who also happens to be a musical genius, returns from Northamptonshire to **Clerkenwell** where as a boy he was apprenticed to a coalman (many boys left home at seven to be indentured for seven years). It was the custom that once a lad had served his time his master gave him money to set up his own business in an area where he was not in competition. Why he was apprenticed in Clerkenwell so far away from home is not known. Why he came back is not known either, what we do know is that he rented a stable here (Rates Book: 'Small Coal Man, £4 p.a.') for a coal store and slept in the long, low room above.

1678 Passionate about music, Britton starts London's first music society (membership ten shillings p.a.). *'The tickle fiddle gentlemen'* of Britton's music club played in the long room above the stable, accessed by rickety stairs. The Society lasted until Britton's death.

The eccentric Catherine <u>Douglas</u>, Duchess of Queensberry, was a regular visitor, while the then-unknown George Frederick <u>Handel</u> spent most of 1711 here with the cultured coalman. Newly arrived in London, it was here that Handel met anyone and everyone in the music world. He played the organ and harpsichord with a friend of Britton's, fellow countryman <u>Pepusch</u> who wrote the music for *The Beggar's Opera* and was organist at Charterhouse. It was only during the last years of his life that Handel became famous, what is surprising is that he was able to ascend the tiny stairs, he was so fat.

One day out on his coal round, Britton's 'cry' was recognised by Woolaston the portrait painter, who invited him up to his studio. The portrait is now in the National Portrait Gallery – not in the main collection, it can be seen by appointment. Dr <u>Garencieres</u>, translator of Nostradamus and physician to the French ambassador, who lived on the other side of **Clerkenwell Green**, became close friends with Britton, as did Henry <u>Carey</u>, who wrote *God Save the King* and *Sally* (pride of our alley).

1714 Britton dies, age 70, after a prank backfired.

The local wag, a JP called Robe, hired a ventriloquist to wait for Britton to come home one dark night and, throwing his voice, ordered the old man to fall to his knees and recite The Lord's Prayer. Britton died in shock four days later and was buried in St James Clerkenwell. After the funeral, friends such as Ned <u>Ward</u> the poet landlord (*London Spy*) were invited back by William <u>Caslon</u>, another friend. Sir Hans <u>Sloane</u> bought Britton's library, but his rare books on Tallis, Byrd and Purcell were sold with his musical instruments.

1753 Britton's books go on show when Sloane founds the British Museum.

1792 Britton's coal yard gives way to the equally famous Bull's Head Pub (see London Correspondence Society).

1836 The London Working Man's Association meets in coffee houses here, founded to launch The People's Charter demanding male suffrage, salaries for MPs (so that working men can run for Parliament) and annual democratic elections. The People's Charter was rejected by Parliament so was taken up by the Chartists, England's first consciously political movement.

....

JOHNSON, Dr Samuel (1709–1784)
Lexicographer

1731 Edward Cave launches *The Gentleman's Magazine* at **St John's Gate**. He wrote most of it himself as *Sylvanus Urban*.

1737 A regular reader of the magazine, with his pupil David Garrick, Dr Johnson leaves Lichfield, Staffordshire for London. They made their way to the St John's Gate, which they *'beheld with reverence'*. Employed by Cave, his first publisher, Johnson moved into the Gate and began work as a 'hack' writer. (It was here too at Cave's office that Garrick made his London acting debut.)

The years spent at the Gate were some of the best of Johnson's life. It may be he remembered the area. As a child he had stayed with his mother at nearby Little Britain. They had made the three-day journey so that little Sam could be 'touched' by Queen Anne to cure his scrofula. It didn't work, he remained scrofulous all his life. Now he is 29, tall, mutters, wrings his hands, twitches, grimaces and looks like a tramp.

There was an official ban on publishing speeches made in the House of Commons but Johnson, with Cave's help, made them up as the anonymous *Senator of Lilliput*. Sam was lazy, with no self-discipline, so had to be locked in a room at the Gate to write.

1744 Publishes *Life of Savage*. A visitor to Cave's office comments how wonderful it is. When they next met, Cave told him that his praise had made the author happy. *'How? We were alone!'* exclaims the visitor. *'You might observe I sent a plate of victuals behind the screen'*, replies Cave (a notoriously stingy editor). *'There skulked the biographer, one Johnson, whose dress was so shabby that he durst not make his appearance.'*

1750 Johnson is appalled to find Elizabeth Clarke Foster, illiterate granddaughter of poet John Milton, begging in the street. She was 61 and ill with asthma. He and Garrick put on a benefit performance of her grandfather's masque *Comus*, which raised £130.

1754 Cave dies. Johnson wrote 'The Life of Edward Cave'.

1762 Finds a publisher for friend Goldsmith's *The Vicar of Wakefield* to save him from the debtors' prison. Johnson founded The Literary Club with his beloved 'Nolly' or 'Goldy' Goldsmith, who he described as an *'eccentric vagabond.'* They sometimes met at The Old Red Lion at **The Angel** (q.v.). Goldsmith worked with Dr Johnson as a book reviewer on *The Gentleman's Magazine* (see also Goldsmith, Oliver).

1775 Writes pamphlets against John Wilkes.

1779 Supports Selina, Countess of Huntingdon in her battle with the vicar of St James, Clerkenwell, who tried to close her chapel in **Exmouth Market**.

1784 Visits Revd George Strahan, vicar of St Mary's, many times. Strahan tended Dr Johnson on his deathbed.

KING'S CROSS WC1

Battle Bridge until 1830

1680 An axe dating from 20,000 BC is found (under present-day **King's Cross Road**) alongside the bones of a straight-tusked elephant.

1830 Battle Bridge loses its ancient name. It became 'King's Cross' when a statue (truly monstrous, by any standards of taste) of George IV was erected where six roads crossed. The edifice was 60 feet high (inside was a public house and a police station) topped by an 11-foot high statue of George (it lasted a mere fifteen years) (see Battle Bridge).

1851 Terminus of the Great Northern Railway sees 250 trains every day. The area was getting blacker by the minute from the coal used by the railways.

1861 Somers Town is demolished to build King's Cross station. Many of the displaced residents moved to Islington.

1860 St Chad's Well, discovered in the time of King Cnut, is covered over for the Metropolitan Railway.

1861 Carlo Gatti, of **Little Italy**, opens a warehouse in **New Wharf Road** to sell ice from wells beneath the **Regent's Canal**.

The wells, 42 feet deep by 34 wide, held 500 tons each. Gatti imported thousands of tons from Norway to supply shops, restaurants and hotels and sold it by the cartload. The massive blocks took six days to reach him via Limehouse Docks. Gatti's Restaurants/ Cafés/Ice Cream Parlours were a familiar sight all over London until customers switched to the new Lyons Corner Houses (1894). His warehouse is now The London Canal Museum and his ice wells are still there.

1864 Dickens publishes *Our Mutual Friend*. The Wilfers' 'Boffins Bower' is in 'Belle Isle', a term of irony for an area where dust heaps (refuse and worse) were piled up. Noxious trades such as Japanning (poor man's lacquer for varnishing wood, metal, leather, papier mâché), lamp blacking factories (pitch is burnt in a chimney crowned with a cone of cloth and fine soot collected to make ink) were carried on, and horse slaughterers and piggeries thrived.

1873 Paul Verlaine, 29, French poet, settles here.

A violent drunk who attacked his own mother, Verlaine was obsessed with fellow French poet, 19-year-old genius Arthur Rimbaud, and left his wife to live with him. Verlaine, devotee of Baudelaire, was a Symbolist, a decadent poet. The pair lived in 8 Great College Street (demolished WWII). By the age of 21, Rimbaud had written some of the world's greatest poetry. They had a famous quarrel here, after which Rimbaud left Verlaine and hid from him in Brussels. Verlaine tracked him down and shot him in the arm, for which he was sentenced to two years' hard labour. On his release he returned to London where he taught French.

1923 *Riceyman Steps* is published, Arnold Bennett's novel about a miserly second-hand bookseller was set in **King's Cross Road**. Many Islington locations are mentioned (see Bennett, Arnold).

1986 Underground disaster. Fire broke out on an escalator that hadn't been cleaned for decades and 'flashed over' the booking hall at Kings Cross station, killing 37 people, many of whom had been directed by confused police into the path of the blaze. London Transport admitted to having ignored 60 previous fire warnings.

1997 Iain Sinclair in *Lights Out for the Territory*, writes about the *'peculiarly seductive electromagnetic field'* around King's Cross which, he said, explained Aidan Dun's prophetic poem *Vale Royal*. Written in 1977, this predicted the spiritual rebirth of Britain, which would begin on the 'sacred patch of ground' between the station and the canal.

1998 Seriously rich people move in. One is Sir Clive Sinclair. Britain's most famous modern-day inventor has returned to his roots. He was born in Islington in 1942 and started his business in **Duncan Terrace**. He invented the pocket calculator and tried to sell it to W.H. Smith, who laughed at him. He also invented the digital watch, a miniature computer called the ZX Spectrum and an odd-looking electric car (the Sinclair C5 was light years ahead of its time. Only 150 people bought it.) His latest invention is an auxiliary motor for bicycles. He predicted that round-the-clock channel trains would make King's Cross 'the most vibrant place in the UK'.

1999 The newly restored Scala Cinema re-opens as a music and arts venue. The long-overdue first stage of £1m refurbishment had begun. The 10,000 residents were fed up with the image of King's Cross created by heroin dealers, hard core porn mags sold round the clock, petrol stations selling £100 worth of condoms every day, 35 brothels and over a hundred kerb crawlers arrested every week. Thirty-five PCs were ordered on special patrol and £37 million invested to rid the area of pimps, prostitutes (now called sex workers) and drug dealers.

2007 St Pancras/King's Cross is set to become London's main international terminus for the Channel Tunnel rail route.

....

KING'S HEAD THEATRE
Upper Street N1

1543 The King's Head pub is first on this site, presumably named after King Henry VIII.
1588 Re-built.
1603 James, King of Great Britain, the sixth James in Scotland, the first in England, great-grandchild of Henry VII, rests here on the last leg of his long journey from Scotland to **Charterhouse** in Clerkenwell, where he will prepare for his coronation. Everyone turned out to see him. England had not had a king for fifty years, no-one could imagine one instead of a queen. The street was renamed King Street in his honour, but it never caught on. **Upper Street** and Lower Road (now **Essex Road**) made geographical sense.
1663 Samuel Pepys of Diary fame is a frequent visitor.
1865 Re-built (present building).
1969 Islington is anything but trendy until Dan Crawford from New Jersey buys the grotty pub and heralds the turnaround in fortunes for poor old **Upper Street**, much of which was boarded up.

Crawford was calling on a very old English concept, pub theatre, not seen (thanks to Cromwell) since Shakespeare's time, when he dispensed with the tatty billiard room to put on plays. He also introduced us to an all-American idea, the dinner show. His vision helped to launch the careers of Amanda Barrie, Lynda Bellingham, Simon Cadell, Tom Conti, Anita Dobson, Dawn French, Hugh Grant, Mark Knopfler (Dire Straits), Maureen

Lipman, Gary Oldman, Bertice Reading, Jennifer Saunders, Mel Smith, Janet Suzman, Imelda Staunton, Tom Stoppard, John Sessions and Victoria <u>Wood</u>.

Comedienne Wood, a staunch supporter of the King's Head, was living in one of Barnsbury's squares while trying to make her mark (lodging in the same house was the writer and TV critic, Clive James). She described the theatre as a *'vital asset'* and a *'tiny powerhouse'*. Actor/director Steven Berkoff said it was *'a sanctuary for every maverick in the theatre world'*. Tom Conti, Quentin Crisp, Rupert Graves, Sheila Hancock, Irene Handl, John Hurt, Ben Kingsley, Joanna Lumley, Anthony Sher, Janet Suzman and Susannah York have all worked here.

1971 Crawford puts in plans to convert the old *'Lit and Sci'* building in Almeida Street into a theatre. He was turned down (see Almeida Theatre).

1978 Thanks to Mr Crawford, Islington is back on London's map as a fun place to be. Islington was re-inventing itself as London's equivalent of 'off- off-Broadway' as the Almeida, St George's, Old Red Lion and, a bit later on, The Hen and Chickens and Lilian Baylis theatres opened.

1999 The longest-surviving fringe venue in London has very little modernisation, no central heating (open fires) videos, taped music, TV ...

The pub has an eccentric life all its own. Bar staff are trained in pre-decimal money on pre-decimal cash registers and takings rung up in pounds shillings and pence. Hanging from the ceiling are old theatre lanterns with coloured gels. After the evening performance music goes on till midnight. There is no resident company, visiting companies rent the theatre on a weekly basis. Reviewers from national papers visits every show. Sheridan Morley, theatre critic: *'(Dan Crawford) ... is a pioneering giant of London theatre ... no-one (except for Peter Hall) has done more for London drama in the last 30 years.'*

The emphasis was on new playwrights and reviving neglected plays which had a chance of transferring to mainstream West End theatres. *Easy Virtue* and *Ketch* transferred to the Garrick. *Kennedy's Children, Mr Cinders, Artist Descending a Staircase* all transferred to the West End and Broadway. *Post Mortem*, by Noel Coward, had never before been professionally performed.

2000 Threatened with closure, a huge banner *'God Save the King's Head'* goes up on St Mary's church opposite.

....

KINGSLEY, Mary (1862–1900)
Mary Kingsley Court N19
1862 Mary <u>Kingsley</u> (niece of Charles *Water Babies* Kingsley, daughter of his brother George), is born in **Upper Street** (address not known). An amateur anthropologist and naturalist she travelled to West Africa to explore Angola and the Congo where she met cannibals. The first woman to climb Mount Cameroon, she wrote *Travels in West Africa* (pub. 1899). Served as a nurse during the Boer War and died of fever.

....

KNIGHTS HOSPITALLERS
Islington: HQ of (English) Knights of St John
1113 A religious Order is set up in Jerusalem, called The Sovereign Military Order of The Hospital of St John of Jerusalem, or The Knights of the Order of the Hospital of St John the Baptist (patron saint of Jerusalem), also known as The Knights of St John, The Knights Hospitallers or simply the Hospitallers.

The Order offered hospitality (original meaning of 'hospital' or 'spital') to thousands of pilgrims who left home every year to brave wild animals, bandits, foreign languages, foreign food (and worse, in anyone's language) foreigners, to see Jerusalem. The Order was international (France used a fleur-de-lys as their emblem, England the lion and the unicorn, Germany the eagle and Holland, an orange).

Rich, powerful and answering only to the Pope, knights wore a long black robe (with a gold-embroidered, eight-pointed cross) in times of war and a white one during peace. The cross's eight points represented the eight languages (tongues) spoken along the pilgrim's route. (The Hospitallers are not to be confused with the Templars, a totally different and quite separate Order set up six years after the Hospitallers.)

Theirs was an intensely religious age, spiritual concerns ruled everybody's lives. Life on earth was so awful, the only comfort was that a better one awaited somewhere else, even if you had to die to get it. Going on a pilgrimage was an insurance against eternal damnation. Anyone who could get to Christ's birthplace was expected to go (just as Muslims are still expected to make the Hadj visit Mecca).

1312 The Templars are disbanded and the Hospitallers receive most of their property.

1381 Wat Tyler takes on the establishment.

1540 Henry VIII closes all religious houses. **St John's Priory**, Islington was one of the last to be suppressed. The English Order was disbanded.

1553 Catholic Mary Tudor revives the Order.

1559 Protestant Elizabeth I disbands it again. Today, the Hospitallers survive in the form of the St John Ambulance Brigade (q.v.), a charitable foundation dedicated to providing First-Aid support.

L

....

LAMB, Charles (1775–1834)
Writer
Islington: Home of 'Elia' (Elia Mews/Street, Charles Lamb Court N1)
Few of the younger generation will have heard of Lamb, but for decades children were reared on Lamb's Tales of Shakespeare (written with his sister Mary), while grown-ups loved his essays written under the pseudonym Elia (pronounced mischievously by Charles as 'a liar') in the London Magazine.

1796 Lamb (21) moves to a house on the corner of High Street and newly built Little Chapel Street (some sources say No. 15, others No. 45, both demolished, now **Chapel Market**) to be near his sister Mary, who was in an asylum (probably Northampton House, **St John Street**, now site of City University) after accidentally killing their mother in a fit of madness.

It was here that Lamb embarked on his literary career. He had moved with his ageing father, deranged by the shock of the murder, and crazy aunt Hetty. The area was still countryside, market gardens and open fields. In January, Charles himself spent six weeks at Balmes Mad House, Kingsland Road (possibly the origin of barmy). Mary, 12 years older and unmarried, adored him and was distraught over his illness. Madness ran in the family (which is why neither of them ever married). She was under enormous stress, working as a dressmaker by day and looking after her much loved but unstable aunt and ageing, ailing parents by night. During a row with a scullery maid she picked up a knife and lunged at her. Her mother tried to intervene, the maid ducked, mother didn't. Mary was committed. Charles, recently discharged from the asylum, witnessed the tragedy.

1797 Mad Aunt Hetty dies.

1798 Publishes a short novel, *Rosamund Grey*.

1799 Old Mr Lamb dies and Charles asks to have Mary discharged into his care. Charles (24) and Mary (36) moved a few doors down to 36 **Little Chapel Street**.

The Lambs attracted a wide circle of friends, old and young, male and female, some educated, some successful, some poverty-stricken, many eccentric. Among them were poets: drug addict schoolfriend Samuel Taylor Coleridge, Robert Southey, Thomas Hood, John Clare, who went mad, Thomas de Quincey who ate opium, the four Williams Blake, Wordsworth, Godwin and Hazlitt (friend Sarah Stoddard married Hazlitt, whom they met when he painted Lamb's portrait, now in the National Portrait Gallery). Another close friend was Harriet Wilkes, illegitimate daughter of the famous radical MP. Her husband William Rough, a lawyer, became Lord Chief Justice of Ceylon. Harriet Wilkes Rough's four children were the only descendants of Wilkes (see Wilkes, John).

1800 Coleridge comes to stay. Charles had fallen in love with Hester Savory (23) daughter of a Quaker goldsmith who lived a few doors away, although they had never spoken. He was drawn to the idea of becoming a Quaker until he attended a meeting, when the contemplative silence put him off. He dubbed Hester 'The Witch of Endoor' (she lived in the end house) and wrote a piece about 'the beautiful Quakers of Pentonville'.

William Wordsworth and his sister Dorothy visit. Charles and Mary took them to St Bartholomew's Fair at Smithfield. 'Wordy', as Byron sarcastically dubbed Wordsworth, wrote about the visit fifty years later in The Prelude. Future poet laureate Robert Southey was another visitor, The Lambs took him to Sadler's Wells to see the 'opera', which was proving very popular.

In 1792 Lamb started working at East India House, Leadenhall Street (demolished 1862, Lloyds Building now on the site) as a clerk in the Accounting Department (he called his fellow six clerks 'a collection of simples'). In 1801 the Lambs moved back to Temple, where they were born.

1823 Charles and Mary rent Colebrooke Cottage, **Colebrooke Row** until Charles retires. After a lifetime in rooms, they now had an entire house to themselves. Better still, it had a garden. The New River (q.v.), which ran in front of the cottage, was well known to Charles. He and Coleridge had swum in it as schoolboys. During one holiday, Charles had set out on his own for Amwell in Hertfordshire to find the source (failed). Charles, ecstatically happy, developed a passion for gardening, especially anemones and roses. From here he could easily walk to work. He was also near his beloved Sadler's Wells, where Joey Grimaldi was one of his favourite performers, and the second-hand book stalls at **Farringdon Market**. He was also near supportive friends: Thomas Hood in **Essex Road**, cousin Charles Lovekin in **Windsor Place**, his solicitor in 3 **Rufford's Row**, and George Daniel in **Canonbury Square**.

Lamb was at his creative peak here and did his best work between 1823 and 1826, the happiest period in his life. Immensely popular, he wrote under the pseudonym Elia, the name he 'borrowed' from a fellow clerk at The South Sea Company. And clearly, he was moving up in the world. Among new friends who now visited the Lambs were painter, Sir Edwin Landseer and banker, Sir Francis Baring. One of Lamb's biographers (David Cecil) compared Lamb's gatherings favourably with those of Shakespeare in the Mermaid Tavern or Dr Johnson's Literary Club.

1825 Adored friend, William Blake dies and is buried in **Bunhill Fields**, the Dissenters graveyard. At a social evening spent at the Lambs, Southey and Lamb discussed the plates for Lamb's *Tales from Shakespeare*, engraved by Blake, a religious fanatic who received commissions from William Godwin. Blake, said Southey, was obviously mad. Lamb, however, who knew all about madness, replied that he was simply a genius.

Lamb's cousin, Charles Lovekin also died. Lamb went to his funeral and recounted afterwards to gales of laughter how the widow, part-howling, part giving directions, had conducted herself, and how Mary had fallen through a chair.

Mary's attacks of mania were becoming more frequent and longer lasting, so Charles took early retirement. and they decided to move to the country.

Lamb's mystified friends couldn't understand his *'voluntary banishment to Enfield Chase'*. Away from Islington he was desperately unhappy and bitterly regretted leaving. He wrote to Hood: *"twas with some pain we evulsed from Colebrook. You may find some of our flesh sticking to the door posts ...'*

1831 Colebrooke Cottage, empty since Lamb moved out, is bought by John Webb, who builds a factory to bottle soda water. Charles sold him some of his furniture which was subsequently given to The Lamb Society (in 1880 another house is tacked on to Colebrooke Cottage, 63 **Colebrooke Row**).

1834 Distraught at the death of his schoolfriend hero Coleridge, walking in Edmonton Lamb stumbles and falls, grazing his face. He died on 27 December, of infection resulting from erysipelas. Buried All Saints, Edmonton, 3 January (Mary lived until 1847).

In 1835, a statue to Lamb was erected in Inner Temple gardens and stolen. A fibreglass copy erected in 1928 was also stolen in 1970. Another was put up in Giltspur Street.

2000 *The Old Familiar Faces* is voted among readers' most popular poems in *Radio Times* poll of the Nation's Favourite Poems of Childhood.

....

LANDMINES

1994 Paul Jackson, Islington Councillor, of **Northampton Square**, expert on microwave technology, wins an award for his high-tech device for locating landmines in the Falklands (1982). His ground probing radar 'electric bloodhound' helped trace skiers buried in avalanches and ended up in the grisly hunt for Fred and Rosemary West's victims in their house of horror (25 Cromwell Street, Gloucester). Jackson helped find the remains of nine women.

1997 The UK Working Group on Landmines is based in **Holloway Road**. A friend of Princess Diana, who campaigned worldwide to get a ban on the use of landmines, after her death Campaigns Officer David Hillman commented that she *'put landmines in every living room'*.

LEAR, Edward (1812–1888)

Artist and nonsense poet

1812 Edward is born at home, Bowman's Lodge, Bowman's Place (used to be an archery practice ground. The site is still just about there) off **Holloway Road**.

The Lear family was large, very large. Edward was the twentieth of twenty-one children, all baptised in the Nonconformist Register. He never knew eight of his brothers and sisters who died young, and barely knew his parents. Edward was reared by his sister Ann. He is the *Book of Nonsense*, *Jumblies* and *Owl and Pussy Cat* man, who gave Queen Victoria drawing lessons at Buckingham Palace and Osborne House, Isle of Wight.

Jeremiah Lear bought Bowman's Lodge and moved his family from Penton Ville to the higher ground and fresher air of Holloway Village in the country. They were here for twenty-three years until he retired to the seaside. Holloway was chosen by Mr Lear, a wealthy stockbroker, for its healthy aspect and convenience to the city, a popular and pleasant place to live (until the railways arrived). George <u>Romney</u> the painter lived nearby, as did famous printmakers James and Robert <u>Pollard</u> (see Pollard, family).

1815 Edward, 3, is held up to his bedroom window to watch the firework display celebrating Wellington's success at Waterloo.

1816 Father in debtors' prison for four years, found guilty of fraud. His mother had to take in male paying guests (Lear's biographers think one may have sexually abused young Edward, accounting for his lifelong melancholy and fear of relationships).

1821 Nine-year-old Edward remembers riding down **Theobald Road** in their gig pulled by Peggy the grey mare, listening to gossip about a local murder.

1827 Mr and Mrs Lear sell Bowman's Lodge (in the 1850s it became a finishing school for young ladies) and move to Gravesend, Kent. Edward, 15, not invited to join them, moved in with sister Ann in rented rooms, 28 **Upper North Street** off Gray's Inn Road.

1837 Smog often covers London so Edward, 25, epileptic, with poor eyesight, asthmatic, depressive and rootless, settles abroad to save what remains of his lungs.

1912 Bowman's Lodge, now LCC stables (horse drawn trams) is converted into The Ideal Cinema. Lit by electricity, it had raked seats and an orchestra. Closed during WWI, the building was taken over by the Ever Ready battery factory.

1999 BBC TV Antiques Road Show. A tiny Lear watercolour is valued at £15,000.

....

LENIN, Vladimir Ulyanov (born in Ulyanov) Ilich (1870–1924)

Islington: Home of the Russian Revolution

1902 February, a Russian Marxist exile in London (one of about 100) receives a letter from Munich asking him to ask Comrade Harry Quelch editor of *Justice* whether he will print Lenin's *Iskra*. Twentieth Century Press, 37a **Clerkenwell Green**, was the publishing arm of the first British Marxist party (Social Democratic Federation). In exile, Lenin, age 32, arrived to plan the Russian revolution, the first of his six visits to London. And so it was that Clerkenwell became HQ of the Russian revolution …

1902 April. Lenin, one of history's giants, the first democratic ruler of Russia, moves to 30 **Holford Square** to mastermind the most disruptive revolution in world history. He took the pseudonym Jacob Richter. He and his wife Nadia Krupskaya rented two rooms for thirty shillings a week.

The couple met when they were arrested in 1895, spending fifteen months in jail together before being sent to Siberia. They breakfasted on bacon and eggs washed down with mugs of beer (tap water would give them typhoid), after which Lenin would head off to Clerkenwell Green. There, Harry Quelch printed the underground newspaper on his flatbed machine, the text set by a Russian compositor in the East End. Seventeen issues, numbers 22 to 38, were printed here between April 1902 and May 1903. Quelch partitioned off part of the printing works as Lenin's editorial base, a table, bookshelf and chair (now listed as an historic monument). They often shared a pint in the nearby Crown. Tom Quelch, Harry's son, working here as a compositor, remembered Lenin as a small, stocky young man with a pointed ginger beard. While Lenin was at Clerkenwell Green, Nadya in Holford Square was busy deciphering cryptograms, warming letters over candles until the invisible ink became legible, and sending coded messages to underground agents operating in Russia. Lenin also spent hours in the old Finsbury Free Library (demolished in the 1960s).

One day, out of the blue, a young (22) man knocked at Lenin's door. His name was Lev Bronstein but he went under the assumed name of Trotsky. Just arrived from Siberia, he warned Lenin that copies of *Iskra* smuggled into Russia via Stockholm through Finland or via Brindisi on to Odessa had been lost, captured or sent to the wrong addresses. What was to be done? Lenin's four page 'spark' which lit the flame of revolution was now printed on thin paper, and smuggled directly into Russia wrapped around the legs of supporters inside their knee-high leather boots. *Iskra* literally walked into Russia.

1903 Lenin and his comrades plan the second Russian Social Democratic Labour Party Congress in one of their favourite meeting places, the upstairs room of The Crown and Woolpack, St John Street. A plaque inside once commemorated the meetings.

British efforts to penetrate the organisation bordered on the surreal. Usually the landlord was told it was a meeting for trades unionists, but this time the room had been booked for 'The Foreign Barbers of London Association'. Detective Inspector Herbert Fitch of Scotland Yard was ordered by his Super to hide in the cupboard but couldn't report back because the meeting was in Russian. Eavesdropping on another meeting at The Old Red Lion, DI Fitch disguised himself as a waiter and managed to get hold of the Minutes and Agenda but when the police arrived Lenin escaped in the food shaft (dumb waiter). By now, a split had occurred in the organisation. Lenin headed the majority Bolshevik faction, which wanted only active revolutionaries in the party, willing to do anything to establish communism. His opponents, the Mensheviks, led by Trotsky, wanted to admit anyone sympathetic to the cause. Lenin won the argument but lost the battle to continue printing *Iskra* in Clerkenwell. The comrades voted to move to Geneva.

1907 May. Comrade (and Comrade-ess) Lenin return to Finsbury for the duration of the Fifth Congress, prohibited by Denmark, Sweden and Norway. They moved into 16 **Percy Circus** (laid out in 1841 on one of Islington's hills, blue plaque on Royal Scot Hotel). The Brotherhood Church, **Southgate Road** was the venue (invited by left-wing Revd Swann, who worked for *The Daily Herald*). The church, paradoxically, was later famous for pacifist meetings attended by Bertrand Russell. The Congress, attended by Lenin, Stalin and Maxim Gorky was besieged by reporters, photographers and detectives. Into the building crammed 336 delegates, including 105 Bolsheviks and 97 Mensheviks. As Lenin couldn't pay the delegates' fares back home, Party members took the hat round. A benefactor, after hearing the speeches, advanced Lenin a £1,700 loan bond which was signed by all the delegates (returned with interest ten years later).

1911 During Lenin's last visit to London, he visits British Communist Theodore Rothstein at 28 **Gladsmuir Road**, Archway.

1912 Harry Quelch, editor of *Justice*, dies. Lenin wrote in his obituary. '*The Russian Social Democratic newspaper had to be printed in London ... Quelch readily made the printing plant available. As a consequence Quelch himself had to squeeze up ... there was no room for another chair.*'

1917 Nicholas II, Csar of Russia, is overthrown. Bolsheviks declare a republic.

1924 Lenin, 53, dies of a stroke. His embalmed body was put on show in the Red Square Mausoleum (long queues until he fell out of favour in the 1990s). Now in storage.

1942 The Russian Ambassador unveils a bust of Lenin in **Holford Square** designed by Berthold Lubetkin and presents it to the borough.

1951 The bust is removed from bombed-out Holford Square and taken to the Town Hall where (until the Liberals won parity and the Soviet dictator became *persona non grata*) 'Comrade Lenin' presided over every full meeting of the Council beneath the red flag of communism. The bust has since mysteriously disappeared from pride of place outside the entrance to the Council Chamber.

1996 The Crown and Woolpack closes. Courage Brewery handed it back to The Brewers Society, who leased it on to The Japanese Canteen.

....

LILLYWHITE, Fred (1792–1854)

Bricklayer turned professional cricketer (MCC 1827–54). Also played for Sussex. Founded the famous sports emporium which still bears his name.

1854 Dies of cholera at home, 10 Princes Terrace, **Caledonian Road**, where he ran a sports shop with sons John and Frederick. His tomb at Highgate Cemetery, complete with cricket bat and balls, was paid for by the MCC.

1863 Son James opens Lillywhite's in the Haymarket, W1.

In 1930 the shop was selling women's aviation suits designed by Amy Johnson.

....

LITTLE ITALY

Area bounded by **Farringdon Road/Mount Pleasant/Clerkenwell Road** EC1.

There have been Italians here since the middle ages, many of whom walked eight hundred miles from Italy. Home of accordionists, ice cream sellers, mosaicists, organ grinders, plaster model makers and street entertainers it is still the centre of Britain's Italian community.

1778 Giuseppe Grimaldi, dentist to Queen Charlotte, arrives. Disenchanted with teeth, crazy about the stage, he became fencing, dancing and ballet master at Sadler's Wells. His illegitimate son Joe, father of English clowns, became actor-manager of Sadler's Wells and topped the bill there for decades.

History will say that three men were responsible for uniting the six states of Italy and turning the country into a republic. One, Giuseppe Mazzini, hounded out of Italy for his republican views, lived, on and off, in **Clerkenwell** for thirty years. He used it as a political base while he plotted to overthrow the governments of several Italian states, wanting neither Pope nor king. The second was Giuseppe Garibaldi, who visited Mazzini in Islington, and the third was Count Camillo Cavour.

1837 Mazzini was an intellectual, a lawyer, son of a surgeon. Garibaldi, the self-educated son of a fisherman, a man of action who said Italy could be taken only by the sword. Count Cavour, the consummate politician, believed political goals could best be achieved through wheeling and dealing. He came to London in 1831 to study the British Constitution. Mazzini, who hated Cavour and considered his methods dishonest, was teaching English to Italian immigrants at the Society for Advancement of Italian Workers, Laystall Street off **Theobald Road** (now Mazzini Garibaldi Club, still the premier Italian institution in London). Although conditions in this area were almost indescribable, Italians, supervised by priests and the Mafia, were clean and well-fed. Medical Officer of Health report: (they are) *'superior' to a similar class of English in the same district ... take more care of their children ... as regards cleanliness ... feeding ... training ... clothing ... sober ... abstemious ... less alcoholism,'*

1844 MP for Finsbury, Thomas Duncombe makes an official complaint in the House about government harassment of Mazzini.

1848 Mazzini helps Garibaldi seize Rome. He expelled the Pope, declared Rome a Republic and became its President. Three months later the French invaded and although Mazzini put up a heroic defence, he was ousted. He returned to Little Italy, where he continued a hand-to-mouth existence.

1861 Population of 899 Italians, 700 by birth. Carlo Gatti started his ice wells in King's Cross (see King's Cross).

1863 Italians get their own church. Architects, builders, masons, mosaicists and painters were brought from Italy. St Peter's, **Clerkenwell Road**, was the first Italian church built outside Italy. The style, use of colour and design were unique in Britain. Garibaldi visited it and both Benjamino Gigli and Enrico Caruso sang here.

Although a Dr Melia travelled Europe to raise money to build the church, local legend has it that Mafia money financed the building through the Sabini family. Darby Sabini, an illiterate boxer and racetrack wizard, was Islington's very own Godfather, king of Little Italy's criminal empire. A gentleman gangster, he was head of the 300-strong Saffron Hill Mob.

1864 Garibaldi, impatient for change, arrives in London and is given the Freedom of the City.

Islington: Home of the Squashed Fly Biscuit

The hero, with his distinctive baggy red shirt and floppy black hat, arrived in Clerkenwell on his one and only visit to England and took the biscuit. Literally. Local Italian bakers created a special biscuit in his honour. Unknown in Italy, the Garibaldi is English, a three-layer biscuit sandwich, the middle layer being a sweet paste of currants known to generations of schoolchildren as 'squashed flies'.

1868 Mazzini leaves Little Italy, his home since 1836.

1872 Mazzini dies in Pisa. His dream of a Republic of Italy came true, but not until 1945.

1879 Signor Terroni opens Britain's first Italian delicatessen in Clerkenwell Road.

1880 Angelo Tomasso leaves Big Italy to make 'hurdy-gurdies' (barrel organs) in Little Italy.

1883 Italians take their statue of Our Lady of Carmel into the streets to celebrate her Saint's Day – the first public Roman Catholic procession in Britain since Henry VIII. The Festival of Our Lady of Carmel is still celebrated on the nearest Sunday to 16 July and attracts 80,000 every year.

1920 Angelo Tomasso churns out 50 barrel organs a week from his Clerkenwell factory.

1929 Italian 'terrazzo' is all the rage. A factory to produce it was set up in **Graham Street** employing men imported from north-east Italy, traditional centre for Roman mosaic. The factory was on the banks of the **Regent's Canal**, which carried imported marble chippings by barge from the Docks. Workers lived in **Vincent Terrace**, **Duncan Terrace**, **Noel Road** and the surrounding area.

1939 WWII. Luigi Finella founds The Mexicano Accordion Band, which played on radio throughout the war and went on ENSA tours.

1940 Mussolini declares war on Britain. MI5 claimed that Clerkenwell's Italian cafés were run by fascist revolutionaries so Italians were classified as enemy aliens and deported to Canada, Australia or the Isle of Man. July, 500 Italians perished on the SS *Andorra Star* bound for Canada. Struck by torpedoes, it sank in 30 minutes.

1948 Angelo Tomasso, 84, is still making, mending and hiring out hurdy-gurdies.

1953 Tomasso, Little Italy's last barrel organ maker, dies (radio/TV killed his trade).

1961 Three thousand people of Italian origin live here.

1997 Gatti's ice wells are still under the London Canal Museum. Battle Bridge Basin, marketed as The Gateway to Europe, is renamed **Ice Wharf**.

....

LONDON CORRESPONDENCE SOCIETY, The (LCS)

1792 The Bulls Head (q.v.) Jerusalem Passage, where republicans met, spawned the most famous and most influential of all political societies, founded by boot maker Thomas Hardy (not the novelist) to show solidarity with the American and French Revolutions. Their hero was Tom Paine, author of *Rights of Man*. The LCS was impatient for parliamentary reform, universal (male) suffrage and yearly Parliaments.

1794 Envious of the American and French Revolutions, members attacked the recruiting offices enlisting men to fight in the war against France. The government, justifiably edgy about republicanism, had them arrested, charged with High Treason and sent to the Tower. A special commission was convened at the Sessions House on **Clerkenwell Green**. The trial lasted eight days. Richard Brinsley Sheridan, MP and playwright (*The Rivals*, *School for Scandal*), member of Dr Johnson's Literary Club, spoke up for Hardy and his members. They were found not guilty and celebrated with a huge triumphal march.

1799 After many attempts at suppression, the whole committee was jailed without trial and the Society declared illegal.

....

LONDON GREENPEACE
Caledonian Road N1
THE MCLIBEL TRIAL

1986 London Greenpeace members distribute leaflets explaining *What's Wrong With McDonalds* outside fast food outlets.

1990 McDonald's issue a writ.

1993 The $multi billion global corporation begins a libel action suing five members. Three apologised; two, Helen Steel (29) barmaid and David Morris (40) postman, wouldn't. With legal aid not available for litigants in a libel trial they had to defend themselves – even though they hadn't written or distributed the leaflet and David was no longer a member. Keir Starmer, Solicitor, of **Doughty Street**, advised them free of charge.

1994 Steel and Morris defend themselves against twelve of the keenest legal minds in the world. McDonalds sued the penniless but dogged duo in Court 35, Royal Courts of Justice. The press headlines went to town: '*Small Fries* v. *Big Burger*.' McDonalds had a £2,000 per day QC backed by a £1,000 a day barrister. The defendants claimed the judge was biased in McDonald's favour when he successfully argued against appointing a jury, saying a jury would not understand the complexities of the argument, although the postman and the barmaid had no such problem. The trial, pencilled in the Court diary to last twelve weeks, took two and a half years.

After two months McDonalds asked for an out-of-court settlement with money going to a charity of the defendants' choice. London Greenpeace refused. The McLibel Support Action Group distributed a further 2 million leaflets. After 102 days, the trial made the record books by being the longest libel case in history. After 199 days it became the longest civil case, after 292 days it became the longest case of any kind in English legal history. 180 witnesses were called and filled 20,000 pages of court transcripts.

1996 The McLibel Support group sets up a page on the Internet, called *McSpotlight*. Trial transcripts were accessed by 14 million visitors. A delighted Auberon <u>Waugh</u> (writer and columnist, editor of the *Literary Review*, son of novelist Evelyn (see Waugh, Evelyn) described it as: '*the best free entertainment in London.*'

1997 Mr Justice Bell takes two hours to read his 45-page summary of his 800-page judgment. Although London Greenpeace lost, the pressure group distributed another 400,000 leaflets. Morris commented: '*the court of public opinion is much more important than a high court ruling*'. An appeal was considered to the European Court of Human Rights.

LUBETKIN, Berthold (1901–1990)

Architect

Opened in 1938, Pine Street Clinic set the example for the post-war welfare state when Finsbury Borough Council pioneered a 'cradle-to-grave' free health service, years before Aneurin Bevan (1945).

Islington: Home of the National Health Service

1930s Finsbury was suffering great social and economic stress. The Council, among the most enlightened of London boroughs, under *The Finsbury Plan* created a Public Health Department. Dr Katial, Chairman, visited an open-plan TB clinic newly-built by Berthold Lubetkin, icon of the modern movement.

Invited to Finsbury Town Hall by Marxist councillors to discuss the proposed health centre, the architect was assured he would be given freedom to experiment. Lubetkin, a Russian, communist unshackled by English tradition, was chosen by the radical councillors although nowhere could have been further from the Bauhaus (German school of modern architecture) than slummy 1930s Finsbury. Lubetkin's design broke with the British tradition of stone and brick in favour of weightlessness. He was determined to use new materials and technology. This was the beginning in Britain of simple, box-style 'minimalist' architecture. Anything not necessary was eliminated. There's no decoration, nothing to distract attention from its function. The parts were prefabricated, machine-made floor joists and window heads were concrete. All rooms faced the sun, with built-in cupboards, glazed walls and flush window frames. Lord Horder, the King's personal physician, went into raptures over it.

1942 The Russian Ambassador unveils a bust of Lenin designed by Lubetkin in **Holford Square** and presents it to the borough. (Whereabouts now unknown.)

1946 Lubetkin, depressed at the fall of the post-war Labour government, is tempted out of retirement by Finsbury Council. He went on to build 'homes fit for heroes' in **Bevin Court** King's Cross and **Spa Green** (site of old pleasure gardens) where each of the one hundred and twenty nine flats was fitted with Britain's first domestic waste disposal system.

1951 Priory Green Estate is built.

1954 130 flats built in Holford Square, one of Lubetkin's last projects before he wound up The Tecton Partnership, predicting that bureaucrats and accountants would soon overrule the judgement of architects.

1998 Lubetkin's Bevin Court and Spa Green get Grade 2 listing.

MacNEICE, Louis (1907–1963)
Poet and broadcaster. Friend of W.H. Auden, Dylan Thomas, Benjamin Britten *et al.*

1947 August, moves to 52 **Canonbury Park South** with Hedli (second wife), Ben, son from his first marriage, Bimba their daughter, and a home help. MacNeice, who had already published twenty books, while here wrote *The Dark Tower* for the BBC with music by Benjamin Britten (1947), *Holes in the Sky* (1948), *Collected Poems: 1925–1948* (1949), *Goethe's Faust* (1951) and *Ten Burnt Offerings* (1952). His sister lived near **Archway** (good for baby-sitting) and George Orwell, whom he knew well, was around the corner in **Canonbury Square**. MacNeice wrote that he had moved into *'a handsome town house in London's Canonbury Park'*. Running the BBC Third Programme poetry outlet, MacNeice gave his drinking buddy Dylan Thomas work. Hedli was spending two months with her parents in Switzerland so Thomas, then at Islington Film Studios (q.v.), stayed with MacNeice at No. 52 and had a good time: *'. . . wine bar at lunch-time, Oval (where I'd never been) in the afternoon & London Casino in the evening'.*

1950 The British Council invites MacNeice to be Director of the British Institute in Athens for a year. He accepted and asked the BBC if Dylan could sit in his chair until he returned. They said no. He packed a reluctant son, Dan (who naturally would much prefer to go to Greece) off to boarding school and found a tenant for 52.

1951 The MacNeices return from Athens. *Ten Burnt Offerings* was broadcast by the BBC. Dan, who hated boarding school, was expelled. Elizabeth Bowen, novelist friend from Ireland and the BBC, told Louis that she was giving up the tenancy of her Regency corner house (once home to Dame Nellie Melba) in Clarence Terrace (Crown Estate) overlooking Regent's Park. MacNeice got friends in high places to pull strings and the family moved there at the end of the summer.

1961 MacNeice (54) arrested for being drunk and disorderly is reporting to the Duty Sergeant on the desk at **Clerkenwell** Police Station.

1963 Bronchitis develops into viral pneumonia. Died 3 September.
2000 Three poems (*Autobiography*, *Prayer Before Birth* and *Soap Suds*) voted among the most popular in *Radio Times* Poll *The Nation's Favourite Poems of Childhood*.

....

MCC (Marylebone Cricket Club)
Islington: Home of Cricket
1752 Organised cricket starts in **Barnsbury** thanks to Thomas <u>Lord</u>, cricket's first official groundsman.

At a meeting at the Star & Garter Club, Pall Mall, Lord was asked by distinguished members (the earl of Winchelsea, et al.) to lease ground at the White Conduit House. They formed the White Conduit Cricket Club (WCCC) and played the first match for Middlesex against Kent at Lord's ground, winning by 304 runs. The game was played on uneven ground with no gloves and no pads. Spectators paid sixpence to get in, cheering the players on (their dogs infuriatingly chasing after the ball) within the wooden paling that fenced in the field. In the days before 'whites' the players could wear anything: striped, checked, spotted shirts, frock or swallowtail coats. Feature articles extolling the charms of Islington as a favourite rural resort visited by city families on Sundays appeared in *The Gentleman's Magazine* and *The Sunday Rambler*. Cricket became all the rage and bats and stumps were hired out to visiting teams.

1755 Rules of cricket revised.

1774 Committee (Duke of Dorset, Lord Tankerville, *et al.*) revises the rules again.

1787 Cricket is such a passion at Lord's that crowds of 5,000 a time turn up to watch and bet on the outcome. Players, fed up with the growing hooliganism, asked Lord to find somewhere else. They moved to smarter Dorset Square, Marylebone and became the Marylebone Cricket Club (MCC). The White Conduit House started its own cricket side, as did The Albion, also in **Barnsbury** (ACC). At Dorset Square the MCC's first match was against WCCC. MCC won by 83 runs.

1800 Women have their own ground in **Balls Pond Road**.

1834 Barnsbury is becoming built-up so the ACC moved from the Albion pub to the Copenhagen (so called after the visit in 1606 of Christian IV of Denmark, who came to London to visit his sister Queen Anne and her husband, James I).

....

McBEAN, Angus (1904–1994)
Theatrical photographer
1945 An early pioneer of Barnsbury's revival as a popular residential suburb, McBean buys 34 and 35 **Gibson Square**.

1949 'Discovers' 19-year-old Audrey <u>Hepburn</u>, whose anorexic waif 'look' is never out of fashion.

Britain knew her hauntingly beautiful face from thousands of soap bar wrappers long before they knew her name. The David Bailey of his day, McBean was sought-after for his surreal poses. Hepburn agreed to front a national advertising campaign for Lacto-Camomile skin moisturiser, £5 for half a day's work. '*What shall I wear?*' she asked. '*Nothing,*' replied McBean. '*I'm not taking my clothes off!*' she protested. So he buried her in sand up to her swan neck, all high cheekbones, huge almond eyes and black fringe. His picture of her was on every billboard in Britain and on every magazine cover. (In the film *Funny Face* (1956) Hepburn plays an actress who finds stardom after being spotted in a photograph.)

1936 McBean is official photographer for Sadler's Wells, Glyndebourne, *Sketch*, *Tatler*, Ivor Novello, Ralph Richardson, Laurence Olivier, Vivien Leigh, *et al*.

1963 Moves to 58 **Colebrooke Row**. When London Underground tried to build a concrete ventilation shaft for the Victoria Line in Gibson Square he helped fight the scheme. McBean was asked to do an album cover for The Beatles, but declined. Eventually, he retired to Suffolk.

....

MEEK, Joe (1930–1967)

Musician and record producer

Britain's first independent record producer competed single-handedly in the 1960s with astonishing success against giants such as EMI, Decca, Pye, Parlophone, Columbia and HMV.

Islington: Home of Indy bands and Telstar

1960 Just months after Joe Orton (q.v.) moves to **Noel Road** Joe Meek arrives at 304 **Holloway Road**, where he spends the rest of his short, seedy life. He was also to meet a violent, tragic, early end just months before Orton. A gifted, promiscuous homosexual like Orton, Meek shared Orton's love of 'cottaging', dicing with danger in the public lavatories along Holloway Road. Unlike Orton, who made it into the Dictionary of National Biography, Meek was hardly known outside the industry. If not for John Repsch, his biographer, it's doubtful he would be remembered.

Mr and Mrs Shenton, who ran the fancy goods shop at 304, sublet the top floors to Meek. He covered the ceilings with acoustic tiles, hung thick curtains on the walls, deadened the floors with carpet and soundproofed the windows. Mrs Shenton screamed at him when molten rubber he had poured under the floor ran down her walls. In his studio, Meek produced unique, outer space sounds. Although this was 1960 and in mono, he heard stereophonically and was the first producer in Europe to use multi-track recording. Successful before moving to 304, he had worked with just about every famous recording artiste in Britain and discovered Adam Faith. Among the young hopefuls who beat a path to his door was Rod Stewart, 16, who lived just up the road at **Archway**. Young Tommy Scott (now Tom Jones) and the Senators drove down from Wales, and he gave Chas 'n Dave, Screaming Lord Sutch, Freddie Starr, Jonathan King and Davy Jones (later Bowie) their first breaks.

1961 *Johnny, Remember Me*, a massive hit for John Leyton, with a synthesiser solo, comes from 304. It was Number One for 15 weeks. Brian Epstein wined and dined Meek, asking him to produce the Beatles, but they couldn't agree terms. In any case, Meek didn't like the Mersey Sound and thought it would be a flash in the pan.

1962 Produces phenomenally successful *Telstar*, played by the Tornados, a unique sound which Meek wrote to commemorate Russia's Sputnik. For over a year it stayed in the Top 20. The single was at Number One for 25 weeks and the EP was Number Four for another 22. They earned him two Gold Discs and he banked £30,000 within weeks of their release. Other hits included *Tell Laura I Love Her*, *Will You Love Me Tomorrow* and *I'll Walk the Line*.

Orton and Meek were both up before the same 'beak' at Clerkenwell Magistrates Court, Meek for importuning, Orton for defacing library books. The experience started Orton's career and ended Meek's (the shame of being in the newspapers depressed Meek and he was never the same again).

1964 Have I The Right by The Honeycombs is another monster hit but does nothing to lift Meek's mood. He was increasingly paranoid, convinced his flat was bugged. He communicated by writing on scraps of paper.

1967 Meek shoots first Mrs Shenton, then himself.

The date, 3 February, is significant. In January 1958 he had predicted the sudden death on 3 February of his hero Buddy Holly and went out of his way to warn the star, but he was a year out. Holly died in a plane crash on 3 February 1959. Meek killed himself on the anniversary. Telstar alone should have made him a millionaire but he died in debt. Like many geniuses he was useless at business, his royalties of £150,000 (rising daily) for Telstar couldn't be touched because of a dispute over copyright.

1996 A plaque to Meek is put on his recording studio with funds raised by his biographer, John Repsch, Secretary of the Joe Meek Appreciation Society.

2000 Jake Arnott writes The Long Firm, a novel featuring Joe Meek.

MILL, John Stuart (1806–1873)

Writer, philosopher, feminist and politician

1805 James Mill, philosopher, marries Harriet Burrow of 12 **Rodney Terrace**, Pentonville and moves into her home.

1806 John Stuart Mill born (the house survived until 1957).

1811 James moves his family from Pentonville to **Newington Green**. John Stuart's favourite book was Daniel Defoe's Robinson Crusoe (did he know that Defoe went to college on Newington Green?). He was already reading Plato in Greek and conversing in Latin. When he grew up, like Lamb, he worked in The East India Company.

1858 Retires from the East India Company.

1859 Publishes On Liberty, saying that people should be allowed to do and think whatever they like as long as they don't harm anyone else.

1863 Publishes Utilitarianism.

1865 Enters Parliament as a Radical MP.

1869 Publishes On the Subjection of Women. Mill donated £20 to the London Patriotic Society, Clerkenwell Green.

MILTON, John (1608–1674)

Poet

Born in London, Milton was educated at Cambridge (where his feminine looks got him dubbed The Lady of Christ's College). In 1642 he supported the Puritan cause and published a number of pamphlets on issues such as divorce and freedom of the press. Obsessed with achieving fame (he said 'fame is the spur'), he died almost unknown outside an exclusive circle of admirers.

1643 A Staunch republican, aged 35, he marries Mary Powell, a royalist, 17, who walks out on him after three weeks. She returned but died in childbirth age 27 after their fourth child. Their first, Anne, was disabled. Son John died young but Mary and Deborah thrived.

Without Mary as secretary, Milton employed Andrew Marvell to help him until at 42, he married Katherine Woodcock (28) from Hackney. She died 15 months later after giving birth to a daughter, who also died. Milton was described as cold and unapproachable, although he did, apparently, save the life of William D'Avenant, hounded out of London during the Civil War.

1667 *Paradise Lost* published. Considered by some to be the greatest poem in the English language.

1670 Milton, age 55 and now blind, woos third wife, Elizabeth Minshull, 24. The couple moved to Artillery Walk, 124/5 **Bunhill Row** – a tiny house with one room on each floor on the edge of a large common (it took four hours to walk round) with one servant and Milton's piano. Anne, 24, Mary, 21 and Deborah, 18, daughters from his first marriage were no longer with him. Anne and Mary were lacemakers and Deborah was a lady's companion in Ireland. Neither Milton nor his wife liked them and the feeling was mutual. When Mary learned her father had remarried she remarked that she'd have been more interested to hear of his death.

1777 Starts *Paradise Regained*. Fans begin to visit him: clergymen, foreigners, nobility, Dryden and, it's said, the Duke of York, future James 11. Everyone except his daughters.

1671 *Samson Agonistes* published.

1674 Deborah, 22, marries Abraham Clarke, an illiterate Dublin weaver. It's said that though she was a teacher, she never taught their daughter Elizabeth to read.

Milton (66) died of gout. Surprisingly, for a man who hated bishops, he was buried not across the road in Bunhill Fields, the cemetery for dyed-in-the wool Nonconformists, but in St Giles, Cripplegate. Widow Elizabeth (35) sold the copyright of *Paradise Lost* for eight pounds and stayed on at Bunhill Row for a further seven years.

POSTSCRIPT: THE MILTONS

1680 Milton's wealthy brother, Judge Christopher Milton (fervent royalist, knighted 1686) of Ipswich, took a London home in **Holloway**. He had two unmarried daughters Sarah, 42, and Anne, 39.

1735 The daughters of Judge Milton, nieces of John, changed their name to Melton. In their nineties (one lived to 94, the other 97) they walked up the steep **Highgate Hill** every Sunday to Highgate Chapel.

1750 Dr Johnson was appalled to find Elizabeth Clarke Foster, Milton's grand-daughter (Deborah's daughter) begging in the street. She was 61 and ill with asthma. He managed to raise £130 from a performance with Garrick of her grandfather's *Comus* (See Johnson, Dr Samuel). She and her husband Tom Foster were able to open a chandler's shop in Upper George's Place, Lower Holloway (renamed **Milton Place** N7).

1754 When Elizabeth Foster (65) died, the Milton line died with her.

MOORFIELDS

Given to the City by the de Fiennes family for the enjoyment of its citizens.

1374 Leased to Thomas atte Ram on condition that he sees to the regular cleansing of the river Walbrook (q.v.). He was allowed to keep anything of value his scavengers found.

1383 'And whereas the watercourse of Walbrook (in the moor fields) is topped up by filth and dung ... punishment may be afflicted on the offenders ...' In it went, offal, filthy rush floor coverings, straw from stables, rotten wood, stale fish, at the dead of night of course!

1415 The fortunes of the various freeholders of the bleak, barren Moor Fields (rented to tenants for a total yearly income of four marks) take a turn for the better when Moor Gate is built and access is made easier.

1473 The Moor Fields are drained again. Ralph Jocelyn, Lord Mayor: *'For repairing the wall of the city: caused the said moor fields to be searched for clay and for brick to be burnt therein.'*

1491 Gardens and walks laid out in the Moor Fields are dispensed with and the land levelled for archery practice.

1512 Roger Archley, a city merchant, *'causes divers dykes to be cast and made to drain the waters of the said moor fields with bridges arched over them but yet it still stood full of noisome waters'.*

1614 Drained, paved and laid out in walks where people parade on summer evenings and on Sundays to show off the latest fashions.

1666 THE GREAT FIRE OF LONDON

As London burned, inhabitants who had survived the plague were homeless and took to Moor Fields. 80,000 fled the city. (Six years later one in four had not returned.) Londoners who couldn't fit into **Bart's** or the sheds at **Smithfield Market** camped outside. The king rode into Moor Fields to be with his people. With St Paul's burning behind him, Charles II spoke from horseback saying that the fire was an act of God, not caused by papists or immigrants. He sent army tents and a shanty town mushroomed. The king ordered parish churchwardens to lodge people in inns, places of entertainment and private houses. Those that could pay should, he would provide funds for those who couldn't. 200 boys from the Bluecoat School were evacuated to Nag's Head, **Holloway**.

John Evelyn, diarist, records that not one of the thousands of homeless camping in fields between the city wall and Highgate begged for alms. They had no need. Within four days everyone had a roof but some moved from centre to centre for charity relief. Many never went back to the city, constant plagues and fires were good reasons not to. To avoid another fire property owners in the city were ordered to re-build using brick (not wood) and to be connected to either London Bridge Waterworks or The New River Company. Those who didn't have the money built shanty towns which developed a life of their own. Surrounded by refuse heaps and open sewers, these makeshift dwellings were eventually replaced with permanent homes.

MOORGATE

1415 Londoners use Alders Gate and Cripple Gate to get to Islington. Men were obliged to practice archery, so a gap was made in the old city wall and a postern (pedestrian) gate built so that city dwellers had direct access to the moors. Stowe: *'Thomas Fawconer, Lord Mayor, caused the wall of the city to be broken toward the said moor and built the postern called Moor Gate for the ease of citizens to walk that way upon causeys towards Iseldon.'*

1672 The Moor Gate is enlarged so that the Trained Bands (see Honourable Artillery Company) could march into the city with their eight-foot pikes upright.

1750 London's traffic is almost at a standstill. City Gates were blamed for holdups (see Traffic).

1761 Because of gridlocked traffic, the authorities ordered the city gates to be removed. The medieval Aldersgate, Cripplegate and Moor Gate which released city dwellers from the smells of London into the fresh air of Islington were demolished (stones were used to repair London Bridge).

1975 February. 42 died, another 74 were injured when a train on the Northern line was driven at full-tilt into the buffers at Moorgate station. No reason was ever discovered for London's worst Underground disaster. The narrow tunnel, packed with wreckage, impeded rescuers. Casualties were rushed to five hospitals, including **Bart's**.

MORE, Thomas (Sir/Saint) (1478–1535)
Catholic martyr

1499 More, law student, takes lodgings in **Charterhouse Square** to be near the Carthusians (some sources say he lived inside the precincts). He stayed four years until he became an MP. Charterhouse was famed for its cosmopolitan intellectual life. More admired the monks and their vows of celibacy. He seriously thought of joining them, not convinced at the wisdom of marriage, particularly for himself. He did marry, though. Twice.

1520 Henry VIII takes More, Prior Docwra of St John's and Baron Berners to meet the king of France at Calais. His yellow tents earned the field where they camped the title *'the field of the cloth of gold'* (today it's still gold, planted with yellow rapeseed).

1529 Henry replaces Cardinal Wolsey with More, who is not pleased.

1535 More watches his friends from Charterhouse being taken to their execution. He was martyred the same year for the same reason, accused of treason, but being an aristocrat was spared the scrutiny of public gaze and had the privilege of being beheaded in private.

1935 Four hundred years after his martyrdom he is canonised.

1960 *A Man for All Seasons*, play by Robert Bolt, became an Oscar-winning film starring Paul Scofield as Thomas More.

MORRIS, William (1834–1896)
Designer, print-maker and poet (born in Walthamstow)
Founded the Socialist League, forerunner of Labour and Communist Party. Lectured to workers at **Clerkenwell Green** *from 1872 until he died. Inspired Arts & Crafts movement. Slogan: 'Have nothing in your home that is not useful or beautiful.'*

1872 Landlords were likely to lose their licence if they let rooms for republican meetings so The London Patriotic Society (LPS), launched to campaign for the nationalisation of land, called themselves The Robin Hood Discussion Society. The Society supported trades unions, was committed to radical reform and, unusually, admitted women. It advertised in *The National Reformer*, selling £1 shares to establish a permanent meeting place. John Stuart Mill, Pasmore Edwards *et al.* bought them and LPS took over No. 37.

1887 Bloody Sunday Police Commissioner Warner banned a march planned for Trafalgar Day to protest against government policy in Ireland. Sunday 13 November, Morris, George Bernard Shaw, Eleanor Marx and Annie Besant led the Clerkenwell contingent singing *La Marseillaise* on a march to Trafalgar Square demanding the right to demonstrate. There were many casualties (see **Clerkenwell**).

1893 Twentieth Century Press, the first legal Socialist (Communist) press opens at No. 37 to print *Justice*, the mouthpiece for the Social Democratic Federation (SDF). Morris sold his library to fund the venture, guaranteeing the first year's rent, and designed the membership card, slogan: '*Educate, Agitate, Organise*.' *Justice* was a weekly newspaper for trades unionists. Harry Quelch, communist editor, was leader of the SDF. The first statement of Marxist theory available in English came from The House on the Green (see Lenin, Vladimir Ilich).

MOUNT PLEASANT EC1

Named with characteristic London irony. Biggest dung hill in Islington (or to use the nicety favoured by Victorians in Dickens' Our Mutual Friend, 'dust mound').

1739 Foul, steaming, stinking mountains of rubbish are landmarks all over Islington. Locals pick over them for bones to sell to soap makers, rags to sell to paper makers and ashes to sell to breeze block makers. Thomas Coram, philanthropist, was so horrified to see babies' bodies thrown on the tips, he started a Foundling Hospital.

1794 THE BRITISH BASTILLE

Yet another prison, officially titled The Middlesex House of Correction, known as Cold Bath Prison, it's the largest in Britain with 1,800 prisoners and 125 staff.

Iron spikes guarded the roof and every wall, not always to keep prisoners in. The government was nervous (with good cause) of the mob. Nicknamed the 'Steel' by inmates (the Bastille), it was financed willingly by nervous ratepayers. There was as much crime inside as out. Turnkeys (warders) earned up to twenty-five shillings a day in bribes. Criminals wore grey uniforms, misdemeanants blue. Protestants had white cards outside their cells, Catholics orange. The filthy conditions inside were much like the 'rookeries' that spawned the inmates. Coleridge in *The Devil's Walk* wrote: '*As he went through Coldbath Fields, He saw a solitary cell, And the devil was pleased for it gave him a hint, For improving his prisons in hell*'. Refined **Cold Bath Square** slid rapidly downmarket. All that remains is the street name.

1820 Crowds gather outside the prison to watch Arthur Thistlewood (50) and his fellow Cato Street (plot to murder Foreign Secretary, Lord Castlereagh) conspirators arrive. Thistlewood was well-known and admired locally as a veteran of the 1816 Spa Fields Riot (q.v.) (some say he organised it). He and four others were charged with High Treason and hanged at Newgate, five were transported. George Cruikshank's imagination was caught by the story and he reconstructed it in a painting.

1821 Six treadmills are introduced to replace the death penalty for minor crimes. They did nothing but circulate air and were made even harder by a regulator fan. Oakum picking was another pointless punishment, 500 in one room spent years un-picking old tarred ship's ropes.

1828 Aris, the corrupt Governor is sacked and replaced by G.L. Chesterton (a forebear of G.K.), a man of integrity who replaced all the staff. Only one suicide was reported in all his 25 years here. Although he didn't think criminals were reformable, he believed in the prison system.

1829 Crime rate rising so the prison is extended.

1830 Government tries to impose stamp duty on the popular press. Clerkenwell was a big printing area and jobs were at stake. Anticipating riots, extra guards were put on the prison.

1842 Pentonville Prison opens in **Caledonian Road**, Barnsbury.

1886 After a hundred years, the 'Steel' closes. When the prison was demolished bricks inscribed by prisoners with their names and dates ended up in a wall on the south side of **Myddelton Passage** near Sadler's Wells (still visible) The General Post Office (GPO) took over the prison and rebuilt it as a sorting office. The 'inmates' (now employees) had progressed from making mail bags to filling them.

1909 Traffic is very slow and the Postmaster General was concerned that the mail was not getting delivered fast enough. An underground electric railway was planned to carry letters and parcels.

LONDON'S ONLY PRIVATE UNDERGROUND RAILWAY

1914 The Post Office starts work on its underground electric railway.

1917 WWI. Tunnelling suspended due to lack of funds. Britain's art treasures were stored safe from Zeppelin raids in the half-built tunnels (Elgin Marbles and other priceless artefacts from the British Museum, The Tate and National Portrait Gallery).

1927 The Post Office high-speed underground railway between Paddington and Whitechapel is completed and opened by George V and Queen Mary.

The electric system was fully automatic and operated around the clock. At 35 m.p.h. compared with 8 m.p.h. average speed overground, mail from Liverpool Street to Paddington took 13 minutes. The railway was nicknamed the Ghost Train because it had no passengers, guards or drivers. 70 feet below ground, 23 miles long, the track a mere 2 feet wide in nine foot, two-way tunnels, it ran every four minutes. Designed solely for letters and parcels it carries mail for 22 out of 24 hours. The carriages, controlled automatically, carried 10 million bags of mail every year between six major sorting offices and two mainline stations.

Halfway along (this part of the tunnel is 6½ miles long) Mount Pleasant Sorting Office covers seven and a half acres. Its 3,000-strong workforce sends 20 million items of mail to 22 million addresses.

1934 Mount Pleasant Sorting Office, the world's largest, pioneers the use of Optical Character Recognition (OCR) for typewritten addresses. One of 80 mechanised letter offices in UK it had the most sophisticated machinery sorting 35,000 letters an hour.

1940 WWII. The Sorting Office is bombed. Operations transferred to the old Aggie in **Upper Street**. The underground railway tunnels were again used to store art treasures. The Post Office didn't return until 1970.

2000 Rumours abound that the Sorting Office is to move to Heathrow.

....

MYDDELTON SQUARE EC1

1631 Sir Hugh Myddelton dies in what one day will be Myddelton Square.

1823 William Chadwell Mylne lays out Chadwell Square. Named after one of the sources of the New River, he was architect and surveyor to The New River Company from 1811 until he died. He designed the astonishing, castellated pumping station in Green Lanes. His father, Robert, also surveyor to The New River Company and St Paul's Cathedral, built Blackfriars Bridge.

Thomas <u>Dibdin</u>, actor-manager of Sadler's Wells, moves into 5 Chadwell Square. He wrote: *'This, not five years since, was an immense field where people used to be stopped and robbed on their return in the evening from Sadler's Wells and the ground floor of the parlour where I sit was as nearly as possible the very spot where my wife and I fell over a recumbent cow.'*

1827 St Mark's Church in the square is designed by William Chadwell Mylne and dismissed by <u>Pevsner</u> 150 years later as: *'the usual Gothic box of the period'*.

1829 When **Chadwell Street** is built, Chadwell Square is re-named **Myddelton Square**.

1908 Fenner <u>Brockway</u>, founder of CND, conscientious objector, Labour candidate for Finsbury Council moves into No. 60, home of the Secretary of the Independent Labour Party. Socialists lived here as a community.

1923 Arnold <u>Bennett</u>'s *Riceyman's Steps* features Myddelton Square.

1931 Gracie <u>Fields</u> moves into No. 30. She was making a film at Islington Film Studios, starring in *Sally in Our Alley*, an early talkie co-written by Archie Pitt (first husband) and Alma Reville (Hitchcock's wife). Director was Monty Banks who became her second husband.

1941 The square is damaged in an air raid.

1962 St Mark's gets a new stained-glass East window. It shows a scene from Sir Hugh Myddelton's life and his Coat of Arms, also Dame <u>Owen</u> and her school (see Owen, Dame Alice), the Angel Inn, Sadler's Wells and the arms of Finsbury, the City and the monarchy.

1975 Lord Brockway unveils a blue plaque on his old home.

NEWINGTON GREEN N1

Select residential area covered in elm trees until the 1600s, when they are cut down (and possibly used to make water pipes (see New River)).

1086 Domesday Book. More live in Newington (pop. 41) than Islington (pop. 27).

1445 27 taxable households. Popular place for prosperous Londoners.

1500s <u>Henry VIII</u> has a hunting lodge here.

1558 Sir Walter <u>Mildmay</u> probably owns land here. Chancellor of the Exchequer and Revenue Commissioner, he issued the new coinage for Elizabeth I. Founded Emanuel College Cambridge. Present at trial of Mary Queen of Scots.

1645 Sir Henry <u>Mildmay</u>, Revenue Commissioner, Master of the King's Jewel House, builds a mansion, The Park, on 44 acres of Newington Green (later Mildmay Nurses' Home was on the site).

1649 Sir Henry is present at the trial of <u>Charles I</u>.

1656 Four houses are built (52/53/54/55), now the oldest surviving terrace in London.

1660 Newly installed Charles II asks Sir Henry Mildmay (who betrayed his father) to produce the king's jewels. Unable to account for missing gems, he was accused of stealing and sent to the Tower.

1664 Sir Henry is deported to Tangier but died on the way at Antwerp.

1667 Charles <u>Morton</u> opens famous Dissenters Academy after the 1662 Act of Uniformity instructs all Ministers to use the Book of Common Prayer or forfeit their livings. Some Nonconformists, Presbyterians and Dissenters, deprived of their livings, banned from preaching within five miles of the City came here. Morton's Academy was on a par with a university, youths were accepted from grammar school.

1675 Daniel Defoe attends Morton's Academy with Samuel Wesley (then spelt Westley) father of John.

1686 Morton emigrates to Charles Town, New England and approves the prosecutions for witchcraft in Salem, Massachusetts.

1690 Isaac Watts is enrolled as a pupil at Morton's Academy.

1702 Reverend Isaac Watts, famous hymnwriter, is appointed Minister at Newington Green Nonconformist Chapel where he stayed until his death. Among the 600 hymns he wrote are When I Survey the Wondrous Cross, Joy to the World, Jesus Shall Reign Where'er the Sun and O God Our Help in Ages Past. He was buried in **Bunhill Fields** and has a plaque in Westminster Abbey.

1763 Samuel Rogers is born in a large house in its own grounds (56–71, corner of **Ferntower/Newington Green Roads**), son of a rich City banker (Corn Hill) and leading member of the local Dissenting congregation.

1781 Rogers starts sending poems to The Gentleman's Magazine at **St John's Gate**.

1784 Mary Wollstonecraft, her sisters Eliza and Everina and friend Fanny Blood open a school. It lasted four years (some sources say two). They became friends with Dr Richard Price, Minister at Unitarian Chapel, who lived at No. 54 (one of the terrace built 1656). He introduced Mary to Dr Johnson.

1786 Rogers publishes Ode To Superstition which is well received.

1789 Dr Price, close friend of Benjamin Franklin, vociferous supporter of American Independence, preaches a sermon in support of the French Revolution at the annual meeting of the London Revolution Society. He dared to tell George III he was 'a servant of the people.'

1792 Rogers publishes The Pleasures of Memory.

1793 Rogers' father dies leaving him very well-off. A generous man with time and money, his friends included Lamb, Hazlitt, Macauley, Sheridan, Southey, Wordsworth, Coleridge, et al.

1803 Rogers, aged 40, now a successful poet, leaves his birthplace and childhood home. He moved to St James' Place, where he gave breakfasts attended by celebrities attracted by his conversation and sarcastic wit. He travelled and became a patron of the arts. His poems were saved from obscurity only because he self-published at enormous cost sumptuous editions illustrated by painters such as J.M.W. Turner and Thomas Stothard.

1807 James Mill moves his family here from Pentonville. John Stuart is 5. (See Mill, John Stuart.)

1880 The ground floors of the seventeenth-century terrace houses, 52/53/54/55 Newington Green are converted into shops.

....

NEW RIVER (The)
Islington: A River Runs Through It

For city dwellers, the scarcity of fresh water has always been a problem. One of the first things William the Conqueror did was divert streams from Islington into the city.

1600 A question is asked in the House about the lack of clean drinking water. William Inglebert, a Londoner, put forward a plan to the Common Council to bring water from

Amwell and St Chad's Well, Ware, Hertfordshire *'via a vault of brick'*. Edmund Colthurst from Bath put in plans suggesting not a vault but an open trench. There was confusion over whose idea it was but John Aubrey, diarist, said it was definitely Inglebert's (in 1935, Finsbury Council renamed Upper Chadwell Street, **Inglebert Street**. The project was put on hold when Elizabeth I's death delayed the Act of Parliament.

1604 Letters Patent to bring water from Hertfordshire are granted to Colthurst.

1606 Act of Parliament authorises Colthurst to bring the water in.

1607 A second Act allows Inglebert to bring water in via his brick vault.

1608 Colthurst asks the Common Council for permission to proceed. He took on a business partner, Hugh Myddelton, MP, goldsmith to James I, and asked for powers granted under both Acts to be transferred to them. After convening, the Council decided to give, not Colthurst, not Inglebert but *Myddelton* permission to proceed.

The New River was not a river but an artificial water supply carried thirty-eight miles from Ware to Islington. Ware, 20 miles away as the crow flies, is 112 feet higher than where the river was to end so the water followed the 100-ft contour line for 40 miles. The drop of only five inches every mile meant the water flowed slowly through Broxbourne, Cheshunt, Enfield, Wood Green, Hornsey, Haringey, Holloway and Islington, ending at Finsbury. The project took Myddelton five years. 150 bridges were built along the route. In some places the river needed an aqueduct so the venture was ambitious and expensive. Water from St Chad's Well and Amwell (later supplemented by the river Lea) flowed via a hand-cut channel, 4 feet deep, 10 feet wide, 60 feet above sea level. Thames Water engineers say they couldn't improve the scheme today.

Once in Islington, the New River was taken around **Canonbury Tower**, the Manor House of Barnsbury (end of Cross Street) diagonally across Lower Street to **Colebrooke Row** alongside Dame Owen School and on to New River Head at The Round Pond, an existing duck pond simply made bigger.

1613 Myddelton's New River will supply the City of London with 38,000 gallons every day, all the fresh water it needs. The New River Company was formed. Myddelton was created a baronet and made Lord Mayor. He built himself a mansion on **Upper Street** (corner of **Almeida Street**, look above entrance to Le Mercury restaurant) near Raleigh (Hogarth painted Raleigh and Myddelton sharing a pipe of tobacco in the Myddelton Arms near Sadler's Wells). The water was piped through hollowed-out elm tree trunks from the reservoir at New River Head to the City across fields or down the centre of streets – hence parts of Islington/Finsbury/Moor Fields were now called Pipe Fields. 160 archery butts were removed to make way.

Islington: Home of Modern Plumbing

The tree trunks were hollowed out, their insides coated with lead to prevent rot and the top tapered to fit (look like giant pencils) inside the wide end (the base) of the next 'pipe'. The joints were secured by giant leather straps with huge buckles. Where water led from the mains into buildings, appropriately located branches were hollowed out and fitted with a huge, quill-like pipe poked through a window. Low-lying houses got water in upstairs rooms, those on higher ground received it via the cellar. The pipes were linked to padlocked turncocks and water was supplied for two to three hours every day to those who could afford to pay.

Because water supply could not be guaranteed, customers installed water tanks (the method continued for 600 years until householders switched to direct supply and did away with water storage). Myddelton's system was so well thought out that it lasted two hundred years until cast iron pipes could be mass-produced. The original wooden pipes were still being dug up as late as 1905 (one is in Islington Museum).

1631 Sir Hugh dies. Despite his enormous contribution to London he seemed never to be free from financial difficulties.

1709 The Water Company needs a prestigious Board Room. The famous Grinling Gibbons (rebus: a cheeky little mouse) was commissioned to carve the wooden friezes, panelling and fireplace. Legend has it that when Sir Christopher Wren and Gibbons were working together on St Paul's, they sometimes lodged here. The Oak Room, a listed building in its own right, is still inside the old Thames Water building (now private flats).

1728 New River Company builds a second reservoir in the open country (**Claremont Square**). It held three and a half million gallons.

1752 Robert Mylne is appointed surveyor. He called his son Chadwell after one of the sources of the New River (**Chadwell Square**).

1807 The tree-trunk pipes are gradually replaced with iron.

1821 Horses arrive at the wind-driven pump house, which can no longer cope with demand. They in turn gave way to steam and then electricity.

1827 Chadwell-Mylne builds an astonishing pumping station resembling a castle at Green Lanes.

1850 The New River Company which, when founded in the 1600s had only the London Bridge Water Company as a competitor, now has eight rivals. Customers paid for water two hours a day, three times a week. Those who could not afford to get connected got water from street standpipes (until deep wells used in industry drew off all the water and the pumps were sealed up and built over).

1852 The Burial Act bans burials in metropolitan areas. Britain finally cottons on to something the Romans always knew: liquid from rotting flesh sinking into the earth may, they ponder, cause typhoid. *Yseldon*, celtic 'place of wells' was no more. The Metropolitan Water Act prohibited standing water. The New River Company's New Reservoir at Claremont Square was drained and the water put into pipes.

1860 Lamb's beloved New River running in front of his old cottage in Colebrooke Row is filled in.

1862 A statue of Sir Hugh Myddelton and drinking fountain on Islington Green is unveiled by Gladstone. It was financed by the New River Company and Sir Samuel Peto, Liberal MP for Finsbury (his company built Nelson's Column in 1843, Peto was created a baronet 1855). Sir Hugh also got a statue outside the Royal Exchange and there's another one (or a copy) in the foyer of Islington Town Hall, which may be from Holborn Viaduct (his name is still there). His portrait hangs in Goldsmith Hall.

1880 After yet another outbreak of cholera The New River Water Company installs filter beds.

1885 A resident of **Claremont Square** complains that the reservoir opposite his house is ugly and forbidding. His letter asking the millionaire New River Company to do something to make it more pleasing to look at. *'It might be made very pretty and a great* *pleasure to the thousands of people who pass by it every day'* was ignored. Today, it's still ugly.

1920 Metropolitan Water Board build their HQ at New River Head. The 200-year-old Oak Room carved by Grinling Gibbons was re-assembled in the Board's magnificent new building.

1930 Thames Water Board Scientific Block for water testing has a preservation order (mentioned in Pevsner's *Buildings of London*).

1963 When the Victoria Line is built the New River is filled in to make a circular reservoir around London (artesian wells) with 21 boreholes for times of drought. 38 million gallons a year were still being abstracted from the old 'New River'.

2000 Thames Water's underground reservoir, carved out of the chalk, stores 33,000 million gallons every winter, enough to fill Lord's cricket ground 200 times over. When the reservoir is full the surplus drains into the New River. A simulated stretch of the river has been created in Canonbury. Fans still walk from New River Head to its source in Herts.

NEW STATESMAN, The

1913 A weekly journal is launched at 14–16 **Farringdon Lane** as a mouthpiece for The Fabian Society.

Fabius was a Roman general famous for his delaying tactics (Fabians want change to evolve naturally). Contributors included G.B. Shaw, Arnold Bennett, G.K. Chesterton, Havelock Ellis, W.B. Yeats and Walter de la Mare. Fabians, launched 1884, helped create The Labour Party. Their policy was *'Dissent. Scepticism. Inquiry. Non-Conformity'.*

Founder Sidney Webb, a clerk in the War Office with a brilliant intellect, was self-educated. His wife Beatrice, from a wealthy family, had the ideas (including Social Security), he actioned them. She also had money, which enabled him to leave the Civil Service and devote his time to politics. (Beatrice had fallen passionately in love with old Highbury boy Joseph Chamberlain who treated her very badly so she settled for Sidney.) He was appointed Professor of Economics at 55 when he founded the London School of Economics. In 1922, age 65, he ran for Parliament and was appointed President, Board of Trade. Made a peer (Lord Passfield), 1929.

OFFORD ROAD N1
Home of hand-blocked wallpaper

1870 John Perry, wealthy entrepreneurial inventor from Cambridge, moves to Islington. He became interested in hand-printed wallpaper and published a book of patterns with John Hanson from his small workshop in **Hanover Yard**.

1875 Perry buys out firms of handblock printers going out of business through mechanisation. Wallpaper was becoming fashionable for those who could afford it (instead of distemper) so Perry built a factory at 142 **Offord Road** (near Arundel Square). He became the leading manufacturer of hand-printed historical/period wallpapers using traditional patterns, many designed by William Morris and Augustus Pugin, which he sold to Sanderson's. Perry invented a machine that used powdered mica (sand) to coat the papers with a satin lustre to protect them from fading.

1941 The firm is taken over by Coles & Sons, Royal Warrant holders, who owned the original 1840 Pugin blocks. The company makes wall coverings for the Queen's Robing Room in Buckingham Palace, for Kensington Palace, the Palace of Westminster, Brighton Pavilion, the Royal Opera House and the White House in Washington.

1966 Benjamin Britten, composer and Peter Pears, opera singer move to No. 99 and stay four years.

Offord Road had another musician who was a household name. Chris Farlowe (born John Deighton, Offord Road, 1940, cousin of Len Deighton, novelist) got to Number One with *Out of Time*, written by Mick Jagger. His house was besieged by the music press and teenage fans. In 1983 he opened *Reckless Records*, a second-hand record shop in **Upper Street** and in the 1990s an antique shop in **Canonbury Lane** called *Out of Time*.

1970 Britten and Pears move to **Halliford Street**, which in 1985 gets a blue plaque.

1997 Britain's last hand-blocked wallpaper manufacturer attracts unwelcome attention when Lord Irvine, Lord Chancellor, commissions Perry's to refurbish his official apartments in the Palace of Westminster, using Pugin's original 1837 blocks.

Perry's have 4,000 blocks with 1,500 original designs dating back to the 1600s. Workers dip 200-year-old, intricately carved wooden (pear or sycamore) printing blocks each weighing 30 lb into coloured matt distemper (chalk base) and press them by hand on to sheets of blank wallpaper. One roll of paper can take a week to produce. Lord Irvine's defence was that the wallpaper is unique, original and would last 40 years.

2000 Newspapers report on the possible impending closure and demolition of the 125-year-old Perry's factory (by contrast Zuber, its French counterpart, is a national monument).

....

OLD PARR'S HEAD
Upper Street N1
1754 The Parr's Head is built on the corner of **Upper Street** and **Cross Street**. Parr was once a household name, having lived to 152.

THE OLDEST MAN IN ENGLAND

Said to have been born in 1483 in Shrewsbury, Old Parr's ancestors also lived to a ripe old age. A countryman, he married for the first time at the age of 80, and fathered two children. Age 102, he was arrested for 'incontinence' (term for adultery) and had to stand in church in front of the congregation in a white sheet, the penance for begetting a bastard. He married again, age 122. At 130 he was still threshing corn and at 152 was brought to London to be exhibited at court but didn't survive long in the noxious climate. Dr William Harvey who conducted the post mortem reported favourably on his internal condition. Parr said he had survived the reigns of ten kings and queens by changing his religion to suit each monarch. His portrait was painted by Rubens, Van Dyck and Blake. He's buried in Poets Corner, Westminster Abbey.

....

ORTON, Joe (1933–1967)
Playwright
1959 Joe Orton and Kenneth Halliwell (met at RADA, 1953) move into a **Noel Road** top

floor bedsit. They painted the walls yellow, the polystyrene ceiling tiles red, grey and pink, stuck black and white tiles on the floor, moved in scores of records and a huge TV set.

1962 The *Daily Mirror* reports on their habit of stealing books from Islington libraries and pasting the covers on the walls of their bedsit, altering the book jackets or rewriting the blurb inside the fly leaf (John Betjeman was depicted in swimming trunks, tattooed from head to foot). Orton and Halliwell appeared at Clerkenwell Magistrates Court (Louis MacNeice, Joe Meek and Bob Geldof also appeared there) and were found guilty of stealing 72 library books, defacing 44 dust covers (now in Islington Library archives) and removing 1,653 colour plates from art books, total damage £450. They were sent to prison for six months.

1963 Orton sells a 45-minute play *Ruffian on the Stair*, written while detained at Her Majesty's Pleasure, to BBC Radio for £65.

1964 *Entertaining Mr Sloane* is a great hit.

1965 *Loot!* is an even bigger hit and in 1970 becomes a film.

1967 Orton wins the *Evening Standard* Drama Award. Giles Gordon, journalist for a quarterly publication, *Transatlantic Review*, taped an interview with him in the tiny Noel Road bedsit. By the time it was published, Orton was dead.

Brian Epstein, who discovered The Beatles, phoned on 9 August, to say a car would call next morning to take Orton to see Richard Lester, Director, *A Hard Day's Night*. But during their own hard day's night, Halliwell bludgeoned Orton to death before committing suicide. The couple were cremated and their ashes scattered in Golders Green Garden of Remembrance. Orton, like Joe Meek, lived in Islington for nine years before meeting with a violent death (see Meek, Joe). For those who believe tragedies come in threes, not long afterwards Brian Epstein was found dead of a drug overdose. Orton and Epstein were 34, Meek 37.

1999 Orton's bedsit in 25 Noel Road is on the market for £100,000 20 people came to view.

....

ORWELL, George (1903–1950)
Writer

Orwell Court N5

1944 Famous author of *Down and Out in Paris and London* (1933) *Burmese Days* (1934) *A Clergyman's Daughter* (1935) *Keep the Aspidistra Flying* (1936) *The Road to Wigan Pier* (1937) *Homage to Catalonia* (1938) *Coming Up for Air* (1939) and *Inside the Whale* (1940) is bombed out of his home near Abbey Road St John's Wood by a doodlebug (V1 rocket). Miraculously, Orwell unearthed the manuscript of *Animal Farm*, his 90-page satire on dictators, from the rubble. He took over the top floor of 27 **Canonbury Square** (blue plaque) and remained the tenant until his death six years later. With him were wife Eileen and adopted baby, Richard.

Christened Eric Arthur Blair, rangy, toothbrush-moustached Old Etonian, Orwell was wounded fighting in the Spanish Civil War (1936–8) and left with a high-pitched voice. Although he had TB he chainsmoked roll-up cigarettes. To simplify his life he wore only khaki or navy shirts. Two years younger, Eileen worked for The Ministry of Food writing exciting information leaflets such as 'A Hundred Ways with a Wartime Potato'. Although Orwell hated London, he and Eileen were blissfully happy in Canonbury Square. He had finally plucked up the courage to leave his well-paid job at the BBC to concentrate on writing. He submitted articles to David Astor (son of Lord Astor) at *The Observer*, introduced by mutual friend Cyril (*Enemies of Promise*) Connolly. He had also accepted the Literary Editorship of *Tribune*, was writing for *Horizon*, *The Manchester Evening News* and the American publication *Partisan Review*. Living in Islington and loving its junk shops (like Evelyn Waugh before him) he penned a feature, *Just Junk . . . 'I could lead you to some first rate* (junk shops) *in the dingier areas of Islington near the Angel and Holloway . . .'* 24 publishers turned down *Animal Farm*. Dial Press in America told him: *'there is no market for animal stories'*. In despair he decided to borrow £200 and self-publish.

1945 August, Frederick Warburg publishes *Animal Farm*. It was an instant international best seller and quickly became a modern classic. Orwell used to go around Islington bookshops, removing copies from the children's section.

1946 March, a growth is discovered in Eileen's womb (probably fibroids) which is removed. The operation was routine but tragically Eileen suffered a reaction to the anaesthetic and died on the operating table. She was 39. Devastated, Orwell returns to Canonbury Square and throws himself into his work.. He attacks old friend Aneurin Bevan and the Labour Party in print for not abolishing public schools, titles and the House of Lords.

1947 Orwell left Islington for Jura, a small Scottish island, to write *1984*. He wanted to get Richard, 4, out of bomb-damaged Islington into fresh country air, where he would have peace to write. But in his heart he didn't wander far from Islington *'. . . He was somewhere in the vague brown coloured slums to the north and east of what had been St Pancras station'* or his old job at the Ministry of Information (*Ministry of Truth*). October, thinking he is better off in town for the winter Orwell brings Richard back to Canonbury Square. Bad move. Britain was hit by a severe fuel shortage with heavy snow and freezing winds. With no coal available Orwell burned peat, furniture and Richard's toys. He returned to Jura and by November had completed the first draft of *1984* before being admitted to East Kilbride TB hospital.

1949 On medical orders, Orwell leaves Jura. In a TB sanatorium in Gloucestershire, he was visited by Sonia Brownell (30). He proposed to her and she accepted. *1984* was published in the UK and in America. Phrases like *'Big Brother'*, *'Newspeak'*, *'Thought Police'* and *'Brainwashing'* entered the language. Orwell was moved to University College Hospital where his doctor had unsuccessfully treated D.H. Lawrence for TB twenty years earlier (1930). Sonia married Orwell in October at his bedside.

1950 January, Orwell has a TB haemorrhage. He was buried at All Saints Church, Sutton Courtney, Oxfordshire. His headstone said simply, as requested, *Here Lies Eric Arthur Blair*.

1997 In a 6-week poll, 25,000 Waterstones bookshop customers vote *1984* the second-greatest book written this century (third is *Animal Farm*).

....

OWEN, Dame Alice (1542–1608)
Philanthropist
Owen Street N1

Alice Wilkes, 15, daughter of Thomas Wilkes, prosperous local brewer and landowner (bought Hermitage Fields after the Reformation), out walking, stops to chat with a dairymaid milking a cow and asks if she can try. As she stands up an arrow lands in her hat. Shaken and grateful for her life, she vows that she will build a school to educate children of the poor of Islington ...

1598 Dame Alice starts building her school on the spot where she almost died (Hermitage Fields was a triangle of land bounded by **St John Street**, **Goswell Road** and **Rawstorne Street**).

1603 James I grants Dame Alice a licence to open a Free Grammar School to *'teach the sons and daughters of the poor, abiding in Islington, Isledon and Clerkenwell'*. And so they were, for over 300 years. Dame Alice, 66, lived long enough to see the launch of her school on her friend, Sir Hugh Myddelton's New River between the Welch Harp and the Turk's Head. Buried in **St Mary's**, her tomb was very grand with sculptures of her children and grandchildren.

1886 Girls are admitted. The boys' school was called Owen's, the girls' school, Dame Alice Owen.

1938 Beryl Grey (Dame) is enrolled as a pupil. One of the first prima ballerinas to keep her own name (English ballet was ridiculed so they changed them to Russian-sounding names).

1958 500 boys, 330 girls.

1977 The Labour Party strongly disapproves of schools which admit pupils by academic selection. Prestigious St Aloysius College and Highbury Grove Grammar were forced to go comprehensive. (See Boyson, Dr Rhodes.) The GLC and Islington Council offered to pay 80 per cent of the removal costs if the Dame Owen Schools moved out of Islington (anywhere outside GLC area, in fact!). After 363 years at **The Angel** the school moved to Potters Bar. The 1613 carvings of Dame Alice, her children and grandchildren were taken to the new school. Among the school's last pupils were John Keeble, Tony Hadley, Gary and Martin Kemp from **Essex Road** and Steve Norman from **Rosebery Avenue**, later famous as *Spandau Ballet*. City University took over the girls' school for its Department of Optometry but the Charity kept the freehold.

1997 Part of the old school playground is Owens Fields Public Garden.

1999 Trustees of Dame Owen Foundation (Worshipful Company of Brewers) have not spent any of its vast fortune on the Islington children it was set up to serve since it moved to Potters Bar. The old site was worth £7m and plans were passed to build a seven-storey block of flats. The High Court however ruled that the school must divide its income of £750,000 p.a. between Potters Bar and Islington, where schools were so bad that even the Labour government is insisting the Council handed education over to private management.

2000 For the first time in 25 years, the Trust is forced to hand over £200,000 p.a. to Islington Schools and to admit a quota of children from Islington.

....

PAINE, Thomas (1737–1809)
Radical

1790 Briefed by on-the-spot reports from Paine, Edmund Burke publishes *Reflections on the Revolution in France*, putting the wind up the propertied classes. 4 November, Paine, itching for a political fight with Burke, booked into the Angel Inn to pen his response, *The Rights of Man*. He estimated it would take four days, in the event he was there four months.

1791 29 January, Paine's 54th birthday, a double celebration. Late the previous night he finished *The Rights of Man, Part One*. He opened a few bottles of wine in the downstairs bar with friend Clio Rickman (*Part Two* was written in Rickman's house). The best-selling book in the history of publishing was dedicated to George Washington.

Paine advocated state grants for education, maternity benefits, child allowances, unemployment benefits and old age pensions. The book was read by the literate poor in factories and mills, many of whom for the first time took an interest in politics. It would lead to Paine being prosecuted for seditious libel.

1791 31 January, under threat of prosecution, Paine takes the manuscript to Joseph Johnson (mentor to Blake, Wordsworth, Wollstonecraft and Coleridge), asking him to get his book on the shelves by 22 February in time for the opening of Parliament and George Washington's birthday.

Johnson received several intimidatory visits from government agents and reluctantly suspended printing. Paine borrowed £40 to self-publish, took the books to Jordan's (Fleet Street printers), asked his friend William Godwin to take charge of distribution and left for Paris, where he had been asked to carry the American flag in the public celebration of the new French Constitution. The book reached the shops in March. According to legend, George III went into a bookshop near Windsor Castle, picked up a copy, read it and put it back, showing no hint of displeasure; nevertheless Paine was indicted in his absence on charges of sedition. The founder of the Declaration of Human Rights died in exile, an American citizen, ignored and forgotten.

1819 Radical politician William Cobbett brings Paine's remains back to England. No-one knows where they are buried. Cruikshank's 1820 cartoon *Coriolanus* (George III) *Addressing the Plebeians* shows Cobbett brandishing the bones of his hero. Paine lapsed into obscurity for 100 years.

1991 An obelisk commemorating him is unveiled in **Angel Square**. As the Angel Inn is no more, his plaque is inside The Old Red Lion down the road. Paine was a drinking man so it's likely he wrote parts of his book there.

....

PARKER, Alan (1944–)
Film director
*Born and brought up in Canonbury Court, **Sebbon Street***.

1997 Reduces hard-nosed Disney chairman to tears with *Evita*, which took two years to make (he read 29 books on Eva Peron). Parker was the discoverer of Jody Foster, who starred in his *Bugsy Malone*, Director of Pink Floyd's *The Wall*, *Angel Heart*, *The Commitments*, *Fame* and *Mississippi Burning*. He worked with the young Oliver Stone on *Midnight Express*, whom, he says, he went to great lengths to avoid.

1950s Living in a council flat, his father paints railings for the electricity board. Parker loved Saturday morning pictures at the Carlton, **Essex Road** and the Odeon, **Upper Street** and says his most vivid memories of Islington were the bombsites and boarded-up war damaged buildings (*The Evacuees*, 1974). Another alumnus of Owen's School (q.v.), he left at 15 and started in the mailroom of an ad agency. He learnt how to direct TV commercials using a 16mm camera. A winner of the BAFTA *Michael Balcon* (see Islington Studios and other entries) Award for outstanding contribution to British film making, he says his worst fear is boring the audience.

Parker's hero, film maker Ken <u>Loach</u> who he says is *'integrity on legs'*, also has links with Islington. He was a member of the Tower Theatre, filmed *Cathy Come Home* in **Popham Street** and is sometimes seen in The Screen on The Green.

PAUL, Robert (1869–1943)
Islington: Home of the Moving Image
1869 Robert Paul, *'father of British Cinema'* is born 3 Albion Place (demolished) off **Liverpool Road**. He was the first Englishman to bring film into the commercial field. Dubbed England's Thomas Edison, he attended Finsbury Technical College.
1895 Paul designs, makes and sells scientific instruments. Commissioned to make a copy of Edison's Kinetoscope (not patented in the UK), he produced a camera that took moving pictures and a device to project them onto a screen.
1896 Visits Finsbury Tech. to show students his films on his 'animatographe'. Paul's first films showed trains entering stations, boats bobbing up and down on the sea and people walking in **Upper Street**.

Each film lasted no more than two minutes, so grainy it looked as if shot in pouring rain. Paul went on to make films showing Princess Maud getting married, The Derby and the Oxford v. Cambridge Boat Race and made a film every week until 1910. 'Paul's Perfect Palpitating Promethean Photos' were shown at the World Fair at the 'Aggie'. His cinematographic enterprises made him wealthy. Firms which had turned out 'magic lantern' slide projectors now made projectors. Local availability of the latest equipment put Islington at the forefront of 'electric theatres' (cinemas).
1897 Stakes out vantage points along the Jubilee route and produces *The Queen's Diamond Jubilee*. Filmgoers could see the procession better than those who had paid £5 for a seat. At the Aggie, Randall <u>Williams</u>, self-styled King of Showmen, staged *'a Phantoscopical exhibition using the electroscope worked by electricity generated on the premises by our own magnificent engine.'* At Myddelton Hall, **Almeida Street**, *the Jubilee Procession (including the historic ceremony at Temple Bar)* was shown along with *'a new and startling train film, a realistic bolster fight and a laughable film of marines at vaulting exercises'*. At Sadler's Wells, a popular film starring James Berry, public hangman of 193 murderers, charted the 'progress' of a convict from his arrest and journey in the Black Maria, to the flogging and hanging beam.

PEABODY, George (1795–1869)
US-born philanthropist
Peabody Yard N1
1827 Age 32, the American philanthropist (his ancestors emigrated from England) settles in London and stays until he dies, age 74.
1866 The first Peabody Estate in Islington is built in Ward's Place, Greenman Street (where Robert <u>Dudley</u>, Earl of Leicester once lived). George witnessed the furore over Charles Dickens' *Oliver Twist* exposing the living conditions in the Clerkenwell rookeries. Those not sleeping in the street lived seven to a room. Peabody gave £500,000 to build cheap rent housing for *'the honest and industrious poor'* (those in regular work) within a ten-mile radius of

The Royal Exchange. Trustees decided his gift must earn 3 per cent interest so that it could be used in perpetuity. Queen Victoria offered Peabody a Baronetcy but he declined it, as he did The Grand Cross of the Order of the Bath (he did accept the Freedom of the City).

PEABODY SQUARE

Four blocks of 155 flats housing 650 tenants, boasted 'model dwellings'. Each had a cooking range, a water boiler, built-in cupboards and a coal store – but no plaster on the brick walls. The flats were for the 'deserving poor' and rigid rules were imposed concerning cleanliness, orderliness and thrift. Passages and steps had to be swept every morning before 10 a.m., sinks, water closets (WCs) and windows cleaned every Saturday, stairs and landings polished every week. Children were not allowed out after 7 p.m. in winter and 8 p.m. in summer. Each block had a communal laundry and a Superintendent who gave tenants a few hours to pay if they fell behind with the rent. Taking in washing or ironing was strictly forbidden, as was the keeping of animals.

1869 Peabody's statue at The Royal Exchange is unveiled by the Prince of Wales in his presence. Six months later, he died in Eaton Square in the arms of his mistress. He was given a magnificent state funeral in Westminster Abbey, the only American ever to be given this honour, but was buried as requested in his home town of Danvers (renamed Peabody), Massachusetts. Other Peabody estates are in Farringdon Lane, Baird, Chequer, Dufferin, Errol, Guest, Roscoe and Whitecross Streets (1882) and Banner Street (1956). Today the Trust runs 73 estates, 13,000 homes and is worth over £800 million.

1997 *A Capital Divided* published by The Peabody Trust mapped social exclusion in London. According to the government's definition of poverty, 100 years post-Peabody Islington still has high infant mortality, high unemployment, 25 per cent on income support and 37 per cent of its children in homes with no wage earner.

PENTONVILLE PRISON
Caledonian Road N1

1842 The New Model Prison opens for business, its grand portcullis entrance designed by Sir Charles <u>Barry</u>. Single cells had hammocks, not beds and the inhumane Silent System was introduced. Prisoners were not allowed to communicate and had to wear masks, sitting in separate boxes in chapel. Elizabeth <u>Fry</u>, famous prison reformer, visited and was horrified: *'separate confinement produces an unhealthy state of mind'*. She was proved right. many prisoners went mad or committed suicide. Seated between Prince Albert and Sir Robert Peel at a dinner at the Mansion House, she made her opinions forcibly known. A scheme was launched to get prisoners to sign the pledge and help them emigrate to Australia. Sheep were taken in to teach shearing. This caused an outcry: criminals must be punished, not taught a trade.

1895 Oscar Fingal O'Flahertie Wills <u>Wilde</u> is brought here to begin two years hard labour before transferring to Wandsworth and Reading gaols.

1897 Having served his sentence with no remission for good behaviour, Wilde is brought back prior to release.

1902 The triple scaffold (three could hang at a time) is brought from Newgate prison.

1910 <u>Crippen</u> is hanged (see Crippen, Hawley, Dr).

1912 <u>Seddon</u> is hanged (see Seddon, Fred).

1916 Sir Roger <u>Casement</u> is hanged for treason.

Casement, (52) was born in Dublin (Ireland was part of the UK, partitioned 1921). A British subject knighted 1910, he had (probably) been spying for the Kaiser. In 1916 he arrived in Dublin in a German U-boat (some say to organise the Easter Rising others say to delay it) and was arrested. An incriminating diary, authenticity disputed, sealed his fate.

1923 Fred <u>Bywaters</u>, ship's purser, is hanged by Tom <u>Pierrepoint</u>. Edith <u>Thompson</u>, a milliner, expecting Bywater's baby, is hanged by John Ellis in Holloway Prison.

Thompson (28) helped her good-looking lover Bywaters (20) kill her husband. She screamed non-stop in the condemned cell from the time her appeal was rejected to the time of execution. At the point of hanging she suffered a miscarriage and haemorrhaged, after which all women about to be hanged wore waterproof knickers.

1941 WWII. Bombed in an air raid, C Block is demolished causing fatalities (the same raid damaged Lenin's old home in **Holford Square**, parts of **Myddelton** and **Granville Squares**).

1946 Albert <u>Pierrepoint</u> hangs William <u>Joyce</u>, dubbed Lord Haw Haw, who broadcast German propaganda to Britain, and Herr Schurch (one of fifteen German spies tried at the Old Bailey). Neville <u>Heath</u>, 30, about to be hanged, had not lost his appetite. He tucked into a traditional English breakfast of eggs, bacon, sausages, tomatoes, fried bread, toast and marmalade and two mugs of tea followed by his last wish, a glass of whisky. In a London hotel bedroom, after mutilating Margery Gardener with a whip, biting off her nipples and thrusting a poker into her vagina, he finished her off by suffocating her. He had met her only 24 hours earlier. Before he could be found he mutilated and murdered another girl in Bournemouth. He often posed either as a peer of the realm or top ranking military officer.

1950 Timothy <u>Evans</u> is hanged by Albert Pierrepoint for the murder of his baby daughter Geraldine, fourteen months, and his wife, age 19.

The previous November, Evans had moved out of 10 Rillington Place and gone to his aunt in Wales, where he reported his wife's death to the police. He said that his landlord Reginald <u>Christie</u> had given his wife 'some stuff' to procure an abortion but she had died. Although Christie had a prison record for violence he convinced the police that Evans was the murderer.

1953 Three years after Timothy Evans dies, Reginald <u>Christie</u> is hanged for the same crime.

The hundreds gathered outside Pentonville were not all local, they had come from Scotland, Ireland, Wales, America and Australia. Seven bodies were discovered at 10 Rillington Place after Christie suddenly gave up the tenancy and moved into Rowton House, **King's Cross Road** (Baron <u>Rowton</u>, philanthropist, politician, private secretary to Disraeli, built hotels for homeless working men in King's Cross, Vauxhall, Stoke Newington, Hammersmith, Whitechapel and Camden. This one became Mount Pleasant Hotel, and then a Holiday Inn). As Christie was eating breakfast in a café in **Pentonville Road**, the new tenant at 10 Rillington Place made the grisly discovery.

10 RILLINGTON PLACE MURDERS

John Reginald Halliday Christie was born 1908 in Halifax. In 1929 he was imprisoned for beating a woman over the head with a cricket bat. In 1933 he was in prison again for stealing a car. He moved to Rillington Place 1938 and started killing women for a hobby in

1943, during the war. By the time Timothy Evans, his pregnant wife and their baby Geraldine moved in, 1948, Christie had already murdered two women there and buried them in the garden. When he was arrested he had on him every single newspaper cutting of Evans' trial. A necrophiliac, he said he couldn't remember how many women he had murdered. There was public outrage that the wrong man had been hanged and the campaign to abolish hanging was stepped up, yet Evans received no pardon, obscure legal arguments being deployed to show that he could have committed the murders.

Rillington Place, re-named Ruston Close, was eventually demolished.

1965 Harold Wilson PM gives permission for Roger Casement's remains to be re-interred in Dublin.

1996 Campaigners win Timothy Evans a pardon.

2000 Novelist Jill Dawson writes *Fred and Edie* about the the Bywaters/Thompson murder.

....

PENTONVILLE ROAD N1

1756 Battle Bridge village is razed to make way for The New Road, built to link Paddington with the Angel.

1773 Henry Penton MP for Winchester, Lord of the Admiralty, builds **Penton Ville**. Designed on a grid, London's first planned suburb was built on 134 acres of rural countryside each side of New Road. Penton was ordered to set his houses 50 feet back, so each had a very long front garden (a few survive near **The Angel**). The Penton family is commemorated in St James', Clerkenwell Close.

1787 St James' chapel is built by subscription.

1791 St James' is declared a Chapel of Ease for St James Clerkenwell.

1800 A map shows Penton Ville, London's First New Town. The part of New Road leading from King's Cross to The Angel is re-named Pentonville Road.

1812 Sir Henry Penton is buried in the vault of St James'.

1819 Thomas Wilson of Highbury Terrace, rich son of a silk mercer, buys a piece of land to build, entirely at his own expense, Claremont Congregational Chapel, seating 1,500. In the event, nineteen worshippers attend (thirteen women, six men).

1828 Painter Richard Parkes Bonington is buried in St James'. He was 27.

Born in Nottingham, he moved with his parents to France when he was 15. His work was much admired by early French impressionists. A regular visitor to London, he died when over here supervising an exhibition of his paintings. The National Gallery, Tate and the Wallace Collection all bought his paintings.

1829 London's first omnibus route opens (see Shillibeer, George).

1837 Joey Grimaldi is buried in St James'.

1840 Claremont Chapel gets a facelift. Brick was considered common so it was covered with white stucco scored to look like stone.

1860 George Betjeman builds his (manu)factory at No. 36 (see Betjeman, John).

1897 Burial ground of St James' opened as a public garden.

1911 Cosy Corner Picture Playhouse corner of Northdown Street/Pentonville Road has the latest Pathé equipment.

1914 New, purpose built King's Cross Cinema opens at 275. Started 1913, work stopped at the outbreak of war and the building was used as a labour exchange until 1920.

1926 Cosy Corner cinema closes, unable to compete with the grand King's Cross one.

1945 Betjeman factory closes.

1951 King's Cross Cinema now a Gaumont.

1962 Gaumont is now an Odeon

1972 The Odeon is a Cine Club (blue movies).

1975 Cine Club closes.

1980 Cine Club is re-opened as The Scala to show films about endangered primates ... First film shown was 1933 *King Kong*, accompanied by noises of tube trains below.

1985 St James' Church is closed. Grimaldi is still there but Richard Bonington moved to Kensal Green cemetery. Plans were passed for offices to be built on the site provided the façade was retained.

1991 The national HQ of The Crafts Council of Great Britain take over the derelict Claremont Chapel.

1998 Newly restored Scala is floodlit and re-opens as an arts venue.

....

PEPYS, Samuel (1633–1703)

Diarist

Islington is mentioned many times in the famous diaries. His entries are so frank he writes in a secret code, cracked only in 1825. The censored diaries were not published until 1893.

1661 Pepys is attending St James' Church, **Clerkenwell** where he has developed a crush on a woman in the congregation. He also visited Clerkenwell Bridewell to see his wife's friend Margaret Pen.

1663 Pepys is a frequent visitor to The King's Head (q.v.), **Upper Street**, The Bottle of Hay, **St John Street** and 'Mother Red Cap', **Holloway Road**, famous resort of prostitutes.

1666 Chronicles the plague and Great Fire of London.

....

POETS

Islington has connections with many poets. Apart from Ben Jonson, England's first poet laureate who acted here and wrote *Bartholomew Fair*, there was Sir William D'Avenant, father of English opera (1656), of Charterhouse Square who succeeded him; John Milton (1661) of **Bunhill Fields**; Ned Ward (1712) of **Woodbridge Street**; Colley Cibber, poet laureate (1733) **Colebrooke Row**; Thomas Hood (1807) of **Essex Road**; Samuel Rogers born at **Newington Green** was offered (1850) but declined the laureateship when Wordsworth died; Robert Bridges poet laureate (1876), doctor at **Bart's** and the Royal Northern, **Holloway Road**; Louis MacNeice (1947) **Canonbury Park South**; Sir John Betjeman, poet laureate (1976) **Cloth Fair**; Andrew Motion of **Tuffnell Park**, who succeeded Ted Hughes as poet laureate in 1999.

....

POLLARD (Robert, James)

Artists

1782 Robert moves to 15 Baynes Row (**Exmouth Market**). Pupil of Richard Wilson RA, painter of landscapes and seascapes, he turned to more profitable print making.

1792 Seventh child, a son, James.

1810 Although they don't get on, Robert and James move from Baynes Row and open a very successful print business at 11 Holloway Place, **Holloway Road**. Some of the best known sporting and coaching scenes of London came from the Pollard studio.

1816 James paints *The Royal Mail Coach at the Peacock Inn* for the George IV birthday procession.

The Peacock and Angel Inns are the Victoria Coach Station of their day. Coaches arrive every ten minutes from 5 a.m. until 11 a.m., at 2 p.m. the rush starts again and continues until dusk.

1821 James exhibits *The North Country Mails at The Peacock, Islington* at the Royal Academy. His father thought he ought to be happy with 50 guineas for it but James held out for more (in 1960 it fetched £19,000 at auction).

1823 James paints *The Peacock Inn* again.

....

PUGIN (Augustus, family)
Architects and designers
Pugin Court N1
Augustus, the famous Gothic revivalist, a French immigrant who spoke no English, became John Nash's right-hand man. He styled himself the Comte de Pugin.

1799 Moves to Islington and publishes a series of water-colours 'Views of Islington and Pentonville'. Catherine <u>Welby</u>, daughter of a local barrister from Inner Temple (dubbed *The Belle of Islington*) out walking stopped to watch him sketch. She was a follower of Revd Edward Irving of Amwell Street.

1802 Marries Catherine in St Mary's. The Pugins lived in Islington for twenty years (1799–1818), possibly in her family home in **Islington High Street**.

1812 Pugin's even more famous son is born, given both parents' names, Augustus Welby Pugin.

1818 *Views of Islington* published by Pugin Snr.

1832 Pugin Snr and Catherine are buried in family vault in St Mary's.

Pugin Jnr was trained by his father. He was commissioned by Sir Charles Barry to decorate the interior for the new Palace of Westminster. His original wooden blocks for handprinted wallpaper are owned by John Perry Wallpapers (q.v.) of **Offord Road**. Tragically, in 1851, he went mad and was an inmate for a year at the world famous Bedlam asylum. His son, Edward Welby Pugin, 17, found himself head of the architect's huge and busy practice. He carried on the business but, mindful of his father's breakdown caused by overwork, retired age 31. He died at 41, the same age as his father.

Q

....

QUAKERS
Islington: Home of the Quakers
1644 George <u>Fox</u>, 20, founder of the Society of Friends, moves to Clerkenwell and preaches pacifism at the Meeting House, **St John Street**.

'Quakers' like 'Methodists' was originally a term of derision. Fox called upon his followers and those in authority to tremble before the Lord. He despised all formal religion and went to church, which he called 'steeple houses', only to interrupt the sermons. Always in and out of prison, he made missionary journeys to Scotland, Ireland, Holland, North America and the West Indies.

1661 Quakers buy Banner Street Burial Ground. They also bought 21 Coleman Street for The Society of Friends Meeting House (name change 1883 to **Roscoe Street**). When George Fox was buried in Banner Street burial ground it was re-named Quaker Garden. When it closed in 1855, a small stone commemorating him was put up.

RADIO DOCTOR (The)

1904 Charles Hill is born in **York Road**, third and last child. Two years later his father (worked for a local piano manufacturer) died. The family moved to Liverpool Buildings, **Highbury Station Road**.

1939–45 WWII. Appointed *Radio Doctor* by the BBC to promote preventative medicine and explain why the war-time diet was such a good one (very little sugar or fat, etc.). Hill gave cosy 'bowel to bowel' talks using the 'everyday language' of 'ordinary people'.

1945 Hill, Chairman British Medical Association, is at loggerheads with Aneurin Bevan in the process of implementing a free National Health Service. Hill argued it would be abused and prove ultimately detrimental for Britain.

1950–63 MP for Luton. (1961 Minister of Housing.)

1963–67 Chairman, Independent Television Authority.

1963 Lord Hill of Luton.

1967–72 Chairman, BBC.

RALEIGH, Walter (Sir) (1552–1618)
Raleigh Mews/Street N1

1575 Ralegh (sic), age 21, moves to **Upper Street** where he (probably) stays six years until he achieves his burning ambition to become one of <u>Elizabeth I</u>'s courtiers.

Raleigh enrolled at the Inns of Court, Middle Temple, to complete his education. His was a typical Tudor house, long, irregular, of wood and plaster with a thatched roof, surrounded by gardens and orchards. December, Raleigh attended Middlesex County Court to stand bail of 100 marks for one of his servants in trouble with the law. His mates were witty and boisterous. Among them was Edmund *Faerie Queen* <u>Spenser</u>, the poet, whose moustache and beard Raleigh joined together with sealing wax while he was sleeping. Another was the Earl of Oxford who liked to shock by calling the Virgin Mary (a Catholic, not a Protestant saint) 'a whore who cuckolded her husband'. Raleigh founded The Friday Club in The Mermaid Inn, Bread St, Cheapside and spent the first Friday evening of every month carousing.

1578 'Ralegh' begins to sign himself Walter Rawley, *Esquire de Curia* of the Court. This meant he had managed to reach Body Extraordinary, a reserve pool of young gentlemen called at any time to wait upon the Queen. Raleigh was young, dashing and good looking.

1580 Committed to Fleet Prison for six days and ordered to 'cool his heels' after a duel following a drunken brawl.

1581 When Raleigh gets to court he is 27, Elizabeth 48. She was still heartbroken over lapdog Dudley, who, declaring undying love for her, secretly married the beautiful widow Lettice Knollys, Countess of Essex.

1584 New favourite, Raleigh is given a lucrative monopoly, the farming of wine 'to make lycences for keeping of taverns and retailing wynes throughout England.' On the Queen's authority he supervised the import of wine and charged every vintner in the land £1 a year for a licence to sell.

One tavern granted a licence was the Queen's Head, Lower Road (Essex Road). The inn lost its original Elizabethan ceiling when a landlord installed a massive snooker table in an upstairs room and the legs went through the floorboards. It still has the original fireplace.

RALEIGH AND TOBACCO

It is not true that Raleigh introduced tobacco into England. He was eleven years old when that was done (1565) by John Hawkins, a chronic snuff-taker who died appropriately of cancer of the nose. Raleigh did however make tobacco fashionable by smoking it instead of chewing, sniffing or growing it for medicinal purposes. He taught the Queen to smoke using a tiny silver pipe, and the habit caught on at Court.

1587 Raleigh sells Ark Ralegh to the Queen, who re-launches it as Ark Royal, flagship of her fleet.

1592 Ten years a courtier, like Robert Dudley before him Raleigh, 38, now wants a wife, home, son and heir. Realising the Queen would never marry him he married Elizabeth Throckmorton in secret. Her Majesty, 59, publicly humiliated, put him in the Tower.

1603 James I, Elizabeth's successor also has him put in the Tower.

1614 Released from the Tower, did he return to his Upper Street home? Two hundred years later, Hogarth painted 'Evening', showing Raleigh sharing a pipe with one of his neighbours, Sir Hugh Myddelton, at an Islington inn.

1618 Having seen off Essex, Francis Bacon indicts Raleigh (on trumped up charges) and successfully argues for his demise. James I ordered that the popular hero should be beheaded on Lord Mayor's Day to distract crowds from his execution. After smoking his last pipe Raleigh made the longest-known speech from the scaffold (45 minutes). Listening to their hero were two grief-stricken members of his fan club, John Pym and John Eliot, who would one day wreak revenge by helping Cromwell execute James' son, Charles I.

No-one is sure where Raleigh is buried. Some say St Margaret's Westminster where there is a stained glass commemorative window, others the crypt of St Mary Beddington Surrey or with his son at St Mary's, West Horsley, Surrey.

AFTERMATH

1624 Sir John Miller of Devon (who has lived in Islington since 1617, just before Raleigh was beheaded) moves into Raleigh's old house on Upper Street.

1640 The house is converted into an inn. Drinkers admired the stained-glass windows with the Raleigh coat of arms.

1790 The Gentleman's Magazine prints a drawing, The North View of the Mansion of Sir Walter Rawlegh at Islington (renamed The Pied Bull, **Upper Street**).

1827 The ancient inn is due for demolition so George Cruikshank and friends come here to toast Raleigh's memory.

1959 A small statue paid for by Anglo-American societies is unveiled by the American ambassador on Raleigh Green, facing Whitehall, near the spot where he was beheaded. Plans are afoot to remove it to Sherborne, Dorset, his old home.

1988 The Pied Bull is renamed The Sir Walter Raleigh.

REFORMATION and Dissolution of the Monasteries

1536 Henry VIII has all wells dedicated to saints covered over, making water even more scarce.

Monasteries, nunneries and priories now belonged to Henry, who made himself head of the Church in England. Pilgrimages to places such as Rahere's tomb (see St John's Priory) were frowned upon. He sold St Bartholomew the Great to the horrid Sir Richard Rich, butchered the Carthusians, sold Charterhouse and St Mary's Nunnery to Sir Edward North, gave St John's Priory to his first daughter, Princess Mary and Canonbury Tower (q.v.) to Thomas Cromwell. St Mary's, **Upper Street** became C. of E. and St Mary's Nunnery church was known as St James'.

1552 The dissolution of the religious houses has thrown hundreds out of work. The homeless and starving once fed by the nunneries and priories roamed the streets begging so a Statute ordered every parish to register their poor and assume responsibility for them. The nobility converted the empty religious houses, making **Clerkenwell** a desirable area to live. Henry VIII's future bride (sixth and last) Catherine Parr, for instance, was living in **Charterhouse Square**.

REGENT'S CANAL N1

The Islington part of the Grand Union Canal was the last link in the great chain of inland waterways which ran from the north of England to the Thames. It's 6 feet deep and 48 feet wide (three barges can pass comfortably). For over half a mile it flows under Islington.

1812 The Regent's Canal Act gives permission for a tunnel to be dug under Islington from The White Conduit House, **Muriel Street** (at Pentonville, during the excavation, the vertebra of a crocodile was found) to Vincent Terrace off **Colebrooke Row**. In places, the tunnel ran under the New River (q.v.). Irish navigators ('navvy' was not a derogatory term) built the canal. It was to keep them in work, barring death by accident, for eight years.

Although only 8 miles long, this stretch of the canal was beset with problems. Thomas Homer, superintendent in charge, absconded with all the money and was given seven years transportation. John Rennie was asked to take over but because of the recent Highgate Hill debacle (the tunnel collapsed) refused, so John Nash was invited to be principal shareholder. Nash, a friend of the Prince Regent, was laying out Regent's Park so had a vision of running the canal through the middle. The venture was beset by problems. The tunnels collapsed, causing many deaths; understandably, labourers were not easy to get. The government tried to force the unemployed after Waterloo to work for nothing but they refused, so it had to lend £200,000 to pay wages.

1820 The canal opens for business. Because tunnelling was difficult the towpath in the

Islington Tunnel was dispensed with. Bargees had to 'leg it' by walking the barge along the roof and sides of the tunnel with the horse plodding overhead.

1837 Despite being very busy (Pickford's alone has 120 barges transporting coal, timber, sand, gravel, metals, corn, hay, refuse and ice) within a very few years the railways took all their business so the canal was a commercial failure. Shareholders tried to sell it to the railways to build a line along its route to the docks.

1930 Barges on the canal are pulled by diesel tugs instead of horses.

1959 The M1, Britain's first motorway, is built. Regent's Canal was commercially defunct.

1970s Houseboats on the canal become fashionable.

RIVERS

1100 In addition to its springs, Islington has two rivers, the Fleet and the Wall Brook (Walbrook), plus a host of minor tributaries feeding the Thames.

Running along the south-west corner of Islington, the Fleet was for centuries an important tributary of the Thames. It had two sources, one at the Vale of Health, Hampstead Ponds, the other at Ken Wood (Kenwood). They ran along Kentish Town Road, under the Regent's Canal and met at Camden Town, where the Fleet went on to King's Cross, Farringdon Road and Holborn Viaduct, joining the Thames at Blackfriars. The river formed a natural defence of the west wall of Roman London and at its widest was 650 feet, navigable until it met another of London's lost rivers, the Bourne (Old Bourne/Holborn). Locals living along its banks gave the Fleet different names. In King's Cross it was the Bagnigge (possibly the name of the landowner), in parts of Clerkenwell it was Turn Mill Brook and at Fagges Well slaughterhouse, for obvious reasons, The Red Fleet.

The Walbrook started near the Angel (where it powered a lead mill until 1800) then ran down to London Wall where it passed into the city via an iron grating in front of Moor Gate. With water costing a penny a pail, the poor built shanties and the rich, houses along its banks. A lane formed alongside the river, the lane became a road, then a high street and then – no more river. The Walbrook is now City Road. Then there was Hackney Brook (Haca was a Dane, Ey was Danish for 'island'). This started at Isledon Road, ran down Gillespie Road into Riversdale Road on to Clissold Park, Abney Park Cemetery and ended when it joined the river Lea. With The Fleet, Walbrook, Hackney Brook, The New River (a canal) and The Regents Canal, Islington must once have looked like Amsterdam or Venice!

ROBINSON, William Heath (1872–1944)

Cartoonist

Islington: Home of the Useless Contraption

*Although Heath Robinson lived in the **Holloway/Highgate** area for 50 of his 72 years, no street is named after him.*

1834 Thomas Robinson, William's grandfather, lives in Coldbath Fields. He started as a bookbinder (first editions of Thomas Bewick) before switching to wood engraving (worked for George du Maurier).

1838 Thomas moves to 1 Upper Grove Cottages, **Holloway** where Thomas (William's father) his second son is born. Thomas was a daredevil who liked to walk along the parapet of Archway's 'suicide bridge'.

1868 The Robinsons are now living in 19 **Benwell Road** from where Thomas Jnr, an illustrator, marries Eliza Heath. Her father owned four pubs. The newly weds moved in with his married sister a few doors down at 29, where their first two sons were born.

1872 William is born in **Hornsey Rise**.

1878 Thomas moves his family back to Benwell Road where his parents still lived (moved from 19 to 37) and his sister still at 29. He now had a whole house, 51. William attended Dame Mole's School then Holloway College private fee-paying schools. Islington still has twenty-six dairy farms and sixteen corn merchants. Once a year the children were treated to a trip to the Eagle Theatre, **City Road**.

1883 The Robinson household at 51 Benwell Road numbers eleven. Thomas and Eliza, the children Thomas, Charles, William, Mary, George and Florence (Mabel died young), Eliza's brother and sister and a servant (a washerwoman came every Monday).

1887 Age 15 enrols at Islington School of Art. His best friend Percy Billinghurst lived at 7 **Highbury Place**, an exclusive area blocked from traffic by a row of white posts. His house overlooked a meadow where sheep grazed.

1892 William and Percy are admitted to the Royal Academy School.

1897 Leaves RA and rents a studio. Trying to sell his paintings to a dealer in **Balls Pond Road** he was advised to 'give up art'.

1903 Marries Josephine Latey, whose father writes for the *Illustrated London News*. The newlyweds moved into a furnished top floor flat next door to the Holloway Empire Theatre (556–564).

1904 Moves to a larger unfurnished flat in Cathcart Hill off **Junction Road**. The *Strand* published two funny drawings, *Child Stealing in Highgate Woods* and *Pickpocketing in Hampstead Lane* which made his reputation as a comic artist. Their children, Joan and Oliver, were born here. Years later, his hilariously funny *How to Live in a Flat* was published to great acclaim.

1912 Name enters *Oxford English Dictionary* after an MP in the House of Commons scathingly likens Austrian aeroplanes to *'Heath Robinson contraptions'*.

....

ROSEBERY AVENUE EC1

Archibald Primrose Rosebery, fifth Earl, Gladstone's Foreign Secretary achieved all three of his stated ambitions in life; to marry Britain's richest heiress (Hannah Rothschild), to become Prime Minister and to win the Derby. The last he achieved three times as an owner, his horses winning in 1894, 1895 and 1905. A Liberal MP, he was also chairman of the first London County Council (LCC). Built in three stages to link Islington with the West End, the road that bears his name bridges the steep Fleet river valley.

1683 Sadler's Wells theatre opens (in what will be Rosebery Avenue).

1800s *Black Dwarf*, a radical magazine of the Regency period, published on premises now occupied by Amnesty International. Clio Rickman, close friend of Tom Paine was a contributor.

1889 800-seat Deacons Music Hall and parts of Spa Green, St John's Terrace, Myddelton Place, Garnault Place, John Street, Cold Bath Square and Mount Pleasant are razed.

Traffic was diverted from **Exmouth Street**, which was pedestrianised. Costermongers moved in and shopkeepers lost trade but stallholders successfully applied to the Vestry for licences.

1950s Rendells Manufacturing Chemists opens.

The strangest aspect of the furore over Marie Stopes' birth control clinic in Holloway (q.v.) is that women had been quietly popping along to **Great Bath Street** ever since 1885, when Walter Rendell opened a shop to sell his very effective Rendell's Pessaries made from quinine to neutralise sperm. In 1917, he moved his shop to **Chadwell Street**. Many women couldn't afford to buy them, which is perhaps why Dr Stopes' clinic was so successful.

ROYAL BALLET, The

Ballet in England was so despised by foreigners, particularly the French, that ballerinas changed their English names to get accepted. Ninette de Valois (Irish-born Idris Stannard) and Lilian Baylis, brought up in South Africa, were determined to set up the English National Ballet company at the 'Wells' to change people's perception.

1931 De Valois, prima ballerina and choreographer, starts with a company of six.

1932 A year for local talent. Alicia Markova (plain Alice Marks from **Finsbury Park**, name changed by Diaghilev) was seldom off-stage. Duncan Grant (later of **Canonbury Square**) did the décor and Elgar's (parents said to have married in St Mary's, q.v.) *Nursery Suite* was performed.

1933 Robert Helpmann and Anton Dolin join Markova at the Wells. The Company performed every Tuesday.

1934 Fifteen-year-old Margot Fonteyn (Fontes) joins the company. First British performance of *Swan Lake* (Pavlova's dresser makes Markova's tutus) and Hogarth's *The Rake's Progress*, first all-British ballet by first all-British ballet company.

1936 The Company has twenty women, twelve men, two choreographers, a conductor and forty students.

1940 Theatre closed during the war. Company moves to Covent Garden.

1957 Royal Charter incorporates Sadlers Wells Theatre Ballet, Sadlers Wells Ballet and Sadlers Wells School of Ballet into the *Royal Ballet*.

ROYALTY IN ISLINGTON

Due to its strategic position in relation to the City the borough has ancient connections with royalty. Among the many royal events connected with Islington have been the following (see individual entries and references for details):

61 Queen Boudicea dies, so legend says, at Battle Bridge. **1016** King Cnut battles with King Edmund Ironside at King's Cross (Chad Street). **1066** William the Conqueror gives Islington to Norman knights. **1170** Henry I is patron of Rahere who built St Bartholomew the Great and Bart's. **1185** Henry II attends the consecration of the Hospitallers' Church. **1199** King (*Magna Carta*) John moves into St John's Priory to prepare for his coronation. **1215** Edward I honeymoons at St John's* Priory and founds the HAC. **1381** Richard II vanquishes Wat Tyler at Smithfield and attends plays at the Clerk's Well and Skinners Well with the Queen. **1399** Henry IV stays at St John's Priory to prepare for his coronation. **1413** Henry V prepares for his coronation at St John's Priory. **1455** Henry VI is arrested in Islington. The Earl of Warwick removes his spurs (symbolic of disgrace), ties his legs to his horse and escorts him to the Tower. **1461** Earl of March is proclaimed Edward IV in St John's Square. **1485** Richard III faces his critics at

St John's Priory. **1487** Henry VII returning to London from the North (where he defeated the impostor Lambert Simnel) is formally met in Islington by the Lord Mayor of London. **1533** Local legend has it that Henry VIII courts Anne Boleyn in secret at St John's Priory. He closed St Bartholomew the Great, St John's Priory, St Mary's Nunnery and Charterhouse. **1551** Princess (Lady) Mary Tudor lives in St John's Priory. **1553** Queen Mary I restores the Hospitallers (Order of St John). **1558** Elizabeth I moves into Charterhouse to prepare for her coronation and visits three more times during her reign. The Ridolfi plot to dethrone her came from there. She visited friends in Islington (Robert Dudley and Earl of Essex in Essex Road, the Fowlers Lords of the manor of Barnsbury, Sir John Spencer and possibly Sir Walter Mildmay and Sir Walter Raleigh). She gave St John's Gate to the censor and disbanded the Hospitallers again. **1603** James I stays at Charterhouse to prepare for his coronation. **1605** Thomas Sleep of Clerkenwell helps Guy Fawkes in his plot to blow up James I. **1649** Thomas Chaloner of Clerkenwell is a signatory on Charles I's death warrant. **1666** The trial of the regicides is held in St John Street. Charles II looks after homeless Londoners in Moor Fields after The Great Fire. **1781** George III visits Aubert the eccentric astronomer in Highbury. **1830** George IV is the eponymous king in King's Cross.

SADLER'S WELLS
Theatre ('The Wells')
Rosebery Avenue EC1

1683 Richard/Dick (some sources say Thomas) Sadler, highways inspector, is hated by his workmen. Digging for gravel to mend the roads, they uncovered two old wells (still there) and almost didn't tell him. Sadler claimed them, transferred his Musicke House from St John's Gate and built a spa and pleasure gardens on the spot.

1733 Colley Cibber (q.v.) from **Colebrooke Row** is resident dramatist. Known for comic portrayals, he wrote 30 plays.

1746 Thomas Rosoman, local architect, knocks down the old Wells and rebuilds the theatre in seven weeks. Owner manager until 1771, he installed seats with shelves on the back (as in today's aeroplanes) to hold bottles of port (made with the theatre's own water supply) and glasses.

1765 Tickets for the Boxes cost three shillings and include a pint of wine.

1786 The show, which lasts three hours, includes a comedy, ballet, tightrope walker, pantomime, operetta and feats by strongmen. The audience could buy wine, lamb chops, ham and pasties to eat in the grounds, *à la* Glyndebourne.

1800 Joey Grimaldi pulls the punters in and the theatre employs 'Master Carey', the great Edmund Kean (q.v.), for the season.

1803 Charles and Mary Lamb bring friend and future poet laureate, Robert Southey here. The 'Wells' had just introduced opera, which was proving very popular.

1807 2,000 cram in to attend a Benefit Night. During a fracas someone called out *'Fight!'*

but the audience, thinking it was *'Fire!'* (a common occurrence) rushed for the exit. Thirty were killed or injured in the panic to get out. The corpses were laid out in the foyer.

1830 St John's Gate is in danger of being demolished so the 'Wells' puts on a benefit, a play about Jack Sheppard, to raise funds.

1844 Islington: Home of Shakespeare

Sam Phelps (the Kenneth Branagh of his day) takes over as actor-manager and revives Shakespeare's plays, rarely seen since 1648 when Cromwell closed the theatres. Phelps lived in **Canonbury Square**. Contrary to expectations, he managed to make Shakespeare pay by presenting 31 of the 34 plays over the next 14 years. He opened with *Macbeth*, which hadn't been seen for 200 years, and played Hamlet for 400 nights to packed houses.

1854 Alcoholism is a big problem. The Total Abstainers take over the 'Wells' for a mass meeting. George Cruikshank, ex-alcoholic, was in the chair.

1862 Phelps retires.

1869 Phelps makes a guest appearance but is saddened by the shoddy appearance of his 'temple'. He became a recluse and died in 1878.

1874 The 'Wells' returns to its watery origins, now a bath house (until the lead is stolen from the roof).

1876 The theatre is now New Spa Roller Skating Rink and Winter Garden with a Pump Room for taking the old spa water.

1877 Mrs Bateman buys the 'Wells' *'the neighbourhood has much improved ... (it) is without a place of amusement and the facilities for getting to Sadler's Wells by trams and omnibuses have greatly increased.'* She started rebuilding the interior the first week of November, the week the great Sam Phelps died.

1891 Charles Chaplin (Senior) is appearing in a variety review. Charlie Chaplin Jnr was two years old. The family lodged in Arlington Way, where Mr Barnett Deitch made ballet shoes for the great Pavlova.

1898 Arthur Wing Pinero writes *Trelawney of the Wells* to express his passion for the theatre.

1906 Closes. It will be 'dark' on and off until the amazing Lilian Baylis rebuilds it in 1931.

1914 WWI. Opens as a 'picture house'. A few films were in colour, frames tinted by hand. It had 3,500 seats and room for 255 standing. The first day's takings were donated to those in distress caused by the war. Films included *The Derby* and *The Lord Mayor's Show*. A favourite cinema snack was pig's trotters.

1920 Islington Council gives planning permission for the 'Wells' to be converted into a pickle factory.

Islington: home of The Royal Ballet and English National Opera

1931 Twelfth Night (6 January), Lilian Baylis, MA, DBE, 'The Lady', after six years of fundraising, opens with Shakespeare's *Twelfth Night*. The leading parts go to two young unknowns, Ralph Richardson and John Gielgud.

The new theatre had 1650 tip up seats, no boxes and no pillars to obscure the view of the stage and no visible support for the dress circle or gallery. Gielgud said it looked like a denuded wedding cake and had awful acoustics. One of Dick Sadler's old wells was at the back of the pit, another under the orchestra. It took Baylis just six years to make a seedy and forgotten theatre world-famous. Lurching from financial crisis to crisis, some nights she urged the audience to throw money at the performers to make sure they got paid. In the Islington tradition, Baylis loathed all forms of elitism and frowned on the idea of a special dress code for the audience.

1932 Walter <u>Sickert</u> gives Lilian Baylis *'The Raising of Lazarus'* to auction at Christie's to help alleviate financial difficulties.

1937 Lilian Baylis dies of a heart attack.

1939 The Wells closes for the duration of the war. Sadler's Wells Ballet transferred to The Royal Opera House, Covent Garden.

1956 Sadler's Wells Ballet gets Royal Charter as The Royal Ballet.

1970 Rudolf Nureyev dances with The Dutch National Ballet.

1988 Houses are knocked down in Arlington Way to build the Lilian Baylis Theatre. One was where Mr Barnett <u>Deitch</u> lived for 28 years making shoes for, among others, Pavlova. Another is where Charlie Chaplin lodged as a boy.

1996 Lilian Baylis' 1931 'Wells' is demolished. English Heritage and The Oxford Archaeological Society sifted the rubble for traces of the previous six theatres on the site.

1998 The 'Wells re-opens with a £30m lottery grant. With a larger stage than Covent Garden, it's the most technologically advanced theatre in Britain.

....

SAFFRON HILL EC1

Thousands of crocus bulbs were brought from Saffron Walden, Essex, in about 1300 and planted on the hill near **Smithfield***. Once grown in England on an industrial scale, saffron was used in cooking to disguise the taste and smell of rancid meat. Nowadays an unbelievably expensive imported luxury (because of labour-intensiveness), it comes from the fragrant yellow calyx of the crocus flower.*

1830s The children of Field Lane, with no access to water for washing, smell so badly, they are barred from school. A Ragged School was set up for them in Caroline Court. 45 boys and girls sat on the floor of one room. The school's back door opened on to a tiny lane, popularly supposed to be the one which led Oliver Twist and The Artful Dodger to Fagin's den. The school moved to a bigger room in White's Yard and a year later to 65 **West Street**.

1843 The school puts an ad in *The Times* for donations. This aroused the interest of Lord Shaftesbury, who became its President. <u>Dickens</u> also visited and left a description of its awfulness. He became a patron and declared it was his favourite charity. His friend Angela <u>Burdett-Coutts</u> (founder of the Society for the Prevention of Cruelty to Children, later NSPCC) paid for washing facilities to be installed. Dickens was a dandy in white trews and purple velvet, which made the children laugh whenever he visited.

1863 When the underground railway is built (see Tube, the) most of Saffron Hill is razed along with the 'rookeries' made famous in *Oliver Twist*.

1865 Land is bought facing Hatton Wall to build a five-storey school.

1879 When **Clerkenwell Road** is built, the school relocates to **Vine Hill**.

Robert <u>Pringle</u>, London's largest supplier of watch and jewellery parts, in Wilderness Works since 1820, was also forced to move. He had fourteen departments including jewellery making, watch making, silversmithing and electro-plating. Wilderness Row, a pedestrian area closed to traffic between **St John Street** and **Goswell Road** where Thackeray once lived was also swallowed up by **Clerkenwell Road**. The terraced Georgian houses-cum-workshops used by 2,000 jewellers, engravers and watchmakers were demolished.

1884 NSPCC take over Field Lane Ragged School. In the 1990s they sold the site for a small fortune.

1996 Smithfield has a new kind of resident living in the new-style rookeries. *YUPs* (Young, Upwardly-mobile Professionals) set up home in the converted warehouses. Saffron Hill where Fagin once lived is now very fashionable.

....

ST BARTHOLOMEW THE GREAT EC1

The oldest church in London. Country house was in Canonbury (until <u>Henry VIII</u>'s purge)

1120 One wintry November day, Henry I's royal yacht, The White Ship, sinks in the English Channel at Harfleur near Rouen. On board was William (17), Henry's only legitimate son. Hard man Henry had only just buried his wife and was said never to have smiled again Henry's servant (minstrel/jester) <u>Rahere</u> was equally devastated. He left Court, joined the Augustinians and went on a pilgrimage to Rome. While there he got malaria and almost died. Coming back he was almost shipwrecked and again nearly lost his life. Then he had a vision of Saint Bartholomew who told him to build a hospital for the poor.

1123 Henry, seeing this as a fitting memorial to his son, gave Rahere a corner of the 'smooth field' – useless, marshy land once used as a Roman horse market. Saint Bartholomew was flayed alive in Armenia (some say India), so butchers adopted him as their patron saint. Smithfield market traders helped Rahere (physically) to build Britain's first public hospital. The site was blessed, the ground drained, foundation stone laid and the hospital dedicated to Saint Bartholomew.

1133 Henry grants the hospital a Royal Charter: *'I will maintain and defend this place even as my crown-and let this place be perpetually defended by the protection of kings.'* A priory was built on to the hospital (revenue from B&B was needed) and Rahere appointed Prior.

1539 Sir Richard <u>Rich</u>, an evil little man, buys the 400-year-old priory from from Henry VIII (stays in the family until 1862). He ripped out the Norman transept and nave (locals successfully petitioned to save the quire as their parish church). Rich converted the Lady Chapel behind the High Altar into a house and moved in. It remained a private dwelling (41 Bartholomew Close) until the 1890s. Only five of the priory's peal of eleven bells escaped melting down.

1595 A gate and gate house are built leading to the old nave.

1697 William <u>Hogarth</u> is baptised. The font is still here.

1724 Benjamin <u>Franklin</u> is taken on by Samuel Palmer's Printing Office in the converted Lady Chapel (see America).

1863 The church is a ruin, open to the sky. The problem was handed over to architect Sir Aston (V&A Museum) <u>Webb</u>, who lowered the floor so that the arches could be seen properly. The original doors were traced and put back.

1900 800 years after his death, Rahere's tomb is opened.

Not only were the garments amazingly preserved, so were the leather sandals strapped to the Prior's holy feet. Shortly after the tomb was re-sealed, one of the church wardens fell ill. Imagining he was dying, he confessed that he had stolen a sandal. Handing it over to the Vestry, he made a miraculous recovery. The tomb was not to be re-opened, however, so Rahere never got his sandal back. It's said that a figure in a cowl haunts the church, looking for his other sandal.

1916 A Zeppelin bomb blasts the façade off the Gate House revealing the half-timbered Tudor original.

2000 Five of the original peal of bells ring in the new Millennium.

....

ST JAMES' Church
Clerkenwell Close EC1

1154 The nuns dedicate their church to St James, patron saint of pilgrims.

1625 The steeple on the medieval church is rebuilt.

1656 Parishioners buy St James and the right to appoint the vicar (still in force).

1687 Daniel Defoe's first child (of eight) Daniel, is christened here.

Islington: Home of The Gun Salute (above a grave)

1691 Sir William Wood (82), knighted by Charles II, Marshal of the Finsbury Archers, is buried in St James'. The Queen's Archer, in 1676 Sir William was the first to wear the Catherine of Braganza Shield. In his honour, three flights of whistling arrows were discharged over his grave, establishing the tradition of the gun salute.

1788 What's left of the medieval nave is falling to bits.

The old church was demolished and a new one built. Local architect, James Carr's design even then was old-fashioned. Reminiscent of James Gibbs' St Martin's in the Fields, the spire was a tribute to Wren. The church had a curved (as opposed to traditional rectangular) west end and a gallery which reflected the social pecking-order of the day: men on the ground floor, women in the first balcony, servants in the second and the 'great unwashed' hidden behind screens. Women tried not to show their ankles so a modesty board (still there) was put up behind the railings on the stairs. The revolutionary organ by George Pike England had no delay between putting fingers on the keyboard and the sound coming out.

Clerkenwell was at the zenith of the watch and clock making industry. Apprentices climbed the spire of St James' each day to watch the ball at Greenwich rise at midday, when they called out 'GMT!', by which their watches and clocks were set.

Until 1918, St James' bell was rung on Shrove Tuesday reminding parishioners to be shriven (absolved of sins) before Lent. It was nicknamed 'the pancake bell'. In the entrance is a memorial to Bishop Burnet of **St John's Square** who wrote *History of the Reformation* and witnessed the Sacheverell riots (q.v.). Locals stoned his coffin as it was brought here. The Benefaction Boards date from Elizabethan times. Church documents from 1561 are in the Greater London Records Office in nearby Northampton Road (see Family Trees). Penton (Penton Ville) family members are buried here.

1834 Johann Steinberg's victims are buried in the churchyard.

At 17 Southampton Street, Pentonville (now **Calshott Street**), a German immigrant killed his common law wife, their four children and finally himself. As was the custom, a stake was put through his heart and his skull cracked open to let the demons out (to give him a chance of getting into heaven). He was buried head-first in an unmarked pauper's grave in Ray Street Cemetery, Hockley-in-the-Hole. The Steinberg house was turned into a tourist attraction by a local entrepreneur who bought the bloodstained clothes, put them on wax effigies and opened to the public. £50 was taken on the first day as queues stretched around the block. Neighbours petitioned successfully to get it closed.

ST JOHN AMBULANCE
St John's Square EC1
Islington: Home of First Aid

How many people know that the familiar angels of mercy belong to the oldest Order in the world, set up in 1099 to minister to sick pilgrims?

1874 Antiseptic is used for the first time during surgery and carbolic acid used as a disinfectant.

Until now no-one had thought of washing down the operating table, nor did surgeons take off their coats or wash their hands before operating. Ordinary people had no money for doctors so kept jam jars of leeches, mustard poultices for asthma attacks, cauterisation irons and wart-eating grasshoppers. Wounds were sterilised using a hot iron. There was no anaesthetic, of course. Nose bleeds were syringed with ice water, burns treated by dredging in flour, wrapping in cotton wadding then being soaked with vinegar.

1877 Sir John Furley and Sir Edmund Lechmere (a fan of **St John's Gate** since he was a local **Charterhouse** schoolboy, see St John's Gate below) found the ambulance movement to administer First Aid for accidents at work, predominantly for those in hazardous occupations such as railwaymen, miners, shipyard and factory workers.

1888 Queen Victoria grants a Charter to The Most Venerable Order of St John (Catholics are holy, Protestants are Venerable), a British Order of Chivalry with the monarch as its head.

1999 Happy 900th Birthday to The Knights of St John! The Order bought the property adjoining the Gate so that St John Ambulance, which had relocated in 1952 (see below) could return where it belonged.

Three thousand Knights of Chivalry and a fleet of 150 ambulance aircraft are recognised diplomatically by 40 countries. Ever-present at football matches, country shows and rock concerts, the new knights of St John (from all walks of life) still wear the eight-pointed cross. They undergo instruction in elementary anatomy and physiology, how to treat fits, fainting, fractures, wounds, haemorrhage, burns, scalds, choking, shock, poisoning and safe transportation of the injured.

ST JOHN'S GATE
St John Square EC1

1504 Sir Thomas Docwra, Prior, rebuilds the South Gate where the Gatehouse keeper and his staff (laymen) live and where visitors book B & B.

1579 Elizabeth I appoints Edmund Tilney/Tylney, Master of the Revels (general name for entertainment at court). He was the official censor, responsible for overseeing plays, players and playhouses. The queen gave him St John's Gate, where he spent the next 30 years (died 1610).

There was to be a censor for the next 400 years (until the Theatres Act of 1968 abolished the post, by then held by the Lord Chancellor). He chose the plays the Queen would see and issued licences to build theatres and put on plays. His job was to look for sedition, as the Queen had many enemies. Shakespeare spent a lot of time with Tylney at St John's Gate, where he had to rehearse his plays when applying for a licence.

Tylney summoned the acting companies to Clerkenwell as soon as he had finished his summer chore of supervising the airing, sponging and brushing of the costumes. Contemporary fashions included goose-turd green, pease-porridge tawny and popinjay blue. Because they had to earn a living by day, actors had to rehearse after dark. This meant elaborate lighting (24 torches and 180 candles), fires to be lit (4,000 sticks of firewood and loads of coal). Painters made canvas houses, castles and villages and wool-stuffed fishes (the audience could tell at a glance which was mackerel and which was flounder). Costumes were designed (armour borrowed) and papier mâché (rags, paper and plaster of Paris) used to make fruits, trees, flowers and monsters. Afterwards, everything was packed into baskets, loaded on to boats on the Fleet and taken down the Thames to Court (usually Greenwich) for opening on Boxing Night.

Theatre under James I was even more popular than it was with Elizabeth I. The king couldn't wait until the traditional Boxing Day to see the latest plays so brought the season forward to November which must have put Mr Tylney in a lather. James was so enamoured of anything to do with theatre that he knighted Tylney, started his own company, The King's Men (formerly the Chamberlain's Men, in which Shakespeare was a shareholder) and saw five times as many plays a year as Elizabeth.

1603 The season is to open with Shakespeare's *Othello* at Whitehall. Shakespeare's company was presenting nearly all the plays: *The Merry Wives of Windsor, Measure for Measure, The Comedy of Errors, Love's Labour's Lost, Henry V* and *The Merchant of Venice* all before *Twelfth Night*. Burbage's company, the Queen's Men (James' wife Anne also loved theatre) were putting on a play, the Boy's Company at Blackfriars another; there were two amateur companies at The Gate rehearsing a masque for the Earl of Pembroke and Ben Jonson was rehearsing a masque starring the Queen with scenery designed by Inigo Jones.

1610 Sir Edmund Tylney, last of Elizabeth I's old friends, dies. James I gave the Gate to Sir Roger Wilbrahim/Wilbraham and the censor's office was relocated to Black Friars.

1703 William Hogarth's father opens a coffee shop in St John's Gate. The menus are in Latin. The venture fails and he is imprisoned for five years for debt.

1731 The Jerusalem Tavern opens in the East Tower. Cave launches *The Gentleman's Magazine.*

1737 Dr Johnson arrives with David Garrick and gets a job with Cave (see Johnson, Dr Samuel).

1750 One of Benjamin Franklin's famous lightning conductors is erected on the Gate.

1754 Cave, 63, dies at The Gate and is buried in St James'.

1781 Samuel Rogers who lives at **Newington Green** starts contributing to *The Gentleman's Magazine.* The popular publication moved to Fleet Street (survived until 1914).

1830 Sadler's Wells puts on a play about Jack <u>Sheppard</u> (q.v.) to raise funds to save the Gate from demolition.

1845 Plans are again afoot to demolish the Gate. A local architect started a *Save St John's Gate* fund, to which a schoolboy fan in nearby **Charterhouse** contributed. The 300-year-old crumbling Tudor brick was faced with ragstone.

1874 Sir Edmund <u>Lechmere</u>, who as a Charterhouse schoolboy had contributed to the fund, buys the freehold and gives it to the Order.

1893 The Gate is given crenellations to reflect the military side of the Order.

1952 St John Ambulance HQ moves to Westminster.

1978 New museum.

1999 St John Ambulance HQ returns to the Gate.

....

ST JOHN'S PRIORY
St John Square EC1

1100 Jordan <u>de Briset</u> (**Briset Street**) who came over with William the Conqueror, gives land in Clerkenwell *'for the maintenance of soldiers against the Turks and infidels'*. Hospitallers painted stone crosses, some red, some white (**White Cross Street**) to mark out their boundaries and built a wharf on the banks of the Fleet (**Fleet Lane**). Patients, too ill to walk to **Bart's**, now arrived by boat.

The Prior of St John's was the third most influential man in England, next in rank only to the king and Archbishop of Canterbury. Not only was he Grand Prior of all England, he was Lord High Treasurer, Chancellor of the Realm and First Baron. St John's, third richest religious house in Britain, besides being huge (the Great Hall was 100 feet long), and the national administration centre, provided B&B for pilgrims (or any visitor in exchange for money or labour) and an armed guard all the way to Jerusalem. It was the biggest, most prestigious hotel in London and royalty often came to stay. A self-sufficient, self-contained community, St John's had ships on the Fleet, orchards, vineyards (**Vineyard Walk**), counting house, dormitories, distillery, brewery, kitchens and fish ponds. There was an armoury, laundry, school and visitors' parlours. The Brothers recruited locally for secular labour including doctors, brewers, bakers, chambermaids, cooks, janitors, millers, slaughterers, pig keepers, laundresses, attorneys and clerks.

Here lived the prior, three chaplains, fifteen deacons, keeper of the keys, parish priest, paying guests, their servants and horses. The Priory had everything except knights, who were usually out of England either in the Holy Land or guiding the faithful there. Hospitality was offered all the way from Clerkenwell to Jerusalem and pilgrims heard eight different languages ('tongues', represented by the eight-pointed star of England, France, Provence, Auvergne, Germany, Italy, Aragon and Castile) along the way.

The waiting list of lads wanting to be a knight was long, but getting accepted was not easy. An English knight of St John had to be of legitimate, noble, birth (four descents on both parents sides), over 20, a bachelor, free from debts, a free man and chaste. If assigned to the military he'd wear a red robe with a white (Maltese) cross, if a Hospitaller, black with a white cross (their successors, St John Ambulance, still wear black and white).

1185 4 March, the Bishop of Jerusalem *'ye Worshipfulle Fader, Araclius, Patriarke Bishop came to this costly pile'* with Henry II to consecrate the Church. Like that of the Templars it was modelled on the Dome of the Rock in Jerusalem. Bigger than the Temple Church, it was the largest round church in England (the crypt survives). The Bishop was on a world fundraising tour to fight the Turks and asked Henry to lead the next Crusade. Henry offered money instead. Heraclius complained: *'We come to seek a king, not money. Every corner of the world sends us money but not one a prince. Here is my head . . . treat me if you like as you did my brother* (Thomas à Becket). *It matters little to me whether I die by your orders or in Syria by the hands of the infidels for you are worse than a Saracen.'*

1199 King John (reluctant signatory of Magna Carta) stays for a month to prepare for his coronation.

1215 Edward I (15) spends his honeymoon here with his bride Eleanor of Castile, whom he had married by proxy, age ten. They had fourteen children.

At each of the twelve places where her cortège made a stopover between Nottingham where she died (1290), and Westminster Abbey where she was buried, Edward built a cross. Charing Cross was the last. (This was the Edward who made his son Edward II first Prince of Wales in 1301, and who executed Scottish hero William (Mel Gibson) Wallace in 1305).

1291 Christians lose the Holy Land. Templars and Hospitallers, booted out of Jerusalem, were homeless. Asked by the Pope to merge, both Grand Masters refused. The Templars, a fighting Order, now had no purpose, but the Hospitallers were still escorting pilgrims to the Holy Land so their Clerkenwell HQ became even more important.

1313 After the loss of Jerusalem there were no more Crusades. The Templars were disbanded. After Edward II had his pick, what was left of their considerable assets and estates was given to the Hospitallers. The Order also inherited the Templar's unpopularity.

1381 The poor hate the Hospitallers, especially the Prior of St John's, the tax-hungry Robert Hales ('Hob the Robber'). The Peasants' Revolt burned down the priory (see Tyler, Wat).

1399 Henry IV is proclaimed king (even though we already had one, Richard). He stayed at the priory to prepare for his coronation and later came back for holidays.

1485 Richard III addresses London's top brass to tell them he has no intention of marrying his niece, Elizabeth of York. It wasn't true, of course.

1533 Local legend has it that Henry VIII has an awayday here with paramour, Anne Boleyn. If so, could it be that their daughter, Elizabeth I, was conceived in **Clerkenwell**?

1540 One of the last religious houses to be suppressed (it brings in revenue), the Priory is pulled down. Sir William Weston, last Prior, is said to have died of a broken heart (although some sources say the last Prior was Sir Richard Shelley). Henry used the remaining buildings to store hunting tents and equipment.

1551 The Lady Mary Tudor moves in. Some say the Priory was left to her in her father's will, others that it was her half-brother Edward VI, who gave it to her. The procession to St John's consisted of: *'Fifty knights afore her and gentlemen in black velvet and chains of gold and more behind each with a peyre of beads in black.'*

1547 The Duke of Somerset wants to strip Westminster Abbey to build Somerset House, his palace on the Strand. Refused permission, instead he blew up parts of St John's with gunpowder and used some of the stone.

1553 Edward VI dies, age 16. Half-sister Mary Tudor is Queen.

Catholic Mary used **Smithfield** for burning Protestants, repaired some of the damage done to St John's by Lord Somerset and revived the Order of St John. 1559, Elizabeth I suppressed the Order again.

1641 Robert <u>Bruce</u> (earl of Elgin and Aylesbury) builds a mansion from the remains of the monastic buildings and uses the crypt as his wine cellar. He named it Aylesbury House. Died 1685. His descendants owned the Priory until 1706.

....

ST JOHN'S SQUARE EC1
(The old Priory precinct)

1461 Handsome, blond, six foot, 19-year-old soldier, the Earl of March is proclaimed Edward IV in the square.

1706 St John's is leased to Presbyterians.

1708 Bishop <u>Burnet</u> retires to No. 36 (renumbered 44) to write *A History of the Reformation.*

The mansion, inherited in his wife's will, had two storeys, three gables, fourteen windows on the front, a forecourt with trees and large grounds at the rear. Steps led up to the front portico supported by Tuscan columns. Burnet gave Sunday evening lectures attended by the nobility including the duke of Marlborough and the duke of Newcastle, who lived around the corner in **Clerkenwell Close**.

1709 Notorious Henry <u>Sacheverell</u>, High Church Tory chaplain who disapproves of religious toleration, gives two sermons in St Paul's accusing the government of jeopardising the established Church. The sermons were printed for distribution. The Bishop of London, none other than Henry <u>Compton</u>, youngest son of Spencer Compton, Earl of Northampton (see Canonbury Tower) supported him.

THE SACHEVERELL RIOTS

1710 Sacheverell is accused in the House of seditious libel (against the Whigs), found guilty, impeached and suspended from preaching. Supporters burned down all Nonconformist meeting houses, including St John's. Bishop Burnet watches, nervous that the fire would spread to his house.

1715 Bishop Burnet (73) dies.

1721 Simon <u>Michell</u>, local JP, rebuilds St John's. He sold it to Queen Anne's Commissioners, C. of E. estates administrators, who reconsecrated it as the Parish Church.

1727 John <u>Wilkes</u>, third of six children, is born in St James' Court.

1817 Bishop Burnet's mansion is now tenements. What had been his hall was a road leading to terraced houses in his back garden.

1840 Scandal! Prince George, cousin of (and once selected as the most suitable husband for) Queen Victoria, marries in St John's Louisa <u>Fairbrother</u>, 31, actress and mother of his three sons. Louisa, at 16, had two sons by Charles <u>Sutton</u>, grandson of the Archbishop of Canterbury. This was a morganatic marriage – the wife being inferior by birth to her husband, neither she nor her children were able to enjoy the privileges of his rank or inherit his possessions.

1840 Smith's Clocks open for business. Their fire-bell *'ignore me at your peril'* alarm clocks were a favourite of workers until well after World War II.

1859 Bishop Burnet's mansion, built for one rich occupant, houses 50 poor ones. In his former front garden were now shops. Many residents were small manufacturers (shoes, boxes, frames and stays). With no clean drinking water their children died of scarlatina.

1931 The Church Commissioners return St John's Church to the Order.

1941 WWII. St John's is bombed.

1958 Lord Mottistone rebuilds St John's Church. It has three original walls and one built in 1721 by Simon Michell. Re-dedicated by Dr Geoffrey Fisher, Archbishop of Canterbury, it's used for investitures and other special occasions connected with the Order.

....

ST JOHN STREET EC1

Known as the Islington Road before St John's Priory (q.v.) was built.

*St John Street starts at **Smithfield** and continues along **Upper Street** and Hollow Way. It was very muddy in winter. Property owners charged drovers a farthing for every horse, bull and cow and one penny for every cart and used the money to repair the road outside their own front doors.*

1530 Roads are virtually impassable. The Statute of Highways ordered property owners to 'mend their ways' (literally – see Traffic).

1720 5 November, Bonfire (Guy Fawkes) Night, an accident at his factory kills John Brock of Brocks Fireworks fame and his daughter. They're buried in St James'.

1849 Opposite the entrance to **Bart's**, workmen dig up stones blackened by fire, covered with ashes and the charred bones of martyrs.

1869 Earl of Northampton gives the old manor house recently vacated by Manor House School for Boys to the Protestant Alliance. (The last earl to live here was in 1677, after which it was an asylum, then a girl's school.) Lord Shaftesbury laid the foundation stone for St Peter's Church, as a memorial in honour of the Smithfield Martyrs (Protestants burned by Mary). There was a procession every year to St Peter's from the Martyr's commemoration tablet on the wall of **Bart's**.

1944 WWII. The Martyr's Church is badly damaged by bombs.

1956 The church is demolished. The parish of St Peter was joined to the parishes of St James and St John. The Martyr Board listing 66 of the martyrs who died from 1400 onwards is in St James'.

2020 (Forecast by Islington Council Planning Department) **St John Street** will become an extension of **Upper Street**, with trendy pubs and eating places tumbling over one another.

....

ST MARY'S Church
Upper Street N1
Islington and the Birth of Methodism

The first church, Our Lady of Islington (statue of the Virgin outside) may have been consecrated around AD 628 when Honorius, Archbishop of Canterbury, divided England into parishes. Islington is the parish of St Mary. St Paul's owned the freehold of St Mary's, which has a Prebendal pew in the Cathedral. A list of the manors of St Paul's at that time shows Islington variously as Yseldon/Iseldon/Eyseldon and Istleton.

1483 Re-built of boulders, pebbles, flint and chalk with a tower, turret and tiled roof. All the other buildings around here were of timber and plaster, indicating its importance.

1539 After the Reformation, Our Lady of Islington becomes plain St Mary's and the statue of the Virgin is destroyed.

1738 On their return from America, John Wesley and brother Charles visit the Vicar of St Mary's, George Stonehouse (they were at Oxford together).

For generations the Stonehouse family had the power to appoint the Vicar of Islington. When George inherited the privilege, to the fury of the churchwardens he appointed himself. He granted the Wesleys and George Whitfield licences to preach. Charles (who wrote *Hark the Herald Angels Sing* here) was taken on as his assistant. John preached here between October 1738 and March 1739, officiating at Holy Communion, births, weddings and funerals.

1739 Middle class parishioners who pay high rents for their pews are outraged to be told by the new preachers that their souls are 'no better than those of the poor'. They complained to the Bishop of London that Stonehouse had invited Methodists to preach. When churchwardens prevented them from entering the pulpit, Wesley preached on the tombstones instead, thus Islington became the birthplace of Methodism. The licences to preach were officially revoked. A disgusted Stonehouse resigned and sold the living.

1751 Old St Mary's is demolished to make way for a new one.

During demolition, a monument dated 1454 was uncovered and the date 1483 found carved into the steeple. Builder (not architect) Lancelot Dowbiggin was buried here eight years later. The remains of Dame Alice Owen's 1613 tomb in the southeast corner of the graveyard were demolished. The bas relief of nine of her children and grandchildren was taken to Dame Alice Owen School and a monument to her raised in the south aisle of the new church.

1772 Revd George Strahan (Strachan in some books), friend of Benjamin Franklin, is appointed vicar, a job he does for the rest of his long life (died 1824) (**Strahan Place/ Terrace N1**). Another friend, Dr Johnson was often seen shuffling down **Upper Street** to help Strahan, who had the reputation of writing turgid sermons so long and rambling that people took playing cards to church. (When Strahan cut himself shaving, the Bishop was heard to remark that he wished he'd cut his sermons instead.) Strahan's father, William, published Dr Johnson, David Hume, Adam Smith and Edward Gibbon.

1784 Strahan ministers the last rites to Dr Johnson.

1800 Despite a growing population, St Mary's is the only established church in Islington, so an Act of Parliament was passed to build Chapels of Ease.

1820 Daniel Wilson appointed vicar. Many of the congregation now went to St Mary Magdalene Chapel of Ease, **Holloway Road**; Wesley's Methodist Chapel, **City Road**; Union Chapel, **Compton Terrace** or Claremont Chapel, **Pentonville Road**.

1824 Revd Wilson introduces a third service on Sundays, all seats free. He was the driving force behind commissioning Charles Barry to build four churches in Islington (see Barry, Sir Charles).

1831 Revd Wilson founds *The Lord's Day Observance Society*. To no avail, shops stayed packed till midnight seven days a week.

1848 Although Elgar's biography says otherwise, some sources say that his parents, William, piano tuner of 6 **High Street** and Ann Greening also of Islington were married here (Sir Edward was cagey about his humble roots).

1886 Revd William <u>Barlow</u> is vicar (until 1902). The population of his deanery (350,000) was bigger than many dioceses (forty parishes) so in all but name he acted as bishop.

1897 Revd Barlow gets his cousin to design him a new vicarage. He is the famous W.H. <u>Barlow</u>, architect of the astonishing 1862 St Pancras Station.

1903 A Grecian-style colonnaded front porch is added.

1934 The new curate is Revd Donald <u>Coggan</u>. In 1974, he became Archbishop of Canterbury.

1938 A stone is found in the crypt, dated between 1100–1150.

1940 WWII. A bomb lands on St Mary's. All that survived was the spire and portico.

1955 The new curate is Revd David <u>Sheppard</u>, who stays until 1958. He played cricket for England and became Bishop of Liverpool.

1956 Duchess of Gloucester opens the rebuilt St Mary's.

1962 A young assistant curate begins his ministry here, ex-RAF radio operator George <u>Carey</u>. He also became Archbishop of Canterbury. Declaring himself at the helm of a sinking ship, he despaired at the British *'allergy to religion.'* He also became a dedicated Arsenal fan and set the C. of E. on its heels when he insisted on the ordination of women priests, although the gay community accuse him of homophobia.

1998 Preparing for the new millennium, St Mary's eight bells, cast in 1754, are rung for the first time in 60 years (the last time was before the war, in 1938).

....

ST MARY'S NUNNERY
Clerkenwell Close EC1

Ecclesia Sanctae Mariae de Fonte Clericorum (the Church of Saint Mary by the Clerk's Well) is by 100 years the first convent to be built in London.

1100 Jordan <u>de Briset</u> gives 14 acres bordering **Clerkenwell Green** to build a Benedictine nunnery. Clerkenwell Green running down to the Fleet was reduced to a wedge-shaped piece of grass between the boundaries of the nunnery and St John's Priory (q.v.).

1154 The nuns dedicate their church to St James, patron saint of pilgrims.

Not all pilgrims headed for Jerusalem, some were on their way to Spain. The trek to Santiago de Compostela (symbol, a scallop shell) was one of the most important Christian pilgrimages then or now. The nunnery had 20 Sisters, daughters of rich men who would have settled large dowries on their daughters had they married, so donated money to the Order instead. It was rich and influential with workmen, servants, chaplains, paying guests and of course pilgrims. Becoming a nun was a good career move, the church had status and power.

As well as the Clerk's Well and the Fleet the nuns had water piped in from Lodder's Well (said to have been on the corner of **St John Street/Goswell Road**). The Three Kings, **Clerkenwell Close**, now occupies the site of the servants' sleeping quarters.

1269 The Prior of St John's gives his neighbour the Abbess a souvenir from the Holy Land, a 'genuine' water pot from the wedding feast in Canaa where Jesus changed water into wine.

1403 The Abbess gives the Prior of Charterhouse permission to lay water pipes across her land. She also built gates facing Clerkenwell Green. Locals burned them down as they encroached on common land.

1539 After Henry VIII, the nunnery, except for the nave of the church, was sold to Henry's executor, Sir Edward <u>North</u>. The last Abbess, Isobel Sackville and Sir William

<u>Weston</u>, last Prior of St John's (q.v.) are buried in the churchyard. Locals were allowed to worship in the old church and still do on the same site today. (Parish records going back to 1561 in the Public Records Office – see Family Trees.)

....

ST MARY'S PATH N1
(Church Lane until 1937)

1714 Church Cottage built for the sexton (caretaker/grave digger), is still there, the oldest domestic dwelling in Islington. Some sources claim this distinction belongs to two houses in **Britton Street**, not so, they were built by Simon <u>Michell</u> in 1723.

1821 A Free Dispensary is opened with two doctors, two surgeons and a resident pharmacist. In its first twelve years, of 31,571 patients treated, 28,620 were cured, 1,318 'relieved', 93 discharged, 124 transferred to hospital, 741 died and 675 were undergoing treatment.

1860 A soup kitchen opens. The massive built-in iron cauldrons with hinged lids were still there in 1951.

1886 New Dispensary built (present building).

1948 The National Health Service is launched and the Dispensary closed.

1951 The soup kitchen, in operation for 100 years, closes.

1990s St Mary's church soup kitchen in the crypt for down-and-outs.

....

SALLY PLACE EC1

Ironically, Republican Clerkenwell spawned the National Anthem, God Save The King. It was also the home of the song that was to make Gracie Fields famous, and may indeed boast the only street ever named after a pop song.

1733 Henry Saville <u>Carey</u> (born 1696) of Great Warner Street (**Warner Street** EC1) was the abandoned illegitimate son of the Marquess of Halifax (Sir George Saville). First published as a poet in 1713 he was friends with John <u>Pepusch</u> and Thomas <u>Britton</u>, and much admired by Joseph <u>Addison</u>. Carey wrote: *God save our gracious king/Long live our noble king/God save the king/Confound their politics /Frustrate their knavish tricks/Long to reign over us/God save the king.* He also wrote *Sally (Pride of our Alley).* *'Of all the girls that are so smart/There's none like pretty Sally/She is the darling of my heart/And she lives in our alley.'*

1743 Living in poverty and mourning the death of his newly born son, Carey hangs himself. At the time of his death he was musician and dramatist for Sadler's Wells (q.v.).

1745 *God Save Our Gracious King* is set to music and sung for the first time in public in Drury Lane Theatre. It struck a major chord at a time when the Young Pretender was campaigning against <u>George II</u> (some sources say a refrain with similar sentiments was sung in 1695 by supporters of <u>James II</u> before <u>William of Orange</u> was imported from the Netherlands).

1787 Henry's son, George Saville Carey also writes songs. His actress daughter Ann (known as Nan or Nancy) had an illegitimate son by an alcoholic who committed suicide at 22. The boy was adopted and brought up as Edmund <u>Kean</u>, first of the great modern Shakespearian interpreters.

1936 Baker's Row/Caroline Place is renamed **Sally Place** EC1.

SANDEMANIAN CHURCH

The Sandemanians were originally called Glasites, after John Glas, who was expelled from the Church of Scotland for objecting to civil interference in church affairs. A 'small and despised set of Christians', they rejected all forms of ritual.

1971 John Glas dies. His son-in-law, Robert Sandeman, an Independent Presbyterian minister, carried on his work. A Sandemanian church was opened in Islington (7 **Barnsbury Grove**), where Michael Faraday, the 'father of electricity', born into the church, preached as an Elder.

....

SANS WALK EC1

Where the Bridewell, Clerkenwell House of Correction or House of Detention used to be is now Sans Walk. Its other boundaries were Corporation Row, **Woodbridge Street** and **Clerkenwell Close**.

Clerkenwell Bridewell catered for three centuries of 'rogues, vagabonds, vagrants, debtors, heretics, papists, blasphemists and unlicensed preachers.' Bridewells or county prisons were so named after a palace built over a well dedicated to St Brigid on the Fleet between Fleet Street and the Thames. Her nickname was Bridey.

The penal code was savage, 220 offences on the Statute Book could (and did) earn the death penalty, including picking pockets. Records show one person imprisoned for stealing a pewter tankard, one a tablecloth, another a piece of bacon. The first prisoner was there for not going to church in over three months. An Act of Parliament decreed that each county must build a Bridewell and they are to be found all over the country. The Baptist's Head, **St John's Lane**, offered prisoners on their way from The House of Detention to Newgate to be hanged, imprisoned or transported their last drink as free men (survived until 1959).

1615 First of seven prisons on this site. The first was Clerkenwell Bridewell, the next four (the second prison was built alongside the Bridewell) were New Prison, followed by the Clerkenwell House of Correction and Clerkenwell House of Detention, each bigger than the last. The Bridewell survived in varied and modified forms until 1886.

1724 Jack Sheppard (20) (original 'Jack The Lad') escapes with girlfriend, Elizabeth Lyon, known as Edgeworth Bess (Edgeworth is Edgware).

1774 Another 'New Prison' built. Under a corrupt administration it's *'a great brothel kept under protection of the law for the emolument of its ministers'*

1775 270 prisoners from Clerkenwell Bridewell, many charged with capital offences, are fettered together for transfer to Newgate. Joining up with another bunch from the New Prison similarly fettered, they raced each other there.

1780 Gordon Riots. 'No Popery' rioters marched through Islington on their way to burn down the Bridewell and release prisoners. The Governor did a deal. He'd free the prisoners if they didn't damage the prison. They agreed (see Gordon Riots).

1818 A new prison is built.

1845 Yet another new prison is built. Clerkenwell House of Detention (largest in London, probably the UK) was built along the lines of 'model prison' **Pentonville** (q.v.). It was a short-stay prison for those on remand. 9,000 prisoners a year included army deserters, cabmen who had offended against the Hackney Carriage Act, failed suicides, vagrants and 'moochers'.

1850 Henry Mayhew is appalled by the number of children incarcerated who had, he said, *not yet cut their wisdom teeth*. Children of eight were deemed to know right from wrong and were therefore culpable. and those as young as twelve could be hanged or transported. Men (5794) and women (2200) too are committed every year, awaiting trial for desertion, jumping bail, etc. After Mayhew's damning visit the county of Middlesex opens an Industrial Home in Feltham (means *home in a field*) for juveniles. This is a Borstal by 1919.

1867 The prison is damaged by the first IRA bomb set off on the mainland (see IRA).

1886 The prison, here since 1611, is demolished (apart from the cells below ground).

1893 Sir Hugh Myddelton Model School for 2,000 pupils built on the site (now part of Kingsway College complex) is opened by the Prince of Wales. Thanks to local care worker John Groom it had a wing for deaf, dumb and blind children (see Groom, John).

1914–18 WWI and **1939–45** WWII. The cells beneath the old prison are used as air raid shelters.

1995 The old cell complex, said to be haunted, becomes a tourist attraction. What visitors see was once the ground floor but because of rising ground levels is now the cellars.

....

SCHER, Anna (1947–)
Inspirational drama teacher
Anna Scher's first teaching post was at Ecclesbourne School.

1968 She takes over an empty chapel in 70 **Barnsbury Road** for an after-school drama club for underprivileged kids. About 70 turned up.

1999 It has 1,000 members, children from 100 schools and a five-year waiting list of 3,000.

A registered charity, its President is Michael Caine. Patrons include Glenda Jackson, Ned Sherrin and Jonathan Miller. Among her first recruits were *Birds of a Feather* duo Linda Robson and Pauline Quirke. When Kathy Burke returned from Cannes in 1998 clutching her award for *Nil by Mouth,* the first person she went to see was Anna Scher. About 10 per cent of her pupils turn professional.

....

SEDDON, Fred
The Murdering Freemason

1910 Moves to 63 **Tollington Park** N4 with his wife, five children (age 1–17) father (73) and a skivvy (housemaid).

Parts of Islington were slums but not Tollington Park. These 'highly desirable residences' had been designed by Roumieu and Gough in 1820, so prestigious that Gough himself moved in. A respectable, middle-class area, this was where Aldermen and JPs lived and the home of William Trounce, founder of the *Islington Gazette*. The miserly Seddon characteristically knocked down the estate agent's price for the elegant, red and yellow brick property to £220. The house with steps leading up to a smart front door had fourteen rooms, an 'area' (for servants) and a basement.

Seddon (40) a freemason, had tiny piggy eyes and a waxed moustache. Superintendent for London & Manchester Industrial Assurance Company, he charged his teenaged sons six shillings a week for bed and board.

1911 Eliza <u>Barrow</u>, a smelly, miserly, middle-aged gin swiller rents the top floor. She had a small fortune which a year later was gone. As was she. The papers were full of the Crippen murder when Eliza Barrow died of 'diarrhoea' and was buried in Islington Cemetery, near Mrs Crippen. Locals, suspicious to read that she had left less than £10, knew she had owned the freehold of the Bucks Head pub, Camden and the barber shop next door. In all she must have been worth about £4,000. Where had it gone? They called in the police who exhumed Ms Barrow and found her body full of arsenic.

1912 At his trial, Seddon upsets Mr Justice Bucknill by declaiming the Freemason's oath: *'I declare before the Great Architect of the Universe, I am innocent.'* The judge, himself a freemason, was so moved he could barely pronounce the death sentence.

18 April seven thousand gather outside Pentonville Prison when Seddon is hanged. His bullied, downtrodden wife re-married and went to live in America. 63 Tollington Park was auctioned, bomb damaged during WWII, converted into flats (1958) and bought by Islington Council (1978). Tenants who knew nothing about the murder have said the house is haunted.

SELLERS, Peter (1925–1980)

Film star

1936 Peter, age ten, starts at St Aloysius College, **Hornsey Lane**, a Roman Catholic school opened 1879 by the Brothers of Our Lady of Mercy.

The school for 160 boarders (boarder bugs) and 200 day-boys (day dogs) admitted all. Peter's father was C. of E., his mother Jewish. Peter was big and clumsy. Practically his only schoolfriend was Bryan Connon, two years younger. They shared a passion for the wireless, especially Will Hay as a bumbling teacher in a second-rate boys' academy. Connon was the straight man, the feed for Peter and they giggled all the way home from school. Connon said Archway Road was the pavement nursery for Peter's Bluebottle on *The Goon Show* and for his Fu Man Chu. Although the school had a drama society Peter, awkward and unpopular, didn't join.

1939 WWII. St Aloysius College relocates to Wisbech, Cambridgeshire. Peter Sellers' schooldays finished at 14 although he remained in touch with the college for many years after. The family moved to Ilfracombe, Devon, where Peter found work in his uncle's theatre.

1955 Michael Balcon films *The Ladykillers* in Frederick (now **Frederica**) **Street**. The robbery scene was filmed outside Stanley buildings in **Cheney Road**. Sellers' first film role, he kept asking Balcon if he was any good. When filming ended a party was given for the residents.

1963 Sellers models his character in *Heavens Above* on one of the Brothers at St Aloysius. He generously donated gifts and money to the school.

1969 Sellers, now rich, likes to drive around the area in his latest flash car. Crossing Archway's 'Suicide Bridge' with Wilfrid Hyde-White one day, he talked a would-be jumper to safety. St Aloysius was forced to go comprehensive (see also Boyson, Dr Rhodes; Owen, Dame Alice and other entries).

1979 Making *Being There* (last film) he telegraphs his old school: *To the boys of St Aloysius College. Peter Sellers was educated here but to no avail he turned out a right twit. See that you don't do the same. Excelsior. Peter Sellers.*

1980 Dies, of a heart attack.

SEVEN SISTERS ROAD N7

1350 Seven elm trees planted at Page Green Tottenham are nicknamed the Seven Sisters.

1831 Seven Sisters Road is built.

1849 One of the worst parts of Islington is The Campbell Bunk. Many of the 68 houses produce convicts.

1852 The seven 500-year-old trees are felled and seven new ones planted by the seven McRae sisters of Tottenham.

1886 Seven wych elms are planted by the seven Hibbert sisters, daughters of a butcher in High Road, Tottenham.

1900 An empty shop at 228 is used as a 'penny gaff' grandly called The Electric Vaudeville.

1909 Islington's first purpose-built cinema is the Finsbury Park Cinematographe at 269 (known locally as The Rink because there's one at the back). White enamel and stone outside, green, pink and white interior décor. Penny-in-the-slot loos kept out undesirables.

1914 The Electric Vaudeville at 228 reverts to a shop.

1923 Montague Pyke's fourteenth cinema, The Holloway Cinematograph at 67 (Devonshire Road, later **Axminster Road**), called Pyke's by the patrons, shows local newsreels, e.g. *Islington Reservists On Parade*.

   Re-named The Palace, locals still called it Pyke's. Patrons were given cough sweets with the ticket to combat thick Woodbine and Player's Weights cigarette smoke.

1923 Finsbury Park Cinematograph at 269 'the Rink' is the first in Britain to show a demonstration of sound on film. An opera singer warbled a chunk of *Carmen* and a ballerina danced Tchaikovsky's dying swan.

1928 Two of the seven wych elms planted by the Hibbert sisters 42 years earlier are blown down in a gale so they're asked back to replace them. Only five turned up, one was ill, another dead (the last Hibbert sister died in 1955).

1930 The Astoria at 232 (Grade 2 listed) built in the style of a Spanish palace opens with a huge orchestra, corps de ballet, dancing troupes and trumpeters from the Life Guards. The foyer resembled a Moorish harem with an illuminated fountain filled with goldfish. Inside was a Byzantine cupola with clouds and stars on the ceiling while the stage was flanked by Andalucian villages and courtyards. There were lavish tea rooms and 200 uniformed staff.

1937 Pyke's closes. Now Safeways.

1939 Paramount Pictures sells Finsbury Astoria to the Odeon chain.

1955 The seven Bastion sisters from Tottenham are televised for the fifth replanting of seven trees. This time it was Lombardy poplars.

1959 During a fight outside Gray's Dancing Academy between the Angel Gang and Finsbury Gang a young PC called to the scene is stabbed and dies.

1960s Concerts at the Odeon draw bigger crowds than films. Top stars appearing included The Beach Boys, the Beatles, Ray Charles, Nat King Cole, Gene Pitney, Duke Ellington and Frank Sinatra.

1970 Rank takes over the Odeon and re-names it The **Rainbow**, dubbed the Madison Square Garden of London. 300 rock shows over the following ten years started with The Who.

1981 The Rainbow closes.

1986 The Red Rose Comedy Club opens. It helped launch the careers of unknowns David Baddiel, Jo Brand, Julian Clary, Alan Davies, Lee Evans, Hattie Hayridge, John Hegley, Eddie Izzard, Paul Merton, Rob Newman, Gerry Sadowitz, Frank Skinner *et al.*

1999 Izzard in cheap PVC jacket and tatty high heels returns to his comedy roots and 200 fans. The next night he faced 11,000 worshippers at Wembley.

SEX PISTOLS (The)
Islington: Home of Punk

Punk was more than a musical style or a fashion statement, for a decade it was an intimidating, in-your-face way of London life. Less of a group than an attitude ('I am the anti-chrrrrrrrrist!!!! I am an anarchissst!!!!'), The Sex Pistols embodied the inarticulate frustration of hundreds of thousands of poorly-educated young, unable to join in a society increasingly driven by money, technology and the Media; those whom Will Hutton in The State of the Nation *identified as the new Underclass.*

1958 John Lydon is born in **Benwell Street**, off Holloway Road. He plays in the bombed-out buildings of one of the roughest areas in London. He attended the local Catholic school, Sir William of York in **Gifford Street** off York Way (near Pentonville Prison).

1974 Age 16, at nearby Hackney College meets soulmate John Beverley (16). Johnny dubbed him Sid after his hamster. When the hamster bit his father, he was called vicious – so Sid was now Sid Vicious, a name he hated.

1975 John's father tells him to cut his long pink hair or get out. He cut it but dyed the left-over bits green.

An assistant at SEX, Malcolm McLaren's shop in the King's Road, spotted John with spiky green hair, teeth to match and a T-shirt with I HATE PINK FLOYD on it. He was invited to audition for a band McLaren was cobbling together. Lydon was dubbed Johnny Rotten because of his bad teeth …

1976 August. Posters around Islington: *The Screen on the Green presents a Midnight Special Sunday Aug 29th Midnight-Dawn. On Stage Sex Pistols+ Clash+ Buzzcocks Tickets £1 from SEX 430 King's Road Chelsea. Tel 351 6764 p.m. or from Box Office Screen on The Green Tel 226 3520*

1977 March, Lydon writes *God Save The Queen* on the kitchen table in his parents' council flat in Finsbury Park while waiting for his baked beans to heat.

The Pistols signed a recording contract with A&M outside Buckingham Palace. Within a week the contract was revoked and A&M had to scrap 25,000 copies (in 1999 one was valued at £2,500). Rejected by EMI, A&M and CBS, Richard Branson of *Virgin Records* signed the band and on 3 April at The Screen on The Green (q.v.) The Sex Pistols performed *God Save The Queen*. The place was packed out, with McLaren at the mixing deck. May, Lydon's *God Save the Queen* (with HM on the cover) was released by Branson. Within a week, despite being banned by BBC, ITV, Capital Radio, W H Smith, Woolworths and Boots, it was number one. July, The Sex Pistols horrified audiences of family viewing show, *Top of the Pops*. November, LP *Never Mind The Bollocks* was released. Lydon was stabbed in the Pegasus pub car park, Highbury. (Chas 'n Dave bought the pub, wheeled in a piano and served pie and mash and jellied eels.)

1978 The Pistols split. Sid died in the USA.

1996 Lydon rehearses in **Brewery Road** off York Way near his old school in Gifford Street. The Pistols were back. 20,000 tickets, £22 each were sold. Also appearing were Iggy Pop, the Buzzcocks and Stiff Little Fingers.

....

SEYMOUR, Robert (1800–1836)

Illustrator

1836 Seymour (36) at 16 Park Place West (377 **Liverpool Road**) has a studio at the end of his long garden. In April the gifted illustrator of <u>Dickens</u>' *The Posthumous Papers of the Pickwick Club* himself became posthumous.

Dickens had written a letter to Seymour criticising the famous artist's work. The pair had met just 48 hours earlier to discuss Dickens' objections, after which Seymour went home and altered his drawings to suit Dickens. The next morning he went to his studio, turned all his Pickwick drawings to the wall, and shot himself. Seymour and his family insisted that it was he, not Dickens who invented Mr Pickwick – not the last time the great writer was to be accused of plagiarism (see Cruikshank, George).

Seymour made his reputation by drawing cockney sportsmen and the story goes that he approached his publisher with a view to producing a book. The publisher said he knew just the man to write the text, Dickens, then enjoying success with *Sketches by Boz*. Seymour had lived in Islington since he left school, lodging at **Canonbury Tower** (q.v.) and 8 **Church Row** off Upper Street. He is buried in St Mary Magdalene, Holloway Road (tombstone now in the crypt). The back door he opened on to the garden that fateful day is still there, as is his sitting room window seat and 1810 fireplace. When Seymour committed suicide both Leech (friend of George du Maurier) and Thackeray, ex-Charterhouse boys, asked Dickens for his job (illustrating *Pickwick*). Dickens rejected both and chose Hablot Brown, who took the name *Phiz* to complement Dickens '*Boz*'. Dickens, from a poverty-stricken background (he was barely educated and looked down upon by the establishment), surely felt a frisson turning down two privileged, wealthy, well-placed ex-public schoolboys. Thackeray showed him his portfolio which Dickens '*Strange to say, did not find suitable*'

2000 Seymour's old lodging house is on the market for £650,000.

....

SHAKESPEARE, William (1564–1616)

1582 Stage-struck Will, 18, a provincial actor, rents a room near Holy Well Lane within walking distance of The Theatre and The Curtain. He joined Robert Dudley, Earl of Leicester's Company. His friendship with his neighbours, the Burbages, lasted until he died,

1595 *Romeo and Juliet* is licensed.

Shakespeare, as author, by law had to pay seven shillings licence fee of St John's Gate (q.v.). and perform his play before Tylney, censor, Master of the Revels. The original script with suggested cuts in the margin still has <u>Tylney</u>'s signature. Tylney's duties were originally confined to plays the Queen would see but he now censored all plays performed in public. Thirty of Shakespeare's plays were licensed at St John's Gate. Once passed, Shakespeare loaded the props, costumes and scenery on to barges on the Fleet to be sent down the Thames to the Globe.

SHEPPARD, Jack (1702–1724)

Highwayman

Sheppard, a popular character and notorious highwayman, was imprisoned five times and escaped four, the last time from Newgate from the third floor above the gate, where he was handcuffed and manacled to the floor.

1724 Hanged at Tyburn age 22 in front of 200,000 spectators

1728 Immortalised as Macheath in John Gay's *The Beggar's Opera*, musical score by local composer John Pepusch, organist at **Charterhouse** (q.v.).

Sheppard was painted by Sir James Thornhill (Hogarth's father-in-law) and interviewed in prison by journalist Daniel Defoe. Harrison Ainsworth's best-selling novel *Jack Shephard* (sic), illustrated by the ubiquitous George Cruikshank, was based on his life. Dubbed a Newgate novel, it was satirised by Thackeray. As was the custom, he was buried in an unmarked grave in unconsecrated ground.

1865 Workmen digging the foundations for the National Gallery in St Martin's Fields unearth Sheppard's remains.

SHILLIBEER, George (1797–1866)

Pioneer of public transport, introduced Monsieur Omnes's bus (omnibus) to London.

1829 Midshipman in Paris during the Napoleonic Wars, he stayed on as a coachbuilder. When M. Omnes launched a horse bus, Shillibeer decided London needed one too, so he came home to make his fortune.

His timing was just right. The New Road was built to link Islington with Paddington (Pentonville Road) and businessmen in the city started moving to the newly-built squares of Islington. Shillibeer, given the first bus route franchise, was first to offer a timetabled service from Paddington to the Bank of England. His depôt was in Carpenter's Mews, **North Road** (now a brasserie). Shillibeer's bus needed three horses to pull it up **Pentonville Hill** but had no brakes for the other side down **City Road** so passengers had to be adventurous. Cheaper two-horse buses and the railways put him out of business but death, like taxes, always being with us, he launched a successful funeral coach firm.

SICKERT, Walter RA (1860–1942)

Impressionist painter, some of his best work was painted in Islington.

1865 Walter Sickert, 5, who grew up to be the most famous British artist of his day, is staying with his great-aunt in **Duncan Terrace**. He had a fistula (see also Dickens, Charles) and needed an operation at St Mark's, **City Road** (1853), a specialist fistula hospital. Fistula, a medical condition, is less of a problem today but once there were fistula hospitals all over the UK. (A fistula is caused by the bursting of an abscess, usually in the canal from the lower bowel to the anus). As a treat, Walter was taken to Sadler's Wells where he would one day tread the boards.

1877 Back in his beloved Islington, in **Claremont Square** he remembers the 'green hill' from childhood. Not a hill and nothing like he remembered, it was in fact the New River Reservoir or Upper Pond. Walter, 16, had left school and acted at Sadler's Wells for the next four years.

1881 Abandons the theatre for painting. Sickert studied in London, France and Italy and married three times. His third and last wife, painter Therese Lessore, shared his passion for Islington. They painted working people (his own working clothes were pink trousers, cowboy hat and comfy slippers) and trawled the music halls for subjects to sketch.

1925 Rents 56 **Noel** Street (**Road** after 1938) overlooking the **Regent's Canal** and paints the view from his studio, *The Hanging Gardens of Islington*. He also painted *Lilac and Thunderplump*, his landlady's daughter and friend giggling and sewing at the window. His brother-in-law gave him a lay figure which had belonged to William Hogarth, life-size, solid wood and very heavy. As it was being lugged upstairs he quipped that it looked like Lazarus being raised from the dead. This became his famous painting, *The Raising of Lazarus*.

1927 Age 67, buys Southey Villa, 15 **Quadrant Road** (demolished to make way for council flats) which survives in his painting *Garden of Love*. The Sickerts lived here for four years, a long time for him. He was now financially successful so could move anywhere (e.g. Chelsea, where his peers were) but loved Islington. Some of Sickert's best paintings were of Collins. He still had his studio in Noel Street but also opened an art school at 1, **Highbury Place**. Here he sketched *The Raising of Lazarus* on the red wallpaper (it may very well still be there).

1931 Moves again. This time to 14 **Barnsbury Park**. He gave up his Noel Street studio but kept 1 Highbury Place. His new address was near **Pentonville Prison**, a useful landmark for directing cabbies. After an evening drinking at the Garrick with Leslie Henson (also of Islington) he hailed a cab intending to visit all the places he had lived during the last 50 years but as he was getting in, the cabby asked *'Pentonville, Sir?'* Sickert was so impressed he let the cabbie drive him home.

1932 Gives Lilian Baylis *The Raising of Lazarus* to auction at Christie's to rescue the near-bankrupt Sadler's Wells. At the handing-over ceremony at the theatre Sickert said: (it is) *'given in memory of my perpetual adoration of Sam Phelps and my gratitude to Isabel Bateman of whose Sadler's Wells Company I was myself a utility member.'*

1939 WWII Terrified of air raids, departs for Bath where he dies three years later. As he spent so much of his life in islington his family gave some of his palettes, etching plates, letters, pictures and photographs, contents of the studio where he painted a sketch for *The Raising of Lazarus*, more than 100 paintings and drawings to the borough.

1970 73 of 'Our Own Sickerts' are exhibited at the Islington Festival. The collection in its entirety had never been on display. His *Tiller Girls* and two paintings of music hall scenes lent to Betty Boothroyd (ex-Tiller girl, ex-Speaker of the House) hang in the red-carpeted, fan-vaulted cloister court of the Speaker's private apartments in the Palace of Westminster. Since 1975, Sickert, for non-art-lovers, is more famous for the story he told Joseph, his illegitimate son, who in turn told it to the journalist Stephen Knight whose bestseller *Jack the Ripper: The Final Solution* is the result. Sickert said that the Duke of Clarence, heir to the throne, had a love affair with Annie Cook, one of his models, and they had a daughter. Sickert was her guardian until she came of age when he became her lover (the affair lasted 12 years) and Joseph was the result. He went on to say that Annie was incarcerated in an asylum by the establishment and her four friends, privy to the royal scandal, were not only murdered but were Jack the Ripper's victims.

1996 The old Glaxo offices bought by City University are converted into The Walter Sickert Hall of Residence.

SKINNER STREET EC1

1390 St Bartholomew's Day. Richard II and his queen Anne of Bohemia watch the Skinners Company perform *The Passion of Our Lord* and *The Creation of the World* at Skinners Well (actual location is not known but the Skinners Company owned the land in Skinner Street).

1409 Another *'Great play at Skynners Welle ... there were to see the same, the most part of the nobles and gentles in England'.*

1816 In the middle of the Spa Fields Riot (q.v.), Able Seaman <u>Cashman</u> loots Beckwith Gunsmiths and was hanged in front of the shop, the last time in England a criminal was executed at the scene of the crime.

1890 Lord Mayor of London opens Britain's first free library with James Duff <u>Brown</u> as chief librarian. It became one of the most important libraries in Europe. Readers reported to Reception with their request, which was brought to them by a librarian.

1894 Finsbury Library is the first in the UK to allow readers open access to shelves (instead of selecting them from a catalogue). For the first time the public was allowed to browse at leisure (see Lenin, Vladimir Ilich).

1912 The People's Picture Playhouse opens at No. 12. A purpose-built barn of a place, it had to be regularly fumigated against vermin.

1920 The cinema is re-named The Globe.

1951 The cinema is now The Rio (closed 1955).

1967 Islington Council demolishes the historically important, world-famous Finsbury Free Library, where Lenin carried out research.

....

SMITH, George ('Brides in the Bath')
Serial killer

1914 Smith moves to 14 Bismarck Road with Margaret Lofty, his (although she doesn't know it) seventh 'wife'. Wife No. 4, Bessie Mundy, died in her bath in 1912 in Herne Bay (he bought a zinc bath on 13 July, beating the shopkeeper down from £2 to £1 17s 6d, then returned it on the 15th, asking for his money back). Wife No. 5, Alice Burnham died in her bath on honey moon in a Blackpool boarding house. The landlady's suspicions were aroused when she criticised him for giving his bride a pauper's burial. He was dismissive, saying *'she's dead isn't she?'*

How or why Smith fetched up in Archway is not known. He came on ahead of his bride to find lodgings. Mrs Heiss, a German, at 16 Orchard Street (now **Wakeham Street**) showed him the rooms and remembered him saying the bath was 'too small'. Suspicious, Mrs Heiss arranged for a policeman to be present when Mr Lloyd returned. After an angry exchange on the doorstop, he left. Unfortunately for Miss Blatch, landlady at 14 **Bismarck Road**, her bath was more than adequate. Smith immediately registered his new wife with the local doctor (Bates, 30 **Archway Road**). The couple spent 17 December settling in with 'Mr Lloyd' carrying out his usual tasks of writing up their wills and seeing to financial formalities. The next evening (18th) Miss Blatch heard a bath being run, then some splashing followed by a long-drawn-out sigh. Suddenly her harmonium in the front parlour pealed forth throughout the house. Mr 'Lloyd' was accompanying himself, singing *Nearer My God to Thee* before popping out to buy tomatoes for supper. When he returned the distraught bridegroom found his bride dead in her bath. At the inquest, exonerated of all blame, he received commiserations. When the drowning was reported in the press, Mrs Crossley, the Blackpool landlady who had a guest whose bride also drowned in her bath, contacted the police.

1915 Smith, born 1872 in Bethnal Green, in a reformatory by nine, in prison by 18, is hanged at Maidstone 13 August, age 43.

1917 After the war German names were unpopular so German Shepherd dogs became Alsatians, and Bismarck Road became **Waterlow Road**.

....

SMITHFIELD

Oldest, largest meat market in the world.

200 AD Outside the north-west perimeter of the Roman wall is a ten-acre flat or 'smooth' field used as a cemetery.

704 The 'smooth field' is known as *Smetha Felde* by the Saxons.

1000 Smithfield Burnings begin on the 'hanging field', a place of public execution for 400 years where criminals were hanged, drawn and quartered and witches burned. The fashion for burning religious recalcitrants started with the Bishop of London, who roasted the wayward on Smetha Felde, a popular Holy Day (holiday) entertainment. Smithfield, world famous for its huge market (London's only medieval market still on its original site) was also used for hawking.

1170 Along with hangings, burnings and jousts, Smithfield now had Bart's Hospital, St Bartholomew's Priory and world famous Bartholomew and Cloth Fairs (q.v.)

1365 During the Hundred Years War, the practising of archery for defence of the realm was compulsory. Edward III ordered that every citizen in his leisure hours and holidays was to practise and not *'waste his time . . . playing football.'*

1369 Edward's edict is backed up by law. The Military Training Act was passed to guarantee trained longbow men in times of war. As there was no open space inside the city walls, Smithfield was used for practice.

1382 Richard II, hero of the Peasant's Revolt marries Anne of Bohemia (sister of good King Wenceslas).

To celebrate, Richard held a huge pageant in Smithfield with jousts. Geoffrey Chaucer, civil servant, author of *Canterbury Tales*, as his MC organised the seating and scaffolding. Competing knights on their way to Smithfield took a short cut through Knight Rider Alley. After a certain number of victories at the jousts they were awarded their spurs, further victories meant they could have them gilded. The goldsmith lived in the alley so it was also known as **Giltspur Street** (still there).

1557 Six local Protestants are arrested at worship. Tried for heresy and burned at the stake they're known as The Islington Martyrs.

1558 Mary Tudor dies. In four years, 200 Protestants had died in the Smithfield burnings. Elizabeth Tudor her half-sister was declared Queen. Another 200 died during her 45-year reign because they were Catholic.

1800 Availability of winter fodder means that Smithfield Market is open for business all year round. Animals were slaughtered on the street and dung flies bred on their entrails in knackers' yards. Hovels around the market swarmed with cat gut spinners, cat meat boilers and purers (dung scoopers), giving it the epithet of *'nosegay of England'*.

1840 3,000 oxen and 36,000 sheep herded down **St John Street** every day.

1849 Workmen find charred bones of Mary's martyrs.

1851 The City buys **Caledonian Fields** to build a new cattle market and Smithfield became a dead meat market. Traders wanted their new market enclosed and made their wishes clear to City of London architect Horace (Tower Bridge) Jones. The underground railway line at Farringdon was later extended to the new market so that meat could be taken straight inside.

2000 Smithfield is still the largest, oldest meat market in the world.

People still come to buy meat as they have for 1,000 years although these days most market days are over by 10 a.m. It's predicted that by 2020 with the increase in vegetarianism, decrease in export (following the BSE crisis), animal rights activists and Mayor Livingstone's proposed congestion charges for incoming vehicles, the market will close. Being so near the wealth of the City, it could be turned into a tourist centre to rival Covent Garden.

....

SOPER, Donald, Baron (1903–1999)

Methodist Minister

'Soap Box Soper' was a popular open-air speaker for many years at **Highbury Corner**. *Famous for his black cassock, socialism, pacifism and teetotalism he remained a lifelong friend of vagrants and alcoholics.*

1928 A young, good-looking priest, Reverend Donald Soper moves into Kelross Road with his new wife. He called himself one of Wesley's travelling preachers and declared it was not possible to be a Conservative *and* a Christian.

1929 Gets the Central Methodist Hall, **Drayton Park** opened. Every year he arranged for 1,000 children of the unemployed to be given a Christmas Morning breakfast.

1930s Revd. Soper's holy picture shows at the Central Methodist Hall draw huge crowds.

1936 Leaves Islington to run the West London Mission, Kingsway Hall.

1955 Petitions to get Ruth <u>Ellis</u> reprieved. Thousands gathered in Hyde Park to hear him debate capital punishment.

1965 Accepts a life peerage and says that the House of Lords is living proof that there is life after death. His opinions were sought right up to the time he died.

....

SPA FIELDS RIOT

(Wilmington Square, Tysoe, Merlin and **Yardley Streets)**

The defeat of Napoleon in 1815 was followed by economic depression causing mass unemployment whose victims, because of the Corn Laws propping up prices, couldn't afford bread.

1816 Meetings are banned under the Seditious Meetings Act and Habeas Corpus (length of time a suspect can be imprisoned before coming before the court) is suspended. At Merlin's Cave (pub) Arthur <u>Thistlewood</u> (hanged four years later for The Cato Street Conspiracy) organised a protest meeting to which he invited famous Sir Henry *'Orator'* <u>Hunt</u> MP. Described in the press as *'an unprincipled demagogue'*, the poor loved him. Word of his visit spread and 20,000 gathered on Spa Fields to hear him. The military was drafted in and soldiers ordered to shoot Hunt if a riot broke out. The field was white with hats, caps and handkerchiefs, Sir Henry having made the wearing of a white hat the official badge of radicals, just as republicans wore red berets during the French Revolution (Radicals were called 'white hats'). The nickname 'radical' was given to all reformers but the political term didn't come about until Sir Henry is imprisoned for a speech he made three years later at the Peterloo Massacre, Manchester.

....

SPAS (and Pleasure Gardens)

Taking the waters first became fashionable in Germany. Islington, prone to springs, cashed in. Pleasure gardens and resorts were laid out around the springs to cater for people who couldn't afford to spend the season in Tunbridge, Bath or Cheltenham so imbibed nearer home in the smaller spas of Islington.

1600s Many people don't take baths or even wash so it doesn't take long for a spa to be topped with thick scum, *'repositories for the dustpans of every housemaid'.*

The fashion was to see and be seen. Visitors were offered a free glass of the water as an inducement to pay for entertainments such as dancing, stunts, freak shows, music, fireworks and ballooning. The genuinely ill responded to adverts boasting the curative effects of this foul-smelling, nasty-tasting liquid (imbibers *'may be briskly moved by one glass'*). Taking the cure was described by John (*Beggar's Opera*) <u>Gay</u> as *'imposed mortifications of the flesh in health's name'.* Mortifications included being wrapped tightly in cold wet sheets. When the lower orders began to 'bib', posh people went elsewhere. One visitor's description of taking the waters: (The spa was) *'full of pot bellied farmers of 60, half palsied and lame artisans with black and calloused hands and many who suffer from severe skin disorders scrubbing from their hardened cuticles the congregated perspiration of ages.'*

As the bathers began to perspire, fleas jumped from them and were picked off by 'dippers', female attendants paid to bring up the water in long-handled ladles or buckets. Daniel <u>Defoe</u> wrote of the spas: *'the ladies are all undress'd'.* Women were driven straight from bed before breakfast still in their nightgowns and carried from their carriages to the waters in curtained sedan chairs. Some spas in Islington stayed in business for as long as the supply lasted, as long as drinking water was suspect (rife with typhoid-carrying bugs), until the 1890s, when the new railways transported passengers out of town to seaside watering holes such as Brighton.

1684 Water from a re-discovered spring opposite Sadler's Wells, when analysed, is found to be similar to that at Tunbridge, so the new spa is called New Tunbridge Wells. Later known as The Islington Spa it had gardens, arbours, tea and coffee rooms and a dance hall. Lubetkin's **Spa Green Estate** (q.v.) is now on the site.

1685 Another old well is found by the owner of The Fountain Inn, Baynes Row (corner of **Exmouth Street** and **Rosoman Street**). The new spa was called The London Spa (now a public house). This bit of Islington/Fiennes/Moor/Pipe fields is now called Spa Fields.

1697 Another old well comes to light. Walter <u>Baynes</u> exploited its (presumed) medicinal properties by building Cold Bath Spa, entrance fee two shillings (old and infirm lowered into the bath via a chair suspended from the ceiling paid an extra sixpence).

1733 <u>Princess Amelia</u> and sister <u>Princess Caroline</u>, daughters of <u>George II</u> visit The London Spaw (Londoners copy Dr <u>Johnson</u>'s pronunciation of 'Spaw') to take the waters. On 2 June it was Amelia's birthday and she was given a twenty-one gun salute as she crossed Spa Fields. Visiting Royalty was a rare event and Islington turned out to see the princesses. The 'quality' didn't usually come to Islington. They hired carriages to frequent Bath, Leamington and Tunbridge. After the princesses' visit, numbers increased to 1,600 a day.

1770 Islington, marketed as a Health Resort, is featured in a magazine article *'Modern Sabbath Day Journeys In Or About London'.*

1870 The remains of Cold Bath Spa are built over.

1894 The great Islington Spa is now a scrubby bit of grass known as **Spa Green**.

....

STOPES, Marie, Dr (1880–1958)
Marie Stopes Court N19
Islington: Home of Birth Control

1921 Marie Stopes Clinic For Constructive Birth Control opens at 61 **Marlborough Road** Holloway N19.

The Mothers' Clinic was a tiny derelict shop squashed between a confectioner's and a grocer's surrounded by battery manufacturers, wheelwrights, welders and furniture removers. The clinic was open every day for free advice on birth control and three women every day were fitted with Stopes' version of the diaphragm (not the Dutch Cap). Stopes said her family planning clinic was the first in the world, it was certainly the first in the British Empire to carry out research into birth control. She was accused of practising genetic engineering and encouraging selective breeding. She took her birth control clinic in a caravan all over the UK, braving men who threw stones at her and jeered: *'Jeanie, Jeanie full of hopes, Read a book by Dr Stopes, But to judge by her condition, Must have read the wrong edition'.* Within five years the premises were too small.

1926 With 5,000 clients on the books, Dr Stopes takes larger premises in **Whitfield Street** W1 (where the clinic still is). The clinic in Holloway was taken over by the Birth Control and Advisory Bureau.

2000 Today there are Marie Stopes clinics all over the world. In London, women can and do terminate unwanted pregnancies in their lunch breaks.

....

SWEDENBORG, Sir William Emanuel (1688–1772)
Scientist and Mystic

An Oxford graduate of Swedish descent, Swedenborg had his first 'vision' in London in 1743. In 1757, he claimed to have witnessed the Last Judgement. He was the author of the well-known witticism, that there is a place in Heaven especially reserved for the English.

1771 Convinced he is divinely inspired, Swedenborg moves in to 26 Great Bath Street (**Topham Street** EC1) and writes *The True Religion*, in which he argued that Christ was not merely the Son of God, but God himself.

1772 Dies on the precise day (29 March) at the precise time he predicted (no, it wasn't suicide).

1783 Robert <u>Hindmarsh</u>, Clerkenwell printer, founds The Swedenborg Society and builds The New Jerusalem Church in Eastcheap. Worshippers called themselves Swedenborgians. <u>Blake</u>, 30, was one.

1798 Holloway becomes The New Jerusalem when Hindmarsh builds a Swedenborgian church in **Camden Road**.

1873 The New Jerusalem Church is built in Park Road (**Parkhurst Road** N7). When the lease expired (some sources say 1954, others 1971) worshippers moved to High Barnet. Today there are 5,000 Swedenborgians in Britain.

TAYLOR (sisters, the)

Nursery rhymesters

1752 Isaac Taylor, 22, of Clerkenwell engraves plates for *The Gentleman's Magazine* at St John's Gate and Mr Chamber's *Cyclopedia* (written in Canonbury Tower, q.v.).

1759 A son, Isaac is born.

1782 Ann is born to Isaac the Younger in **Upper Street** opposite St Mary's. A year later, sister Jane is born in Red Lion Street (now **Britton Street**) Clerkenwell.

1804 Ann and Jane Taylor's *Original Poems For Infant Minds* is published.

1806 The sisters publish *Rhymes for the Nursery*. Jane, who died young, wrote *The Star*, probably the most famous nursery rhyme in the English language. *'Twinkle, twinkle little star, How I wonder what you are, Up above the world so high, Like a diamond in the sky'* was published in their *Rhymes for the Nursery*. Kate <u>Greenaway</u> later republished it in *Mother Goose*, a compendium of old nursery rhymes.

1999 Nelson Mandela, President of South Africa, sings *'Twinkle, twinkle little star'* with children at his farewell party.

TERNAN, Ellen (1839–1914)

Actress

The secret teenage mistress of Charles Dickens lived off St Paul's Road. He fell in love with her not long after she moved here. Today, his museum in Doughty Street sells cameos of her but for years she was hardly known.

1855 Ellen (16) moves into Park Cottage on the corner of Northampton Park and St Paul's Place off St Paul's Road. The cottage was squeezed between the North London Railway, cattle market and brickfields. Plots for new houses were marked out with poles and reminded the sisters of gibbets. Her mother used her maiden name Frances Jarman as a stage name. Sam <u>Phelps</u>, actor-manager of **Sadler's Wells** was doing well with Shakespeare, so was able to offer regular work to Frances and her actress daughters Fanny (known for her green spectacles) and Maria. However it was teenage Ellen, born in Rochester near Dickens' own birthplace, who made history.

1857 Dickens takes friend and fellow-adulterer, Wilkie Collins' play, *The Frozen Deep*, to Manchester. The Ternans, Frances, Fanny, Maria and for the first time, Ellen (17) were on tour with it.

Dickens, 44, father of ten children, married 22 years, was totally smitten by Ellen. When he returned he broke the bombshell to Catherine, his plump, middle-aged wife, that they were to have separate bedrooms. She was devastated. Dickens was a frequent visitor to Park Cottage and ordered a bracelet to be sent to Ellen but it was delivered in error to Catherine who was distraught. Dickens denied any romantic interest, feigned fury and ordered Catherine to make amends by calling on the Ternans to take tea at Park Cottage. Not long afterwards (according to Anny Thackeray) Charles Dickens Jnr, who was older than Ellen, bumped into his father and 'Miss whatever the actress' name is' on Hampstead Heath and the jig was up. Ellen later appeared before Queen Victoria in a royal command performance by the Sadler's Wells company.

1861 Dickens leaves Catherine. The Ternans move out of Park Cottage.

1870 Dickens dies writing *Edwin Drood*, a story of a man leading a double life. The couple had thirteen years together but none (according to Dickens' daughter Kate) were happy. Ellen, 31, knocked ten years off her age, married a man of 22, moved to Margate and had children. Her family did not discover her secret until she died, age 75. Her son burnt all her papers.

1879 Catherine Dickens is buried with a baby daughter at Highgate Cemetery.

....

THEATRES

Modern day Islington has eleven theatres.

1174 Parish Clerks produce plays outdoors to teach the Scriptures. The Clerk's Well in the Fleet Valley with its steep banks provided a natural amphitheatre.

1560 Fortune Theatre built in Playhouse Yard between Golden (Goldyng) Lane and White Cross Street.

1576 Thousands trek across Finsbury fields to go to The Theatre, Britain's first purpose-built playhouse in Holy Well Lane.

1577 The Curtain opens in the same lane. John Aubrey, eighteenth century gossip columnist, wrote: '*The Greene Curtaine is a kind of Nursery or obscure Play House somewhere in the suburbes, I think toward Clerkenwell*'.

1599 The Red Bull, **Sekforde Street** opens. The Prince's Men use the Fortune Theatre, The Queen's Men use The Red Bull.

1656 Cromwell gives Sir William D'Avenant permission to stage opera in Rutland House, **Charterhouse Square**.

1660 Charles II grants a theatre patent (monopoly) to D'Avenant who transferred his theatre to Dorset Gardens (Duke's Theatre).

1683 Sadler's Wells (q.v.)

1850s Upper Street: The Golden Mile for Music Halls (see Music Halls)

1935 Michel Saint-Denis arrives in London from Paris and opens his London Theatre Studio in **Upper Street** with George Devine (founds the English Stage Company at The Royal Court).

1952 Tower Theatre.

1959 Brian Way sets up Theatre Centre in **Noel Road** so that out-of-work actors can keep working. He helped Pam St Clements, Geraldine James, Ben Kingsley, Anthony Sher and Juliet Stevenson on the road to stardom.

1961 Little Angel Puppet Theatre opens in the old Band of Hope, **Dagmar Passage**.

1968 Anna Scher takes over an old chapel in 70 **Barnsbury Road** to open an after-school drama club for underprivileged kids (see Scher, Anna).

1969 Dan Crawford buys **The King's Head** (q.v.).

1978 Almeida Theatre opens. George Murcell, actor (died 1998), opens a replica of Shakespeare's Rose Theatre in St George's Church, Tufnell Park. Sarah Miles acted here as did Anna Carteret. Closed 1998 it reopened 2000. Landlords at the Old Red Lion, **St John Street** turned their upstairs sitting room into a fringe theatre where the New Play Festival is held every year. 350 scripts are received, 12 get through.

1980 Britain's first performing arts training school founded 1911, the Italia Conti Theatre School arrives in **Goswell Road**.

1986 The Hen and Chickens, Highbury Corner opens a theatre in its upstairs room. Its 60 Edwardian seats started life in Drury Lane.

1988 Houses knocked down in **Arlington Way** to build The Lilian Baylis Theatre (q.v.). The People's Picture Palace, **Holloway Road** is converted into the National Youth Theatre of Great Britain.

1996 Rosemary Branch re-opens with a Stephen Kirk play on the history of Islington (which he hopes to turn into a film). Kirk is the producer of *Pretty Woman*, *Back To The Future* and *Top Gun*. Christopher Richardson opens the Pleasance London. He saved The Unicorn Children's Theatre (Leicester Square).

2003 Lease expires on Tower Theatre.

....

TOLPUDDLE STREET N1
The Tolpuddle Martyrs (q.v.)

1834 George Loveless of Tolpuddle, Dorset consults reformer Robert Owen about how to start a Union. *The Society of Agricultural Labourers* is formed. Trying to get the weekly minimum wage increased from nine shillings, Thomas Standfield and his brother John, George and his brother James, James Hammett and James Brine were convicted of administering 'illegal oaths for seditious purposes' under the Mutiny Act of 1797.

1834 The Government reduces the agricultural wage to six shillings a week. George Loveless and the others were sentenced to transportation (permanent exile). In Australia they were separated, sold for £1 each and sent to work in chain gangs. 120,000 trade unionists gathered on Copenhagen Fields then marched to Whitehall with a petition. 5,000 special constables were sworn in to keep the peace. Robert Owen led the procession and presented the petition to Home Secretary Lord Melbourne, who refused to accept it. When they took it to the king (William IV), the government called out troops.

1836 Thanks to Dr Thomas Wakley, MP for Finsbury the Martyrs are granted a free pardon and allowed home (see Wakley, Thomas). Scattered all over Australia, they first had to be found.

1837 George Loveless returns from Australia and is given a huge welcome at The White Conduit House. Tom Wakley was Guest of Honour.

1838 After four years, James Loveless, James Brine, Thomas and John Standfield return home.

1839 James Hammett the sixth and last Tolpudddle Martyr, returns home.

1984 The Tolpuddle Tree, a sycamore, is planted in Caledonian Park by Norman Willis of the TUC.

1986 Tolpuddle Street, a new road, replaces Culpeper and Mantell streets.

....

TORRENS, William (1813–1894)
Torrens Flats EC1

Liberal MP, Anti-corn law Irish lawyer elected to represent Finsbury for 20 years (1865 to 1885). He helped set up the London School Board Act to provide free education for children up to the age of 14.

1865 Brings in the Torrens Act *'Improvement of Artisans and Labourers' Dwellings.'* He was challenged by fellow MPs over his definition of *'not fit for habitation'*, asked to qualify how 'stinking' was the cess pit, how 'crowded' was crowded, how far away was the dung heap and how nearby was the knacker's yard.

1894 Dies of injuries sustained in a traffic accident.

....

TRAFFIC (Problem, the)

The area having long been the main gateway to the City of London from the North, Islington's present-day problems with traffic have their origin in the mists of time ...

1364 Edward III orders tolls to be collected to repair Holloway Road.

1664 First permanent toll gates erected.

1750 City Gates blamed for causing bottleneck at Islington.

1761 Medieval Moor Gate, Alders Gate and Cripple Gate leading to Islington are demolished to improve traffic flow.

1812 New North Road from the City to Archway is built, as is Arch Way Road.

1818 One horse on a canal can transport 45 tons of cargo. The **Regent's Canal** was built but rapidly superseded by railways.

1829 George <u>Shillibeer</u> (q.v.) is given the first bus franchise.

1846 Traffic is almost at a standstill. What we need is trains ... The North London and Midland Railways carved up Islington, hundreds of tenements were demolished and the residents thrown on to the streets without compensation.

1860 Traffic is almost at a standstill. What we need is trains underground ... The world's first underground railway, the Metropolitan line ran from Paddington to Farringdon.

1865 Traffic is almost at a standstill, toll gates were blamed for causing holdups and demolished.

1897 Traffic is almost at a standstill. It's all the fault of private horse-drawn carriages. What we need is buses ...

1899 Traffic is almost at a standstill. What we need is trams ...

1935 Traffic is almost at a standstill. It's the trams. Take away the tracks and have trolley buses instead ...

1959 Traffic is almost at a standstill. All the fault of trolley buses which slip off overhead wires causing snarl ups.

1993 Traffic is almost at a standstill, it's the cars. What we need is a No Stopping Red Route from the Archway to the Angel.

1999 Traffic is almost at a standstill. What we need are tolls and trams ...

2000 March. *Highbury & Islington Express* headline: 'A Borough That's Going Nowhere'. It takes 25 minutes for cars/buses to get from **Islington Green** to the Town Hall, **Upper Street** (half a mile) Traffic is static from **Hornsey Rise** to **Archway** roundabout, **Stroud Green Road** is gridlocked and the Victoria Line conks out at **Finsbury Park**. *What we need*, says Mayor Livingstone, *is a £5 congestion charge (toll) for motorists entering London ...*

....

TUBE (The)

Islington: Home of The Underground Railway

1863 The Metropolitan Subterranean Railway terminates at Farringdon. It followed the course of the old river Fleet from King's Cross Road to Mount Pleasant, ploughing through **Saffron Hill** rookeries, wiping out the notorious Chick Lane slums toward **Smithfield**. *Punch* dubbed it *The Sewer Railway*. Carriages were open trucks, but 30,000 passengers cheerfully boarded on the first day.

The world's first underground railway wasn't all underground, much of it was open to the elements (the same bits are open today). The only real tunnel went through Mount Pleasant. A trench was dug, retaining walls built then the opening covered. People were nervous of their homes collapsing, **Exmouth Street** giving special cause for concern because of extensive tunnelling. Punch ran a <u>Leech</u> (contemporary of <u>Cruikshank</u> and a **Charterhouse** boy with Thackeray) cartoon showing a stoker's head appearing through the kitchen floor: *'Excuse me marm, can you 'blige me with a scuttle o' coal?'*. *The Times* thundered: *'It is an insult to common sense to suppose people would prefer to be driven amid palpable darkness through the foul subsoil of London'*. But they did. The Underground carried nine million passengers in the first twelve months.

Trains were considered vulgar and were used mainly by the labouring class. The station was in **Farringdon Street**, the nearest place to the City where it could be built. (The faience-covered Farringdon and High Holborn station entrance was put up in 1922. Reverted to just Farringdon, 1936. 1990s campaign to change it to Clerkenwell so far failed.)

TURNMILL STREET EC1

Place of ill-repute

1190 The rich site their houses on the banks of the Fleet and build their 'necessity houses' (bog houses or 'bogs') over it.

1191 Richard of Devizes, monk and chronicler of London is shocked by *'actors ... smooth skinned lads, Moors, pretty boys, effeminates, belly dancers sorceresses, extortionates, night wanderers, magicians, beggars and buffoons ...'*

1417 The stewes (brothels) enjoy increased business after those inside the city walls are suppressed by the Lord Mayor (Dick <u>Whittington</u> was not Mayor this year, he was MP for London, see Whittington, Sir Richard). The Mayor tried to close these too but had no jurisdiction outside the walls, parts of which were a mere 150 yards from the City. (Brothels were called stewes, because prostitutes, to show they were clean, stewed publicly in barrels of hot water. This did not prevent a pandemic of venereal diseases.)

1562 418 Clerkenwell residents, 112 of whom live in Turn Mill Street, are assessed for the Poor Rate.

1597 *Henry IV*. <u>Shakespeare</u> has Sir John <u>Oldcastle</u>, youthful Henry's drinking partner, rollicking in the taverns and brothels in Turnmill Street (see Oldcastle, Sir John).

1614 Turn Mill Street, also called Tryl Mill Street and Turn Bull Street, is still infamous for brothels.

1782 The Castle Inn is rebuilt.

1811 Only pub in the UK with a pawnbroker's licence (hence the three golden balls on the inn sign).

A ROYAL VISIT

Hockley-in-the-Hole was the place to go for prostitutes, bear baiting, and gambling, a favourite haunt of the <u>Prince Regent</u>. One night, out of money, George asked the landlord to lend him some and left his watch as security. Next day he sent a messenger from the palace to return the money, retrieved his watch and granted the pub a pawnbroker's licence in perpetuity. Still in force. There's a painting inside showing the story.

1899 Booths Gin moves to the banks of the Fleet from Cowcross Street around the corner where it has been since 1687 (once had to drill only 100 feet for an unlimited water supply). Other local industries also included snuff, liquorice making and hair powder manufacturing. E.W. Mountford, who designed Old Bailey (Central Criminal Courts of Justice) and City University, designed the Booths Gin Distillery. Pomeroy, who worked with Mountford on the Old Bailey, carved the bas reliefs showing the stages of gin making. When the distillery closed in 1929, his façade was re-erected in **Britton Street** (Mountford House).

....

TYLER (Wat)
Revolutionary
1381 The Peasants Revolt

Wat Tyler (Tegheler/Helier) and his men marched on a city in turmoil, with a weak civic government, to inspect the Chancellor's audit, attack the Knights Hospitallers' Clerkenwell HQ and execute the hated Prior Hales, Lord High Chancellor, first Baron of England.

Tyler was an ex-soldier with a gift for leadership, a discharged non-commissioned officer from The Hundred Years War with France. He had been batman to Sir Richard Lyon, who treated him badly, and so was one of the first to lose his head. The Essex contingent was led by Jack Straw. Nearing Clerkenwell, they razed the Fleet prison whose inmates joined the march. Wat and his men camped on Clerkenwell Green and set fire to St John's Priory (q.v.).

While Wat marched into London, Straw and his gang went up to Highbury Castle (q.v.), dismantled it and set fire to the contents (never rebuilt, **Leigh Road** is the filled-in moat). The ruins became famous as Jack Straw's Castle.

The boy king, Richard, was at Mile End parleying with Thomas Farringdon of the East End contingent. Baron Hales and the Archbishop of Canterbury were hiding with Richard's mother in the Tower. Guards made no attempt to protect Hales or the Archbishop as Wat and his men broke down the door to the Queen Mother's private apartments and laughingly kissed her before allowing her to leave. They dragged Sudbury and Hales out and beheaded them. (Some versions say it was *John* Tyler, *not Wat*, who killed Hales on Tower Hill.) Hales, 60, lies buried in the Priory Church, **Clerkenwell** with other knights of the Order of St John.

15 June, Richard, with William Walworth, Lord Mayor, meets Wat at **Smithfield**. The king's men lined up outside **Bart's**, Wat's men were opposite, outside the market. Walworth owned many of the brothels burned down by the rioters and was a founder of **Charterhouse**, which he assumed (wrongly) Wat also intended to burn down. Richard, with bodyguard Squire Standish and Mayor Walworth attending, met Wat alone in the middle of the square. All were on horseback. Wat couldn't resist the grand gesture. He nonchalantly bent down, scooped water from a puddle, rinsed his mouth and with an expression of contempt spat it out at the feet of the king. A furious Walworth caught him off-guard and stabbed him. (The perfectly preserved knife, a twelve-inch long, double-ridged dagger, Fishmongers' Hall's most treasured possession, is remembered in the Arms of the

City. '*Walworth slew rebellious Tyler in his alarmes, the king therefore did give in lieu the dagger in the City Armes.*') Standish quickly drew his sword and finished Wat off. He and Walworth were knighted on the spot. Leaderless and demoralised, Wat's followers were escorted by Richard past the still-burning St John's, out on to the Moor Fields where they dispersed. Despite his status as local hero, Tyler, has never had a memorial.

U

UNION CHAPEL
Compton Terrace N1

1799 Spiritually unfulfilled by C. of E. worship and its hierarchical structure churchgoers start worshipping in an abandoned chapel in Highbury Grove. They call themselves Unionists.

1804 The congregation sever connections with St Mary's, appoint their own minister and attract worshippers from every background. Meetings were so popular, the Unionists were given permission to build a Chapel of Ease and appointed Henry Leroux, a Huguenot architect.

1806 Leroux completes **Compton Terrace** (q.v.). It consisted of the dainty Union Chapel (meaning meeting house to distinguish it from church) flanked by two houses either side.

1844 Congregation is 300.

1859 Congregation is 700. The tiny Georgian chapel was bursting its seams.

1876 Unionists re-name themselves Congregational Unionists because the impetus of worship comes from the congregation. Dr Henry Allon, minister (friend of Asquith, Earl of Oxford who lived around the corner in **St Mary's** Road, now **Grove**, and his sister Evelyn who lives at 21 **Douglas Road**) bought 18 and 19 Compton Terrace to build a larger chapel. James Cubitt, author of '*Design for Congregations*', was commissioned.

Getting away from the conventional design of churches, he considered naves and aisles inappropriate as the emphasis should be on the congregation not the altar. Union Chapel made his name as an architect, only one of three Cubitt chapels to survive (others are in Cambridge and Newcastle upon Tyne).

1877 Union Chapel is opened by Gladstone who speaks to full congregations here and is a regular worshipper, as were the Betjeman family (see Betjeman, Sir John) who lived at No. 13. 2,000 seats in pews arranged around the pulpit in a semi-circle gave an unrestricted view from any position and enabled every worshipper to see, hear and participate. A Sunday School was built at the back for 1,000 children. Organist W.H. Monk wrote *Abide With Me*; another, Henry Gauntlett, wrote *Once in Royal David's City*. The chapel was well attended until after WWII. Wealthy Congregationalists who lived in Highbury New Park drifted away when they couldn't get their carriages around the new trams in Upper Street (see Traffic).

1883 The Pilgrim Fathers Society, Plymouth, Mass. send a piece of the 1620 Plymouth Rock. (It's in the glass case above the door to the right of the pulpit.)

1888 Bicycles become affordable. Whole families cycled into the country on a Sunday and the congregation dwindled.

1889 The Victorian chapel, already out of proportion to the Georgian terrace, gets a huge tower – so is top-heavy as well.

1892 The minister quips that his parishioners are leaving *'either for Hampstead or heaven'*. The new railways which were polluting the inner city made it easier for people to live further out and many moved to the newly built suburbs.

1980 The congregation numbers twelve. Union Chapel was under threat of demolition.

1986 Revd Dr Janet Wootton revives its fortunes by hiring it out for filming (Anthony Hopkins and Demi Moore, *Shadowlands*); concerts (Jools Holland, Jo Brand, Rory Bremner, Eddie Izzard, The Pretenders) and rehearsals by companies appearing at the Almeida and Sadler's Wells (q.v.). She got into hot water when a theatre company put on *Bad Boy Johnny and The Prophets of Doom* in which a naked woman offers her body to the Pope. Accused of blasphemy, Revd Wootton pointed out that Union Chapel had no altar and had never been consecrated.

UPPER STREET N1

(Anglo-Saxon 'stroet' means 'houses on both sides'.) From medieval times the main route north out of the City.

1575 Walter Raleigh (q.v.) is living here.

1600 The Long Causeway, a raised pavement, is built at the Angel, enabling pedestrians to walk on dry land, not a sea of mud and worse.

1603 James I rests at **The Kings Head** on the last lap from Scotland to **Charterhouse** (q.v.).

1619 The Long Causeway is extended and repaved.

1784 Mary Wollstonecraft opens a school.

1808 Benjamin Disraeli's family live in Trinity Row (9 Upper Street, now 215).

1851 The Golden Mile (for Music Halls). Kate Greenaway moves opposite **Islington Green**.

1854 Jones Burial Ground, an old plague pit at the back of the Lansdowne Arms (The Fox/Slug and Lettuce), opens as New Bunhill Fields. Residents rested in peace for 120 years until the site was developed (re-interred 1997).

1861 Foundation stone laid of The Agricultural Halls (q.v., now Business Design Centre).

1862 Mary Kingsley is born in Upper Street (address not known). (See Kingsley, Mary.)

1863 Retailer William Whiteley, keen to build a department store, considers Upper Street but, shrewd businessman, predicted (correctly) that when the railways opened at either end (**The Angel** and **Highbury Corner**) the street would lose its carriage trade and go downmarket, so built his famous emporium at Westbourne Grove, Bayswater instead.

1865 The Manager of the National Provincial Bank at 173 (managers lived above the bank) has tennis courts laid out in his back garden.

1881 The London Road Car is horse-drawn with an external staircase to take passengers to the top deck.

1887 Islington Chapel and a school with thirty classes opens on the corner of **Gaskin Street** and Upper Street. 1,000 at a time worshipped here.

1900s The Electric Theatre, 75 Upper Street, opens with *The Birth of Christ*. Uproar from churchgoers! When film censorship started three years later the censor banned religion, the monarchy and white women seen with black men.

1911 The Empress, a purpose-built cinema, opens (now Screen on The Green).

1923 The Town Hall opens (today TV and film makers, e.g. *Our Friends In The North* and *This Life* use the Council Chamber).

1935 Michel <u>Saint-Denis</u>, one of the most influential men in theatre (see Theatre) opens his London Theatre Studio in the old Providence Baptist Chapel, **Providence Place** (behind Screen On The Green, now National Asthma Campaign HQ).

Saint-Denis introduced theatre in the round and founded The National Theatre. The <u>Ustinov</u>s didn't know what to do with young Peter, 16, so Mrs Ustinov, an artist who painted scenes from the theatre, farmed him out to Saint-Denis, a friend. Described by Ustinov as a '*tweedy pipe smoker with yellow hair*', Saint-Denis also nurtured the careers of Edith Evans, Marius Goring, Alec Guinness, Laurence Olivier and Michael Redgrave.

1938 Rattling trams give way to quieter trolley buses.

1951 Empress Picture Theatre renamed the Rex.

1968 Romaine Hart inherits the Rex and makes it her very own Screen on the Green (now one of Britain's longest-surviving independent cinemas).

1969 Dan <u>Crawford</u> buys **The Kings Head** (q.v.).

1971 Malcolm <u>Heaysman</u>, manager of Beck's at No. 52 is murdered (q.v.).

1978 Islington Chapel, corner of Gaskin and Upper Street, is a recording studio. Sisterwrite, the first feminist bookshop in the UK, opens. The five-woman co-operative was the first to promote and sell radical feminist literature from all over the world. '*Run by Women for Women about Women*' (since closed).

1980 Striking staff members of *Time Out* set up *City Limits*, a rival listings magazine at 313 Upper Street.

1981 Tariq <u>Ali</u> opens *The Other Book Shop*, No. 328.

1990 Upper Street sees mounted police when Islington Council introduces Mrs Thatcher's hated Poll Tax. Councillors leaving a meeting at Town Hall had missiles thrown at them.

2000 Upper Street has 80 eating places and pubs.

....

WAKLEY, Dr Thomas, MP (1795–1862)
Wakley Street N1

Medical reformer, Coroner for West Middlesex, friend of William Cobbett and Dickens, started The Lancet (1823–) to expose nepotism in hospitals.

1835 Surgeon son of a Devon squire, Wakley becomes MP for Finsbury (until 1852). An Islington radical, he was dubbed the 'Member for Medicine' and campaigned against the Poor Law. He advocated free museums and art galleries, affordable housing for working people, a minimum guaranteed wage and warned against food adulteration. In his maiden speech he announced that he would be moving a resolution to have the transportation sentence on the Dorset farm labourers, the Tolpuddle Martyrs (q.v.) commuted. The speech followed his presentation of 13,000 signatures on a petition.

HOW WAKLEY GOT THE MARTYRS PARDONED

The men were prosecuted under an old 1797 Law of Mutiny rather than the correct one covering the unlawful administering of oaths, which carried a lighter sentence. Wakley's argument was that if the Dorset men were guilty, so was every freemason, because Lodges had a secret oath for members. Wakley argued that every single member of every single lodge would fall within the meaning of the 1797 Mutiny Act and it was time to put an end to one law for the rich and another for the poor. He secured a full pardon for the Tolpuddle Martyrs.

1836 Two years into their life sentence, the six Dorset labourers are granted a free pardon and brought home from Australia.

1865 Wakley castigates Clerkenwell Workhouse (*Guardian* offices on the site) in the *Lancet* as the worst in London.

1883 Clerkenwell Workhouse, publicly shamed by Dr Wakley, is demolished.

WAUGH, Evelyn (1903–1966)
Novelist

1928 Waugh moves to 17 **Canonbury Square** with his new wife, also Evelyn (friends call them he-Evelyn and she-Evelyn).

Waugh was ecstatically happy and very much in love. His book on Rossetti was doing well and *Decline and Fall* getting excellent reviews (Arnold Bennett called it a *'brilliantly malicious satire'*, which guaranteed success). Waugh was hard at work on a biography of local preacher, John <u>Wesley</u>. His wife, the Honourable Evelyn Gardner, was truly grand (her mother, Lady Burghclere, was sister of Lord Caernarvon, whose money helped unearth Tutenkhamun's tomb). On a Christmas cruise she fell ill, he nursed her through pneumonia. It was touch-and-go, but she outlived him by 30 years.

Self-confessed snob, Waugh started on *Vile Bodies* but, finding the social round tiresome, went to write in peace in Oxford. While he was away, party-person she-Evelyn, house-sharing with their close buddy, Nancy Mitford, fell passionately in love with John Heygate, another mutual friend. Furious, Waugh moved out of Canonbury Square and filed for divorce. Evelyn eventually married Heygate. Broken-hearted and publicly humiliated, Waugh published *A Handful of Dust*, one of the most depressing novels ever. He later remarried.

The Waughs' great friend Nancy Mitford, an even bigger self-confessed snob, creator of 'U and non-U', was the great-granddaughter of a Southwark brush maker. Her grandfather, Thomas Milner Bowles, was the illegitimate son of Susan Bowles and Thomas <u>Milner-Gibson</u> MP with whom she had been in service. Her sister Diana was married to Fascist leader Sir Oswald <u>Mosley</u>, and was interned for part of WWII in Holloway Prison (q.v.).

1966 Waugh dies.

1996 Evelyn Gardner dies.

WESLEY, John (1703–1791)
Islington: Home of Methodism
Wesley lived 56 of his 88 years here.

1714–20 Age 10, introduced to the area after the Duke of Buckingham nominated him for one of the few free places at **Charterhouse**. He was very happy here and returned to study or visit all his life.

1739 Middle class parishioners at St Mary's (q.v.) who rent their pews are outraged to be told by Wesley that their souls are equal to those of the poor. Thanks to the churchwardens who prevent him entering the pulpit, Islington becomes, by default, the home of Methodism.

1740 The licence to preach issued by Revd <u>Stonehouse</u> is officially revoked.

Banned from preaching inside any C. of E. church, Wesley preached anywhere he could. He travelled four thousand miles, preached 40,000 sermons and spent fifty-two years travelling. Jeering mobs stoned him, the Church denounced him but he brought hope to millions.

Wesley preached at a derelict gun foundry owned by the HAC (q.v.) in what will soon be **City Road**, where cannons were once cast for Cromwell in the Civil War. On Sunday evenings, thousands came with lanterns across the fields and there was standing room only. Soon there were two regular services, at 5 a.m. and 9 p.m. so that worshippers could attend their own churches to take communion (Wesley attended St Luke's, Old Street all his life). He took over the lease and built the world's first Methodist Chapel. Floorboards were nailed together to make a three-tier pulpit.

1742 His mother, Susannah <u>Wesley</u> is buried across the road in Nonconformist Bunhill Fields.

1746 Opens the first free dispensary in London staffed by an apothecary and a surgeon (500 patients in the first five months). Wesley pioneered the use of electricity for the treatment of melancholia (depression), forerunner of electro-convulsive therapy (ECT). He opened a book shop, a school and a refuge for widows with children, and lent money to parishioners who wanted to open businesses in the area.

1777 Lease runs out on the foundry (St Luke's took it over for an asylum while George <u>Dance</u> was building a new one in **Old Street**). Wesley bought land for a permanent chapel and put in plans which were passed subject to the chapel being hidden from the road, so as not to offend Anglicans. Some sources say his friend Dance designed it. Wesley was delighted with his new chapel which he said was *'perfectly neat but not fine'*. He preached in the Mother Church of World Methodism (still here) for the rest of his life.

1780 Wesley publishes *Primitive Physic*, still in print and still relevant (in 1996 Glenda Jackson MP opened Archway Clinic of Herbal Medicine).

1790 Dies 2 March and is buried in his garden.

1963 14 million Wesleyan Methodists throughout the world celebrate the 260th anniversary of his birth.

1984 Museum of Methodism opens in the crypt of his church.

....

WHITE CONDUIT (The)
Barnsbury Road N1

1430 Margery, daughter of Sir James Bernersbury, grants land to **Charterhouse** Monastery (q.v.).

1611 Thomas <u>Sutton</u> pipes water from a well to Charterhouse School. He covered the conduit and faced it with white stone, so it was known thereafter as The White Conduit (name inscribed above the present Penny Farthing pub).

1649 Famous London landmark. Its water became famous for baking the best bread rolls in London so a large house nearby capitalised on its location and called itself White Conduit House Tea Rooms.

1700 Rebuilt. Situated on high ground, it had fine views of the city, with its forest of Wren spires and the magnificent dome of St Paul's.

1754 Bought by its competitor, the owner of The Angel Inn (q.v.) around the corner, who made it fashionable (<u>Goldsmith</u> was a frequent visitor). Grounds stretched as far as present day **Cloudesley Square**. Cows kept in the meadow supplied the house with fresh milk, cream, butter and cheese.

1784 **Lord's Cricket Ground.** Organised cricket starts here with Thomas <u>Lord</u> (q.v.).

1790 Thomas <u>Rowlandson</u> RA paints a cricket match on White Conduit Fields.

1837 George <u>Loveless</u>, the first Tolpuddle Martyr to return from Australia, is given a huge welcome. Tom <u>Wakley</u>, MP for Finsbury who petitioned to reprieve the Martyrs was Guest of Honour. <u>Dickens</u> was a frequent visitor. *In Sketches by Boz*, The White Conduit House features in *'First of May'*.

1849 House demolished. Barnsbury was completely built up and views of the city had gone.

....

WHITECROSS STREET EC1

The Hospitallers painted stone crosses red or white (White Cross Street) to mark out their boundaries.

1560 The Fortune Theatre is built in Playhouse Yard, Goldyng (name of the landowner) Lane (**Fortune Street**).

1640 Theatres are closed. Puritans rule London.

1691 George <u>Fox</u>, founder of the Quakers, is buried in the Quaker Burial Ground.

1742 Samuel <u>Whitbread</u>, who served his apprenticeship in Clerkenwell, opens a small brewery here. He brewed Pale, Strong and Amber beers (by 1800 he owned fourteen pubs). By 1999, Whitbread was the UK's leading food and drink conglomerate.

1813 There are more debtors than can be accommodated at Marshalsea, Fleet or King's Bench because families go with the debtor into prison so a new debtors' prison opens (the Bankruptcy Act of 1869 abolished imprisonment for debt).

1983 Children from Prior Weston School take part in James Galway's *Pied Piper* at The Barbican.

....

WHITE LION STREET N1

1594 The Wyte Lyon Inn is used by drovers (sign is a White Lion rampant).

1714 Re-built.

1743 A turnpike is built for access into Islington.

1898 White Lion Inn re-built.

1972 No. 57 becomes infamous as the educationally experimental White Lion Free School where fifty pupils choose what/if they will learn.

....

WHITTINGTON, Richard

Lord Mayor of London, died 1423

Whittington Grove/Hospital/Park/Place/Terrace and **Villas**; **Fitzwarren Gardens** N19 (he married Alice Fitzwarren); **Pauntley Street** N19 (his place of birth);

Mercers Place, **Road** and **Terrace** owned by Whittington's livery company (silk mercers).

TURN AGAIN, WHITTINGTON

1370s Legend has it that when Whittington arrived in London he got a job as a clerk in **St John's Priory** (q.v.). Other sources say his father sent him to London to follow a mercer's apprenticeship (if so he would have been about twenty-one when he finished indentures and trudged through Islington). Legend also has it that he left the City via what became **New North Road**, **Canonbury Road** and **Holloway Road**. Thirty-two successive mayors of London, led by the Mayor of Islington, have walked the walk every year, until 1999 when someone changed the route via St Paul's Cathedral and the Tower of London (because it's prettier). It's very unlikely he was going home, since his father, Sir William Whittington (contrary to legend, Dick was not a poor boy from a poor family), lived in Pauntley, Gloucester in which case he would have been heading west not north.

At the bottom of **Highgate Hill**, a steep, 400 foot ascent, Dick stopped for a rest. Looking down, he saw the city lights twinkling and heard The Great Bell of Bow (rung every night at 9 o'clock to warn approaching travellers the City gates were about to close and to tell London apprentices they could put down their tools). He imagined it was urging him to go back and try again and that if he did he would be Lord Mayor of London – which he was in 1397, 1416 and 1419 (some sources say he was mayor four times, having one year temporarily stood in for his successor).

1423 Whittington is buried in St Michael Paternoster Royal in the City. He left money to rebuild **Bart's**.

1473 William Pole, a rich merchant, victim to leprosy, establishes a leper colony (Lazar House) and Spital (hospital) on Highgate Hill. A stone cross was put up on the roadside to warn passers-by. Locals called it the Whittington Stone, so his story has already passed into legend.

1538 Lazar House Chapel is suppressed by Henry VIII but the hospital is allowed to continue and eventually becomes The Whittington.

1608 Whittington Stone is erected on Highgate Hill.

1689 Sir Christopher Wren rebuilds St Michael's (where Whittington was buried), burnt down in the Great Fire.

1744 The Whittington Stone gets a pavement around it. In 1795, according to *The Gentleman's Magazine*: *A stone at the foot of Highgate Hill was supposed to have been placed there by him on the spot where he had heard Bow bells. It had a pavement around it 18 feet in circumference and this stone remained until 1795 when a parish officer had it removed, sawn in two and placed in two halves on each side of Queens Head Lane in Lower Street. The pavement he converted to his own use and with it paved the yard of The Blue Last pub* (now the Marlborough Head. Irate locals forced him to replace it).

1965 Borough of Islington Coat of Arms includes part of Whittington's (yellow rings).

THE LEGEND OF PUSS-IN-BOOTS

1460 Richard Whittington, great-nephew, builds a mansion in Pauntley. In it was a stone bas relief sculpture of a boy with a cat.

1605 A new play opens, *The History of Richard Whittington*. A cat featured in the script.

1860 Gloucester Council is putting in a sewer and drainage system, where the house of

Dick Whittington's nephew once stood. Labourers dig up a sculpted bas relief dating from the 1400s of a boy with a cat in his arms (now in Gloucester Museum).

1939–45 St Michael's in the City where Whittington was buried is bombed.

During restoration a mummified cat was found in the rafters. Was it buried with Whittington? Was it the custom to put a mummified cat in a church roof? Did a cat chase a bird and couldn't get down again? The vicar was so annoyed by visitors asking to see it, he burnt it.

1964 A cat is added to the Whittington Stone.

1967 St Michael's is rebuilt. The stained glass window shows Dick Whittington with a cat.

....

WILKES, John (1727–1797)

Politician (see previous references)

Destined to be both local and international hero, Wilkes is remembered for many reasons, not the least for being a self-confessed, debauched sex maniac, who was sent to the Tower for calling the king a liar.

The principal founder of radical movements in Britain, Wilkes proved it was possible to achieve political change by harnessing the disparate political energies of *'the inferior set of people'*. He broke down the secrecy which surrounded parliamentary proceedings by printing debates in the House, brought about his one-man Magna Carta, bill of rights, which forced MPs to make pledges to those who elected them, helped to end the tradition of press ganging men into the armed forces, instigated shorter parliamentary terms and fathered more equal representation in Parliament. He also established the principle that general arrest warrants in which no one was named were illegal.

1727 St James' Court, **St John Square**, a prosperous, residential area, John, third of six children, is born to Sarah and Israel Wilkes, who are very well off.

Israel was a distinguished member of Distillers Company at a time when a glut of cheap corn was making distillers of cheap rotgut gin rich. He married the cultured, educated, intelligent, only-child and heiress of a rich tanner from Bermondsey. The couple kept a coach and six with a Coat of Arms on the panels. Israel spoiled John and as his father's favourite, he was given plenty of money. More influential was his Presbyterian mother who instilled in her children 'unbending non-conformity'. John Wilkes was sent to boarding school in Hertfordshire and completed his education at the University of Leyden.

1746 Wilkes graduates and returns home to St John Square to celebrate his twenty-first birthday with his family. His father gave him land in East Anglia and an income of £350 p.a. He married Mary Mead, rich heiress, owner of the 25-bedroom manor of Aylesbury. The marriage failed.

1747 Father dies leaving three sons and two daughters. First son Heaton inherited the business and built a new distillery; second son Israel settled in New York (a descendant founded *The Edinburgh Review*), one daughter was married three times to rich businessmen; the other, Sarah, was an eccentric recluse (said to be the inspiration for Dickens's Miss Havisham).

1762 Wilkes founds The *North Briton* – a weekly, provocative, satirical newspaper equivalent to today's *Private Eye*.

1763 23 April, Issue 45. Wilkes writes a piece calling the king, in effect, a liar.

He criticised the King's Speech in the House of Commons at the opening of Parliament making him the first to say publicly that the monarch could be wrong. Charged with treasonous libel, Wilkes was cast as the hero and <u>George III</u> the villain in a drama which was to last fifteen years. The article brought Wilkes international fame, it also prevented him from taking his seat in the House of Commons for eleven years. 30 April, general warrant issued for the arrest of the writer, printer, publisher, sellers, anyone connected with issue 45. No names were mentioned because no-one knew who they were. Despite Parliamentary privilege, Wilkes was arrested and put in The Tower. The case hinged on this issue of whether an MP could be arrested. 6 May, the Court discharged him on grounds of privilege. Boswell: *'This morning the famous Wilkes was discharged from his confinement and followed to his house ... by an immense mob who saluted him with loud huzzas while he stood bowing from his window.'* 6 July, Wilkes had won his argument that general warrants, issued with no named person, were illegal. He was released, charged the government with robbery (of his person) and was awarded £1,000 damages, a huge sum.

1764 Clerkenwell Green: Wilkes speaks to thousands on *Liberty* before leaving for Paris. He was declared an outlaw in his absence and expelled from the House of Commons.

1768 Wilkes surrenders his outlawry at the Court of the King's Bench. He received a £1,000 fine (exact amount of damages awarded to him for false arrest) and 22 months in Fleet prison.

1769 January, one of the two largest City wards, Farringdon Without unanimously adopts Wilkes as their Alderman. February, for the third time Middlesex electors vote in Wilkes as their MP. For the third time Parliament refused to let him in. Middlesex freeholders adopted him as their candidate for the next election, which he won unopposed. The Court elected Henry Luttrell to oppose Wilkes for a second poll. (Wilkes 1,143 votes. Luttrell 296.) 15 April, Parliament declares election null and void because Wilkes is in prison. Luttrell was admitted to the House of Commons. 17 April, 2,5000 Middlesex freeholders proposed they should not pay Land Tax because they were not represented in Parliament. Their slogan *'No Taxation Without Representation'* became the rallying cry of America. May, crowds sing *'God Save Great Wilkes, our King'* whenever the national anthem is played. 60,000 petitioners demanded unsuccessfully that Wilkes be recognised by Parliament as the lawful MP for Middlesex.

1770 April, Wilkes is released from prison and takes up his post as Alderman for Farringdon Without.

1772 Appointed Sheriff of London and Middlesex.

1774 Winning his fourth election and finally allowed to take his seat in the Commons as the Honourable Member for Middlesex, his previous three expulsions were expunged from official records. Voted Lord Mayor of London, he conferred the Freedom of the City on William Pitt and Lord Nelson. The days of *Wilkes and Liberty* riots were over.

1777 Gives public support for the independence of the American Colonies in the House of Commons.

1779 Made City Chamberlain.

1780 Wilkes is a 'hero' of the Gordon Riots (q.v.). He took personal charge of the defence of the besieged Bank of England, centre of Capitalism. Many of the rioters were veterans of the *Wilkes and Liberty* demonstrations which had championed his election 15 years earlier, yet the great Radical personally threw rioters in the Thames, shot at what were, ostensibly, his own ranks and killed several.

1797 Reconciled to George III, Wilkes, champion of American Independence, is appalled by the rumblings in France to get rid of their monarchy. Age 70, he retired from Parliament, an *'extinct volcano'* and wasn't missed, having not made a speech in the House for nine years.

1799 Wilkes dies, dubbed in his obituary *'The Last Englishman'*. He was buried in Bunhill Fields, the only place Nonconformists could go.

Statue in New Fetter Lane EC1 (*'Champion of English Freedom'*) unveiled 1988, the only cross-eyed statue in London. Two pubs (neither survives) in N1 commemorated Wilkes: The North Briton, and The Three Johns (Wilkes, his lawyer John Glynn and John Horne (Horne Tooke, Wilkes supporter imprisoned and acquitted for High Treason).

WILLIAM THE CONQUEROR (1027–1087)

1066 After Hastings, gives land owned by the English aristocracy to the Norman barons who came over with him and introduces the manorial system into England.

The lord of the manor rented land to tenant farmers, villagers used 'no-man's land' or common land (non-fertile, woodland or waste land) for grazing animals. At some point the lordship became separated from the Baronetcy. Until 1937 both could be bought and sold.

William commandeered everything outside the City despite the fact the City owned the huge county of Middlesex of which Islington was part. (The City didn't get Middlesex back until 1130.) He granted parts of north Islington to Geoffrey de Mandeville (who hands it on to Ralph de Berners, who in turn gives parts to the canons of St Bartholomew the Great, q.v.), the canon's burh/**Canonbury**); south Islington to de Briset (who gives parts to the Knights of St John (q.v.) and to Benedictine nuns); the high burh/**Highbury** to De Reman, whose descendants give it to the Hospitallers (q.v.) and, possibly, de Fiennes gets central Islington (his descendants give parts to the City). De Bruis gets the Lordship of **Tottenham** and calls the manor house Bruis Castle. William diverted some of Islington's many streams into the City (one in Highbury Fields fed into Cripplegate until 1811).

1068 Domesday Book (The Great Survey). Population is 77. Almost twice as many live in Newington as in Islington proper. The Domesday Book lists 27 communicants in the parish of St Mary, 41 at **Newington** and 9 at Tollington (**Hornsey**).

WOLLSTONECRAFT, Mary (1759–1797)

Writer and feminist

Islington: Home of Feminism

1784 Encourages her sister Eliza (Bishop) to leave her husband. They open a school with their other sister Everina and friend Fanny Blood, first in **Upper Street**, then at **Newington Green**.

1786 Mary travels to Portugal alone to visit Fanny Blood, her closest friend. Heartbroken when Fanny died in childbirth (as she herself was later to do), on her return Mary closed the school. Her sisters secured teaching posts and Mary was appointed governess to Lord Kingsborough's children in Ireland.

1795 Alone and abandoned by Gilbert Imlay, father of her daughter Fanny (named after her closest friend), after two years in Paris, where she was witness to the French Revolution Mary returns to Islington. She settled in **Finsbury Square**, where she attempted suicide by taking laudanum but survived. In the summer she travelled through Scandinavia with one-year-old Fanny. On her return, feeling no better, she jumped off Putney Bridge.

1795 Moves from Finsbury Square to **Cumming Street**, Pentonville. Her *Letters Written During a Short Residence in Sweden, Norway and Denmark* were published and raved over by Shelley, Coleridge, Southey and Wordsworth. Her *A Vindication of the Rights of Woman* was re-printed. She was re-introduced to William <u>Godwin</u>, publisher, novelist, Dissenting minister-turned-professional atheist, anarchist, philosophical representative of English Radicalism and seminal figure in the spread of republicanism. It was a meeting of two great minds. Godwin had a huge following among young people (Shelley worshipped him) and featured among Mary's heroes. By December, Mary was pregnant by him.

1797 March, they marry in Old St Pancras Church. That August, in the newly built apartment in the new suburb of Somers Town, her second daughter, Mary, was born. She became very ill. Godwin sent for Dr Poignant (apt name), chief obstetrician at Westminster Lying-in Hospital. Without washing his hands (hygiene as yet undreamed of) he examined her internally and infected her womb.

4 September, Mary is worse. Midwife, Mrs Blenkinsop, as was the custom with breast fever, brought in a litter of puppies to suckle. 7 September, Mary worse still. Godwin called in Anthony Carlisle, distinguished surgeon at Westminster Hospital. 10 September, Mary dies of puerperal fever/septicaemia.

BIRTH OF FRANKENSTEIN

Fanny Imlay, Mary's fatherless daughter, three years old, committed suicide at 21. Mary Godwin, destined to be partner to the love games played by the poet Shelley, wrote *Frankenstein*, the world's first science fiction story, about an artificially-created monster (bits and pieces from charnel houses) who vows vengeance against the man who gives him life and then disappears alone into the Arctic wastes.

....

WOODBRIDGE STREET EC1

(Red Bull Yard until 1778)

1581 Thomas <u>Sekforde</u>/Seckford /Sackford lives on his estate, bounded by St James Walk, Aylesbury Street, St John Street and Corporation Row. He founded Sekforde Hospital and Almshouses in *Woodbridge Suffolk*, hence **Woodbridge** and **Sekforde Street**s. MP for Ipswich, Grays Inn barrister, he was Master of Court of Requests and Surveyor of Court of Wards and Liveries.

1599 Red Bull Theatre opens.

1604 The Queen's Men perform at The Red Bull.

1627 The Red Bull puts on Shakespeare but the actors are so bad they're booed off stage.

1633 Despite the law that only two theatres are allowed to open (Duke's and Drury

Lane), the Red Bull (whose owner and patrons couldn't give two figs about the law) switches to comedy, starring, for the first time in England, female actors.

1661 <u>Pepys</u> visits, one of an audience of a hundred, to see *'All's Lost but Lust'* starring England's first actress in The Queen's Men Company. He wasn't impressed.

1665 Red Bull Theatre closes.

1712 Ned <u>Ward</u>, humorist, satirist, coarse poet, publisher of *London Spy* (*sketches of London life*) opens a pub in Red Bull Yard (directly opposite Jerusalem Passage off Aylesbury Street). In *British Wonders* he wrote: '. . . the Bulls and Bears, Old Dung hills, Night men, Slaughterers, Jayls, Butchers Dogs and Hogs that dwell, In sweet St James Clerkenwell . . .' He became close friends with Thomas <u>Britton</u> and attended his musical concerts, likening the players in the long, cramped room to *'sweaty dancers at a Buttocks Ball'*. After Britton's death Ward, with friend William <u>Caslon</u>, arranged a sale of his effects to help his widow.

1778 Red Bull Yard name changes to Woodbridge Street.

....

WORLD WAR ONE (1914–1918)

1916 St Bartholomew the Great succumbs to a Zeppelin bomb which blasts the gatehouse, revealing the original (1559) half-timbered Tudor building.

1917 Islington's 3,000 Germans are interned or deported.

Tunnelling for the new GPO underground railway at Mount Pleasant Sorting Office was suspended (see Mount Pleasant). Excavations were used to store the Elgin Marbles and other priceless artefacts from the British Museum, The Tate and National Portrait Gallery.

1918 People need news of the war. Cossors Aberdeen Works, **Highbury Grove** couldn't make radios quickly enough to meet demand. Their 'Melody Maker' was such a best-seller, impatient customers were offered self-assembly kits.

1921 Veterans still unemployed three years after the war try unsuccessfully to seize the Town Hall, then occupy **Essex Road** Library for six weeks.

....

WORLD WAR TWO (1939–1945)

A total of 958 Islingtonians died and 78,000 homes were damaged. Over a third of Londoners not yet recovered from the first war and knowing all too well what the second would bring moved out during the next six years. Great Sutton Street, Northburgh Street and Dallington Street – a densely populated industrial quarter where people walked to work – were to become after the war a commercial area. Air raid sirens were dusted off and tested. Night raids meant any glimmer of light would guide an enemy bomber. Blackout curtains went up at the windows, street lights and traffic lights were masked, torch beams stuck over with two layers of paper, smoking in the street was banned and the edges of pavements painted white to indicate the road.

To fool enemy paratroopers, all signposts, milestones, station names were removed and shop signs painted over if they showed destinations (such as The Islington Bakery). Men became Local Defence Volunteers (The Home Guard/'Dad's Army'). Iron railings were removed for the war effort and housewives asked to donate saucepans to make aeroplanes. During air raids people were forbidden to shelter in underground stations so bought platform tickets and went down anyway. At Christmas they decorated the platforms with streamers and bunting.

Huge silver barrage balloons as big as houses appeared over Islington to deter dive-bombers. Filled with gas they were tethered by heavy steel cables. A shortage of glass meant that people took their own tankards to the pub. Because of the threat of poison gas every man, woman and child was given a rubber gas mask to carry in a box. Schools relocated, children were evacuated to the countryside. Cinemas closed – including Essex Road Coronet and *The Flying Scotsman* cinema coach, which was needed as a people carrier. The Savoy in **Holloway Road** was the only new cinema to open in Islington during the war. When theatres were closed for the duration, Sadler's Wells was forced to tour. Those few lucky enough to have television sets wouldn't watch again until service resumed in 1946.

Caledonian Market was closed and used for storage of munitions. When it finally re-opened it was no longer in Islington, but at the Elephant and Castle. Luigi Finella of Little Italy (q.v.) set up The Mexicano Accordion Band, which played on radio throughout the war and went on ENSA tours. Islington squares were dug up and used for air raid shelters, as were the cells under Hugh Myddleton School. Peter Sellers' old school, St Aloysius College, relocated to Cambridgeshire for the duration. The Aggie was closed. Exhibitions including the Motor Show, Crufts and the Military Tournament transferred to other venues and never returned. The Betjeman factory in **Pentonville Road** was closed. Their Tantalus had become obsolete, there were no more servants to steal the Scotch. Thanks to Cossor's (q.v.), the radio trade took off, indispensable for news of loved ones fighting at the front.

1940 Ships bringing goods to Britain are sunk by U-boats so food, soap, petrol, coal and clothes (schoolboys had to wear short trousers to save material) were rationed. Everyone was given a ration book and told to register with one grocer for their allotted 4 oz of butter and bacon and 12 oz of sugar a week and with one butcher for 4 oz of meat. When Mussolini declared war on Britain, Italians in Little Italy, here since the Middle Ages, were officially classified as enemy aliens and deported. In July, 500 perished on the SS *Andorra Star* bound for Canada. Islington Film Studios released films which reflected the times: *They Came By Night*, *For Freedom* (about the sinking of the *Graf Spee*), *Neutral Port Uncensored*, *Alibi* and *We Dive at Dawn*. A Highbury resident telephoned Scotland Yard to report that German paratroopers had captured the local film studios (they were film extras). A bomb landed on St Mary's and uncovered stones dated 1100. All that survived was the 1750 spire and the pseudo-Greek colonnaded front portico, stuck on in 1903. The church would not be rebuilt until 1956. 15 October, a bomb hit gas and water mains under an air raid shelter in **Goswell Road**. 200 perished. Their bodies were never recovered.

1941 The (now listed) 250-year-old Oak Room in Thames Water Building, **Rosebery Avenue** is dismantled and stored for the duration. Lady Diana Mosley, wife of the British fascist leader, was interned in Holloway Prison (q.v.), which was later severely damaged in an air raid, as was Pentonville. (C Block was demolished, causing several fatalities.) **Holford Square** was badly damaged as were **Myddelton Square** and **Granville Square**. Parts of **Charterhouse** were gutted by incendiaries (fire bombs). Islington sponsored its very own Spitfire Mark VI, sent to Gibraltar to be used in training.

1942 The Russian Ambassador unveils a bust of Lenin in Holford Square and presents it to the borough as an expression of solidarity.

1944 Flying bomb hits the Gaumont in Holloway Road, ripping through the roof before exploding. A fire bomb landed on Mount Pleasant Sorting Office (q.v.) so the Post Office moved to the Aggie and did not return until 1976. Mount Pleasant's underground railway tunnels were used to store art treasures. George Orwell, bombed out of St John's Wood, moved to **Canonbury Square**.

1945 Islington is bombarded with VIs, small jet-propelled pilotless aircraft called flying or buzz bombs, and their successor, the V2. One of the last V2 rockets to be launched hit **Highbury Corner**, killing 24 and seriously injuring 155. The crater became today's roundabout. The five (some say 22) houses in **Compton Terrace** nearest Highbury Corner were so badly damaged they had to be demolished.

Peace breaks out, and Islington is looking the worse for wear: **Charlton Place**, where Dickens' friend Caroline Chisholm once lived, was earmarked for demolition, **Camden Passage** was a sorry sight. St John's church, **St John's Square** was burnt out, its four walls open to the sky. Another V2 had devastated **Farringdon**. News editors agreed not to publish photographs, believing that war-weary demoralised locals would not want to see more of their beloved city gone.

Postscript

Smithfield, the oldest meat market in the world, is still with us, as is St Mary's Church in Upper Street, Bart's Hospital and the crypt and Gatehouse of old St John's Priory (although in some quarters feelings run as high today against Islam as they did in the days of the Knights Hospitallers). Battle Bridge has its old name back. The King's Head, Britain's first fringe theatre, is still just about with us and the Little Angel Puppet Theatre is hanging on. The traffic problem is as bad as ever so Mayor Livingstone is suggesting a new toll (congestion charge) for those coming into London and affluent residents are trying to release parts of the old river Fleet from its cast-iron corset (sewer pipe). The battles Islington fought have, in the main, been won. The Church of England is still (just about) the established church but no longer cares if you're a Quaker, Methodist or Chinese Baptist, let alone a Roman Catholic. We have a free press (almost) the vote, free education and heath care, abortion on demand and old age pensions. Marxism has come and gone (although there are still sporadic demonstrations against capitalism) and women are liberated. Nelson Mandela is back home and Tony Blair PM has pushed through the Good Friday Peace Agreement, the minimum wage, abolished the House of Lords (just about) and granted Wales and Scotland independence.

But Islingtonians are as feisty as they ever were running 650 voluntary organisations, many of which are eco-activist or campaigning bodies. Although Charter 88 is still battling for constitutional change, others such as Index on Censorship, Greenpeace, International PEN, the Green Party, Friends of the Earth, UK Working Group on Landmines *et al.* set their sights much further afield.

Once, a flag, the red flag of communism no less, from the 1950s to the late 1990s, flew on the town hall. To visit Islington was a bit like popping over to Boulogne for a bit of a duty free and stumbling across the French Revolution. That was when Islington was infamous, dubbed the People's Republic, furthest left of Leninist Labour boroughs which dismissed the District Auditor as 'Thatcher's Puppet', before the cover-up of paedophilia in its children's homes, before Ofsted closed its education department and privatised its schools, before the death of a Labour councillor in October 1999. The council comprised 26 Labour councillors and 26 Liberal Democrats. No Tories and no 'Others'. Labour had full control through the casting vote of the mayor. After the death of the councillor, the leadership suspended council meetings to prevent the Liberal Democrats taking advantage of their new majority of one until the by-election in Hillrise ward which the Lib Dems won, taking control of a council run by Labour for 30 years. In 1982 when a solitary SDP counciillor was elected, the issues of the day included banning Robertson's gollies, *Baa Baa Black Sheep* and black bin liners as presenting a negative picture of black people. The Women's Committee supported five-year jail sentences for men who '*use emotional coercion within a sexual relationship*', grants for gym mats for lesbian self-defence classes and non-sexist jigsaws for the under-fives to whom were also given an Anti-Racist Adviser. The Liberal Democrats took control of Islington Council on 13 January 2000. A line has been drawn under its colourful, controversial past. Has the new millennium heralded the end of an era? Are we all Lib Dems now?

Bibliography

British Encyclopedia (vols 1–10), Odhams, 1933

Concise Dictionary of National Biography (The Softback Preview by arrangement with Oxford University Press, Vols 1–3), OUP, 1994

(The) London Encyclopedia, edited by Ben Weinreb and Christopher Hibbert, Papermac, 1990

(The) Official Centenary History of Arsenal Football Club, by Phil Soar and Martin Tyler, Hamlyn, 1986

(The) Official Journal of the William Britain Collectors Club

Ackroyd, Peter, *Blake*, QPD by arrangement with Sinclair-Stevenson, 1995

Arundell, Dennis, *The Story of Sadler's Wells*, David & Charles, 1978

Chute, Marchette, *Shakespeare of London*, Dutton, New York, 1949

Coote, Stephen, *A Play of Passion: The Life of Sir Walter Ralegh*, Macmillan, 1993

Drabble, M. and Stringer, J., *Concise Oxford Companion to English Literature*, OUP, 1990

Draper, Chris, 'Islington's Cinemas and Film Studios', Islington Libraries, undated

Emmons, Robert, *The Life and Opinions of Walter Richard Sickert*, Lund Humphries, 1992

Evans, Hilary and Mary, *The Man who Drew the Drunkard's Daughter, The Life and Art of George Cruickshank*, Frederick Muller, 1978

Forster, John, *The Life of Charles Dickens*, Chapman & Hall, 1876

Gimarc, George, *Punk Diary*, Vintage, 1994

Hillier, Bevis, *Young Betjeman*, Cardinal, 1989

Kronenburger, Louis, *The Extraordinary Mr Wilkes*, New English Library, 1974

Lawson-Dick, Oliver, *Aubrey's Brief Lives*, Mandarin, 1992

Parsons, Tony, *Dispatches fron the Front Line of Popular Culture*, Virgin, 1994

Prance, Claude A., *Companion to Charles Lamb*, Mansell, 1983

Repsch, John, *The Legendary Joe Meek*, Woodford House, 1989

Rothstein, Andrew, *A House on Clerkenwell Green*, Marx Memorial Library, 1983

Rose, June, *Marie Stopes and the Sexual Revolution*, Faber & Faber, 1992

Rude, George, *Wilkes and Liberty*, OUP, 1962

Smith, Frank O.M., 'This insubstantial pageant': The Story of the Tavistock Repertory Company, Ashford Press, 1982

Somerset, Anne, *Elizabeth I*, Phoenix, 1997

Spielmann, M.H. and Layard, G.S., *The Life and Work of Kate Greenaway*, Bracken, 1986

Spoto, Donald, *The Dark Side of Genius, The Life of Alfred Hitchcock*, Frederick Muller, 1988

Stow, John, *A Survey of London* (1598), Routledge, 1893

Tomalin, Claire, *The Invisible Woman, The Story of Nelly Ternan and Charles Dickens*, Penguin, 1991

Walker, Alexander, *Peter Sellers*, Coronet, 1981

Willats, Eric, A., *Streets with a Story: The Book of Islington*, Islington Local History Education Trust, 1988

Wilson, A.N., *A Life of John Milton*, Mandarin, 1996

Index of Names

Adams, Douglas; author, 1, 18

Addison, Joseph; MP, publisher 40, 175 (also Steele, Richard)

Agas, Ralph; surveyor, 111

Ainsworth, Harrison; author, 67, 89, 106, 182

Ali, Tariq; journalist, 2, 197

Allison, George; football manager, 9

Allon, Dr Henry; Methodist minister, 195

Ansell, Henry; teetotaller, 112

Archley, Roger; merchant, 136

Atye, Arthur; politician, 29

Aubert, Col. Alexander; eccentric 29, 96, 97

Aubrey, John; diarist, 11, 142, 190

Audley, family, 39

Austen, Thomas; developer, 96

Aveling, Edward; Marxist agitator 99

Avery, William; manufacturer, 54

Babbage, Charles; mathematician, 10, 29, 82

Bacon, Sir Francis; politician, 10/11, 30, 157

Bailey, James; showman, 4, 23

Baker, Roy Ward; film director, 102

Balcon, Michael; film producer, 85, 102, 116

Barlow, Revd William; vicar of St Mary's, 27, 173/4

Barlow, W.H.; architect, 27, 174

Barrett, Mick; republican, 110 (execution of)

Barrow, Eliza; murder victim, 177

Barry, Sir Charles, architect, 12, 13, 26, 55, 151

Bawden, Nina; author, 24

Baxter, George; print-maker, 46

Baylis, Lilian; theatre owner, 113, 161, 163, 183

Baynes, Walter; developer, 55, 77, 187

Beardsley, Aubrey; illustrator, 15/16

Beck, Frederick; toyshop owner, 25

Bell, Vanessa; author, 28

Benham, Canon; Dickens indexer, 68

Bennett, Arnold; author, 16, 80, 89, 119, 144

Berners, Sir James; landowner, 11

Bernersbury, Margery; benefactor 11, 35, 199

Besant, Annie; feminist, 53, 138

Betjeman, Ernest; manufacturer, 17

Betjeman, family; furniture makers, 17, 106, 195, 207

Betjeman, George; manufacturer, 17, 153

Betjeman, Gilbert; musician, 17

Betjeman, John (gndfr of John), 17

Betjeman, Sir John; poet laureate, 12, 17/18, 25, 70

Bewick, Thomas; engraver, 1

Billington, brothers; hangmen, 104

Binnie, Sir Alexander; engineer, 7

Bird, John; magazine editor, 70

Birkbeck, Dr George; educationist, 83

Blair, Tony; Prime Minister, 13, 18, 71, 115

Blake, William; artist and poet, 40, 124 (death of), 145

Blishen, Edward; author, 18

Blondin, Charles; tightrope walker, 23

Blood, Fanny; author, 204

Blore, Edward; architect, 41

Boadicea/Boudicca, Queen (of Iceni tribe), 11, 15

Bolton, Prior William; architect 27, 29

Bondfield, Margaret MP; trade unionist, 62

Bonington, Richard Parkes; painter, 153 (burial place of)

Booth, Cherie (m. Blair) QC, family of, 19/20

Booth, John Wilkes; assassin, 4, 19

Booth, Junius; actor, 4, 19

Bottomley, Virginia; Health Minister, 14, 71

Bourchier, John (Lord Berners), 11

Bowen, Elizabeth; author, 131 (friend of MacNeice)

Box, Sidney; film producer, 86, 116

Boycott, Rosie; magazine editor, 20, 50, 70, 81

Boyson, Dr Rhodes (Sir), MP; educationist, 20/1

Bridges, Robert; poet, 14, 21 [b]

Britain, family; toymakers, 21/2

Britten, Sir Benjamin; musician, 22, 76, 144, 145

Britton, Thomas; coalman, impresario; 117, 175 206

Brock, John, firework manufacturer, 172 (accidental death of)

Brockway, Fenner (Lord Brockway); campaigner, 26, 70, 113, 140

Bronowski, Jacob; scientist and writer, 25, 31

Brown, James Duff; librarian, 184

Bruce, Robert (e. of Aylesbury), 171

Bruckner, Anton; composer, 83

Budgell, Eustace; suicide, 55

Bunyan, John; preacher and poet, 22

Burdett-Coutts, Angela; philanthropist, 106, 164

Burke & Casey; republicans, 109

Burke, Edmund; political philosopher 148

Burnet, Bishop, 171

Burnett, Fanny (s. of Dickens), 67, 69 (death of)

Bywaters & Thompson; murderers, 152

Caley, John; keeper of records, 78 (death of)

Carey, George; vicar of St Mary's, later Archbishop of Canterbury 174

Carey, Henry (Lord Hunsdon), 76

Carey, Henry Saville; poet, f. of Kean, 117, 175 (suicide of)

Carr, James; architect 50

Carrier, Robert; chef, 12, 25, 114

Carton, Ronald; crossword compiler, 27

Casement, Sir Roger; plotter, 152 (execution of)

Cashman, Able Seaman; looter, 183 (execution of)

Caslon, William; type-founder, 4, **31/2**, 43, 206

Castle, Barbara (Baroness); campaigner 18, **32/3**, 70, 113

Cave, Edward; publisher, 4, **33**, 118, 168

Cavell, Edith; nurse, **33**

Cavendish, William (Newcastle), 49

Cavour, Count Camillo; diplomat, 127

Cecil, William (Lord Burghley), 37

Chaloner, James & Thomas (yngr), 49, 62, 70

Chaloner, Sir Thomas; diplomat, 49, 75

Chamberlain, Joseph MP, 101

Chamberlain, Richard, family, 82, 101

Chambers, Ephraim; encyclopaedist, 30

Chaplin, Sir Charles; comedian, 4, **34**, 57, 163

Chapman, Herbert; football manager, 8

Charles II, Stuart, King of England, 15, 66, 136, 140, 166

Chaucer, Geoffrey (as ADC to Richard II), 185

Cheeseman, Wallace; philanthropist, 81

Chesterton, G.L.; prison governor, 138

Chisholm, Caroline; philanthropist, 10, 70, 208

Christie, Reginald; serial killer, 152/3 (Rillington Place murders)

Chubb, Charles; locksmith, 12 (death of)

Cibber, Caius; sculptor, 16, 55

Cibber, Colley; actor-playwright, 55 (Charlotte, dr.), 162

Cloudesley, Richard; landowner 54/5

Coade, Eleanor; manufacturer, 42

Cobbett, William MP; radical 52, 149

Coggan, Donald; vicar of St Mary's, later Archbishop of Canterbury 174

Cohen, Stanley Cllr; politician 28

Coleridge, Samuel Taylor; poet, 123, 124 (death of), 138

Collinson, James; artist, 106

Compton, family (Northampton), 27, 30/1, 46, 48, 58/9 (rel. to Spencers), 60, 63, 111, 172

Coram, Thomas; philanthropist, 138

Coventry, Sir Thomas, politician, 30

Cowper, William; poet, 6

Crane, C. Howard; US architect, 5, 45

Craven, Thomas; developer, 77

Crawford, Dan; theatre owner, 5, 98, 114, 120/1, 190, 197

Crippen, Dr Hawley Harvey; murderer, **60-62**, 99, 101, 113, 152

Croft, Michael; theatre producer, 107

Cromwell, Bridget, d. of Oliver, 63

Cromwell, Oliver; politician, 40, 49, **62**, 66, 88, 157

Cromwell, Thomas; politician, 29, 36, 96

Crosse, John; brewer, 48

Cruden, Alexander; bookseller, 17, **24/5**

Cruft, Charles; dog showman, 23, **63/4**, 99, 106, 112

Cruikshank, George; cartoonist, 3, 41, **64/5**, 67, 89, 106, 138, 149, 163, 182

Cubitt, James; architect, 195

Culpeper, Nicholas; herbalist, 51

D'Avenant, Sir William; playwright, **66**, 76, 135, 190

Dance, George, & son; architects 43, **65/6**

Daniel, George; satirist, 28 (death of)

Dawes, John; developer, 27, 31, 96

De Barowe, Lady Alicia, 95

De Berners, Ralph, family (Bourchier), 11, 26, 95, 137, 204

De Briset, family, 169, 174, 204

De Bruis, family (Bruce), 171, 204

De Clifford, George (Cumberland), 38

De Fiennes, family (Fiennes), 82, 135, 204

De Mandeville, Geoffrey, 11, 204

De Manny, family (de Mauny), 11, 34, 42

De Valois, Dame Ninette; ballerina, 113, 161

Deeping, Warwick; author, 99

Defoe, Daniel; author, 4, 23 (burial place of), **66**, 134, 141, 166

Deitch, Barnet; shoemaker, 34, 164

Dexter, Walter; campaigning editor, 69

Dibdin, Charles; theatre manager, 111, 140

Dickens, Charles; author, 6, 10, 43, 65, **67-69**, 90, 164, 200

Disraeli, Sir Benjamin MP; Prime Minister, 56, **69/70**, 196

Docwra, Sir Thomas; Prior of St John's, 137, 167

Douglas, Catherine (Duchess of Queensberry), 117

Du Maurier, George, painter-author, **73**, 90, 159

Duane, Michael; headmaster, 20

Dudley, family (Northumberland), 29, 36, 51

Dudley, Robert (Leicester) 75, 76, 150, 157

Duncan, Helen; convicted witch, 105

Duncombe, Thomas MP; campaigner, 10, 70, **73/4**, 128

Earlom, Richard; engraver, 78

Edmund ('Ironside'), King of England, 15

Elgar, Sir Edward; musician, 173

Elizabeth I, Tudor; Queen of England, 36/7, **74-6**, 96, 100, 122, 156/7, 167/8

Ellis, Ruth; last woman hanged, 50, 105, 186

Epstein, Brian; Beatles' manager, 146

Essex, Earl of, 11

Evans, Timothy; hanged for crime he did not commit 152/3 (Rillington Place murders)

Evelyn, John; diarist, 136

Fagan, Michael; oddball, 107

Fairbrother, Louisa; actress, 171

Faraday, Michael; scientist, 12, **79**, 176

Farlowe, Chris; singer, 145

Farringdon, Thomas; landowner, 194

Fawkes, Guy; plotter **81**

Fell, Margaret; wife of Fox, George, 3

Fields, Gracie; entertainer, 45, 57, 140

Fiennes, Ralph; actor, 34

Finella, Luigi; accordionist and bandleader, 129, 207

Fisher, Sir Thomas; minister, 12, 93

FitzStephen, William; chronicler, 47, 51, **83/4**

Fleetwood, Gen. Charles; Cromwellian 23, 63

Fonteyn, Dame Margot, ballerina, 161

Foster, Elizabeth Clarke; g/dtr. of Milton 118, 135

Fowler, Sir Thomas; courtier, 12, 75

Fox, George; Quaker founder, 3, **155/6**, 200 (burial place of)

Foxe, John; cleric and author, 91

Franklin, Benjamin; printer, politician, polymath, 4, 32, 141, 165, 168, 173

Frederick, Hanover; Prince of Wales, 92 (accidental death of)

Fry, Elizabeth; prison reformer, 151

Fry, Roger; poet and playwright, 28, **85** (and s. Sara)

Furley, Sir John and Lechmere, Sir Edmund; founders of St John Ambulance 167

Garencieres, Dr; translator of Nostradamus 50, 117

Garibaldi, Giuseppe; revolutionary, 127, 128

Garrick, David; actor-manager, 118 (pupil of Johnson), 135, 168

Gatti, Carlo; ice maker and restaurateur, 119, 128

Gay, John; poet and lyricist, 40, 103, 106, 187

Geldof, Sir Bob; musician, **86**

Georges I-V, Hanover family; Kings of England, 9, 16, 60, 149, 175, 187 (family), 193/4 (Prince Regent)

Gibbons, Grinling; woodcarver, 143

Gigli/Caruso, performances, 128

Gilbert, Roland; architect, 51

Giles, Carl; cartoonist, 6

Gillray, James; cartoonist, 64

Gissing, George; author, **87**

Godwin, William; anarchist publisher, 149, 205

Goldsmith, Oliver; poet, 31, **87**, 118, 200

Gordon, Lord George; rioter 87/8

Gough, Piers; architect, 2

Grace, Dr W.G.; cricketer, 14

Grant, Duncan; designer, 28, 161

Green, Charles; balloonist, 88

Greenaway, Kate; illustrator, **89/90**, 196

Grey, Dame Beryl; ballerina, 148

Grey, Lady Jane, 29, 36

Griffiths, Catherine; campaigner, 104

Grimaldi, Giuseppe; f. of Joe, 90, 127

Grimaldi, Joe; clown-impresario 64, 78, **90**, 123, 127, 153 (burial place of), 162

Groom, John; philanthropist, 70, **90/1**, 177

Grossmith, brothers; actors, 27

Gwynne, Nell; courtesan, 15, 16, 110

Hales, Robert; Prior of St John's, 95/6, 170, 194 (murder of)

Hall, Dr John; s.-in-law of Shakespeare, 58, 59

Halley, Edmond; f. of Edmond, 93 (d. in suspicious circs.)

Halley, Edmond; astronomer, **93**

Hallidie, John; engineer, 7

Halton, Sir William; landowner, 12, 93

Hancock, Thomas; inventor, 88
Handel, G.F.; musician, 40, 117
Hardie, Keir MP; Prime Minister, 97
Hardy, Thomas; bootmaker and radical, 51, 129
Harmsworth, Sir Harold (Viscount Rothermere), benefactor 7
Harvey, Len; boxer, **94**
Harvey, William; court physician, 11, 14, 145
Haselrig, Sir Arthur MP, 63 (murder of)
Hastings, Jack (e. of Huntingdon), 54
Hatfield, James; lunatic, 16
Hawes, Dr William; philanthropist, 76
Robinson, William Heath; humorist, 63, **159/60**
Heath, Neville; murderer, 152 (case and execution of)
Heaysman, Malcolm; murder victim, 3, 197
Henry VIII, Tudor, King of England, 3, 5, 13, 42, 47 92, 96, 122, 137, 140, 158, 170, 201
Henson, Leslie; actor, 97
Hepburn, Audrey; actress, 132
Hicks, Sir Baptist JP, 94
Hill, Dr Charles; 'Radio Doctor', **156**
Hillman, David; campaigner, 108, 124
Hindley, Myra; murderess, 105
Hindmarsh, Robert; printer, 48, 188
Hitchcock, Alfred; film director, 5, 85, **101-3** (career of)
Hogarth, William; artist, 6, 16, **103/4**, 142, 165, 168 (f. of Wm.)
Holmes, Sherlock; detective, 14
Homer, Thomas; canal overseer, 9, 158
Hood, Thomas; poet, 76, **108**, 123
Hook, James RA; painter, 46
Hooke, Robert; surveyor of London, 16
Hooke, Theodore; poet, 108 (friend of Lamb)
Hornby, Nick; author, 9, **109**
Horsley, William; composer, 41
Houghton, Prior; Catholic martyr, 35/6 (execution of)
Howard, family (Norfolk), 37, 38, 39, 75, 91
Howard, John; penal reformer, 16
Hunt, Sir Henry ('Orator') MP; radical, 52, 186
Hyde, William JP, 88
Inglebert, William; benefactor, 141/2
Irvine, Lucy; castaway, **110**
Irving, Washington; US author, 4, 31
Izzard, Eddie; comedian, 180
Jackson, Glenda MP; actress and campaigner, 3, 8, 78

Jackson, Paul, Cllr; inventor, 124
Jacques, Martin; Marxist editor, 114
James I, Stuart, King of England (VI of Scotland), 39, 96, 120, 148, 157, 168, 196
James II, Stuart, King of England, 59, 175
Jennings, Joseph; architect, 92
Johnson, Bryan; author, 114 (suicide of)
Johnson, Dr Samuel; writer and lexicographer, 33, 77, 87, **118**, 135, 168, 173 (death of)
Johnson, Joseph; publisher, 149
Jones, Henry; headmaster, 21
Jones, Inigo; architect, 14, 168
Jones, Paul; singer, actor, 25
Jonson, Ben; playwright, 13, 39, 49
Joyce, William ('Lord Haw Haw'); traitor, 152 (execution of)
Kean, Edmund ('Master Carey'); actor, 162, 175
Keeler, Christine; sometime courtesan, 28, 105
Kent, Monsignor Bruce; campaigner, 26, 73
Kingsley, Mary; author, 121, 196
Kirkham, Pamela (Baroness Berners), 13
Klein, Dr; campaigner, 114
Lackington, James; bookseller, 43, 83
Lamb, Charles; essayist (also Mary, s.), 28, 34, 65, 108, **122-4**, 162
Landells, Ebenezer; publisher of Punch, 12
Lasky, Harold J.; film producer, 116
Latey, Josephine (m. W. Heath Robinson), 160
Laurel, Stan; comedian, 4, 34
Lear, Edward; artist and poet, 106, **124/5**
Lechmere, Sir Edmund; benefactor, 169
Leech, John; cartoonist, 41, 193
Leighton, Archibald; bookbinder, 78 (death of)
Lenin, V.I.; revolutionary, 54, 70, **125/7**
Leroux, Henry; architect, 27, 195
Lewson, Jane; wealthy recluse, 55
Leybourne, George; entertainer, 56
Leyburne, Sir Francis, courtier, 37
Lilburne, John; dissenter, 22, 63
Lilley, Peter, MP; politician, 18
Lillywhite, Fred; sports retailer, **127**
Livingstone, Dr David; explorer, 83
Lloyd, Marie; music hall entertainer 82
Loach, Ken; film director, 114, 150
Lord, Thomas; groundsman, 12, 111, 132, 200
Lovelace, Ada; d. of Byron, asst. of Babbage, 10
Loveless, George; Tolpuddle martyr, 9, 191, 200
Lovell, Thomas; speaker of the House, 76
Lubetkin, Berthold; architect, 83, **130/1**

Lydon, John; singer, 107, 180/1 (Sex Pistols)

MacNeice, Louis; poet, **131/2**

Marconi, Aldo; inventor, 99

Marx, Karl; political philosopher, 53

Marx, Eleanor; feminist, 53, 138

Mary I, Tudor, Queen of England, 29, 36 (death of), 47, 122, 170/1

Mary Stuart, Queen of Scots, 37

Matthews, Sir Stanley; footballer, 9

Mayhew, Henry; social worker, 177

Mazzini, Giuseppe; revolutionary, 74, 127/8

McBean, Angus; photographer, 25, 56, **132/3**

McKennal, Sir Bertram; sculptor, 97

Medwin, Michael; actor-producer, 25

Meek, Joe; record producer, 107, **133/4**

Michell, Simon; builder, 171

Mildmay, Sir Henry; Commissioner, 140

Mildmay, Sir Walter; Chancellor, 74, 140

Miles, Sir Bernard; actor-manager, 31

Mill, John Stuart; philosopher, 53, **134**, 141

Miller, Sir John, 157

Milner-Gibson, Thomas; benefactor, 41, 70, 198

Milton, Christopher; judge (brother of John), 135

Milton, John; poet, **134/5**

More, Saint Thomas, Catholic martyr 11, **137** (death of)

Morris, Sam; entrepreneur, 24

Morris, William; poet, designer, Socialist 46, 53, 54, 70, **137/8**

Mortimer, Raymond; writer, 27 (death of)

Morton, Charles; dissenter, 66, 70, 140

Mosley, Lady Diana; internee, 105, 207

Mosley, Sir Oswald; politician, 12, 105, 198

Mottistone, Lord; archaeologist, 42, 172

Mountford, E.W.; architect, 46, 194

Mozart, Wolfgang A.; musician, 14

Murcell, George; actor-manager, 190

Murphy, Fred; serial killer, 56

Myddelton, Sir Hugh MP; developer 103, 139 (death of) 142/3, 148, 157

Mylne, William Chadwell; architect 139, 143 (f. Robert)

Naoroji, Prof. Dadabhar MP, 82, 83

Nash, John; architect, 7, 158

Neville, John (Lord Latimer), 42

Newbery, John; publisher, 30, 87

Newell, Mike; film director, 98

Newland, Abraham; banker, 100

Newnes, George; publisher, 81

Nichols, John; magazine editor, 101 (death of)

Nollekens, Joseph RA; artist, 51

North, Sir Edward (Lord North); politician, 36, 74, 75, 158, 174

Oakes, John; campaigner, 97

Oates, Titus; spy, 95 (Bran Tub Plot)

Okey, Colonel; regicide, 95

Oldcastle, Sir John (Lord Cobham); Lollard, 50, 193

Olivier, Sir Laurence; actor-manager, 25, 57

Orton, Joe; playwright (with Halliwell, Kenneth), 56, 77, 113, 133, **145/6**

Orwell, George (E.A. Blair); author, 28, 98, **146/7**, 208

Osborne, John; playwright, 57

Owen, Dame Alice; benefactress, 19 (as Wilkes), 140, **147/8**

Owen, Robert; trade unionist, 10, 191

Paine, Thomas; republican, 4, 111, **148/9**, 160

Parker, Alan; film director, **149/50**

Parr, Catherine, family, 36, 42, 158

Parr, 'Old Parr'; oldest man ever, **145**

Paul, Robert; cinematographer, 46, **150**

Payton, John; campaigner, 25, 70, 113/4

Peabody, George; US philanthropist, 4, 115 (P. Trust), **150/1**

Pears, Sir Peter; singer, 22, 144

Peck, Frederick; architect, 23

Peel, Sir Robert MP; Prime Minister, 52, 53

Pellew, Adml. Edward (Lord Exmouth), 78

Penton, Sir Henry MP; developer, 6, 153

Pepusch, John; musician, 40, 117, 175, 182

Pepys, Samuel; diarist, 120, **154**, 206

Perceval, John (e. of Egmont), 60

Perceval, Spencer MP; Prime Minister 60 (assassinated)

Perry, John; wallpaper printer, 144

Peto, Sir Samuel MP, 143

Pevsner, Sir Nikolaus; architecture writer 6, 73

Phelps, Sam; theatre owner, 28, 163, 189

Pierrepoint, Albert; hangman, 105, 152

Pierrepoint, Tom; hangman (br. of Albert) 152

Pinchbeck, Christopher; jeweller, 1

Pinero, Arthur Wing; playwright, 163

Pinter, Harold; playwright, 3, 31

Plath, Sylvia; poet, 28

Poirot, Hercule; detective, 43 (TV home of)

Pole, William; philanthropist, 7, 201

Pollard, Robert and James; print-makers, 1, 77, 78, 106, 125, **154/5**

Popham, Arthur; museum curator, 28

Price, Dr Richard; Unitarian minister, 141

Princesses Amelia and Caroline, drs of George II, 187

Pringle, Robert; jeweller, 164

Pugin, family; architects, 73, **155**

Quelch, Harry; printer (and Tom, son), 54, 125, 126, 127 (death of H.), 138

Rahere; Prior of St Bart's, 165, 166

Raleigh, Walter, Sir; courtier, 3, 11, 75, 76, **156-8**, 196

Randell & Evans; brickmakers, 64

Ray, Cyril; humorist, 56

Rennie, John; engineer, 43, 158

Repsch, John; biographer (of Meek), 134

Rich, Sir Richard; landowner, 158, 165

Rickman, Clio; radical publisher, 149, 160

Ridolfi; plotter, 37 (Ridolfi Plot), 162

Rimington, Stella; head of MI5, 27

Rogers, Samuel; dissenter, 141, 168

Rogers, Thomas; architect, 51

Romney, George RA; painter 125

Ronalds, Francis; inventor, 97

Rosebery, Archibald (5th Earl), 82, 160

Rosoman, Thomas; architect, 77, 162

Rothstein, Theodore; friend of Lenin, 126

Roumieu and Gough; architects, 2, 177

Rowlandson, Thomas RA; painter, 200

Rushdie, Salman; author, 114

Russell, Bertrand; philosopher, 26, 126

Sabini, Darby; gentleman gangster, 128

Sacheverell, Revd Henry; plotter, 2, 171

Sachs & Walters; murderers, 104

Sackville, Elizabeth; Abbess of St Mary's, 174 (burial place of)

Sadler, Richard; developer, 162

Saint-Denis, Michel; theatre producer, 190, 197

Saunders, Dr William, physician 96

Saunders, John; benefactor, 42

Savile, Margaret Fowler, 12

Scher, Anna; drama teacher, 12, **177**, 190

Scoles, Joseph; architect, 73

Secombe, Harry; entertainer, 3, 57

Sedding, John; architect, 78

Seddon, Fred; murderer, 113, 152, **177/8**

Sekforde, Thomas MP, benefactor, 205

Selina, Countess of Huntingdon; Nonconformist 77, 78 (death of), 88, 118

Sellers, Peter; comedian, 8, **178**

Sellon, Revd; vicar of St James, 77

Seymour, Robert; illustrator, 31, 65, 67, **181** (death of)

Seymour, Sir Thomas; courtier, 42

Shakespeare, William; playwright, 50, 168, **181**

Sharpe, Granville; campaigner, 89

Shaw, G.B.; playwright, Socialist 53, 138

Shaw, Norman; architect, 90

Sheppard, Jack; highwayman, 40, 51, 106, 163, 176, **181/2**

Sheppard, Revd David; vicar of St Mary's, 174

Sheridan, Richard Brinsley MP; playwright, 129

Shillibeer, George; transport pioneer, **182**, 192

Shrubsole, William; musician, 77

Sickert, Walter RA; painter, 12, 98, 101, 164, **182/3**

Sinclair, Iain; author, 120

Sinclair, Sir Clive; inventor, 120

Sleep, Thomas; Catholic plotter, 70, 81

Smith, Chris MP; campaigner, 18, 81, 83, 115

Smith, George; murderer, 8, 101, 113, **184** ('Brides in the Bath' murders)

Smith, John; politician, 18 (death of)

Soper, Revd Donald; Methodist minister, 45, 98, **186**

Southey, Robert; poet, 123

Spence, Sir Basil; architect, 25, 27

Spencer Sir John, family, 29, 58/9 (rel. to Comptons)

Spenser, Edmund; poet, 156

Standfield, Thomas; Tolpuddle martyr, 9, 191

Stanley, James (e. of Derby, Lord Strange), 30, 63

Starmer, Keir; solicitor, 129

Steel & Morris; 129/30 (McLibel Trial)

Steinberg, Johann; murderer, 166/7

Stevens, Cat (Yusuf Islam); singer, 107

Stewart, Rod; entertainer, 8

Stonehouse, George; vicar of St Mary's, 173 (b. of Methodism), 199

Stopes, Dr Marie; campaigner, 70, 81, 107, 161, **188**

Stowe, Harriet Beecher; US author, 2, 78

Strahan, Revd George; vicar of St Mary's, 118, 173

Strahan, William (f. of George), 4

Strauss, Johann; musician, 56

Straw, Jack MP; Home Secretary, 32, 105

Straw, Jack; revolutionary, 96, 194

Street-Porter, Janet; broadcaster, 2

Sutton, Thomas; benefactor, 39, 82, 114 (arms of), 199

Swedenborg, Sir William; visionary, **188**

Swinnerton, Frank; author, 80

Tandy, Jessica; actress, 5, 98

Taylor, Ann and Jane; children's rhymesters, 90, **189**

Tealby, Mary; philanthropist 14/15, 106

Ternan, Ellen; actress, **189/90**(as mistress of Dickens)

Terroni, Sgr; delicatessen owner, 128

Teschemacher, Edward; songwriter, 100

Thackeray, William Makepeace; author, 41

Thistlewood, Arthur; plotter, 138, 186

Thomas, Dylan; poet, 86, 131

Thoresby, Ralph; antiquary, 106

Tomasso, Angelo; barrel-organ maker, 128, 129 (death of)

Torrens, William MP; reformer, 70, **191/2**

Trinder, Tommy; comedian, 57

Tuffley, Mary, wife of Defoe, 66

Tuffnell, William (Joliffe); landowner, 12

Turpin, Dick; highwayman, 106

Tyler, Wat; revolutionary, 51, 80, 96, **194/5**

Tylney, Edmund; master of revels, 75, 84, 168, 181

Tyrwhitt-Wilson (Baron Berners), 12

U2; pop group 109 (first London appearance of)

Ustinov, Peter; actor, raconteur, 197

Vagg, Sam Collins; music hall turn, impresario, 56

Vasso, Madame; clairvoyant, 34

Verlaine, Paul; poet, 119

Wakley, Thomas; MP; reformer 70, 80, 191, **197/8**, 200

Walker, Alexander; film critic, 25

Walpole, Sir Robert MP; Prime Minister, 60

Walton, Sir Izaac; author, 51

Walworth, Sir William; Lord Mayor of London, 35, 194

Ward, Ned; satirist, 206

Watt, James; engineer, 43

Watts, Isaac; hymnist, 23, 141

Waugh, Evelyn; author, 28, 130 (Auberon, s.), 147, **198**

Way, Brian; actor, 190

Webb, John; soda water manufacturer, 124

Webb, Sidney & Beatrice; social educationists, 144

Webb, Sir Aston; architect, 165

Weekes, Sidney; designer, 98

Welby, Catherine (w. of Pugin); 155

Wellington, Duke of, 41, 92

Wesley, John; Methodist minister, 40, 66 (Samuel, father of J.), 77, 83, 100 (death of) 111, 173, 198/9

Wesley, Susannah, mother of John, 199 (burial place of)

Weston, Sir William, Prior of St John's, 170, 175 (burial place of)

Whitbread, Samuel; brewer, 43 (death of), 200

Whiteley, William; retailer, 196

Whittington, Sir Richard; Lord Mayor of London, 7, 114 (arms of), **200-202**

Wilde, Oscar; writer and wit, 104, 151

Wilkes, Alice - see Owen, Dame Alice -

Wilkes, Harriett; d. of John, 123

Wilkes, John MP; radical politician, 23, 24, 52, 70, 80, 88, 104, 118, 171, **202-4**

Willan, Monica; campaigner 14

William I (Conqueror), King of England, 11, 84, 95, 111, **204**

William III, King of England (d. of Orange; also Mary, Q.) 59-60

Williams, Randall; 'King of Showmen', 150

Wilson, Henry; architect, 78

Wilson, John & Elizabeth; transport pioneers, 97

Wilson, Revd Daniel; vicar of St Mary's, 173

Wilson, Thomas; benefactor, 101, 153

Wollstonecraft, Mary; author and feminist, 70, 81, 83, 141, 196, **204/5**

Wood, Sir William; king's archer, 166 (burial of)

Wood, Victoria; comedienne, 121

Woodfall, H.S.; author, 30, 56

Wootton, Dr Janet; Methodist minister, 196

Wordsworth, William; poet, 123

Wren, Sir Christopher; architect, 201

Wright, Billy; footballer, 9

Yvele, Henry; architect, 35